CULTURAL ENCOUNTERS

Published under the auspices of the
CENTER FOR MEDIEVAL AND RENAISSANCE STUDIES
University of California, Los Angeles

Auto de fe in the Plaza Mayor, Madrid

CULTURAL ENCOUNTERS
The Impact of the Inquisition in Spain and the New World

EDITED BY

Mary Elizabeth Perry
and
Anne J. Cruz

UNIVERSITY OF CALIFORNIA PRESS
Berkeley   Los Angeles   Oxford

University of California Press
Berkeley and Los Angeles, California
University of California Press
Oxford, England
Copyright © 1991 by
The Regents of the University of California

**Library of Congress Cataloging in
Publication Data**
Cultural encounters: the impact of the Inquisition
in Spain and the New World / edited by Mary
Elizabeth Perry and Anne J. Cruz.
   p.   cm.
Papers presented at an international confer-
ence held March 25—27, 1988 in Los Angeles,
Calif., sponsored by the University of California,
Irvine, the University of California, Los Angeles,
and the University of Southern California.
Includes bibliographical references and index.
   ISBN: 978-0-520-30124-5 (pbk. : alk. paper)

   1. Inquisition—Spain—Congresses. 2. Inquisition—Mexico—Congresses. 3. Indians of
Mexico—Congresses. I. Perry, Mary Elizabeth,
1937–   . II. Cruz, Anne J., 1941–   .
III. University of California, Irvine. IV. University of California, Los Angeles. V. University of Southern California.
BX1735.C84 1991
272'.2—dc20
            90–22450
            CIP

CONTENTS

PART II • PERSECUTION AND PERSISTENCE

PART III • BIBLIOGRAPHICAL ESSAYS

ACKNOWLEDGMENTS

The essays included in this volume were selected from papers presented at the international conference, "Cultural Encounters: The Impact of the Inquisition in Spain and the New World," which took place March 25, 26, and 27, 1988, at the University of California, Los Angeles and the University of Southern California. Under the auspices of the UCLA Center for Medieval and Renaissance Studies, and sponsored by the University of California, Irvine, the University of California, Los Angeles, and the University of Southern California, this scholarly reunion formed part of the international observance of the quincentenary of Christopher Columbus's voyage to the New World.

The conference's main purpose was to bring together scholars in several disciplines—anthropology, ethnology, history, and literary studies—from leading universities in North America, Europe, and Latin America, and, for the first time in Inquisition studies, to provide a forum in which to exchange recent research findings and take stock of the status of Inquisition studies in the United States and abroad. The essays included herein testify eloquently to the success of the conference in its endeavor to broaden discussion of the role of the Spanish Inquisition in Hispanic society, and to investigate in depth the Inquisition's powers, not only in Spain, but in the New World.

For their support of the conference and the publication of the present volume, we are grateful to the National Endowment for the Humanities, the Comité Conjunto Hispano-Norteamericano para la Cooperación Cultural y Educativa, the UC-MEXUS Consortium, the UC Irvine School of Humanities, the USC College of Letters, Arts, and Sciences;

the USC Doheny Library; and the Del Amo Foundation Committees at UCLA and the University of Southern California. The conference Planning Committee gave us expert advice during the crucial early stages of the conference: we thank members Carroll B. Johnson, UCLA; Henry Ansgar Kelly, UCLA; Carlos Otero, UCLA; and Jaime Rodríguez, UCI. We especially wish to recognize María Cristina Quintero, who organized the USC colloquium; Fredi Chiappelli, Director of the UCLA Center for Medieval and Renaissance Studies; Robert I. Burns, S.J., UCLA; and Michael J. B. Allen, who is now Director of the UCLA Center for Medieval and Renaissance Studies. Susanne Kahle, UCLA Center for Medieval and Renaissance Studies, deserves a special note of thanks for her invaluable assistance to the conference and this volume.

Finally, we would like to thank the session chairs, the conference participants, and the members of the Southern California community; their dialogue has strengthened and enriched the essays in this volume. We are grateful especially for the opportunity to work with Fredi Chiappelli and Joseph Silverman before their untimely deaths. We thank Susan Isabel Stein for translating the Spanish essays with thought and care, Nicholas Goodhue for his expert copyediting, and Annie Reynoso for her skilled word processing.

Our greatest thanks are due those scholars who generously allowed us to engage their research in the growing critical discourse on the Spanish Inquisition, and with whom we have worked these past months in bringing this volume to light. To them we extend our most sincere admiration and gratitude.

Mary Elizabeth Perry
Anne J. Cruz

INTRODUCTION

Mary Elizabeth Perry and Anne J. Cruz

Ferdinand and Isabel revived a long dormant medieval institution when they received permission from Pope Sixtus IV in 1478 to name inquisitors in the cities and dioceses of their domain. Directing their newly appointed inquisitors to defend the true faith, the Catholic Kings set into motion a machinery that would quickly expand beyond investigations of apostasy and heresy. The Spanish Inquisition established permanent tribunals in major towns and cities, developed a large bureaucracy to carry out investigations in most communities of the realm, and permeated all areas of human life, both private and public. Franciscan missionaries carried the Inquisition to the New World, where it ran headlong into the clash between Iberian Catholicism and Native American beliefs. From its quiet beginning as a papal court of inquiry restricted in the thirteenth century to the Crown of Aragon, the Spanish Inquisition thus became a major theater for cultural encounters among the many peoples throughout the Hispanic world.

A *suprema*, or council of clerics appointed by the Spanish Crown, supervised the vast bureaucracy of the Inquisition on both sides of the Atlantic, but the documents from its voluminous records show that the Inquisition represented more than the Crown or an official elite. Although the Crown appointed as inquisitors clerics with degrees in law or theology, the people who answered their questions as witnesses or suspects often spoke of ideas and beliefs remote from theological and juridical scholarship. Instead, they related both the extraordinary and ordinary events of their everyday lives. Inquisitors could not merely impose official views but were required to hear and record all testimony.

Their careful records thus reveal a continuous interweaving of various cultures, religions, and political power that reflects the social and intellectual climates of Spain and the New World and that documents the complexities of those same social groups they attempted to contain.

Historically, the Inquisition has provided a rich source of study for scholars of anthropology, history, and literature. From the "Black Legend" descriptions of sixteenth-century writers, even to current social history, Inquisition studies have proved to be controversial, contradictory, and provocative. Several recent conferences indicate growing interest in Inquisition scholarship. The 1978 international symposium held in Cuenca, Spain, addressed the historical origins and implications of the Inquisition. In that same year Inquisition specialist Gustav Henningsen organized an international symposium in Denmark, and historian Angel Alcalá organized the conference held in 1983 in the United States which focused on the mentalities of the Inquisition. Other recent symposia addressing the Inquisition have been held in Brazil, Paris, Rome, and Illinois.

The essays in this volume developed from papers presented at an international and multidisciplinary conference held in Los Angeles in 1988 that for the first time addressed the complex interactions between Hispanic cultures and the Spanish Inquisition. Representing the most innovative scholarship to date, these selected essays offer a comprehensive review of previous studies, investigate major issues, and explore and present new perspectives on the cultural significance of the Inquisition in Spain and the New World.

The volume is divided into three parts, beginning with *Part I: The Inquisition and the Limits of Discipline,* which examines the methods used by the Inquisition in its attempts to control diverse populations in both Spain and the New World. The anthropological and historical studies in this section focus on the uses and limitations of the Inquisition and other forms of discipline imposed on Native Americans and such marginalized groups in Spain as sorceresses, visionaries, and prophets.

The Inquisition had labored diligently in Spain to contain populations of *conversos* (Christianized Jews) and *moriscos* (Christianized Muslims), increasingly catechizing these communities and monitoring their external behavior. In the process of colonization—indeed, as an integral part of this process—the measures of control adopted by the Counter-Reformation resurfaced in Spanish efforts to subdue native cultures in the New World. Here the Holy Office faced not simply a problem of containing religious minority groups, but the complex task of organizing a colonial society of non-Spanish speaking Indians. In their contributions to this section, J. Jorge Klor de Alva and Roberto Moreno de los Arcos both examine the Indian Inquisition, but they reach implicitly contradictory conclusions about its effectiveness.

Anthropologist Klor de Alva argues that the Indian Inquistion failed to carry out the Christianization of Native Americans. Instead, Spanish authorities turned to penitential discipline as a means of "colonizing souls." Noting the comparatively small number of Inquisition cases against Indians, this scholar concludes that neither the royal decree of 1571 proscribing prosecution of the Indians, nor humanitarian arguments to protect them, provide satisfactory explanations. Klor de Alva looks instead at the military and strategic requirements for subduing the indigenous peoples of so many city-states, and he argues that the penitential discipline promoted by confession and missionaries served Spanish interests far more effectively than did severe punishments of a few Indians by the Holy Office.

Studying the arrival and development of inquisitional jurisdiction in the Americas, historian Roberto Moreno de los Arcos distinguishes between the Inquisition and the institution that dealt specifically with Indians, variously called the Indian Inquisition, the Protectorate of Natives, or the Indian Tribunal of Faith. In contrast with Klor de Alva, he details how the Indian Inquisition gained both jurisdictional and ecclesiastical control over the Indians by utilizing theological arguments. Outlining its development, Moreno de los Arcos studies the Indian Tribunal's rationale for power in its conceptualization of the Indians as idolaters, and the resultant need for exorcism and conversion. He concludes that, although the Inquisition was prohibited from punishing Indians for transgressions of faith, the institution that administered their punishments originated from and remained analogous to it.

The limits of the Inquisition were determined as much by the social need for certain practices as by the impossibility of total control in an essentially heterodox culture. In her essay on *curanderos* and the Inquisition in colonial Mexico, anthropologist Noemí Quezada argues that a shortage of doctors prevented the Holy Office from carrying out a widespread prosecution of native healers. She investigates the role of traditional healers in the diverse cultures of New Spain, and views them as serving an important function within the communities of Indians, mestizos, and blacks. Citing several trials of curanderos, she reveals how, despite their unorthodoxy, they were allowed to practice among their own peoples so long as they avoided certain traditions such as ingesting hallucinogens. Quezada explores the contrasting values of European medical practices against non-European traditions of communal healing regarded as superstitious by the Spaniards.

Love magic, the subject of María Helena Sánchez Ortega's essay, represents another popular activity that often came under the scrutiny of the Inquisition. To read her essay is to enter into a feminine world of spells, incantations, and invocations meant to attract and hold men. Through a meticulous reading of Inquisition documents on the trials of several sorceresses and their clients, Sánchez Ortega discovers the complex rituals through which women in early modern Spain conjured demons as well as saints in their attempts to control men's wills.

Despite prosecutions of many accused sorceresses, the Holy Office could not stamp out the popular practice of love magic. Examining the ways through which women subverted the very system that oppressed them, Sánchez Ortega shows that their interest was less amorous than economic: underlying the sorceresses's imprecations is the pragmatic realization that women need male support in order to survive in a patriarchal society.

Like those of Quezada and Sánchez Ortega, the two essays by historians Richard Kagan and co-authors Angus MacKay and Geraldine McKendrick examine popular cultural practices questioned by the Inquisition and discuss why they should draw the attention of an institution established to prosecute apostates and heretics. MacKay and McKendrick study the phenomenon of visionaries in Spain and their treatment by the Inquisition. Noting the prominent role played by women, they focus on several female visionaries, including Sor María de Santo Domingo, an ignorant peasant woman who was often consulted by Cardinal Ximénez. To the authors, her case illustrates how women were actively encouraged to adopt a visionary spirituality by such great religious figures as Saint Ignatius Loyola and Ximénez, and how the Franciscan order in particular espoused female spirituality. In their essay, MacKay and McKendrick point out that belief in these women's messianic prophecies, especially by the monarchy, in fact protected them from the Inquisition.

Richard Kagan cites three cases—a soldier, a lawyer's daughter, and a Portuguese nun—in which prophecy won considerable fame for these otherwise ordinary people. Church ambiguity about prophecy and the difficulties of distinguishing false prophets from true prophets prevented the Inquisition from taking a more active role in attempting to control those who said they were relaying messages from God. In fact, Kagan argues, the Holy Office only prosecuted those "plaza prophets" whose prognostications constituted a direct political threat to the monarchy. Kagan challenges the conclusion of other historians that the Inquisition did not serve as an instrument of royal absolutism, and he argues instead that the practice of the Holy Office must be seen within the limitations of a specific political context.

The survival of cultures persecuted by the Inquisition provides the focus for *Part II: Persecution and Persistence*. In his essay on family and patronage, historian Jaime Contreras questions the customary polarized conceptualization of conversos opposed to Christians. Using a sociological perspective to reexamine the presence of this minority group in sixteenth-century Spain, he notes its existence as one dependent upon secrecy and clandestinity. His study posits the importance of lineal and kinship relations as a means of creating and maintaining a separate identity—both social and personal—not only within the majority group, but also in opposition to it. Thus, to Contreras, the crypto-Jews hold an intermediary position between conversos and emigrant Jews who fled Spain to practice their religion elsewhere.

Conversos are also the subject of Stephen Haliczer's essay, which argues that a unique combination of popular and official culture promoted their persecution by the Spanish Inquisition. Citing the case of 1491 in which Jews were accused of ritually murdering a Christian child in La Guardia, he writes that popular anti-Semitism combined with official belief in demonic power and transformed Jews and Christianized Jews into agents of the Devil. Conversos thus became a target for displaced aggression in Spain that took the form of widespread witch-hunts through most of the rest of Europe, and the *Santo Niño* became a symbol that inquisitors and the populace alike would use to justify their persecution.

Through a variety of literary sources, Joseph Silverman traces the Spanish obsession with lineage, with "clean" blood as opposed to tainted *marrano* and converso origins. Presenting several variations on the theme of fear of the Inquisition, this literary scholar shows how different authors utilize similar anecdotes to lament the destruction of a pluralistic society. In his readings of Lope de Vega's play *El niño inocente de La Guardia*—which dramatizes the legend addressed earlier by Stephen Haliczer—as well as the *Lazarillo de Tormes* and the writings of Fray Antonio de Guevara, he argues that the expression "to know other people's lives" exposes a new "mode of scrutiny," which functions as a weapon of intolerance and oppression in the hands of the inquisitors.

Yet Silverman notes that, through the undetermined nature of his literary hero, Cervantes is one writer who employs the maxim positively and gives it revolutionary force. The fact that the author reveals neither

Don Quixote's birthplace nor his lineage nor even his family name is significant in not only liberating Don Quixote from the fears of having a past, but also allowing a vision of a Spain that might have been. Don Quixote's curiosity about others derives not from a will to destroy, but from the need to create an alternative world, one which Silverman calls a "parenthetical paradise of Art."

Literary critic Moshe Lazar traces the survival of Anussim or crypto-Jewish culture, its religious devotion and continued "Jewishness" despite the forcible conversion to Christianity of Sephardic Jews. Challenging critics who have questioned the Anussim's ability to retain over several centuries a hidden religious life, and recalling Jaime Contreras's argument that stresses the clandestine existence of crypto-Jews, Lazar details how, despite the burning of their sacred books, the Anussim procured and kept hidden many Bibles, prayer books, commentaries on Jewish law, essays on Jewish history, and cabalistic and other mystical treatises that maintained their faith. When the texts were not available, they memorized a Judaism rescued from the scorched parchments and, ironically, from inquisitorial documents themselves.

Lazar demonstrates how accusations and confessions echo the Anussim's frequent themes of guilt over their conversion or their life as crypto-Jews, of dreams of leaving the Christian lands for Jerusalem or Constantinople, and of the hope of messianic redemption. This scholar claims that, in particular, the fragments of psalms and sentences recorded in Inquisition trial documents in Portugal, Majorca, and New Spain, as well as in Spain, confirm the Anussim's knowledge of the most important prayers of the Sephardic ritual and bear witness to the depth and continuity of their faith.

Historian Stanley Hordes notes the persistence of a pluralistic society in New Spain despite Inquisition persecution of crypto-Jews. After 1596, when cases of Judaizing declined in the Mexican Inquisition, many immigrants from Spain and Portugal actively participated in the developing economy of New Spain, even as they preserved their crypto-Jewish identity. Noting the significance of extended group relationships among these people, Hordes shows that Jaime Contreras's proposal to use family, kinship, and lineage as a basis for studying conversos is valid as well for the crypto-Jews of the New World.

In his study of cases of crypto-Jews before the Mexican Inquisition, Hordes argues that Spain's changing relationship with Portugal resulted in increased Inquisition prosecutions of Judaizers in New Spain in the periods following 1580, when Philip II assumed the Portuguese throne, and 1640, when the Portuguese rebelled against their Spanish rulers. He thus expands upon Richard Kagan's argument for the political significance of the Inquisition as a vehicle for the monarchy, and he underscores the bonds between the Inquisition in the New World and Spain.

Part III: Bibliographic Essays begins with a summary by Jesús Martínez de Bujanda of recent historiography on the Inquisition in Spain. This scholar points out that as a result of the numerous studies, catalogs, and computerized data bases that have appeared since 1977, contemporary scholars are much better informed about Inquisition documents. Equally important, the climate of study has evolved from a polemical confrontation between the traditional Catholic perspective and the progressive liberal viewpoint to what he terms a more "serene" approach that aims toward a higher degree of objectivity and impartiality. Such early histories of the Inquistion as José Antonio Llorente's *Historia crítica de la Inquisición* and Henry C. Lea's monumental *A History of the Inquisition in Spain* have recently been reedited; the latter has been translated into Spanish and its document references updated. According to Martínez de Bujanda, the latest scholarly work on the Inquisition focuses on its role as a political and religious tribunal as well as on its role as an institution for social and religious control. He concludes his essay with a valuable list of these works published from 1977 to 1988.

Historian Richard E. Greenleaf presents an authoritative compendium of the historiography of the Mexican Inquisition. Professor Greenleaf traces the evolution of diverse interpretations and methodologies applied to the Inquisition in New Spain, from its earliest primitive period (1522–1569) when Spanish Catholicism first clashed with native beliefs, through the establishment of the Tribunal of the Holy Office (1571–1700), whose main function was to control the influx of seditious literature, to the Inquisition in Bourbon Mexico (1700–1820) and its preoccupation with non-Catholic foreigners. This thoughtful essay devotes specific sections to scholarship published both on Indians' cases before the Inquisition, as well as on cases of crypto-Jews. In his final section, Professor Greenleaf notes the problems of interpretation that face scholars who study the Inquisition, and he urges them to leave aside clichés as they continue to analyze documentary evidence.

Whether exploring the uses of the Inquisition, its limitations, or scholarship that has been published on it, the essays in this collection provide a unique analysis of the Inquisition as a forum for the meeting of diverse and, at times, even opposing cultures. Despite the violence of the encounters and the inexorable changes that ensued, what emerges from the inquisitorial documents is a vivid lesson in survival, one that sketches clearly and with great poignancy how various groups in different cultures strove to endure.

Although the immediate scholarly purpose of the anthology is to reach a more profound knowledge of the Inquisiton, analogies are certain to be drawn between events in the sixteenth century and those of our own, as the Spanish Inquisition's power is representative of oppressive institutional forces that exist to this day. For a clearer understanding of the systematization of this power, attention must be given both to the means of repression and to its reception and subversion by those groups it intends to constrain. The essays in this volume not only expand in great measure our comprehension of the Spanish Inquisition and its interrelations with Hispanic and Native American cultures, they also point to the larger lesson that cultural difference cannot be sustained without a continual process of social resistance.

PART ONE

The Inquisition and the Limits of Discipline

Colonizing Souls: The Failure of the Indian Inquisition and the Rise of Penitential Discipline

J. Jorge Klor de Alva

When you tell someone your secret, your freedom is gone.
—FERNANDO DE ROJAS, *La Celestina*

On a November morning in 1539 don Carlos Ometochtzin, the native leader of the former city-state of Texcoco, was taken out of the prison of the Holy Office garbed in the typical sanbenito cloak and cone-shaped hat of the sentenced offender. He was paraded through the streets of downtown Mexico City, candle in hand, to a scaffold surrounded by the multitude that came to witness his sentencing and abjuration, and later to see his strangled body burn at the stake.[1] For the majority of the natives, it would be unfortunate that never again would an anti-Spanish rebel meet his end at such a public spectacle. In less than a decade, the stake where individual bodies were set ablaze was replaced by the local controls of provisors (or vicars-general) of the dioceses or archdioceses[2] and, even more important, by the confessional, its penances, its magical threats, and its very real capacity to command the submission of tens of thousands of wills to the nascent colonial structure. The two related processes alluded to by these events—the failure of the Indian Inquisition and the consequent rise of penitential discipline, whose control mechanisms played a leading role in the colonization of the Nahuas (the Aztecs and their linguistic and cultural neighbors)—are the subject of this essay.

From the beginning of the colonial effort in New Spain, ambivalence about the Holy Office limited its utility as an instrument for the domination of natives. For instance, the movement to exclude the Indians from the authority of the Inquisition reached an early climax in 1540, when the apostolic inquisitor, Fray Juan de Zumárraga, received a reprimand from Spain for imposing the death sentence on the *cacique* don Carlos.[3]

Fig. 1. Two figures in penitential costume.

The Indians, however, continued to be processed by the Inquisition throughout the decade. And although official warnings to avoid treating the natives with severity were heard, no official prohibition against trying them outside the local dioceses or archdioceses was issued until 1571, when Philip II formally removed the Indians in the Spanish colonies from the jurisdiction of the Holy Office.[4] Despite a previous absence of legislation specifically excluding the Indians, some form of proscription nonetheless existed, because it appears that only one case involving Central Mexican Indians came before the Holy Office from 1547 to 1574.[5] Ambivalence is further suggested by the fact that out of 152 *procesos* acted upon between 1536 and 1543, the years of greatest inquisitorial persecution of natives, only about nineteen involved Indians (see Table 1.1) and the number accused was quite small, approximately seventy-five.[6]

Given the seemingly endless possibilities—painfully brought home to us by the experiences of some contemporary nation-states—for forcing subordination through a "culture of terror,"[7] why were so few natives tried, tortured, or executed by the Inquisition? And why was colonial policy so inconsistent that the Indians ended up beyond its grip altogether, although no law demanded that that be the case until 1571, while the need for maximizing control was fully recognized as critical, by both Church and Crown, prior to this date? As is usually the case when spectacular forms of oppression give way to their more subtle varieties, the reasons commonly offered for the Spanish retreat from an aggressive application of such a powerful instrument for subjecting natives have centered on an assumed rising cry of humanitarian sentiment,[8] which is said by some[9] to have echoed the following orders issued in 1540 to the apostolic inquisitor, Archbishop Zumárraga:

> since these people are newly converted . . . and in such a short time have not been able to learn well the things of our Christian religion, nor to be instructed in them as is fitting, and mindful that they are new plants, it is necessary that they should be attracted more with love than with rigor . . . and that they should not be treated roughly nor should one apply to them the rigor of the law . . . nor confiscate their property.[10]

But the implementation on humanitarian grounds of these instructions could not have been the primary force that led to the exemption that was generally observed. First of all, the Visitor General Francisco Tello de Sandoval, who replaced Zumárraga in New Spain in 1544 and was responsible for making known the New Laws of 1542—the laws that exhibited the greatest degree of toleration Charles V was able to muster on behalf of the Indians—not only was *not* instructed to avoid trying natives when acting as apostolic inquisitor but, on the contrary, during his three-year term failed to dismiss the cases against the Indians that came before the Holy Office.[11]

Second, although we know from the effects of the writings of Bartolomé de Las Casas and those of other reformers that this movement could have an influence on the formation of colonial policy,[12] the reform was focused on limited circles during the middle decades of the century and was more successful among Spanish rulers in the Old World than among colonial officials, who had to face the very real wrath of the settlers when they ventured arguments on behalf of the Indians. Fur-

TABLE 1.1 Mexican Inquisition of Indians in the Sixteenth Century 1522–1594 (Archivo General de la Nación, Inquisición [Mexico])

YR[a]	No/Sex	Doc	Idol	Sacrifice	Sorc/Witch	Super[b]	Pact/Devil	Biga	Concu	Relig/Crime	Heresy
22	1m	Pro[c]							x		
28	1m	Den			x						
36	2m	Pro	x	x							
36	1m	Pro			(performance as interpreter)					x	
36–37	1m	Pro	x		x						
37	2m	Pro			x						
38	1m	Pro						x			
38	1m	Inf	x								
38	?	Pro	x								
38	1m	Pro	x								
39	1m	Pro	x (Don Carlos Ometochtzin "Proceso criminal")								
39	2m, 1f	I, Pro	x						(hid idols)	x	
39	1m	Pro						x	x		
39	1m	Pro							(hid idols)	x	
39	3m	Pro					(spoke against Church)			x	
39	1m	Pro	x						(hid idols)	x	
39–40	1m	Pro	x (absolved, lack of proof even after torture)								
39–40	1m	Inf	x						x		
40	?	Frag.	x								

YR	No/Sex	Doc	Idol	Sacrifice	Super	Pact/Devil	Sorc/Witch	Biga	Concu	Relig/Crime
40	1m	Den	x (hid idols)				x			x
40	2m	Pro	x							x
44	–	Inf	x (Yanguitlán, outside Nahua area)							
44–46	2m	Pro	x (Yanguitlán, outside Nahua area)							
44–47	3m	Pro	x (Oaxaca, outside Nahua area)							
46–47	1m	Pro	x							
47	1m, 1f	Causa	x							
47	1m	Inf	x ("sacrifices and ceremonies . . . according to their ancient customs")							
57	1m, 1f	Pro			x (buried pagan in churchyard)					x
74	1f	Pro							(blasphemy)	x
81	1m	Den						("lewd acts with a dead woman and his mother-in-law")		x
94	4m	Pro							(theft from Inquisition)	x

[a] YR = year, No/Sex = number/sex, Doc = document type, Idol = idolatry, Sacrifice = sacrificial rites, Sorc/Witch = sorcery/witchraft, Super = superstitious acts or beliefs, Pact/Devil = pact with devil, Biga = bigamy, Concu = concubinage, Relig/Crime = miscellaneous religious crimes.

[b] There are no cases for superstition, pact with Devil, or heresy (by the seventeenth century these accusations were made primarily against women, especially mestizas, mulattoes, or members of the other castes [see Quezada in this volume]).

[c] *Proceso* (trial case), *Denuncia* (accusation), *Información* (testimony), *Fragmento* (incomplete text, not possible to ascertain its status), Causa (trial case with accusation).

thermore, in the New World much if not most of the legislation that favored the indigenes over Spanish interests was generally disregarded or
selectively applied.[13] As a consequence, the disputes of the intellectuals,
particularly those that took place in Spain,[14] had very limited practical
significance in New Spain unless they reflected policy implications that
supported the powerful sectors that ruled the colony. These facts point
to the difficulties that undermine any categorical conclusion concerning
the timing and role played by the toleration movement in the collapse
of the Indian Inquisition. Thus, when it comes to measuring the relative
strength of the forces that acted to remove the Indians through the Holy
Office, it may be more profitable to pay attention to the everyday exigencies of colonial control than to the royal fiats or the juridical or theological arguments that sometimes informed them.

THE INQUISITION AND THE ECONOMY OF PUNISHMENT

Although its ostensible function was to safeguard the orthodoxy of the
faith, the Holy Office was recognized to be and constantly was used as
an important tool for social and political control since its founding in
the thirteenth century.[15] In the New World the history of the Inquisition
is primarily the story of the struggles over power and truth that marked
the changing fortunes of the various ethnic, racial, and social sectors.[16]
Following the defeat of the Mexicas of Mexico-Tenochtitlán in 1521,
Cortés and the Franciscan friars put the Holy Office to work to secure
their predominance over both upstart Spaniards and recalcitrant Indians. By the surprisingly early date of 1522 an Indian from Acolhuacán
appears to have been formally accused of concubinage, thereby becoming the first person in Mexico to be tried by an agent of the Holy Office.[17]
This presaged the use of inquisitorial punishment to regulate the behavior of Indians and Europeans that was generalized the following
year, when two regulations were issued whose topics fit well into the
hands of the Cortesian band. One edict, aimed at Europeans, opposed
heretics and Jews; the other, whose vagueness was more a license to prosecute than a guide to proper behavior, was "against any person who
through deed or word did anything that appeared to be sinful"![18]
    In New Spain the regulatory possibilities of the latter ordinance were
especially clear to those who interpreted the culture of the Nahuas as a
satanic invention, and who used this as a justification for persecuting indigenous religious and sociocultural practices as criminal. Indeed, as the
military and political hegemony of the Spaniards solidified, this popular
interpretation was implemented as an apparatus of control by turning

Fig. 2. "Discipline of players and gamblers and punishment of one who had ridiculed our holy faith, by order of Cortés."

social customs and beliefs, acceptable in the native moral register, into sins, subject to temporal and symbolic punishment according to the Spanish criminal/canonical code. The tracing of both European and New World moralities onto the same penal map resolved the problem of cross-cultural (national) jurisdiction immediately. Thus, the Franciscan friar Martín de Valencia, who read into many aspects of the native cultures the authorship of the Devil, began to persecute recently baptized Indians in his capacity as commissary of the Holy Office immediately after his arrival in 1524. By 1527 his zeal was such that he had four Tlaxcalan leaders executed as idolaters and sacrificers,[19] even though the previous year the Franciscans had lost control of the Inquisition to the Dominicans.[20] In turn, the Dominican leaders of the Holy Office lost no time setting the institution to the task of stopping Cortés and his Franciscan allies from monopolizing the mechanisms of social and political domination; they sought to accomplish this power shift primarily by processing scores of their rivals as blasphemers.[21] However, with the arrival of the first viceroy in 1535, and the initiation of Zumárraga's episcopal tribunal the following year, the attention of the Holy Office shifted from the highly partisan contests between Spaniards[22] to the need to organize a colonial society primarily out of Nahuatl-speaking Indians.

It is hard to imagine a more difficult project: political and religious resistance, demographic ratios, language barriers, cultural distances, and extensive geographic spaces stood in the way, and the Spaniards had few precedents they could follow with confidence. Neither the confrontations with heretics, apostates, or non-Christians back home, nor their experiences with the far less socially integrated tribal and chiefdom communities in the circum-Caribbean area, prepared the Spaniards for the encounter with the city-state polities of New Spain. In Central Mexico cultural, regulatory, and security concerns contrasted sharply with those faced in Spain; there, not only did a variety of effective mechanisms of social control exist that could not be duplicated in the New World, but the problems of ethnic diversity in the peninsula tended primarily to affect civic unity rather than to challenge political stability or cultural viability, as was frequently the case in Mexico.

Consequently, from the time of the fall of Tenochtitlán, the primary requirement for the establishment of a colony was tactical and ethnographic knowledge, which called for the development of new disciplinary and intelligence techniques.[23] To gain control, the Spaniards needed information about the topography and natural resources of the land, the political and social organizations and their jurisdictions, the geography of economic production, the type and extent of religious beliefs and rituals, the meanings and implications of ideological assumptions and local loyalties, and the nature and exploitability of everyday practices. All these data had to be elicited, translated, interpreted, and ordered within familiar conceptual categories that could make practical sense of the land and the people in order to form the New Spain out of highly ethnocentric and aggressively self-interested city-states.

To this effect, what today would be called ethnography drew the attention of some of the early conquerors (particularly Cortés himself),[24] priests, and secular officials, so that by the early 1530s missionary-ethnographers were formally instructed to collect the information needed to found a productive and peaceful colony.[25] Of the various institutions charged with the creation of new knowledge about the Indians, the Inquisition seemed to hold the most promise. After all, it enjoyed overwhelming support on the part of Church and Crown, and it appeared to have access to the maximum force needed to extract confessions, draw forth information, and punish those who remained silent or otherwise resisted its claims.

A close study of trial records nonetheless suggests that the efficacy of the Holy Office as a punitive system and the quantity and variety of information the inquisitors could elicit were limited by a number of factors. First, quite apart from the ruses and manipulations that sometimes precipitated inquisitorial accusations (*denuncias* or *informaciones*), charges were formally restricted to the types of crimes and breaches legally recognized as within the competence of the Holy Office. These included a significant but extremely small number of categories of acts that needed to be controlled by the colonial powers (see Table 1.2, A). Second, there were legal restraints upon the interrogative procedures used that made it difficult for important but excludable information to enter the record. Third, the extreme and public nature of the penalties could serve as a warning to many but did so at the price of moving the key rebels who resisted the colonial order further underground, where it became more difficult to uproot them.[26] Fourth, the cultural and demographic barriers between Indians and Europeans, the Holy Office's legalistic procedures, and the Inquisition officials' constant concern with status—all called for levels of financing, energy, and personnel that spelled the need for the institution to focus its attention and resources on what it knew best and ultimately feared most: heresy and deviance among Europeans. Not surprisingly, of the 152 procesos tried by Zumárraga's tri-

TABLE 1.2   Inquisition Cases in New Spain
(Archivo General de la Nación, Inquisición [Mexico])

Type of Offense	Indian Inquisition	Non-Indian Inquisition
A. 1522–1557		
Idolatry[a]	15	
Bigamy/concubinage	5	
Sorcery/witchcraft	2	
Misc. religious crimes	2	
B. 1536–1543[b]		
Blasphemy		56
Judaizing		19
Heresy		8
Lutheran heresies		5
Clerical crimes		5

[a] Includes dogmatizing against the beliefs of the Church, hiding idols, and performing sacrifices.

[b] Of a total of 152 cases, 93 concerned offenses restricted to Europeans, 19 involved Indians (approximately 75 individuals).

bunal, ninety-three were for crimes associated almost exclusively with Europeans: blasphemy, heresy, Judaizing, and clerical crimes (Table 1.2, B).[27]

Together, these restrictions contributed to making the Inquisition a poor mechanism for meting out the type of punishment needed to effectively regulate masses of unacculturated Indians. But what ultimately marginalized the Holy Office from the efforts to subjugate the native populations was the widespread deployment, during the first half of the century, of two related practices: sacramental confession and missionary ethnography. Because each of these was far more pervasive and intrusive than the Inquisition, together they were more efficient at gathering the kind of information needed to transform the Nahuas into disciplined subjects. Elsewhere I take up the role of the penitential system as an inciter of discourse on the self and as an apparatus of self-formation;[28] here my sole concern is to study how, in the first half of the sixteenth century, a shift took place from the inquisitorial techniques of random investigation and selective punishment to a technique of penitential discipline that sought to affect each word, thought, and deed of every individual Indian.

FROM PUNISHMENT TO DISCIPLINE

The responsibility for the forced acculturation of the Indians moved from the Holy Office to the (seemingly) less stringent local offices of the bishops (known as the *provisorato del ordinario*) in 1547 (see Moreno de los Arcos, this volume). The archival record attests to the timing of this de facto shift in jurisdiction because only one relevant case[29] appears between that date and 1574,[30] by which time the Holy Office had already lost its official jurisdiction over the indigenes (see Table 1.1). Although the change of venue is nowhere explicitly explained or noted, the letters sent to Zumárraga in 1540, after he had had don Carlos executed, suggest the outline of a new policy. Translated into today's analytical language, the critical points in the instructions to the archbishop could be summarized—and were justified then—as follows:

1. *Punishment, by functioning as part of a regime of exercises aimed at disciplining through indoctrination, is to be discreet and to have the self (mind/soul), rather than the body, as its object.* That is, instead of torture, rigorous punishments, or scandalizing executions, what was needed was for the Indians "first to be very well instructed in and informed about the faith . . . because gentleness should be applied first, before the sore is opened with an iron."

2. *The source and end of the discipline are to be invisible.* For instance, "the little property they possess" should not be confiscated "because . . . the Indians have been greatly scandalized, thinking that they are burned on account of the great desire for these goods."

3. *The discipline is to be made imperceptible by appearing to be evenly applied throughout the whole social body.* In effect, instead of teaching them a lesson through rigorous persecution, "the Indians would be better instructed and edified if (the Inquisition) proceeded against the Spaniards who supposedly sold them idols, since they deserved the punishment more than the Indians who bought them."[31]

I will continue by analyzing the meaning and implications of each of these points.

PUNISHMENT AND THE DISCIPLINING OF THE SOUL

Scholars have made much of the humanism the first point seems to imply. The call for tolerance is an echo of the arguments developed in the late 1530s by Las Casas[32] to attack the superficial and sometimes violent means with which the Spanish officials and Franciscan friars sought to impose the new faith on the Indians. However, a survey of the methods used by the missionaries during these early years attests to the futility of Las Casa's appeals for moderation.[33] It could not have been otherwise. The popular idea that natives needed to be treated in a special manner (because they were new to the faith, because they had a weak understanding, or because they were inclined to vice, etc.) originally arose out of very real political exigencies, although the specific conclusions may have been drawn from speculative reflections on ethnographic data or theology. However contradictory, policy was primarily driven by the pragmatic requirements of the colony, although, as is the case today, in official discourse the need to control was frequently masked by lofty language that expounded on the humanity of subordinates.

A particularly vivid example of the rhetorical, rather than empirical, nature of assessments of native capacity to acculturate is suggested by the following fact: almost *thirty* years after the letters to Zumárraga were written, the priest Sancho Sánchez de Muñón, while advising the king about the need to establish a Tribunal of the Holy Office in the New World, could still argue that

> [the Inquisition] would be one of the most important things in the service of God, for use against the Spaniards, mulattoes, and mestizos who offend our Lord [but] *for now it should be suspended in what concerns the natives because they are so new to the faith, weak [gente flaca], and of little substance.*[34] [My emphasis]

In effect, the movement toward leniency was less the product of the reformers' rejection of the spectacular punishment of criminal acts, which continued for the Indians in an attenuated form at the local provisorato del ordinario level, and more a recognition, on the part of most priests and secular officials, that what colonial order called for most was the eradication from Indian life of the myriad of seemingly banal deviations from Spanish cultural habits and social customs. The friars, in their letters, sermons, doctrinal works, and detailed manuals for confessors, were quick to argue that every gesture and thought, from those associated with sexual life and domestic practice to the magical and empirical procedures employed in agriculture, the crafts, and social relations, had to be disciplined, retrained, and rechanneled, so as (I would add) to serve the interests of those who wielded power in the colony.[35]

To discover and punish these minute illegalities, systematic and pervasive forms of intervention were necessary. In this situation the Inquisition's attention to the scandalous cases of a few indigenous cult leaders[36] was clearly a dangerous and wasteful display of colonial power. Furthermore, too much delinquency went unperceived by most Spaniards and was primarily confined to the private or local spheres, which were too numerous to be handled with the juridical safeguards called for by the inquisitorial process. Meanwhile, as these minor infractions continued to escape the grip of the authorities, they helped to reinforce and legitimate sociocultural and political alternatives to the habits and practices necessary for the formation of a homogeneous, predictable, and submissive population.

Although the need to impose some form of consistent and uniform discipline had been coming to light since the early 1530s, a substantial division in the Spanish perception of the level and nature of native resistance to Christianity made it impossible to implement one. On the one hand, Zumárraga's Inquisition, charged with defending the assumptions and practices that articulated Hispanic culture, had the debilitating effect of propagating the idea that native heterodoxy continued primarily as a result of heretical dogmatizing by a few indigenous religious leaders. On the other hand, some of the Franciscans, especially Motolinía,[37] a key figure in the Christianization process since 1524, were claiming that the natives were seeking salvation by the millions and were quickly forgetting the beliefs of the past. On one level, these representations were slowly being challenged by the ethnographic studies undertaken during this time, primarily those begun by Olmos in 1533.[38] On another level, the varieties of regional experiences and the urgent need for immediate control were leading some priests to the realization that local knowledge of the Indians was fundamental to the development of the type of discipline capable of forming "docile bodies."[39] If this latter call for widespread, rather than selective and exemplary, intervention had failed, the Indian Inquisition might have continued—as it did for the other more assimilated racial castes.

The Indian Inquisition, however, did end. And, in particular, its demise came about because it had been organized to function only among the baptized, who presumably already shared with the inquisitor the basic idea of what was and was not an infraction. If this is the case, it follows that the Holy Office was ill suited to discipline a people who did not share its basic cultural or penal assumptions. Before the spectacle of the stake could move beyond striking fear in the hearts of the natives to transforming their behavior permanently, they had to know the prohibitions of the Holy Office and accept the illegality of the things prohibited. Only an efficient system of indoctrination could make these prerequisites a reality.

But an effective proselytizing strategy had to go far beyond violent or physical coercion, the performance of baptisms, or the teaching of the rudiments of the Christian doctrine. It had to penetrate into every corner of native life, especially those intimate spaces where personal loyalties were forged, commitments were assessed, and collective security concerns were weighed against individual ambitions. Thus, "the invasion within"[40] could not be done by scare tactics, whose ultimate result would more likely be resistance than acquiescence, but rather by shifting the moral gears to produce social and political effects that favored the interests in stability and productivity of those in power. An operative indoctrination that could produce such results had to begin with the widespread, but localized, imposition of a constant regime of moral calisthenics through corporal and magical punishments (like the threat of the fires of Hell). These exercises, backed by the threat of the provisors, had to have as their aim the retraining of the individual in order for him or her to internalize a Christian form of self-discipline that would ultimately make external force secondary or unnecessary.[41] This intrusive strategy sought to constitute the most discreet punitive mechanism possible: a fear of divine retribution nourished by a scrupulous consciousness of one's wrongdoings. And where this failed, as it very frequently did, it excused the policing intervention of the priest, with his threats of supernatural punishment, corporal penance, and public shaming and ridicule. It also permitted pious neighbors to force the sinner to behave properly by threatening to exclude him or her from the moral and civic community. It was a brilliant experiment in mass subordination: the costly punishment of individual bodies by colonial officials or the Inquisition could be replaced, for the most part, by the economical disciplining of myriads of souls.

THE INVISIBLE ORIGIN AND OBJECT OF DISCIPLINE

The authorship and end of inquisitorial punishment were always evident. The *source* was obvious to all: Spanish hegemony—a force coming ultimately from the same external apparatus that inflicted innumerable other penalties and burdens. To the Indians, almost all of whom remained unacculturated in the 1540s, its ends were equally apparent: to deprive the accused of his or her traditions, the guiding memory of the ancestors, personal liberty and dignity, corporeal well-being and temporal property, and life (or so it must have seemed after the execution of the cacique don Carlos). Since at this early date the crimes the Inquisition sought to punish were not generally regarded as illegalities by the still unacculturated community, the Holy Office depended primarily on the exercise of power rather than assent. It therefore lacked the legitimacy to turn scandalous punishments into moral lessons.

In contrast, the transparency of the discipline the friars sought to establish had as its source a continuous and permanent project of acculturation at the margins of Spanish life. The ritual origin and legitimating structure of this program of assimilation, which historians traditionally identify as "conversion,"[42] was a baptism which, in the early colonial situation, the friars had effectively transformed into a new social contract. Thus, unlike inquisitorial punishment, which turned the native subject into an object of punitive force, baptism, the voluntary acceptance of a new social pact, could force each party to it to participate *as an active agent* in his or her own punishment.

On one level, this new social contract was put into effect by the forces that were slowly appropriating for themselves the authority to determine both the rules of civic life and the nature of the new colonial truths. At the points of general concentration, and therefore penetration, these forces appeared in the form of local priests who (genuinely, for the most part) sought the temporal and symbolic (or supernatural) well-being of the Indians. Their good intentions had the rhetorical and emotive capacity to transpose agency, making the initial phases of indoctrination appear to be the voluntary acceptance of new rules of behavior and new codes of belief. Colonial power thus could circulate at a symbolic level that erased in its very movements the origins and ends that drove it. At another level, the new social pact, by resting on the rhetoric of magic,[43] could be enforced by the manipulation of punitive signs,[44] whose supernatural source was continually preached and whose human origin could thus remain hidden from the believers. The source of the new discipline was consequently made invisible by making it appear as if its fountainhead were either the individual, who voluntarily assumed it, or a deity who commanded it from above: Its end, the peaceful subordination to and productive loyalty on behalf of the colonial powers, was reconstituted as the personal quest for temporal well-being and supernatural salvation.

THE UBIQUITY AND UNIFORMITY OF DISCIPLINE

The letters to Zumárraga underlined how important it was that inquisitorial punishment appear to be justly assessed and evenhandedly applied. As already noted, this was not possible as long as the Holy

Office had jurisdiction over such a culturally heterogeneous population as the one in New Spain. By weaving the new discipline into the personal and public strands of native and Spanish lives, however, the friars could be seen to cover with it all social and cultural sectors. The widespread use of an apparently common Christian doctrine, penal code, and ritual cycle was at the heart of this tactic.

Furthermore, by introducing the Christian sacraments in ways that made them coextensive with the life-cycle rituals of everyday indigenous life, the missionaries attempted to reify these rites and their meanings so that they would appear to be normal and universal. The ultimate result was to make the Christian practices accessible through the native registers of common sense, thus giving them the appearance of being natural and ubiquitous, while freeing them of the need to justify themselves on other grounds. Of course, the sporadic public punishment of non-Indians that continued after 1547 reinforced this image of penitential discipline as general and uniform.

In effect, the domestication and normalization[45] of millions of unacculturated Indians by dozens of friars needed far more than an Inquisition. It called for a new regime of control that acted upon the soul to create self-disciplined colonial subjects. Unfortunately, an analysis of the methods used to effect this end, primarily through a penitential discipline founded on confessional practices, is beyond the scope of this volume, but it is taken up elsewhere.[46]

NOTES

1. Archivo General de la Nación (hereafter AGN), Inquisición, tomo 42, expediente 1.

2. Greenleaf, "The Inquisition and the Indians of New Spain: A Study in Jurisdictional Confusion," 141. See Moreno de los Arcos, this volume.

3. García Icazbalceta, *Don Fray Juan de Zumárraga: Primer Obispo y Arzobispo de México* 4:170–173.

4. Greenleaf, *Zumárraga and the Mexican Inquisition, 1536–1543*, 74; idem, "The Inquisition and the Indians," 141.

5. AGN, Inq., tomo 42, exp. 1.

6. Greenleaf, *Zumárraga*; idem, "The Inquisition and the Indians," 139.

7. Taussig, *Shamanism, Colonialism, and the Wild Man*, 3–36.

8. See Gibson, "Indian Societies under Spanish Rule," 367.

9. See Greenleaf, *Zumárraga*, 14.

10. García Icazbalceta, *Don Fray Juan de Zumárraga* 4:171.

11. AGN, Inq., tomo 34, exp. 6; tomo 37, exps. 6–10, 12.

12. See Hanke, *The Spanish Struggle for Justice in the Conquest of America*.

13. See Gibson, *The Aztecs Under Spanish Rule: A History of the Indians of the Valley of Mexico, 1519–1810.*

14. See Hanke, *Aristotle and the American Indians: A Study in Race Prejudice in the Modern World.*

15. Tentler, *Sin and Confession on the Eve of the Reformation.*

16. Alberro, "La Inquisición como institución normativa"; idem, *La actividad del Santo Oficio de la Inquisición en Nueva España, 1571–1700*; Behar, "Sex and Sin, Witchcraft and the Devil in Late-Colonial Mexico."

17. AGN, Inq., tomo 1, exp. 1. Roberto Moreno de los Arcos disputes the occurrence of this case, whose record is physically missing from the Archivo, because of the early date (personal communication). I suggest the utility of inquisitorial powers was recognized well enough in the first post-Contact decade (see Table 1.1 and Greenleaf, *Zumárraga,* 7–44) as to make this precipitate exercise of them plausible.

18. AGN, Catálogo de Inquisición, tomo 1, exps. 2, 3.

19. Gibson, *Tlaxcala in the Sixteenth Century,* 34. Neither the date (1526 or 1527?) nor the number of victims (four or six?) is beyond dispute.

20. Greenleaf, *The Mexican Inquisition of the Sixteenth Century,* 11.

21. Greenleaf, *The Mexican Inquisition,* 7–40; Baudot, *Utopía e historia en México: Los primeros cronistas de la civilización mexicana (1520–1569).*

22. Greenleaf, *The Mexican Inquisition,* 1–44.

23. Alberro, "La Inquisición"; idem, *La actividad del Santo Oficio.*

24. Cortés, *Cartas y documentos.*

25. See, especially, Baudot, *Utopía e Historia.*

26. Klor de Alva, "Martín Ocelotl: Clandestine Cult Leader."

27. Greenleaf, *Zumárraga,* p. 14.

28. See Klor de Alva, "Sahagún and the Birth of Modern Ethnography: Representing, Confessing, and Inscribing the Native Other" and "Contar vidas: La autobiografía confesional y la reconstrucción del ser nahua." My book on the subject, tentatively titled *The Confession of the Other: On the New World of Colonialism, Anthropology, and Modernity,* is in progress.

29. AGN, Inq., tomo 42, exp. 1 (dated 1557).

30. AGN, Inq., tomo 48, exp. 1.

31. García Icazbalceta, *Don Fray Juan de Zumárraga* 4:170–173.

32. Las Casas, *Del único modo de atraer a todos los pueblos a la verdadera religión.*

33. See Motolinía, *Memoriales; o, Libro de las cosas de Nueva España y de los naturales de ella*; idem, *Historia de los indios de Nueva España.*

34. Quoted in Cuevas, *Historia de la iglesia en México* 1:380.

35. See *Doctrina cristiana en lengua española y mexicana por los religiosos de la orden de Santo Domingo*; Molina, *Confesionario mayor en la lengua mexicana y castellana.*

36. See González Obregón, *Proceso inquisitorial del cacique de Tetzcoco*; idem, *Procesos de indios idólatras y hechiceros.*

37. Motolinía, *Memoriales,* 120.

38. See Baudot, *Utopía e historia*, 19–81, 129–245.

39. On discipline and the formation of "docile bodies" see Foucault, *Discipline and Punish: The Birth of the Prison*, 135–169.

40. Axtell, *The Invasion Within: The Contest of Cultures in Colonial North America*.

41. See Klor de Alva, "Sin and Confession among the Colonial Nahuas: The Confessional as a Tool for Domination."

42. Cf. Klor de Alva, "Spiritual Conflict and Accommodation in New Spain: Toward a Typology of Aztec Responses to Christianity."

43. On the rhetoric of magic see, for instance, Taussig, *Shamanism*.

44. On punitive signs see Foucault, *Discipline and Punish*, 95; Fabian, *Language and Colonial Power*.

45. On "domestication" and "normalization" as the results of disciplinary practices see Foucault, *Discipline and Punish*.

46. See nn. 28 and 41 above.

BIBLIOGRAPHY

Alberro, Solange. "La Inquisición como institución normativa." In *Seminario de historia de las mentalidades y religión en el México colonial*, edited by Solange Alberro and Serge Gruzinski. Departamento de Investigaciones Históricas, Cuaderno de Trabajo 24. Mexico City: Instituto Nacional de Antropología e Historia, 1979.

———. *La actividad del Santo Oficio de la Inquisición en Nueva España, 1571–1700*. Colección Científica, vol. 96. Mexico City: Instituto Nacional de Antropología e Historia, 1981.

Axtell, James. *The Invasion Within; The Contest of Cultures in Colonial North America*. New York: Oxford University Press, 1985.

Baudot, Georges. *Utopía e historia en México: Los primeros cronistas de la civilización mexicana (1520–1569)*. Translated by Vicente González Loscertales. Madrid: Espasa-Calpe, 1983.

Behar, Ruth. "Sex and Sin, Witchcraft and the Devil in Late-Colonial Mexico." *American Ethnologist* 14 (1987): 34–54.

Cortés, Hernán. *Cartas y documentos*. Introduction by Mario Hernández Sánchez-Barba. Mexico City: Editorial Porrúa, 1963.

Cuevas, Mariano. *Historia de la iglesia en México*. 4th ed. 5 vols. Mexico City: Ediciones Cervantes, 1942.

Doctrina cristiana en lengua española y mexicana por los religiosos de la orden de Santo Domingo. 1548. Reprint. Madrid: Ediciones Cultura Hispánica, 1944.

Fabian, Johannes. *Language and Colonial Power*. New York: Cambridge University Press, 1986.

Foucault, Michel. *Discipline and Punish: The Birth of the Prison*. Translated by Alan Sheridan. New York: Vintage Books, 1979.

García Icazbalceta, Joaquín. *Don Fray Juan de Zumárraga: Primer Obispo y Arzobispo de México.* Edited by Rafael Aguayo Spencer and Antonio Castro Leal. 4 vols. Mexico City: Editorial Porrúa, 1947.

Gibson, Charles. *The Aztecs Under Spanish Rule: A History of the Indians of the Valley of Mexico, 1519–1810.* Stanford: Stanford University Press, 1964.

———. *Tlaxcala in the Sixteenth Century.* Stanford: Stanford University Press, 1967.

———. "Indian Societies Under Spanish Rule." In *Colonial Spanish America.* Edited by Leslie Bethell. New York: Cambridge University Press, 1987.

González Obregón, Luis, ed. *Proceso inquisitorial del cacique de Tetzcoco.* Mexico City: Archivo General y Público de la Nación, 1910.

———. *Procesos de indios idólatras y hechiceros.* Mexico City: Archivo General de la Nación, 1912.

Greenleaf, Richard E. *Zumárraga and the Mexican Inquisition, 1536–1543.* Washington, D.C.: Academy of American Franciscan History, 1961.

———. "The Inquisition and the Indians of New Spain: A Study in Jurisdictional Confusion." *The Americas* 22 (1965): 138–166.

———. *The Mexican Inquisition of the Sixteenth Century.* Albuquerque: University of New Mexico Press, 1969.

Hanke, Lewis. *The Spanish Struggle for Justice in the Conquest of America.* Boston: Little, Brown and Co., 1965.

———. *Aristotle and the American Indians: A Study in Race Prejudice in the Modern World.* Bloomington: Indiana University Press, 1970.

Klor de Alva, J. Jorge. "Martín Ocelotl: Clandestine Cult Leader." In *Struggle and Survival in Colonial America.* Edited by David G. Sweet and Gary B. Nash. Berkeley, Los Angeles, London: University of California Press, 1981.

———. "Spiritual Conflict and Accommodation in New Spain: Toward a Typology of Aztec Responses to Christianity." In *The Inca and Aztec States, 1400–1800: Anthropology and History.* Edited by George A. Collier, Renato I. Rosaldo, and John D. Wirth. New York: Academic Press, 1982.

———. "Sahagún and the Birth of Modern Ethnography: Representing, Confessing, and Inscribing the Native Other." In *The Work of Bernardino de Sahagún: Pioneer Ethnographer of Sixteenth-Century Aztec Mexico.* Edited by J. Jorge Klor de Alva, H. B. Nicholson, and Eloise Quiñónes Keber. Vol. 2 of Studies on Culture and Society. Albany: Institute for Mesoamerican Studies. Austin: University of Texas Press, 1988.

———. "Sin and Confession among the Colonial Nahuas: The Confessional as a Tool for Domination." In *Ciudad y campo en la historia de México.* Edited by Richard Sánchez, Eric Van Young, and Gisela von Wobeser. 2 vols. Mexico City: Instituto de Investigaciones Históricas, Universidad Nacional Autónoma de México, 1990.

———. "Contar vidas: La autobiografía confesional y la reconstrucción del ser nahua." *Arbor* 515–516 (1988): 49–78.

Las Casas, Bartolomé de. *Del único modo de atraer a todos los pueblos a la verdadera religión.* Edited by Agustín Millares Carlo. Translated from the Latin by Atenógenes Santamaría. Mexico City: Fondo de Cultura Económica, 1942.

Molina, Alonso de. *Confesionario mayor en la lengua mexicana y castellana.* 1569. Reprint, with introduction by Roberto Moreno. Mexico City: Universidad Nacional Autónoma de México, 1984.

Motolinía, Toribio de Benavente. *Memoriales: o, Libro de las cosas de Nueva España y de los naturales de ella.* Edited by Edmundo O'Gorman. Mexico City: Universidad Nacional Autónoma de México, 1971.

———. *Historia de los indios de la Nueva España.* Edited by Edmundo O'Gorman. Mexico City: Editorial Porrúa, 1973.

Taussig, Michael. *Shamanism, Colonialism, and the Wild Man.* Chicago: University of Chicago Press, 1987.

Tentler, Thomas N. *Sin and Confession on the Eve of the Reformation.* Princeton, N.J.: Princeton University Press, 1977.

TWO

New Spain's Inquisition for Indians from the Sixteenth to the Nineteenth Century

Roberto Moreno de los Arcos

It is common knowledge that the Tribunal of the Holy Office of the Inquisition was expressly prohibited from interfering in cases involving Indians. "Thank God," the distinguished Spanish historian Guillermo Céspedes del Castillo adds recently in the volume dedicated to the colony from his *Historia de España*.[1] What has not been made common knowledge is that this does not imply in any way that the Indians were exempt from punishment for transgressions of the faith. In effect, throughout the entire colonial period and well into the nineteenth century, there existed an institution expressly dedicated to punishing the Indians' religious offenses, identified by various names: Office of Provisor of Natives, Tribunal of the Faith of Indians, Secular Inquisition, Vicarage of the Indians, Natives' Court. This institution generated an enormous number of trials, very few of which have come to light.[2]

Ignorance of this tribunal's existence is based partly on the fact that historiography on the colonial Church is basically furnished by clergymen and Catholics eager to exalt Spain's efforts in America and to cover up the incidents that might appear negatively to liberal minds. The undeniable existence of the Holy Office of the Inquisition has been so well documented—so worn out yet so poorly understood by politically liberal writers—that this other capacity the Catholic Church had (and still has) to inflict punishment should have been discovered. What is evident is that a great number of colonial books do exist, clearly revealing all the details of the inquisitorial procedure regarding Indians, but it seems that we cannot see the forest for the trees.

Most of the known trials of that tribunal have been published and studied as "sources" of indigenous ethnohistory. This they are, in effect, but primarily they are trials that can be used as a source for many other investigations, although it seems to me that the first one should be the study of the particular institution that generates them. In and of themselves, like any other documents, they are of no use as a study of what they do not contain.

It would be unjust to affirm that there has been a universal ignorance of this institution's existence. Obviously, those who created it knew about it, as did those it punished. I am more concerned with emphasizing the recent investigations of this institution, and I will refer to only two.

At the end of the nineteenth century, a Mr. Carrión, a Protestant, published a gallery of renowned Indians.[3] Among the Indians in that gallery was a Dominican Indian, Friar Martín Durán, whose existence was invented, and who was supposed to have been burned at the stake by the Holy Office for heresy. Don José María Vigil, director of the Biblioteca Nacional at the time, consulted with the scholar don Joaquín García Icazbalceta regarding this case. The latter had already published a letter debunking the myth, and with his characteristic prudence, had arrived at the conclusion that the falsifier's intention was to create the existence of a pre-Lutheran Indian in sixteenth-century New Spain. Among Icazbalceta's many arguments refuting the truth of this history is that of jurisdiction. He demonstrates that an Indian would have been subject to trial not by the Holy Office but instead by the authority of the ecclesiastical judge (i.e., the bishop or archbishop) through the Natives' Court.[4]

Much more recently, Professor Richard E. Greenleaf, with great insight and acumen, has clarified the issues. In an article published in 1965 in *The Americas*, he studies both tribunals, the Holy Office and the Office of Provisor, along with what he terms "jurisdictional confusion." This article allows us to clarify the underlying causes regarding the punishment of the Indians' transgressions of the faith as well as to establish a historical perspective of the facts. In this first essay, Professor Greenleaf's principal subject is the Holy Office.[5] His second article, published in the same journal in 1978, deals with inquisitorial trials against Indians as ethnohistorical sources and presents a compilation of invaluable information on this theme. It also includes a list of trials initiated against Indians, derived from the Archivo General de la Nación (AGN), principally from the Inquisitorial branch, as well as half a dozen from the National Welfare branch.[6] In these investigations as well as in the author's other works dedicated to studying the Holy Office, the problem I am focusing on has been well outlined.

My investigation of the subject takes a different approach. It focuses uniquely on the Office of Provisor, ignoring the Holy Office completely, except when for some reason they coincide. This is, in short, the history of an institution's ecclesiastical-jurisdictional power over the Indians. As can be easily understood, this is a major undertaking that must confront enormous difficulties. We are dealing with vast documentation generated throughout three centuries, very difficult to access, of the dioceses and archdioceses of Mexico City (in this case the sources are located in part in the AGN, Bienes Nacionales, and in part in a locale which I cannot recognize since the destruction of the Mitre in the earthquake of 1985), Oaxaca (which involves its own difficulties), Chiapas (which is organized and now publishes a bulletin), Yucatán, Michoacán (now publicly accessible since it is considered the property of the Instituto Nacional de Antropología e Historia), and Guadalajara. The undertaking is impossible without a team of historians. I trust I will be able to organize one and offer the initial results by 1992, with catalogs of the trials and lists of the provisional judges of each diocese. The bibliography of the colonial books I have discovered on this material is presented in this essay and will soon be published, in an identical edition, as the *Bibliotheca Superstitionis et Cultus Idolatrici Indorum Mexicanensium,* beginning with Diego de Balsalobre's classic treatise. In this essay, I offer a summary of the problem and will allude to the progress of the investigation.

No one is unaware that the Church's power over society, like that of the state, has two axes composed of its authority and its territory—that is, its jurisdiction or power to set standards, to revise sentences, to correct, and to punish, and the territory or demarcation within which all of this can take place. As an example that will serve for what follows, we remember that many medieval Spanish cities contained more or less isolated precincts known as Moorish mosques and Jewish synagogues. Civil jurisdiction over these spaces fell to the state; the Church had no jurisdiction over them. The Christians would enter by force in order to baptize Moors and Jews, thus making them liable to ecclesiastical jurisdiction. They were prosecuted afterward if they willingly apostatized or attempted conversion through peaceful entrance into the precinct, a privilege enjoyed only by the Franciscan order. Those who were Christianized in this way were known as *moriscos* or *judíos conversos.* If this was not the case, then they maintained their own faith and could not be forced, a fact which is, it will be recalled, the cornerstone of Friar Bartolomé de Las Casas's argument in his defense of the Indians.[7] Jurisdiction and territory are also the axes in the Americas of what Ricard, a Catholic, called "spiritual conquest,"[8] and Duviols, a liberal, called "destruction of the indigenous religions."[9]

Primarily, jurisdiction over the "faithful" is exercised by the bishop or ecclesiastical judge within the confines of his territory, which are almost always clearly delimited. The necessity of conserving the faith and its orthodoxy led to the creation, generalized in the Old World, of the Tribunal of the Holy Office of the Inquisition against Heretical Perversity and Apostasy. Its jurisdiction, which was above that of the bishops, exceeded the diocese but not the kingdom. The principal crimes that it originally prosecuted were Christians' acts of heresy, that is, departure from or error concerning dogma in its two forms, material (i.e., through ignorance or confusion) and formal (through pertinacity),[10] and apostasy, or the rejection of the true faith in order to embrace another religion, which was fundamentally the case with the *conversos*.[11] This last crime was punished with the severest penalties. The catalog of punishable crimes expanded with the passage of time, and the Tribunal of the Holy Office gained enormous importance and respect. It is worth remembering here that "inquisition" simply means "investigation." It was the tremendous weight of the Tribunal of Faith that led to the semantic change, so that its exclusive claim to inquisition was recognized and sanctioned.

The encounter with the New World created many problems. To understand what occurred jurisdictionally, we must refer to the theological underpinnings. The Holy Scriptures, dictated by the Holy Spirit, say in the New Testament that Christ's apostles preached throughout the entire world.[12] Such a decisive affirmation thus authorized created quite a difficulty for Catholic theologians, since the New World was populated by millions of human beings, none of whom were Christian. In the face of such a reality, some explanation had to be found. The most ingenious theologians postulated that the intentionally lost apostle, St. Thomas, had preached in the Americas. The foundations were taken from the indigenous myths like that of the priest Quetzalcóatl, whose alleged kindheartedness the Catholic priests were set on promoting. This thesis, which also occurred in Peru with some variations, arose in the sixteenth century and was expunged by the nineteenth.[13] It did not actually flourish, because among other things, it implied the brutal fact that the entire continent had apostatized. The practical solution was to declare that the existence of the New World was a mystery and that the Indians were "gentiles" (that is, without ever having received Christian doctrine), and to set about evangelizing them. The Church was able to do this because they deemed the Indians "idolaters," among other negative things.

Idolatry is an unpardonable error for Christianity. It consists of offering *latria*, or worship and service owed solely to God (the worship of the saints is called *dulia*), to an idol, an image created by human beings.[14]

Fig. 3. "Bonfire of clothing, books, and items of idolatrous priests burned by the friars."

That the Indians were idolaters provides one of the principal justifications for what Spanish historiography continues to call the "just titles"
of the conquest of the New World. This implies that if Spain had conceded the existence of the Indians' own religion, it would not, in terms
of what has been said above, have had Christian jurisdiction over them.
As far as civil jurisdiction was concerned, the Indians were alleged to
be, among other things, drunkards and sodomizers.

In spite of some heroic attempts to slacken the zeal, Spain proceeded
with the conversion of New World Indians. The process turned out to
be more difficult than had been anticipated. The main problem is that,
in spite of the friars' investigations which are our principal sources, the
Indians had their own religions and were unfamiliar with Christianity,
unlike the Moors and the Jews, who had centuries of contact with Christians. The two religious mentalities confronted each other without mu-
tual understanding: one exclusive, that of the Christians, and one inclu-
sive, that of the indigenous peoples. This reality has been conceptualized
in terms of "syncretism" or "nativism," and yet these terms are not completely satisfactory. The fact is that the Christian Church expanded its
battlefronts. It did not simply have to contend with the heretical deviations or the apostasies with which it was familiar in the Old World, but
now saw itself forced to employ its imagination regarding the novelties
that the Evil Spirit manifested in America.

The Church held that the Devil was the guilty party. I have already
compiled some notes toward an essay that could be entitled "The Devil
in the New World."[15] He was the one responsible for the veil that hid
these lands and peoples from European eyes. He had fooled the Indians
into worshipping him with *excrements* in place of the *sacraments* of the
Church of God and as a mockery of divinity. He was responsible for the
fact that the Indians committed crimes against the faith after having
been baptized. All of this resulted in the primary necessity of exorcising
lands, animals, plants, and people. This resulted, I believe, in the initial
Franciscan practice of limiting the baptismal rite. It also resulted in indispensable and constant vigilance in order to detect and punish all deviations, that is, to exercise ecclesiastical jurisdiction.

According to Llorente, inquisitional jurisdiction was introduced in
America when, by order of Charles V, the cardinal inquisitor Adriano
named don Alfonso Manso, bishop of Puerto Rico, and Friar Pedro de
Córdoba, vice-provincial of the Dominican Islands, as inquisitors of the
Indies and other islands on 7 January 1519.[16]

Regarding New Spain, jurisdiction arrived with the famous "first
twelve" Franciscans headed by Friar Martín de Valencia. This privilege

was derived from Pope Adrian VI's bull dated 10 May 1522, entitled *Exponi nobis* and known as *Omnimoda,* which stated that "in case there were no bishops," the friars could act as secular clergy and exercise the jurisdiction corresponding exclusively to the bishops.[17] This produced two interesting historical outcomes. The first generated a peculiar conflict that lasted for almost three centuries regarding the Spanish state's efforts to secularize the Indian parishes, finally achieved with great effort around 1770. The second concerns the topic I am now addressing.

The first twelve Franciscans received episcopal jurisdiction as well as jurisdiction of the Holy Office and that of inquisitors of the Indies, on their passage through the West Indies.[18] The Franciscans arrived in New Spain with this power, prepared to exercise their authority. The head of the faculty was, obviously, Friar Martín de Valencia. We have incomplete information about the number of trials he initiated, but as he formed part of that reality which severely punished apostates, we know that in 1526, one year after the evangelization of Tlaxcala, he ordered the hangings of at least six men and one woman from among the "most principal caciques" in various *autos de fe,* as attested in diverse sources and portrayed in two illustrations in the codex that accompanies Muñoz Camargo's work.[19] I have always believed that these acts deprived Valencia of the honor of sainthood that his order wished to bestow upon him.

Since jurisdiction could be delegated and the Franciscans had complete control in this area, it is on record that in the following year, 1527, Friar Toribio de Benavente, the humble Motolinía of our literature, sentenced the conquistador Rodrigo Rangel to one day at mass with a candle and nine months in a monastery for blasphemy.[20] Scant information exists regarding this primitive inquisition by the secular clergy.

I do not know whether it was intentional, but everything seems very well thought out. The Spanish Crown sent to Mexico Franciscans whose vocation was conversion, as we noted earlier. The first bishop of Mexico, Fray Juan de Zumárraga, was also Franciscan, with ample experience in the extirpation of witchcraft in the Basque provinces. The "elect one," as he was called, arrived in New Spain with episcopal jurisdiction in 1528. Since it fell to Zumárraga, Friar Martín de Valencia and his companions immediately yielded the jurisdiction they had exercised for four years, "although he refused it," according to the document of cession.[21] In 1534, Zumárraga was invested by delegation with the office of inquisitor. In this capacity he carried out dozens of trials, among which many of the published ones are of increasing interest.[22] The most well known is that of the cacique don Carlos de Texcoco, which ended with his death at the stake in 1539.[23] When the king found out about it, he

Fig. 4. "Great punishment of five major caciques and one woman for
obstinancy and returning to idolatry after becoming Christians."

angrily issued a decree condemning Zumárraga's action, saying that since the cacique's life could not be returned to him, all his belongings should be returned to his kinsmen, and he prohibited the maximum penalty for Indians, "tender shoots in faith."[24] This decree thereafter saved Indians from execution on grounds concerning the Christian religion.

The following and third chapter on jurisdiction concerned the inspector Tello de Sandoval, who, between 1544 and 1547, was employed as apostolic inquisitor and carried out various trials.[25] Zumárraga had been tacitly relieved of this function, although his episcopal jurisdictional powers were not suspended.

Between 1548 and 1569, jurisdiction reverted to the bishops, since the Holy Office had not named any inquisitors. Very little is known about the trials during these years. At any rate, the *Omnimoda* bull was not abolished, and the evangelists were able to exercise their authority in areas without bishops. Between 1561 and 1565, Friar Diego de Landa authorized trials in Yucatán leading to harsh denunciations which he was able to dispel in Spain, aided by the aforementioned bull.[26] As far as we know, the missionaries exercised jurisdiction in areas without bishops (as in the case of the Jesuits in Baja California in the eighteenth century—a fact which certainly must have terrorized the enlightened Hegel).

After much hesitation, the Spanish Crown resolved to reestablish the Inquisition in American territories in 1569.[27] Their purpose had much to do with the prosecution of the old crimes of heresy and apostasy that were its traditional target, given that the colonies were being infiltrated in an effort to avoid the Old World tribunals, as was amply demonstrated later on. In the document regarding the creation of the Holy Office in America, the king expressly prohibited interference in Indian cases and preserved the bishops' authority.[28] Beginning at that time, in civil as well as ecclesiastical matters, New Spain was decidedly split into two republics, that of the Indians and that of the Spaniards (including all types of Europeans, criollos, mestizos, blacks, mulattoes, etc.).[29]

Consequently, after 1571, when the Holy Office of the Inquisition was formally established in Mexico, two tribunals of the faith existed until 1820, at which time the first tribunal was definitively closed and the bishops published edicts proclaiming their recuperation of total jurisdiction.[30] We are thus studying a very active institution that arose in 1548 and disappeared—if indeed it has formally disappeared—quite recently. It is well worth our efforts to make a thorough study of it.

NOTES

1. Guillermo Céspedes del Castillo, *América hispánica (1492–1898)*, vol. 6 of *Historia de España*, ed. Manuel Tuñón de Lara (Barcelona: Editorial Labor, 1983), 241. The sentence is as follows: "As if something were lacking to intensify the change, the Inquisition was established in the Castilian colonies in 1571, without, thank God, jurisdiction over the Indians."

2. Cited in n. 30 below.

3. Antonio Carrión, "Indios célebres de la República Mexicana; o, Biografías de los más notables que han florecido desde 1521 hasta nuestros días" (1860), in Anastasio Zerecero, *Memorias para la historia de las revoluciones en México* (Mexico City, 1869), 485–493.

4. Joaquín García Icazbalceta, *Carta a José María Vigil aclarando un proceso de la Inquisición en el siglo XVI* (Mexico City: José Porrúa e Hijos, 1939), 32. The letter is dated 31 May 1885. Icazbalceta states clearly: "The bishop knew of the trials for Indians through the Protectorate of Natives, who would afterward perform the autos de fe in which the prisoners were, in general, bigamists or sorcerers, and the punishment commonly consisted of whipping. After the case that caused the inhibition (that of the cacique don Carlos de Texcoco), no Indian was ever burned at the stake for heresy or any other charge."

5. Richard E. Greenleaf, "The Inquisition and the Indians of New Spain: A Study in Jurisdictional Confusion," *The Americas* 22, no. 2 (October 1965): 138–166.

6. Richard E. Greenleaf, "The Mexican Inquisition and the Indians: Sources for the Ethnohistorian," *The Americas* 34, no. 3 (1978): 315–344.

7. Concerning these aspects, refer to the classic work by Henry C. Lea, *Historia de la Inquisición española*, trans. Angel Alcalá and Jesús Toribio, ed. Angel Alcalá, 3 vols. (Madrid, 1983), vol. 1, chaps. 1–3.

8. Robert Ricard, *La conquête spirituelle du Mexique: Essai sur l'apostolat et les méthodes missionaires des Ordres Mendiants en Nouvelle-Espagne de 1523–24 à 1572* (Paris: Université de Paris, Institut d'Ethnologie, 1933).

9. Pierre Duviols, *La destrucción de las religiones andinas (Conquista y colonia)*, Universidad Nacional Autónoma de México, Instituto de Investigaciones Históricas, Serie de Historia General, 9 (Mexico City, 1977), 480.

10. For example, see L. Bouyer, *Diccionario de teología* (Barcelona: Editorial Herder, 1983), 313–314.

11. Bouyer, *Diccionario*, 86–87.

12. *Biblia de Jerusalén* (Bilbao: Desclee de Brouwer, 1981). Matthew 28:16–20: "The eleven disciples went to Galilee, to the mount which Jesus had indicated. And upon seeing him, they worshiped him; yet, some still doubted. Jesus went to them and said: 'I have been given all the power of heaven and earth. Go, then, and make all the people disciples, baptizing them in the name of the Father, the Son, and the Holy Ghost, teaching them to obey all that I have commanded. And thus I will be with you forever until the end of the world.'"

13. Jacques Lafaye, *Quetzalcóatl y Guadalupe: La formación de la conciencia nacional en México*, pref. Octavio Paz (Mexico City: Fondo de Cultura Económica, 1977), 484. For another excellent summary of the topic in a study prior to Lafaye's, see Alfredo López Austin, *Hombre-dios: Religión y política en el mundo náhuatl*, Universidad Nacional Autónoma de México, Instituto de Investigaciones Históricas, Serie de Cultura Nahuatl, monografía 15 (Mexico City, 1973), 212. To know the colophon of such an extravagant thesis, refer to Severando Teresa de Mier, *Obras completas: El heterodoxo guadalupano*, with the brilliant preliminary study and selection of texts by Edmundo O'Gorman, vols. 81, 82, 83 (Mexico City: Universidad Nacional Autónoma de México, Coordinación de Humanidades, Nueva Biblioteca Mexicana, 1981).

14. Bouyer, *Diccionario*, 324–327.

15. The "Respuesta" anticipated Guillermo Porras Muñoz, *El clero secular y la evangelización de la Nueva España* (Mexico City: Universidad Nacional Autónoma de México, Academia Mexicana de la Historia, Coordinación de Humanidades, 1987), 66.

16. Juan Antonio Llorente, *Historia crítica de la Inquisición en España*, pref. José Jiménez Lozano, 4 vols. (Madrid: Hiperión, 1981), 4:2, 160–162.

17. I am transcribing the original Latin provided by Friar Gerónimo de Mendieta, *Historia eclesiástica indiana*, ed. Joaquín García Icazbalceta (Mexico City, 1870), 192–193: "Et insuper, ut melius praefata conversio infidelium fieri valeat, et saluti animarum omnium in praefatis terris Indorum pro tempore degentium provideatur, volumus, et tenore praesentium de plenitudine potestatis concedimus, ut praefati praelati fratrum, et alii quibus ipsi de fratribus suis in dictis Indiis commorantibus, duxerint commitendum, in partibus in quibus nondum fuerint Episcopatus creati (vel si fuerint tamen infra duarum dietarum spatium ipsi vel officiales eorum inveniri minime possint) tam quoad fratres suos et alios cujuscumque ordinis qui ibidem fuerint ad hoc opus deputati, ac super Indos ad fidem Christi conversos, quam et alios cristicolas, ad dictum opus eosdem comitantes, omnimodam auctoritatem nostram in utroque foro habeant, tantam quantam ipsi et per eos deputati de fratribus suis, ut dictum est, judicaverint opportunam et expedientem pro conversione dictorum Indorum, et manutentione ac profectu illorum et aliorum praefatorum in fide catholica et obedientia sanctae Romanae Ecclesiae; et quod praefata auctoritas extendatur etiam quoad omnes actus episcopales exercendos, qui non requirunt ordinem episcopalem, donec per Sedem apostolicam aliud fuerit ordinatum." This also appears in Francisco Javier Hernáez, S.J., *Colección de bulas, breves y otros documentos relativos a la Iglesia de América y Filipinas*, 2 vols. (Brussels, 1879), 1:382–384, but the Spanish translation speaks of the "omnímoda potestad y autoridad" (385).

18. It is evident that the inquisitorial power of the first twelve was delegated by those who exercised this same authority in the Indies, since they received no express or direct authority from the Spanish inquisitor general. Apart from the sentences known to have been executed, the source is Friar Antonio de Remesal, O.P., *Historia general de las Indias Occidentales y particular de la gobernación de Chiapa*

y Guatemala, ed. Carmelo Sáenz de Santa María, S.J., 2 vols., Biblioteca de Autores Españoles, vols. 175 and 189 (Madrid: Ediciones Atlas, 1964–1966), 2, 2: 122: "When in 1524 Friar Martín de Valencia and his Franciscan priests came to Mexico, Friar Pedro de Córdova was still alive, and due to the inquisitorial power that he had, he was named commissioner of all of New Spain, with authority to punish criminals in certain cases, keeping to himself the knowledge of the more serious crimes, for although Friar Martín de Valencia had been granted many privileges by Pope Leo X . . . regarding matters that concerned the Holy Office of the Inquisition he had no papal brief, nor any particular privilege, nor orders from the Spanish inquisitor general." Friar Agustín Dávila Padilla, O.P., adds information in his *Historia de la fundación y discurso de la Provincia de Santiago de México, de la orden de Predicadores,* pref. Agustín Millares Carlo, 3d ed. (Mexico City: Editorial Academia Literaria, 1955), 1:41–42: "And as the sons of God easily recognize and love one another, the spirit of the blessed Father Martín de Valencia, Guardian of San Francisco of Mexico, was well loved. This father was an eminently virtuous man, and likewise esteemed the great Friar Domingo de Betanzos's virtue, for it seemed to him that whenever Friar Domingo de Betanzos was present, everyone was quiet, and where he resided, all were obedient: and in all serious and didactic matters he was recognized as the authority. It is a characteristic of humble people to see themselves as inferior to others and to esteem them, feeling that they are more worthy of honor than themselves. The holy Guardian did not feel that it was his place to carry out the duties of inquisitorial commissioner by apostolic authority, but he held the position because he deserved even higher honors. He began to arrange with his friars to procure the good Friar Domingo de Betanzos for this office. At this time there was no bishop in the area, and a bull issued by Adrian VI gave episcopal cases as well as the apostolic commission for those of the Holy Office of the Inquisition to the prelate of San Francisco, with a declaration from the pontiff that authority could be turned over to the prelate of the order of preachers who assisted in that area . . . ; and thus ordained by the words of the bull to carry out the office, and because the city wanted him to do so, Friar Martín de Valencia stepped down and the blessed Friar Domingo de Betanzos took over the duties." Refer to Joaquín García Icazbalceta, "Autos de fe celebrados en México," *Obras,* 10 vols. (Mexico City: Victoriano Agüeros, 1896), 1:271–275.

19. García Icazbalceta, in his text quoted in the preceding note (p. 275), refers to an "ancient manuscript from Tlaxcala" he had examined in which he discovered that Valencia "gave sentences of capital punishment." Although it is unclear whether there were one or three individuals executed by the Franciscan commissioner, Icazbalceta is inclined "favorably" to believe that it occurred in only one case.

In René Acuña's recent excellent edition of Diego Muñoz Camargo's *Descripción de la Ciudad y provincia de Tlaxcala de las Indias y del mar Océano para el buen gobierno y ennoblecimiento dellas,* facsimile ed. (Mexico City: Universidad Autónoma de México, Instituto de Investigaciones Filológicas, 1981), we find the hanging of a Tlaxcaltecan cacique for relapsing into idolatry, as well as of five "very important caciques" and a "woman from that area" for apostasy (fols. 261v, 262v). There are also two burnings at the stake for "pertinacity." The illustration of the hangings reads *quintlatique*, which surely means that afterward, "they were burned."

20. The brief sentence was published by Mariano Cuevas, S.J., *Historia de la Iglesia en México*, 5 vols., 5th ed. (Mexico City: Editorial Patria, 1946–1947), 1:248. It also appears in Friar Toribio de Benavente or Motolinía, *Memoriales; o, Libro de las cosas de la Nueva España y de los naturales de ella*, ed. Edmundo O'Gorman (Mexico City: Universidad Nacional Autónoma de México, 1971), 431.

21. "Carta de Fray Martín de Valencia y otros religiosos al emperador," Tehuantepec, 18 January 1533, in Salvador Escalante Plancarte, *Fray Martín de Valencia* (Mexico City: Editorial Cossío, 1945), i-xi. It is obvious that Zumárraga's resistance to receiving ecclesiastical jurisdiction was based on the fact that he was only bishop-elect. In 1533 or 1534 he returned to Spain, where he was confirmed, at which time he acquired inquisitorial jurisdiction. He was given the title of inquisitor by don Alonso Manrique, archbishop of Seville and inquisitor general, in the city where his see was located on 27 June 1535. Joaquín García Icazbalceta, *Don Fray Juan de Zumárraga, primer obispo y arzobispo de México*, ed. Rafael Aguayo Spencer and Antonio Castro Leal, 4 vols., Colección de escritores mexicanos, vols. 41–44 (Mexico City: Editorial Porrúa, 1947), 3:71–73.

22. Luis González Obregón, *Procesos de indios idólatras y hechiceros* (Mexico City: Archivo General de la Nación, 1912). The trials date from the period 1536–1547.

23. Luis González Obregón, *Proceso criminal del Santo Oficio de la Inquisición y del fiscal en su nombre contra don Carlos, indio principal de Tetzcoco* (Mexico City: Eusebio Gómez de la Puente Editor, 1910).

24. García Icazbalceta, *Don Fray Juan de Zumárraga*, 4:65–89, includes the transcription of an inventory of papers from the cathedral office in 1746. Entry number 76 reads: "Another letter from . . . the inquisitor general reprimanding the famous señor Zumárraga for having tried an Indian cacique for idolatry and thereafter sentencing him to death and burning him at the stake; dated in Madrid, 22 November 1540." The royal decree of reprimand is found in the same volume (4:172–173) and is dated Madrid, 22 November 1540.

25. Francisco Tello de Sandoval's inquisitorial power over "any people whatsoever" in New Spain was conferred by Juan Tavera, archbishop of Toledo and inquisitor general, in Valladolid on 18 June 1543. Refer to Vasco de Puga, *Cedulario de la Nueva España*, pref. María del Refugio González, facsimile ed. (Mexico City: Centro de Estudios de Historia de México Condumex, 1985), fol. 97r. Richard E. Greenleaf, *La Inquisición en Nueva España, Siglo XVI*, trans. Carlos Valdés (Mexico City: Fondo de Cultura Económica, 1981), 85–92, deals with the trials initiated by Tello.

26. Refer to France V. Scholes and Eleanor B. Adams's excellent book, *Don Diego Quijada, alcalde mayor de Yucatán, 1561–1565*, 2 vols., Biblioteca Histórica

Mexicana de Obras Inéditas, vols. 14 and 15 (Mexico City: Antigua Librería Robredo de José Porrúa e Hijos, 1938).

27. José Toribio Medina, *Historia del Tribunal del Santo Oficio de la Inquisición en México*, expanded by Julio Jiménez Rueda (Mexico City: Ediciones Fuente Cultural, 1952), 33–34; Greenleaf, *La Inquisición*; 168–169.

28. The creation of the Holy Office was sanctioned in a decree issued by Philip II in the Pardo on 25 January 1569, *Recopilación de leyes de los reinos de las Indias*. Prólogo por Ramón Menéndez Pidal. Estudio preliminar por Juan Manzano Manzano. 4 vols. (Madrid, Ediciones Cultura Hispánica, 1973), bk. I, tit. XIX, leg. 1. Along with this text, some *Instructions* were issued which, as far as I know, remain unpublished in the National Historical Archive in Madrid. One of them states: "You are advised that, in the execution of your duties, you are not to take proceedings against the Indians of your district, because for now and until you are ordered to do otherwise, it is our will that you only act against Old Christians and others within these Spanish realms against whom it is customary to take proceedings." In *Historia de la Inquisición en España y América*, ed. Joaquín Pérez Villanueva and Bartolomé Escandell Bonet (Madrid: Biblioteca de Autores Cristianos, Centro de Estudios Inquisitoriales, 1984), this decree can be found on p. 717 and pp. 727–728. It is stated explicitly in the *Recopilación*, bk. VI, tit. I, leg. 35, that jurisdiction over the Indians belongs to the bishops. See one very late attempt (1767) by the Spanish Inquisition to intervene in Indian cases on behalf of an Indian priest acting as petitioner, along with the negative judgment of the primate bishop Lorenzana of Toledo (1773), in Roberto Moreno, "Dos documentos sobre el arzobispo Lorenzana y los indios de Nueva España," *Históricas* 10 (Sept.-Dec. 1982): 27–38.

29. Refer to a summary illustrative of this problem in Roberto Moreno, "Los territorios parroquiales de la ciudad arzobispal, 1524–1974," *Gaceta Oficial del Arzobispado de México*, 7a época, 22, nos. 9–10 (Sept.-Oct. 1982): 151–182.

30. In a more extensive work in progress, I am concerned with various aspects of the Office of Protectorate: its jurisdictional and administrative functions, prosecuted crimes (mainly concubinages, idolatries, superstitions, sorceries), public autos de fe, fool's caps, and other indications of public humiliation, and so on. Obviously these functions are practically identical with those of the Holy Office. I also address the so-called problems of jurisdiction with both tribunals.

Regarding procedure, refer to, among other texts, Gonzalo de Balsalobre's classic *Relación auténtica de las idolatrías, supersticiones, vanas observaciones de los indios del obispado de Oaxaca, y una instrucción y práctica . . . para el conocimiento, inquisición y extirpación de dichas idolatrías y castigo delos reos* (Mexico City: Viuda de Bernardo Calderón, 1656), 22 f.

As one example of a trial at the beginning of the eighteenth century whose procedure was normal but whose object was anomalous, refer to Roberto Moreno, ed., "Autos seguidos por el provisor de naturales del Arzobispado de México contra el ídolo del Gran Nayar, 1722–1723," *Tlalocan* 10 (1985): 377–477.

THREE

The Inquisition's Repression
of *Curanderos*

Noemí Quezada

As an ethnologist, I have focused my interest on the *curanderos*, or folk healers, of colonial Mexico in order to explain both their persistence and their continuity in medical practice. I also wish to define the role of the curanderos and to examine their importance within this evolutionary social process, for the curanderos' knowledge and skills contributed to the health of the oppressed and led to the formation of a traditional mestizo medicine that syncretized Indian, black, and Spanish folk medicines. These categories of analysis confirm the important social function of traditional medicine and its practitioners who offered a solution to the health problems of the majority of the population of colonial Mexico.

The necessary existence and function of the curanderos in New Spain can be attributed to the scarcity of doctors.[1] The authorities allowed for their presence and practice with a degree of tolerance that came to characterize the prevailing social relations in the American colonies, allowing not only for the continuity of traditionalist medicine but also for the beliefs and practices of the ancient pre-Hispanic religions as a means of resistance.[2]

The Crown was politically conscientious in establishing a legal medical system for Spaniards, thus protecting the health of the group in power. The Indians, and eventually the blacks and mixed castes, were assigned the practices of the curandero. Yet this division along class lines went ignored; Spaniards frequented the curandero as much as the other groups. Given its social dynamics, traditional medicine permeated the entire New Spanish society.[3]

If the curanderos were necessary, then why were they pursued, tried, and punished by the Holy Office of the Inquisition? The contradiction presents itself in ideological terms: on the one hand, their services were required as experts on the human body, as able surgeons, and as superior herbalists; on the other hand, they were harshly repressed for the magical part of their treatment, which frequently contained hallucinogens and which the authorities, according to the Western world view of the time, viewed as superstitious.[4] The authorities intended to prove that medical expertise derived solely from Spanish medical knowledge; they would thus invalidate the entire medical practice of all other practitioners and justify their condemnation.

THE CURANDEROS AND THE HOLY OFFICE [5]

From the very beginning of the conquest of New Spain, the Spanish Crown attempted to impose a Catholic world view upon which to base a system of normative practices that would organize the entire society within the framework of religion. The problems presented by the social and ideological heterogeneity of New Spain were extremely difficult to solve. The colony's reorganization was carried out along administrative, economic, and political lines, but resulted in a different dynamic on religious and cultural levels. The goal was to unify the entire society under the Catholic faith, which in actual practice was interpreted and molded according to each social group's conception. Despite the Church's efforts to disseminate its official doctrine through regular and secular clergy with the support of the civil authorities, the various social groups—mixed castes, Indians, and marginalized Spaniards—perceived Catholicism as an ideal impossible to live up to on a daily basis. Thus, the religious beliefs of New Spain reveal a process of syncretism reflecting popular religion and culture.

At times even unconsciously, civil and religious authorities strove to achieve their assigned goal of social integration; unity, however, was at best superficial in a society where diverse ideologies coexisted and interrelated, ultimately resulting in a less strict and orthodox situation than in Spain.[6] The unification of Spanish society under the reign of the Catholic monarchs, as well as the Church's gradual loss of political power as it increasingly came under monarchical control, had repercussions in the American colonies, where the lack of jurisdictional limits over control and conservation of the faith led to frequent confrontations between civil and religious authorities. To maintain order and to ensure the system's equilibrium, constant vigilance was needed via the institution created in Europe in the thirteenth century and adopted by the Catholic kings at the end of the fifteenth century:[7] the Tribunal of the Holy Office of the Inquisition, which functioned as a disciplinary apparatus, "an organism of internal security,"[8] controlling dissidents within the religious, moral, and social order.

The first missionary friars were invested with the powers of the secular clergy where there was no priest or bishop, and they were responsible, among their other duties, for the detection and punishment of all violations of the faith.[9] No case of *curanderismo* appears registered under the first commissioners of the Holy Office.

Fray Juan de Zumárraga, the first bishop of New Spain, received inquisitorial powers in 1535, and he established the episcopal inquisition with a tribunal and inquisitorial functionaries in 1536. Under his supervision, which lasted until 1543, twenty-three cases of witchcraft and superstition were tried, probably including some cases of traditional medical practices.[10]

Petitions first circulating in the middle of the fifteenth century explained the need to establish a Tribunal of the Holy Office which, like that in Spain, would have total disciplinary control, thus avoiding the frequent abuses and jurisdictional equivocations of the civil authorities. Philip II authorized the tribunal in 1569 with royal letters-patent, and it was established in New Spain in November, 1571. As in Spain, the New Spanish inquisitors were, above all else, men of law who scrupulously carried out their duties in order to maintain social control.[11]

After Zumárraga had condemned the cacique of Texcoco to the stake for idolatry in 1539, causing him to be removed as inquisitor, the question arose as to whether the Indians should suffer inquisitorial penalties since the Crown was legally responsible for their guardianship and protection.[12] Fully aware of the abuses committed by the provincial commissioners supervised by the bishops during the episcopal inquisition, Philip II decided to leave the Indians outside the control of the Holy Office and placed them under the ordinary jurisdiction of the bishops.

Although the royal decision was respected, inquisitorial commissioners did receive accusations against the Indians. For some of these commissioners the separation of jurisdictions was quite clear;[13] for others, confusion, jealousy, or the belief that the crime merited inquisitorial punishment incited them to apprehend, reprimand, and threaten the Indian curanderos.[14] Once the denunciation was issued, it was important to determine whether it concerned "pure Indians" or mestizos; to remove all doubts, the Holy Office thus required that the commissioners formalize the proceedings with documents such as testimonies.[15]

Of the thirteen cases concerning Indians found among the proceed-

Fig. 5. "Punishment of a cacique of Tlaxcala for falling into idolatry after becoming a Christian."

ings I have examined, that of Roque de los Santos, who was accused as a mestizo, appears to be illegal. During the course of the trial, it was discovered that he was an Indian; nonetheless, he was sentenced, and it remains unclear whether sentencing occurred because he was part of the same trial as Manuela Rivera, "La Lucera," or because the inquisitors decided that the punishment was appropriate for a mestizo. Proof of this racial status was furnished in a document not included in the proceedings. He was sentenced to be paraded in a cart preceded by a town crier who announced his crimes, to receive two hundred lashes, and to labor eight years in a mining hacienda.[16]

THE CURANDEROS PUNISHED BY THE HOLY OFFICE

Of the seventy-one delations and denunciations which the Holy Office received against curanderos, fourteen warranted attestations and were dismissed after being considered inappropriate. Twenty-two cases were tried which called for testimony; in fourteen cases the inquisitors decided in favor of public or private reprimand, two suffered public humiliation, only one had a public auto de fe in the Church of Santo Domingo, and one was exiled. These were the maximum punishments suffered by the curanderos.

The first cases specifically recorded in the registers of the Inquisition as offenses of curanderos were those of Francisco Moreno, a thirty-year-old Spaniard accused of healing by incantation in 1613, and the mulatta Magdalena, for having taken peyote as a divinatory aid.[17]

From this time until the beginning of the nineteenth century, the accusations against the superstitious curanderos give descriptions of the therapies that identified specializations and the use of herbs and hallucinogens in the curative ceremonies. Most importantly, they attempted to understand the practitioners of traditional medicine and their patients, disclosing the latter's reactions and fears regarding the unknown, the mysterious ways of those who dealt with their health, and patients' belief in their powerful supernatural faculties.[18]

It was also a common belief that bewitchment and all incurable illnesses resulted from hatred or unrequited love. Between these two poles revolved the relationships of New Spanish men and women; seeking good health, they appealed to the curanderos, yet when undergoing treatment, sometimes positive and other times negative, they often fell into the contradictory position of thinking they had violated the norms imposed by the Holy Office. This reaction, quite natural for the times, accounted for the detailed records of the inquisitors which have fur-

TABLE 3.1

Año	Nombre del Curandero	Grupo	Cargo	Delación	Confiscaciones de Bienes	Carcel	Tormento	Sentencia
1613	Francisco Moreno	español	curandero ensalmador	X				
1614	Magdalena	mulata	curandera adivina, tomaba peyote	X				
1621	Ana de Carnaval	negra	curandera hechicera, daba bebedizos	X				
1627	Isabel de Arias	mulata	partera supersticiosa	X				
1627	Ana de Valencia	s/cons.	partera supersticiosa	X				
1664	Estefanía de los Reyes	mulata	curandera, partera y adivina	X	X			se proseguirá su causa
1678	Inés	mulata	curandera hechicera	X		X		
1685	Agustina Rangel	castiza	alumbrada, pactaria, hechicera y curandera	X	X	X	X	Abjuración de Levi. Auto Público. Paseo c/pregonero, 2000 azotes. Serv. en Hosp. 2 años.
1689	María Calderón	mestiza	curandera supersticiosa	X				
1690	Francisco	indio	curandero	X				
1696	Indio	indio	curandero y adivino. Tomó *pipiltzintzin*	X				Se envía la Instrucción al cura para que haga las diligencias
1701	Esteban Lorenzo	mulato	curandero hechicero	X				
1709	Agustina de Lara	española	curandera, partera y hechicera	X				
1713	"La Lora"	india	partera, cambia voluntades	X				
1713	Mulato	mulato	curandero, desliga, cambia voluntad	X				
1713	Diego de Alanís	mulato	curandero, uso de yerbas	X				
1716	Indio	indio	curandero, usaba peyote	X				
1716	Beatriz "La Piatzin"	mulata	curandera, hechicera y adivina	X				
1716	Jusephe	mulato	curandero supersticioso	X				
1717	María de Escobar	mestiza	curandera, sobadora	X		X		reprensión, prohibición ejerc.
1717	Juana de la Pompa "La Cirujana"	española	curandera de maleficio y adivina	X		X		se fugó de la cárcel, se depositó en un convento
1718	Juana de Santa Ana	española	curaciones supersticiosas	X				
1719	Dominga de Meza	mulata	curandera de maleficio, desliga	X				

Año	Nombre	Casta	Descripción				Observaciones
1723	Josefa de Zarate "Madre Chepa"	mestiza	curandera supersticiosa, partera y adivina		X	X	reprensión en público
1725	María "La Durana"	s/cons.	curandera supersticiosa	X		X	reprensión, presa en un recogimiento de Puebla que se hagan las diligencias
1729	Sebastiana "La Caballero"	mulata	curandera, sobadora			X	que se hagan las diligencias
1729	Francisca de Avilés	española	curandera supersticiosa			X	
1730	Mariana Adad de Mosqueira	s/cons.	curandera, cura enf. incógnitas			X	
1730	Feliciana de la Garza	india	curandera supersticiosa			X	por ser india no toca al Santo Of. se recomienda reprensión
1730	Dominga "La Pasillos"	mestiza	curandera, cura y provoca maleficio			X	el capellán envía las diligencias al Santo Oficio.
1733	Manuela Rivera "La Lucera"	castiza	curandera supersticiosa	X		X	5 años presa. Vergüenza: 25 azotes c/ pregonero, 6 meses de servicio en un hospital
1733	Roque de los Santos	indio o mestizo	curandero supersticioso, cura maleficio	X		X	paseo en carroza, 200 azotes con pregonero, vendido su trabajo por 8 años a una Hacienda
1733	Miguel Sánchez de Arteaga	indio o mestizo	curandero supersticioso			X	
1733	Gertrudis	mulata	curandera, partera y hechicera			X	
1733	Ma. Concepción "La Salvatierreña"	mulata	curandera supersticiosa y maléfica	X		X	Vergüenza: paseo por las calles c/preg. 25 azotes, reprensión severa, confesión sacramental
1737	Manuel José de Motezuma	castizo	curandero, usaba pipiltzintzin	X		X	cárcel para aclarar por 3 días
1737	Sebastián Salvador	indio	curandero supersticioso (maestro)	X		X	
1737	Joseph González	mestizo	curandero (alumno)	X		X	reprensión pública severa y prohibición del ejercicio

TABLE 3.1 (continued)

Año	Nombre del Curandero	Grupo	Cargo	Delación	Confiscaciones de Bienes	Carcel	Tormento	Sentencia
1743	Lucía "La Berrueto"	española	partera	X				se hagan las testificaciones se remiten los Autos al S.O.
1744	María Teresa	mulata	hechicera	X				
1752	Manuela	española	curandera supersticiosa	X				reprensión en la Audiencia del Tribunal. Prohib. del ejercicio
1753	Marcela	s/cons.	partera, hechicera	X				
1760	María de los Dolores	mestiza	curandera de maleficio	X		X		reprensión severa, se la ponga en libertad
1764	Isabel María	india	curandera hechicera	X				se le mire con benignidad, por su rusticidad no se le concede intención herética
1764	Pascual de Salazar	mestizo	curandero, hechicero y adivino	X				
1766	Petra de Torres	española	curandera y partera supersticiosa	X				reprensión, no use del ejerc.
1768	Juan Miguel Escandón "Churumbelo"	mulato	curandero supersticioso	X		X		represnión
1771	Pascual de Morga	mulato	curandero supersticioso	X				reprensión
1772	Juana María Nava	india	curandera y partera maléfica	X		X		se ordena se le ponga inmediatamente en libertad
1772	José Quinerio Cisneros	mulato	curandero supersticioso	X	X	X	X	cárcel en San Juan de Ulúa, destierro 10 años, Confes. Sacram.
1772	Santiago de la Cruz	indio	curandero (maestro)	X				reincidente, castigado por S.O.
1774	Lugarda	india	curandera supersticiosa	X				
1774	Joseph "El Zapatero"	s/con.	curandero supersticioso	X				
1777	Juan Luis	negro	curandero y adivino	X				reprensión, no use del ejerc.

Año	Nombre	Casta	Descripción				Observaciones
1782	Matiana Saldaña "La Pastora"	mulata	curandera, partera sortílega	X			reprensión
1782	Ma. Tiburcia "La Gachupina"	española	curandera supersticiosa	X	X	X	se le siga causa
1784	María Margarita Reyes	mulata	curandera supersticiosa	X		X	se reprenda al cura por den de arresto sin autorización
1784	Petra Narcisa	mulata	curandera y pactaria	X			que se suspenda, despreciada
1784	José Antonio Hernández	español	curandero supersticioso y arbolario	X		X	sospechoso de Leví, preso por orden del Protomedicato
1787	José de Roxas	mestizo	curandero supersticioso	X		X	se fugó de la cárcel
1789	Francisca	española	curandera supersticiosa	X			
1790	Rosalía de Aguilar	s/con.	curandera supersticiosa	X			se encontró curaba enfermedades corrientes, 1805 acusada por sus maldades públicas
1792	Dominga "La Polla" o Juana Ma.	mestiza	hechicera maléfica	X		X	se hagan diligencias
1792	Agustina Carrasco	s/con.	partera maléfica	X			
1793	Pascuala	mestiza	curandera	X			
1796	María Fernández	negra	curandera supersticiosa	X			no fue localizada
1798	Lorenza	s/con.	partera hechicera	X			despreciada
1798	Miguel Ponce	castizo	curandero, hechicero, pactario y adivino	X		X	reprnesión
1800	Juan o Mariano "El Cojo"	mulato	curandero supersticioso	X			difunto, nadie lo conocía
1800	Juana María Apodaca "La Chalis"	india?	curandera supersticiosa	X			se formalice su expediente, que el padre la reprenda
1806	Santos Bernabela	india	curandera supersticiosa, polvorista	X			despreciada por ser india, prevengase al tribunal corresondiente

nished us with all the cultural data needed to confirm the continuity of curanderismo within medical practice, to determine its changes, and to specify the concepts and judgment of that medical practice, formed, on one side, by the curanderos defending their practices and, on the other side, by the inquisitorial authorities who wished to repress them.[19]

THE ACCUSATIONS

Self-accusations were unusual, perhaps because the curanderos did not consider their practice a crime. Only Francisco Moreno and Mariana Adad denounced themselves. The former found out in an Edict of Faith that the occupation of spell-caster (*ensalmador*), which he had practiced for many years in various cities in New Spain, was prohibited; presenting himself before the inquisitorial commissioner of Oaxaca, he sought clemency through his open declaration of ignorance. In her report, Mariana minutely describes her case, from predestination since infancy through her initiation and practice; she was confident that the inquisitors would assess her healings as a gift from God.[20]

Delation was the most frequent reason for detention given in the reports, and it is not surprising to discover that the majority of the delators were the former patients of the accused curanderos. On occasion, knowledge of an edict that had been posted on the doors of the church and had been read by the priests during mass on Sundays or holy days aroused unrest and fright, unleashing in turn a series of accusations made by the informers "in order to relieve the conscience."[21]

When the informer presented him- or herself before the inquisitors at the Holy Office in Mexico City, the provincial commissioner or priest with inquisitorial authority swore to keep the secret. The informer was asked what type of declaration he or she was prepared to make, since the kind of process depended upon whether it was merely a delation or an actual accusation. The prosecutor of the Holy Office made the accusation after hearing the attestations and presenting the case before the qualifying judges.

In spite of the declaratory oath, it is probable that the actual reasons for a delation were hatred or resentment when the cure had negative results, at times worsening the patient's condition, or when the curandero had refused to attend a sick person.[22] In those cases where the remedy had positive results, the patients, having disobeyed the faith by resorting to forbidden practices and specialists, sought to lighten the punishment they believed they deserved by accusing someone else. Neither family nor romantic ties were exempt in these circumstances.

Feelings of impotence in the face of illness, fear of the unknown, envy, competition, and fear inspired by love, all impelled New Spaniards to the Holy Office.[23]

Delations presented through public rumor were received and investigated. Between one and four attestations were sufficient to ensure continuation of a case. In some cases, the curanderos' public reputation became an issue with the priests or civil authorities, as it caused a public disturbance and loss of control over the faithful; the priests then had the responsibility of making the accusation to the Holy Office.[24]

When provincial commissioners or priests with inquisitorial authority were involved, they usually sent the complete delations and reports to the commissioners of the Holy Office beforehand, so that upon receiving a response from the qualifying judges they would know how to proceed with each case.[25] Inquisitors were responsible for the most stringent enforcement of the rules and regulations of the Holy Tribunal. They often expedited the *Instructions* to ensure the correct methods of inquiry and to obtain greater information in order to standardize judgment by the qualifying judges, thus avoiding, wherever possible, errors that might discredit the prestige and deplete the treasury of the Holy Office.[26] There were few cases where the accused could not be located, either because too much time had transpired between the crime and the accusation, or because he or she had died.[27]

THE TRIALS

Once the delation or report was received and the trial subsequently endorsed, the first step was to call upon the witnesses, dismissing those cases where interrogation revealed that they had been motivated by hatred, desire to defame, or other similar reasons. Witnesses presented by the informer or called by the commissioner were advised of their responsibility and the importance of their testimony, as well as of the punishment incurred if their testimony should prove false or motivated by hatred or enmity. In accord with the rules, witnesses were assured of and sworn to secrecy.[28]

The purpose was to gather as much information as possible in order to continue the trial or to dismiss it. Although the number of witnesses in the cases of curanderos varied depending upon the offense committed, it was usually determined by the conscientiousness of the commissioner. For example, more than twenty witnesses were called in the trial of María Tiburcia, while eleven were called in the trial of Manuela Josefa; in general, the average number was four or five witnesses. In the case of Petra Narcisa, six testimonies were presented, and since the information was considered insufficient to decide the case, the trial was rescheduled and six other witnesses were called in order to define the charges.[29] Moreover, it was common to request testimony from the curanderos' former patients, relatives, or assistants.[30]

DETENTIONS AND IMPRISONMENT

The judges ruled whether or not to proceed with the trial on the basis of the testimonies, with the prosecutor of the Holy Office presenting the formal accusation.[31] Once the decision to proceed had been made, the accused was detained and placed either in the secret jails of the Holy Office, in the curate jail, or in the royal jails; in some cases, women were taken to houses of correction.[32] The goal was to interrogate the accused as many times as necessary.

When the prisoner was placed in the jail of the Holy Office, a very meticulous physical description was made, along with a description of all articles of clothing, other personal belongings, and bed clothes.[33] In six cases the prisoners' belongings were confiscated, and in only one was it noted that they were "few and poor." The other five cases make no mention of the value, from which we can infer that the total was unimportant. Transfer of prisoners from the interior of New Spain to the jails of the Holy Office in Mexico City was done infrequently, since the expense was covered by the prisoner's own possessions. Where there were no possessions, the tribunal covered the expense, ordering a careful examination of "the quality of the person and the nature of the offense, and the trial to take place only under great consideration."[34]

There were anomalies in the detentions; for example, when Miguel Antonio and his wife presented themselves to denounce Manuel José de Moctezuma, all three were imprisoned. The curandero was set free, but the denouncers were detained for an additional period of three days and received a sharp reprimand for having taken *pipiltzintzin*, a hallucinogen recommended by Manuel José.[35] Priests who made arrests without the authorization of the Holy Office were also severely reprimanded, and if the civil authorities tried to make arrests, the inquisitors protested the encroachment on their jurisdiction.[36]

The length of time in prison varied with the duration of the trial; in general, it fluctuated between the three and five years it took to complete the trial. Only the prison cells of the Holy Office were safe and adequately guarded; in other locations the prisoners were able to escape. One curandera did so by burning down the door; although she was able to escape, she was captured because she was very ill. "El Churumbelo" escaped through the rafters of the jail ceiling, but he was captured and returned to prison. María Margarita, with the help of her daughter, escaped in shackles. Among the fugitives was José de Roxas, arrested for teaching forbidden prayers to children; he was the only fugitive who was never captured.[37]

THE CONFESSION AND TORTURE

The interrogations of the curanderos proceeded in the usual way. In general, they accepted the charges and confessed correspondingly; only Agustina Rangel denied the eighty charges imputed to her. "La Cirujana," feigning insanity and sickness with hallucinations of snakes, almost managed to deceive the inquisitors and avoid indictment.[38] The interrogations provided proof complementing the accusations against the prisoners. For example, Lorenza, an elderly midwife, never "wished to declare the kinds of herbs" that she used in her healings. In these cases, specialists were sought to identify the medicinal plants in order to determine if they were prohibited.[39]

All of the punitive rules and regulations of the Holy Office were based on physical punishment: not only torture but deprivation of liberty, imprisonment in dark, humid cells, solitary confinement, whipping, and even the public exhibition of the prisoners in specific clothing and the parading of male and female prisoners naked to the waist were all degradations not easily forgotten by the individual or society. That was, after all, the objective: to conserve a vivid memory of the punishment.

In two cases of curanderos, both were tortured in order to obtain confessions: José Quinerio Cisneros, a mulatto whose file contains the decree that torture be applied, because of his reluctance, "one or more times, as much as is necessary,"[40] and Agustina Rangel, aware of the inquisitorial mechanisms, who declared that she thought she was pregnant, since she "finds herself with great pain in the belly and hips." This excuse most probably postponed both trial and torture.[41] Despite the torture, Agustina continued to deny the eighty charges pressed by the prosecutor, repeating before the inquisitors that if she had cured people, it was by "the grace of God and of the Holy Virgin and Santa Rosa," who helped and advised her, Santa Rosa entering her body to cure the sick. The qualifying judges were the ones who asked the prosecutor to torture her, to see if she would confess the truth.[42] Convinced of her revelations, she insisted on denying the charges even after torture. When she was sentenced in October 1687, two years after she had been detained, she again denied the charges. Not until February 1688, when the sentence was carried out, did she admit to them.[43]

THE SENTENCES

The most frequent punishment against the curanderos was a reprimand with a prohibition against their practices. In most cases, the reprimand took place privately before the commissioner, the notary, the prosecutor, and the inquisitorial witnesses, gathered together at the trial's final hearing when it took place in Mexico City. In other places, it was made before the representatives of the Holy Office. Public reprimand was carried out by the same officials with six, eight, or more witnesses.[44]

The reprimand was meant to be a lesson to the accused, and the justification was that in many cases no other punishment was applicable, since "because of their backwardness they cannot be charged with any heretical intention," or because they had committed the offenses "without malice, only in order to avoid working and to swindle innocent people."[45] The reprimand was severe and its threat was important. The tribunal took harsh measure against recidivists. After the reprimand, the prisoners would make an oath promising not to repeat the offense. Juan Luis, a black man, was warned he would receive public reprimand of twenty-five lashes at the church door if he did not honor his oath.[46] "La Cirujana" was a recidivist, who, because of her illness, did not receive any major punishment and was placed in a convent.[47] Moreover, reprimands were issued against ignorant witnesses and denouncers.[48]

PUBLIC PUNISHMENT

Public punishment functioned as an educational ritual of inquisitorial power. The principal assumption was that exemplary punishment would prevent New Spaniards from committing offenses. Francisco Peña is emphatic about the concept of punishment: "The primary objective of the trial and death sentence is not to save the soul of the accused but rather to procure public welfare and to terrify the populace."[49]

The penitents, carrying candles, gagged, and wearing tunics, cone-shaped hats, and nooses, covered with symbols indicating their offenses, were exhibited publicly, their crimes published and repeated by the town crier. The prisoner was thus penalized not only by inquisitorial authority but by the entire society as well, represented by those participating in the ritual. People who attended the ritual liberated themselves through self-expression in the ceremony, and they learned from the punishments not to commit the same offenses. They saw the penitents' sufferings in these rituals that catalyzed the repressive New Spanish society. The goal of publishing the penalties was to avoid social transgression, disequilibrium, and rupture.

Few curanderos received these punishments. Two women suffered public humiliation. Manuela "La Lucera," after a long imprisonment of five years, was paraded in 1734 through the customary streets by a crier who finally gave her twenty-five lashes at the pillory; the second part of her sentence consisted of working in a hospital for six months.[50] "La Salvatierreña," a forty-six-year-old free mulatta, was led through the streets by a crier promulgating her offense and received twenty-five lashes at the pillory; she was sentenced to prison and severely reprimanded, being required for one year thereafter to make her confession at the main altar, and to pray three Salve Reginas and three Apostles' Creeds after mass.[51]

The maximum penalty for the curanderos was the abjuration *de levi*, a formal oath to avoid this sin in the future. The only one who received it was Agustina Rangel. Before it was carried out, she embraced Christianity and accepted the accusation made against her. The abjuration took place in the church of Santo Domingo on 8 February 1688. At the end of mass, she offered a votive candle to the priest and performed the abjuration in expiation of her sins. The following day, 9 February, she was "taken on a beast of burden, naked to the waist, wearing the aforementioned noose, and cone-shaped hat, and led through the customary streets," with the crier announcing her offenses as he led the way to the pillory where she received two hundred lashes. On 12 February she entered the Hospital of the Conception of Jesus of Nazareth to serve the poor for a period of two years. Her file states that she served the entire sentence, obtaining her liberty in February 1690.[52]

José Antonio Hernández, a Spaniard whose case required ten witnesses and whose trial lasted four years, was kept prisoner by order of the board of royal physicians who charged him with being a curandero and an herbalist. The qualifying judges finally found him to be "a suspect de levi against the Holy Catholic Faith," but there is no definitive sentence.[53]

Finally, José Quinerio Cisneros, accused of being a superstitious curandero, received the following sentence: exile from the towns of Madrid, Mexico, and Salamanca for "a period of ten years, during which the first two are to be spent in the Castillo de San Juan de Ulúa, assigned to royal tasks, on prebend and without salary." After one month in San Juan, he made his confession, and did so also at Easter. Every Saturday he offered part of the rosary to the Virgin Mary.[54]

CONCLUSIONS

The beliefs, practices, and behavior of the curanderos punished by the Holy Tribunal were as follows:

1. The belief that they should not infringe upon established religious norms. They were convinced that they should heal the sick through their therapeutic techniques and with the aid of supernatural beings, whether originating in Catholicism or in other religions.
2. The use of hallucinogens that served not only as medication but also as a means of achieving a magic trance, consciously seeking auditory and visual hallucinations that would allow them to establish contact with supernatural beings.
3. The presence of prayers, images, and sacred and at times consecrated relics in the curative ceremonies.
4. Divination as a means of making both diagnosis and prognosis.

New Spain's classist society, with its heterogeneous culture, included several conceptions and practices of the curanderos. While Spanish curanderos argued that they healed people "through the grace of God," the mestizos, mulattoes, Indians, and blacks followed a traditional method based on their teachings and practices. The supernatural beings invoked in the curative ceremonies correspond to the world view of each group. For the Spaniards they were the Catholic deities: Jesus Christ, the Virgin, the Holy Trinity, the Holy Spirit, various saints, and the Devil. They cured with their dialogues, revelations, and even through bodily possession, but always within the framework of individual healing. The other groups however, while acknowledging and invoking Catholic deities, fundamentally perceived pre-Hispanic deities in the hallucinatory episodes; and while these divinities aided, directed, and prescribed, it was the curandero who healed, involving both the patient and the assistants in a collective healing.

The curanderos appeared as transgressors of established morality, since they were said to have participated in condemned practices such as concubinage, homosexuality, and promiscuity. Yet the vast majority of the curanderos were exempt from punishment, as their herbal medicine did not merit any type of condemnation, and they were eventually permitted the use of officially sanctioned images and relics. The Holy Office's response confirms that the medical practice of the curanderos was viewed and accepted as a necessity. It was within reach of the general populace; the curanderos were as poor as their patients, since in the confiscation of personal belongings, no curandero with money was ever found. The colonial curandero thus served a specific function by offering a solution to the health problems of most of New Spain through the use of an efficient traditional medicine.

NOTES

1. Documents from the Archivo General de la Nación (México) (hereafter AGN), Protomedicato, tomo 2, expediente 8, fol. 272.

2. AGN, Protomedicato, tomo 3, exp. 8, fol. 159: The intendant of Guanajuato stated that in that town there was no medical facility and that common cures were provided by women who practiced with extreme conscientiousness, employing domestic medicines.

Tomo 2, exp. 8, fol. 159: A mayor affirmed that if no doctor was available, it was common practice to employ a curandero "because as ignorant as they might be, they had more experience and knowledge than everyone else."

3. Ibid., tomo 3, exp. 8, fol. 159: In 1799 the viceroy of New Spain issued an edict affirming that "there is no prohibition against the curanderos giving aid to the infirm in the dwelling areas of Indians."

4. The hallucinogens most frequently ingested were peyote (*Lophophora Williamisii*), ololiuqui (*Rivea Corymbosa*), and *Ipomea Violacea* and *pipiltzintzin* (*Savia Divinorum*). AGN, Edictos, tomo 2, fol. 87: The Holy Tribunal of the Inquisition circulated the first edict published in 1617, followed by many others during the colonial period, which stated that the use of hallucinogens would be harshly punished.

José Toribio Medina, *Historia del Santo Oficio de la Inquisición en México* (Mexico City: Universidad Nacional Autónoma de México, Miguel Angel Porrúa, 1987), 160. Regarding the prohibition of peyote and other hallucinogens, the inquisitors reasoned that ingestion established an implicit pact with the Devil, because "they estrange the senses and create visions and phantasms."

5. The following research has been carried out in the Instituto de Investigaciones Antropológicas, Universidad Nacional Autónoma de México.

6. Richard E. Greenleaf, *Inquisición y sociedad en el México colonial* (Madrid: Ediciones José Porrúa Turanzas, 1985), 9. Greenleaf affirms that in colonial Mexico neither the Tribunal nor its agents were able to exercise control over the ideas of the colonial population or the Indians.

7. A. S. Turberville, *La Inquisición española* (Mexico City: Fondo de Cultura Económica, 1971), 30.

8. Greenleaf, *Inquisición*, 6.

9. Ibid, 19. Bull issued by Leo X in April 1521 and confirmed by Adrian VI in the Bula Omnimoda in 1522.

10. Medina, *Historia*, 24–28.

11. Julio Caro Baroja, *El Señor Inquisidor y otras vidas por oficio* (Madrid: Alianza Editorial, 1968), 21.

12. José Miranda, "Indios." In *Los tribunales de la Nueva España* (Mexico City: Universidad Nacional Autónoma de México, 1980), 165. Miranda notes that the Indians, "due to their actual situation—due to the difference in civilizations—had to be juridically assigned to a special category as Spaniards, that of the uncouth and the poor, and were therefore subjected, like the latter, to a system of guardianship and protection, for it was assumed that conferring upon them a status of equality with the common citizens, i.e., the Spaniards, or even with those who were not citizens, i.e., the castes, would only create prejudice against them."

13. AGN, Inquisición, tomo 830, exp. 11, fol. 156. The commissar of Aguascalientes declared: "Because she is a pure-blooded Indian whose practice and punishment do not concern the Holy Office, let her be merely sternly reprimanded."

Tomo 1433, exp. 25, fol. 224: The commissar of Masaya, Nicaragua, has determined that "because she is an Indian, let the accused be placed in the file with the despised ones, forewarning the corresponding commissioner of the Indians."

14. Ibid., tomo 842, fol. 104. In Bolaños, Jalisco, Juana Ma. Nava, a recidivist Indian, was detained and imprisoned for being an evil curandera. The Holy Office sent an order to the commissioner "to free her immediately," warning him: "Do not for any motive apprehend anyone who has been accused."

15. Ibid., tomo 824, exp. 13, fol. 213. On certain occasions it was difficult to determine whether or not "pure Indians" were involved, as occurred with the commissioner of Querétaro, since Miguel Sánchez's parents were unknown. Tomo 1468, fol. 85: In the case of Juana Ma. Vanegas, "La Chalis," it was suggested to the priest of Paso del Norte that he formalize her file, as it was unclear whether or not she was an Indian. Tomo 1182, fol. 69: In the case of the Indian woman Lugarda, the denouncer's husband was called in to testify.

16. Ibid., fols. 60–63; Miranda, "Indios," 172. Miranda points out that "Indians could not be fined by law but could only be sentenced to lashes, forced labor, torture, or death. A sentence of forced labor was not carried out in galleys or other state institutions (prisons or otherwise) but rather in private institutions such as workshops, bacon shops, bakeries, etc., whose owners bought the labor of the prisoner for the duration of the sentence."

17. AGN, Inq., tomo 878, exp. 853, fol. 510, and tomo 302, exp. 8g, fols. 128–130.

18. Ibid., tomo 1150, exp. 10, fol. 136. As the commissioner of Salamanca, Guanajuato, notes in 1772, "these territories are very contaminated with similar superstitions, the people even desire to believe thus and do not wish to believe

that the illnesses they suffer are the will of God our Father, but rather they vacillate and then believe that they are bewitched, from which follow all the inconsistencies . . ."

19. There is abundant information from the inquisitorial records which facilitates a reconstruction of various aspects of New Spanish popular culture; one source on traditional colonial medicine is Gonzalo Aguirre Beltrán's *Medicina y magia* (Mexico City: Instituto Nacional Indigenista, 1963).

20. AGN, Inq., tomo 878, exp. 83, fol. 510, and tomo 830, exp. 3, fol. 49. Nicolau Eimeric and Francisco Peña, *El manual de los Inquisidores* (Barcelona: Muchnik Editores, 1983), 132. Eimeric indicates the great precautions that the commissioners must have taken in these cases, since people might accuse themselves in order to avoid punishment brought on by another's accusation.

21. AGN, Inq., tomo 746, fol. 522: In "observance of the Holy Office," the Indian Miguel Juan presented himself before the priest of Chapa de Mota to accuse Diego de Alanís, a mulatto. Tomo 862, exp. 37, fol. 288: The priest carried out his duties in the name of the Holy Office in order to locate curanderos or idolaters in Tixtla, and thus found the Indian Sebastián Salvador.

22. Ibid., tomo 862, exp. 30, fol. 216: The curandero Manuel José de Moctezuma, a *castizo*, was denounced by the mulatto Miguel Antonio for refusing to cure his wife. Tomo 785, exp. 12, fol. 253: Luis Antonio Contreras threatened to denounce María Teresa in the Holy Office and finally actually did so, for her refusal to remove a spell she had cast on him because of jealousy. Tomo 674, exp. 12, fol. 96: María Calderón was accused by Nicolás Ramírez, husband of the sick woman, who was called later to testify.

23. Ibid., tomo 1036, exp. 10, fol. 189: The accuser Nicolás Saucedo had been bewitched by his brother Pascual de Salazar for having taken away his rifle. Tomo 337, exp. 14, fol. 4: Juan Conquero, a Portuguese man, denounced his concubine, Ana de Carvajal, a black woman, for having bewitched him; he had tried to leave her but found to the contrary that every day he loved her more. Tomo 848, fol. 28: During trial, Manuela "La Lucera" denounced Roque de los Santos, with whom she had an "illicit relationship."

24. Eimeric and Peña, *El manual*, 145: Eimeric indicates that a trial by interview was called for, in which the inquisitor brought in witnesses to clarify public rumors.

AGN, Inq., tomo 1028, exp. 7, fol. 245: The vicar of Tlanepantla reported as a public error the healings of the Spaniard Petra de Torres, and called two witnesses to testify. Tomo 1427, exp. 14, fol. 78: Dominga "La Polla" was imprisoned by the mayor of the district of Querétaro, as there were many accusations made by the sick people of the Barrio de Santa Ana, where she worked. Tomo 1168, exp. 16, fol. 232: Juan de Córdova "heard it said" that Joseph "El Zapatero" was very sought after as a curandero.

25. AGN, Inq., tomo 767, exp. 33, fol. 534: Fray Juan de Zapata, a conventional Augustinian, wrote to the Holy Office and asked for its judgment regarding the superstitious cures of "La Cirujana." Tomo 826, exp. 14, fol. 336: The

chaplain of Aguascalientes sent the report so that the Holy Office would make a judgment on the case of Juana de Bustos.

26. Ibid., tomo 543, exp. 3, fol. 13: In the case of Esteban Lorenzo, the *Instructions* were sent to the priest of Metepec to proceed properly and make more information available to him. Appropriate formalities were recommended in the following cases: tomo 826, exp. 52, fol. 15: "La Caballero," in Izúcar; tomo 826, exp. 43, fol. 446: Francisca Avilés, in the Sultepec mines; and tomo 826, exp. 54, fol. 535: Lucía Berrueto, in Sultepec.

27. Ibid., tomo 1365, exp. 4, fol. 23: In Querétaro, Jerónimo Ortiz was called on to testify, but the black woman María Fernández could not be found, accused ten years after the crime had been committed, so that "no investigation of her manner of living was possible." Tomo 1397, exp. 14, fol. 205: In the case of the mulatto Juan "El Cojo," four witnesses were called; it was decided, however, that since "nobody knew him, nor did he appear in the parish register," he was already dead.

28. Eimeric and Peña, *El manual*, 140. Refer to the examination of witnesses.

29. Ibid., 165: Eimeric notes that the excessive number of witnesses was liable to extend the trial, although he believes that at times more witnesses than the stipulated number were necessary. AGN, Inq., tomo 1300, exp. 12, fol. 187–259; tomo 964, exp. 6 fols. 354–373; and tomo 1228, exp. 12, fols. 347–393.

30. Ibid., tomo 811, exp. 16, fol. 463–470: In the case of "La Durana," two of the witnesses were her children. Tomo 1300, exp. 12, fol. 254: A doctor appears among the witnesses, called to testify and give his opinion as a specialist.

31. Ibid., tomo 598, exp. 15, fol. 538: The prosecutor requested the detention of Estefania de los Reyes. Tomo 322, exp. 2, fol. 154: Agustina Rangel was formally accused by the prosecutor.

32. Ibid., tomo 844, exp. 6, fol. 509.

33. Ibid., tomo 322, exp. 2, fol. 142. This is what occurred with Agustina Rangel.

On the secret jails and the buildings occupied by the Tribunal of the Holy Office, refer to Francisco de la Maza, *El palacio de la Inquisición* (Mexico City: Instituto de Investigaciones Estéticas, 1951), 82 pp., illustrations and plans.

34. AGN, Inq., tomo 75, exp. 22, fol. 170: *Instructions* sent by Pedro de los Ríos, notary of the Holy Office, to the commissioners in 1572. Medina, *Historia*, p. 22: Pedro de los Ríos was named Notary of the Secret and arrived in New Spain with don Pedro Moya de Contreras, inquisitor general, in 1571.

35. AGN, Inq., tomo 862, exp. 30, fol. 217.

36. Ibid., tomo 1240, exp. 14, fol. 350; tomo 1427, exp. 14, fol. 78: The mayor made Dominga "La Polla" a prisoner and brought her before the commissioner of the Holy Office, who assured him that imprisonment was not necessary.

37. Ibid., tomo 767, exp. 33, fol. 534; tomo 1053, exp. 7, fol. 433; tomo 1240, exp. 14, fol. 350; and tomo 1176, exp. 5, fol. 105.

Eimeric and Peña, *El manual*, 117: Peña comments that "the fugitive, as a result of his evasion, transforms himself into an outlaw."

38. AGN, Inq., tomo 322, exp. 2, fol. 172 and tomo 767, exp. 33, fol. 530. Eimeric and Peña, *El manual*: 148–151: Eimeric includes feigning insanity and illness among "the ten deceptions of the heretics in order to respond without confessing."

39. AGN, Inq., tomo 1313, exp. 12, fol. 4, and tomo 1240, exp. 14, fol. 350: It was recommended to the priest of Guanajuato that in the presence of a notary "he make identification carefully by an apothecary or herbalist if one is available in that place . . . or if not, by two local elders of good conscience and who have knowledge of herbs . . . and if there is rosemary or peyote, or any other herb commonly applied to some superstitious use."

40. Ibid., tomo 1150, exp. 10, fol. 231.

41. Ibid., tomo 522, exp. 2, fol. 152. Eimeric and Peña, *El manual*, 187–188. Peña's note reads: "What can be done if the accused individual who is to be interrogated is a pregnant woman? She should not be tortured or terrorized, lest she give birth or abort. Other means should be employed to extract from her the confession before she delivers. After delivery there is no obstacle."

42. AGN, Inq., tomo 522, exp. 2, fol. 154.

43. Ibid., fol. 209.

44. Ibid., tomo 862, exp. 37, fol. 297: Joseph González was severely reprimanded in the presence of six or eight persons and forbidden to practice as a curandero.

45. Ibid., tomo 1036, exp. 10, fol. 196, and tomo 1254, exp. 9, fols. 144–145.

46. Ibid., tomo 1111, exp. 57, fol. 456.

47. Ibid., tomo 767, exp. 33, fol. 534, and tomo 964, exp. 6, fol. 375.

48. Ibid., tomo 1228, exp. 12, fol. 390, and tomo 767, exp. 30, fols. 480–491.

49. Eimeric and Peña, *El manual*, 151. Medina, *Historia*, 35 ff. for the descriptions of the autos de fe in which the accounts of the assistants are transcribed and in which the social and religious ritual of the punishment is discernible.

Michel Foucault, *Vigilar y castigar* (Mexico City: Siglo Veintiuno Editores, 1980), 48–52, analyzes the transcendental significance of public execution on both the social and individual levels.

50. AGN, Inq., tomo 848, fol. 12: Patients who accepted the cure were sentenced to six months' service in a hospital.

51. Ibid., tomo 844, exp. 6, fol. 543.

52. Ibid., tomo 522, exp. 2, fols. 209 and 226–233. Medina, *Historia*, 333, registers this case among those who abjured that day in Santo Domingo. On the procedure of abjuration as a consequence of slight suspicion, see Eimeric and Peña, *El manual*, 190–191.

53. AGN, Inq., tomo 1235, exp. 1, fols. 186–187.

54. Ibid., tomo 1333, fol. 359.

FOUR

Sorcery and Eroticism in Love Magic

María Helena Sánchez Ortega

During the sixteenth, seventeenth, and eighteenth centuries—and even now in some rural areas—Spain maintained a long and extensive tradition of magic. Men and women of all ages and social conditions passionately practiced some of these rituals that the Church considered superstitions. One large group of magicians of both sexes—although some Inquisition tribunals prosecuted more women—claimed the power to cure illness, especially when caused by dark forces. The Inquisition prosecuted them for the improper use of Catholic liturgical prayers. A second large group composed mainly of men were feverishly caught up in the search for enchanted treasures, supposedly hidden by both Muslims and Jews at the time of their expulsion from the Iberian peninsula. Monks and priests, intellectuals, peasants, and city dwellers all formed silent partnerships with *judeoconversos* and *moriscos,* the former members of the expelled ethnic groups.

Largely carried out by men, this "masculine magic" employed—or at least claimed to employ—knowledge derived from such sources as astrology, the cabala, readings of the psalms, and the more popular esoteric books; thus we may also call it an "educated magic," although in most cases the protagonists were no more than simple amateurs with very vague notions of the specializations that experts—among whom we must include the level-headed men of science—had practiced for centuries. Women were not completely absent from these silent partnerships, although their role was always that of extra or assistant in the complicated maneuvers intended to disenchant hidden riches.[1]

Inquisitorial proceedings clearly distinguish another group of women as equally involved in magical practices, with the primary goal being seduction and conquest of a suitor. This third type of magic had a distinctly amorous nature, not only in its objectives, but also in its cants, invocations, and rites.[2] The Spanish Inquisition prosecuted all of these men and women equally for their deviation from one of the fundamental dogmas of the Catholic Church, the exercise of free will, and for the misuse of the sacred liturgy and of the names of God, the Virgin Mary, and the saints. The practice of love magic was also condemned for its invocation of evil spirits—such as the Lame Devil (el Diablo Cojuelo), Satan, Barabbas, and similar demons—that allowed the possibility of establishing some kind of inadvisable pact with Evil. The "diabolical pact" had already been clearly defined and repudiated by ecclesiastical authorities since well before the establishment of the Spanish Inquisition.[3] Fortunately for our sorceresses and amateurs, however, as well as for the solutions to their problems by means of magic, the attitude of the judges and prosecutors of the Spanish Holy Office were never so strict as in other areas, and even in the most extreme cases, prisoners usually received penalties limited to whipping and exile.[4]

The inquisitional archives constitute the best source available for studying the three types of magic referred to above. On the basis of these sources, I have cataloged the following summary of superstitious practices and sorcery performed by women who were concerned about the absence or possible loss of love.

LOVE MAGIC

In my analysis of the relaciones de causas (the lists of prisoners sent by every local tribunal to the central or supreme council) that I have been able to study to the present, the rituals practiced by the Catalan, Valencian, Andalusian, and Castilian sorceresses, as well as those tried by the tribunals of Las Palmas in the Canary Islands, belonged to a common store. Transmitted orally, and slowly elaborated over an undetermined period of time, they probably originated in the early Middle Ages.[5] Little by little the sorceresses incorporated themes and rites into a common repertory, which immediately "traveled" over all of Spain as a result of the women's great mobility. The sorceresses tried by each tribunal frequently came from areas quite distant from where they had finally been denounced and detained, and, as we shall see, many led restless lives, continually moving from place to place.

As these women came into frequent contact with one another, their consultations rarely ended after visiting one "expert." Each chance occasion—a gypsy who entered the house asking for alms, a traveler who arrived at the town, a short trip made to another city—provided an opportunity for making contact with some new professional who contributed original solutions and new methods. For in effect, the practice of sorcery is almost a profession for many women, and this double aspect of professionalism and geographical mobility explains the fundamental sameness of these practices, which offer few variations throughout the entire Iberian peninsula.

The study of the various tribunals reveals very similar profiles, and according to the goals and content of these rituals, the characteristics of "love magic" may be classified in the following manner:

First, there is a cluster of romantic procedures or spells, aimed always at uncovering the intentions of the man. These procedures are divided according to the instruments needed for the divination:

a) procedures carried out with beans, cards, a sieve, scissors, or other similar instruments;
b) divinations that make use of fire, spells that employ alum and salt, spells with "saucepans," "flasks," and similar items;
c) spells with various other objects such as a rosary or oranges.

Second, we can distinguish a cluster of rites with either an obvious or an underlying erotic content. Their erotic content may be termed implicit or explicit:

a) explicit: those rites which employ menstrual blood, semen, pubic hairs, and similar items;
b) implicit: those prayers and rituals whose goal—as stated in the documents—is to achieve "illicit" contact in a more or less implicit manner, such as the conjuration of the shadow-broom, and other similar cases.

Finally, there are a series of cants and invocations of spirits which may be accompanied by a generally uncomplicated ceremony, such as gesturing with the hands, or showing oneself at a window, with the conjuration or recitation of the decisive act. These cants are meant to appease some suitor, to regain his love, to make him return and visit the enamored woman, and other similar goals. I am grouping them under the heading of "the power of the word," because without the sorceress's conviction and force in reciting them, no one would seriously believe in their effect:

a) cants to placate a man and obtain his favors such as "Furious you come to me" ("furioso vienes a mí"), and "Hello, hello, man" ("hola, hola, varón"), and conjurations to the sun, moon, and stars;

b) conjurations to obtain a visit from the man, such as conjurations of the door and window;
c) magic cants to obtain the love of a suitor and avenge his neglect, such as the cant to the Lonely Soul [Ánima Sola], to Santa Marta, to "wicked" Marta, to Santa Elena, to San Silvestre, and to San Onofre.

As we have seen, the sorceresses' objectives completely justify the label of "love magic," and this has appeared to be the appropriate name for the practices generally carried out by women, but the seeming passion of these sixteenth-, seventeenth-, and eighteenth-century women deserves to be examined with greater thoroughness. In reality, and as is readily apparent in these supplications to the spirits, the presence of a suitor represents more of a material necessity than a truly amorous one. More than any other, our sorceresses' most frequent conjuration, that "[man's name] come, *giving me what he has and telling me what he knows,*" demonstrates that the desired "friend's" presence basically meant the support of someone who would help the women overcome life's difficulties in a society controlled by men economically as well as religiously. The single woman not only saw herself obliged to fight against material adversity, but also became suspect to her neighbors, unless she placed herself under the tutelage of some mystic "spouse" by following the path of the nuns and *beatas.* Isolated in society, unable to count on any masculine support, whether real or sublimated, she risked falling into the category of witch, especially if she had reached middle age. The sorceresses and their clients, therefore, were deeply invested in winning over and retaining the man who, in this case without any extraordinary powers, could ward off poverty and social marginalization. The fundamental goals underlying their rites were those of women who desperately sought men's redeeming company by:

a) determining a man's amorous intentions;
b) obtaining a man's love;
c) recovering and retaining the love of a scornful man.

AMOROUS ANXIETY IN FEMININE SORCERY

The long tradition and repeated practices of the cants, rites, and conjurations in the Middle Ages and the following centuries amassed so many possibilities for the woman in search of a stable companion that without having to analyze all the categories previously mentioned, and examining only the most frequently recited phrases and refrains,[6] we penetrate the very heart of "feminine magic," discovering the most intimate aspects of the sorceresses and their clients during these rituals. Judging from the cants recited by the sorceresses in order to attain the secret desires of their clients, love was the chief aim of these women of the Habsburg regime, who so readily solicited "love magic."

Despite their assertions, these enamored women were not satisfied merely with having their love reciprocated. Their aspirations and amorous passion extended to the total control of the beloved's will, and the reasons for desiring such control had little to do with the admired mystical sighs of their religious sisters' passion. Our enamored women, practitioners of magic, were essentially pragmatic souls who realized that they must obtain masculine support at all costs, so as not to be socially devalued.

Yet the purely amorous or erotic aspect of most of these practices is undeniable. Refrains of a basically impassioned nature are recited in all the rites and conjurations. In a client's name, a sorceress entreated the immediate appearance of the man, they ordered him to return if he had gone away, and repeated, through various chants, the desire that he be consumed with passion. This was only one facet of love magic, however, and we need to examine and learn about the others. Let us first examine the emotional characteristics of our foremothers.

The usual divinatory practices with beans or cards tell us very little regarding feminine emotions. The expert restricted herself to telling fortunes and inquiring about the possible appearance of the man. The extremely long conjuration of the beans recited by a sorceress named Castellanos who was tried by the Toledo tribunal contains only one enlightening phrase. After a tedious conjuration in which the beans were tossed to reveal the future, and after naming the Virgin, the saints, and such elements as the sea, the sands, the ground, and the seven heavens, the conjuration included only the following phrases:

> Así como esto es verdad
> me declaréis lo que os fuere preguntando . . .
> habas que me digáis la verdad
> desto que os fuere preguntando
> si hubiere de venir fulano[7]

> [Just as this is true
> You will tell me what I ask . . .
> Beans, tell me the truth
> About this which I ask you
> If (man's name) will come]

Other sorceresses stated the case even more concisely. Isabel Bautista, also tried by the Toledo tribunal,[8] recited a long conjuration, repeating only:

Si fulano ha de venir
salga en camino

[If (man's name) is coming
Let him be on his way]

In spite of their complexity, neither the conjurations recited before tossing the beans nor fortune-telling with cards offers much information about the emotions of the women tried by the Inquisition, except for their desire to conjure a man who would take an interest in them.

Fortunately for us, the conjurations and practices of love magic were so numerous that other sorceries and cants reveal, little by little, the most recondite thoughts of these enamored women as well as the extent of their desires. Love magic is a process through which we can observe the various stages of love as well as the diverse psychological states which the lovers—men or women—experienced in their erotic-emotional relations. The sorceries of the beans and the cards would have been useful only during the initial anticipatory phase when the beloved had not yet appeared, or resisted doing so. The professionals would employ these sorceries only for women wishing to know whether or not they were to achieve this essential goal, but they still reserved a vast repertory for future situations that might occur once the coveted suitor had been trapped, such as the need to arouse a passion not overly potent, to achieve the beloved's constancy, and—admittedly—to calm the anxieties and thirst for revenge of a rejected woman. The professional sorceress applied each phrase on the conjurations, according to the specific needs and circumstances of the women, since they hid nothing regarding their personal situations. This specificity created an entire range of psychological nuances that must also be taken into account.

Clients requesting the appearance of a man, therefore, consulted the beans or the cards—a common occurrence, judging by the frequency with which these conjurations were solicited. But the woman visiting the sorceress was not always lonely or frustrated, and almost as frequently we encounter in the trials other sorceries, such as the oranges and the rosary, which confirmed that love had finally arrived, albeit without the desired intensity. Once again the enamored woman had to resort to an expert who could change the course of her future by bringing the will of her man to a more complete state of submission.

The phrases in the sorceries requiring a rosary or some oranges as the divinatory instrument allow us to understand the second stage of the amorous process. Esperanza Badía, for example, tried in Valencia, held a rosary and recited a long and complicated conjuration in which she invoked various demons and other magical characters, ending with the following phrase:

> Venga el corazón de fulano
> atado, preso y enamorado[9]
>
> [Let the heart of (man's name) come
> Bound, captured, and enamored]

The same phrase also appears in the conjuration employed in the sorcery of the oranges, in Castile as well as in Valencia and the rest of the peninsular regions. It thus constitutes a veritable leitmotiv expressing the central message of such apparently diverse practices. The preliminary phrases vary, the conjured "diabolical" beings may be different, but the essential phrase is always the same: "Let the heart of [man's name] come / Bound, captured and enamored" [Venga el corazón de fulano / atado, preso y enamorado].

The fundamental goal now became retaining the male lover. The conjuration accompanying the sorcery of "the palms" was recited with this goal in mind. The sorceress would pat the length of her arm with the palm of her hand in order to uncover the intentions of the absent man and would again recite a very similar phrase. Laura Garrigues, a sorceress in the 1655 Valencian auto de fe, stated quite bluntly:

> Fulano,
> donde quiera que estés,
> te envío este clavo
> te doy este martelazo
> Por mi amor presto vengas
> por mi amor, preso y atado[10]
>
> [(man's name,)
> Wherever you are,
> I send you this nail
> I strike you with this passion
> Soon you will come for my love
> For my love, captured and bound]

Like the other sorceries, the sorcery of the palms circulated in multiple versions over the entire Iberian peninsula, but the variations occurred principally at the beginning of and in addition to, the mantic practice.[11] The central phrase, however, is very similar in all cases and confirms that this sorcery belongs to the second amorous phase together with the sorceries of the rosary and the oranges. In Castile, María Castellanos recited it as follows:

Yo, María, te llamo Francisco,
que vengas por mi amor gimiendo y llorando[12]

[I, María, call you, Francisco,
To come for my love, moaning and crying]

With this variant, this singularly interesting woman, to whom we shall refer again, introduces us to a new phase in love magic beginning with the conjurations and rites in which the symbolic value of fire intervenes: conjurations of salt and alum and sorceries of "pans" and "flasks" or "phials." In the latter, the name varies in different regions according to the language, but the examples all reveal the intimate feelings of women in search of love.

The conjurations of alum and salt were recited in order to divine the future. The sorceress threw a fistful of salt or a bit of alum into the fire so that she could interpret the flame. In all cases the sorceresses began to reveal a state of mind in which impatience appeared to have played an important part. The woman reciting the conjuration did so on behalf of someone whose anxiety was much more intense than in the former cases. In the simplest versions, as in Gerónima González's case in the Valencia auto de fe, the invocation is simple:

Sal, salida . . .
assi como moros ni cristianos
pueden estar sin ti
que Fulano no pueda estar sin mi[13]

[Salt, pouring forth . . .
Neither Moors nor Christians
Can be without you
Nor can (man's name) be without me]

However, the use of fire seemed somehow to stimulate and to contribute to a new psychological state in those women who resorted to the help of sorceresses, as we can clearly observe in the conjuration of alum. María Antonia de Neroña, also from Valencia, explicitly indicated her desire to inflame her beloved's heart:

No pongo alumbre
sino el corazón y entrañas de Fulano[14]

[I do not use alum
But rather the heart and soul of (man's name)]

Gerónima González uses a very similar phrase in the same alum ritual:

Así queme el corazón de Fulano
y arada en amor mío[15]

[Thus burn the heart of (man's name)
and plow in my love]

The formula is repeated in Castile (in the version of our friend Castellanos) in even more explicit form. The beloved must be consumed with love and visit the woman who loves him.

. . . Que así como te has de quemar
se queme el corazón de Fulano
porque me venga a ver[16]

[Just as you will be burnt up
(man's name)'s heart must be inflamed
So that he comes to see me]

Of course, all of these imprecations, which are in general quite poetic, were accompanied by flames and were directed toward the powers of Avernus, who conferred upon them their magical aspect; we are, however, more concerned with analyzing their psychological content and scope.

As we can see, the emotional temperature of the love-magic enthusiasts rose quite a few degrees thanks to the use of fire, and we begin to understand their real intentions toward their suitors. The enamored women of the Habsburg regime wanted absolute control over the will and movements of the men they had snared, and this wish is an essential chapter in their magic manipulations and anxieties, clearly manifested in the fact that the experts' conjurations employed no instrument or ceremony. The unadorned word is the fundamental factor here, and it is an indispensable key to our elemental "psychoanalysis" of love magic.[17]

When the professional sorceress resorted to magic cants, the relationship had apparently reached its worst state. The man was scornful, he missed assignations, and the woman also suspected the presence of another woman on the scene. To revive his interest, it now became necessary to resort directly to evil forces. St. Marta, Marta "the wicked," and the entire chorus of devils already familiar to the client—Satan, Barabbas, the Lame Devil—were invoked directly or indirectly, but with almost no instruments or paraphernalia.

At this point the enamored woman had to placate her companion's anger, and the sorceress placed at her disposal a wide variety of "appeasing conjurations" to rekindle his passion, mainly through the influence of St. Elena or St. Marta. The sorceress would also endeavor to reinstill in the man the need to see his abandoned lover. The conjurations aimed at changing the man's angry attitude were usually short and extremely graphic. No doubt the women of the Habsburg regime feared their companions' violent tempers, proof of which is frequently documented in the declarations. Prudencia Grillo, tried by the Toledo tribunal, justifiably resorted to magic because she was afraid of being locked in a castle by the man on whom she depended.[18] Other women also speak of the bad treatment they received at the hands of their husbands or lovers, and of attempts on their lives in various forms. One woman even stated that she was fed ground glass in a murder attempt.[19] Given the men's violence and mean temperament, it is not surprising that these women viewed sorcery as a far more satisfactory recourse than the customary Christian prayers and resignation recommended by their confessors.

In any case, a brief reading of one of these women's versions confirms their obvious fears. Undoubtedly the man's presence is as much feared as desired. Laura Garrigues, for example, tried in Valencia in 1655, would conceal her hand inside her clothes when she saw her angry lover approach, and pulling her pubic hairs, would repeat:

Furioso vienes a mí
furioso vienes a mí
tan fuerte como un toro
tan fuerte como un horno
tan sujeto estés a mí
como los pelos de mi coño
están a mí[20]

[Furious you come to me
Furious you come to me
As strong as a bull
As hot as an oven
You will be as subject to my will
As the hairs of my cunt
Are to me]

The best-known and most widely spread refrain, however, contains a somewhat mysterious formula—surely a synthesis achieved after centuries of use—that gives it even greater poetic charm. Most likely its obscure meaning and brevity contributed at the same time to its enormous divulgation and popularity during the sixteenth and seventeenth centuries:

Con dos te miro
con cinco te ato
tu sangre te bebo
el corazón te parto[21]

[With two I watch you
With five I bind you
Your blood I drink
Your heart I rend]

Laura Garrigues also knew a version of this conjuration which reveals more clearly the need to control an overly impetuous man:

Con dos te miro
con tres te ligo y ato
la sangre te voto
el corazón te parto
con las parias de tu madre
la boca te tapo
¡Hale, asno!
sobre ti cabalgo[22]

[With two I watch you
With three I bind and tie you
Your blood I curse
Your heart I rend
With your afterbirth
I cover your mouth

(The sorceress covered her mouth here)

Come along, ass!
I'll ride you]

It is not difficult to infer, after reading this brief imprecation, that the magic enthusiast believed she would shut the mouth that insulted her, subjecting it to her will in the same way as women dominated the little asses that so frequently served as ladies' mounts precisely because of their inferior strength and docility. The version Isabel Bautista used in Castile confirms and expands my point:

Con dos te miro
con tres te tiro

con cinco te arrebato
calla, bobo, que te ato
tan humilde vengas a mí
como la suela de mi zapato[23]

[With two I watch you
With three I toss you
With five I captivate you
Quiet, fool, I'll bind you

(At this point the sorceress would slap her knee as a sign of command, and finish:)

You will come to me humble
As the sole of my shoe]

As shown above, enamored women understood quite well the mean temperament of their companions, but surely this formed part of the rules of the game. It was extremely important to placate their tempers in order to achieve a reconciliation. The amorous encounters and visits—which were most likely at night, judging by the extramarital nature of the majority of the relationships—rekindled the love interest. Without a doubt, the man's return constitutes an important motive for anxiety. His arrival is impatiently awaited, but he does not appear. The lover goes to her window, opens the door and looks down the street. He is nowhere to be seen; feeling exasperated, she nevertheless continues to wish for his presence, perhaps with increased anxiety. The conjurations of the door and the window reflect perfectly the scene I have just described.

In the conjuration of the door, like that of the window, the woman who recited went outside and looked down the street, where she supposed the man she wanted to attract would appear. Laura Garrigues did not object to going outside in broad daylight to call her lover:

Fulano
ni tú me ves
ni yo te acierto
yo te llamo con el Padre . . .
tan humilde
tan sujeto
vengas a mí
como mi señor Jesucristo
subió al santo árbol de la cruz

a morir por ti y por mi
Amén

[(man's name)
You do not see me
Nor have I found you
I call you in the name of the Father . . .

(Here the sorceress invoked the powers of the Holy Trinity, and this was followed by the supplication and command:)

so humble
so subjected
You will come to me
As my lord Jesus Christ
Climbed the Holy Tree of the Cross
To die for you and me
Amen]

Evidently the sorceress tried to evoke the sacred figure's proverbial docility and resignation before a superior will. But, as the reader can imagine, the inquisitors were not partial to complex poetic associations.[24]

María Antonia de Neroña, also of the Valencian tribunal, preferred to act at night, apparently at ten o'clock sharp. She would then invoke the lover, calling him three times, imagining him with a noose around his neck, that is, bound like a prisoner pleading for help:

Fulano, Fulano, Fulano,
por la calle abajo te veo venir
una soga de ahorcado traes a la garganta
a grandes voces diciendo
Fulana, váleme . . .

[(man's name, man's name, man's name,)
from down the street I see you coming,
A hangman's noose around your neck
Clamoring in a loud voice,
(woman's name,) help me . . .]

Repeated again and again, the refrain emphasizes not only the attempt to draw the companion's attention, but the woman who is to help him as well. The woman then denies him her aid, however, and turns him over to the conjured demons so they may penetrate the man's heart, provoking the same anxieties and pain she has suffered, as she recites this magic prayer:

... No te quiero valer
válgate Barrabás y Satanás
y todos los diablos que allá están
todos os juntaréis
y en el corazón de Fulano entraréis
y este cuchillo de cachas negras
por el corazón le clavaréis
tantas ansias le daréis
que a mi casa le traeréis

[I don't wish to help you,
Let Barabbas and Satan help you
And all the devils who are there
You will all gather together
And this black-handled knife
You will plunge into his heart
You will cause him so much anguish
That you will lead him to my house]

The basic intention is evident, but the woman is not satisfied with this wish alone, and she adds one of the refrains frequently repeated when the woman's anxiety led her to the brink of desperation:

... Y no le dejaréis
reposar, ni comer, ni dormir
ni en la cama reposar
sino conmigo pensar

[... And you won't let him
Rest or eat or sleep
He will not rest in bed
But will think only of me]

The rest of María Antonia de Neroña's conjuration is explicit in this invocation "of the window":

... Que venga con ansias y pena
en su corazón
por verme y hallarme

[... Let him come with anguish and sorrow
In his heart
To see me and find me ...]

The only instrument the woman employed during this ceremony was the black-handled dagger that was to be thrust in the windowsill at the opportune moment—an obvious symbol of the forgetful lover's heart.[25]

María Antonia de Neroña was one of the women who best expressed her love frustration in these cants. Her trial summary included a similar cant bidding the man to visit her again. On this occasion María Antonia was even more decisive: the man should appear bound and held fast by his most delicate parts:

> A Fulano veo venir
> soga de ahorcado trae tras él . . .
> estas le traeréis
> de su coxón
> de su riñón
> de su baçón
> de las telas de su corazón[26]
>
> [I see (man's name) coming
> A hangman's noose after him . . .

(At this point she conjured the demons who were in this case, interestingly enough, feminine.)

> You will bring him
> By the balls
> By his kidney
> By his spleen
> By his heartstrings

Yet most of the sorceresses are not as explicit or rhetorical as María Antonia de Neroña. Gerónima González conjured the street and called the demons, limiting her entreaty:

> ¡Ah de la calle!
> ¡ah, so compadre!
> . . . Satanás, Barrabás y Lucifer
> que me den a saber si Fulano vendrá[27]
>
> [Hey, the street (repeated)
> Hey, mate!

(The invocation of the demons continued and was much longer than in Neroña's version, surely because Gerónima González emphasized the ceremony's magic aspect rather than merely stating her desires, which were limited to one phrase:)

. . . . Satan, Barabbas, and Lucifer
Let me know if (man's name) will come]

Laura Garrigues employed a brief and disconsolate imprecation to make her man return. She then entreated him by invoking such magic characters as María de Padilla, of the so-called Circle of the Castilian king Pedro I, who bewitched men and subjected them to her will with a ring containing an enchanted demon, and condemned the souls to hell, diabolical figures, like the "desperate souls":

Vecino y compadre,
gran señor de la calle
Fulano solía venir a verme
y ahora no viene
yo quiero que venga
y me lo has de traer
yo te conjuraré

[Neighbor and mate,
Great lord of the street,
(man's name) would come and see me
And now he does not come
And you are to bring him to me
I will entreat you . . .]

As with María Antonia de Neroña, Laura also added her wish that the demons penetrate this man's heart to induce such anguish that he would not rest until he had sought her out.[28]

At this precise psychological moment, these semi-abandoned women employed very simple ceremonies, whose symbolic value was as evident as the use of fire. In general, the rites associated with the door, the place where one awaits the appearance of the beloved man, were limited to sweeping the threshold and conjuring him. Laura Garrigues awaited nightfall, left the door of her house ajar, and recited:

Conjúrote, puerta y quicial
por donde Fulano ha salido
ha de volver a entrar[29]

[I conjure you, door and side-post
where (man's name) went out
He must enter again]

The pleas of the sorceresses and their clients directed to the stars, the moon, and the sun follow the same pattern we have seen during this stage, as the woman attempts to retrieve her man but also desires to avenge herself for his absence. These cants addressed to the stars praise their beauty—"Maiden star, the highest and most beautiful . . ." [Estrella doncella, la más alta y la más bella]—and entreat them to penetrate the ungrateful heart painfully. One of the most ancient is the prayer by the beata of Huete, from the Cuenca tribunal of 1499; she invokes nine stars in all and then proceeds to the cant's central message:

Al monte Synay iréys
e nueve varas de amor me saquedes
por la cabeza de Santa Cruz las hinquedes
e de la cabeza al coraçón al riñón
y al taso o al baço
y a las andas del espiñaço
e las tresientas coyunturas
que en su cuerpo son
que no pueda comer ni beber
hasta que a mí venga a bien querer
e a aver plaçer[30]

[You will go to Mount Sinai
And bring me nine staffs of love
You will drive them into the head of the Holy Cross
And from the head to the heart
And from the heart to the kidney
And to the taso or the spleen
And all along the spine
And the three hundred joints
in his body
So that he can neither eat nor drink
Until he comes to love me well
And to take pleasure in me]

The conjuration of the stars appears frequently in the Castilian tribunals at Cuenca and Toledo, and the well-known refrain from this conjuration, "So that he can neither eat nor drink . . ." [que no pueda comer ni beber], constantly accompanies other invocations throughout the following centuries. The Castilian Juana Dientes disrobed and let down her hair before reciting it, perhaps as a means of invoking the physical encounter with the lover; we must not forget that during this time, nudity and untied hair had sinful erotic connotations. Her conjuration was even more forceful than that of the religious devotee from Huete, who does not invoke the demons Beelzebub and Satan conjured by Juana:

Y con la fragua de Belzebú y Satanás
siete rejones le amolad
e con el coraçón de Fulano las lançad
para que ningún reposo pueda tomar
hasta que venga a mi mandar
Diablos del horno
traédmelo ayna
diablos del peso
diablos de la plaça
traédmelo en dança
diablos de la encrucijada
traédmelo a casa[31]

[. . . and with the forge of Beelzebub and Satan
You will sharpen seven daggers
And thrust them into (man's name)'s heart
So that he shall have no rest
Until he answers my command
Devils from the furnace
Bring him to me now
Devils of the scales
Devils of the plaza
Bring him dancing to me
Devils of the crossroad
Bring him to my house]

The proceedings against Isabel Bautista contain another conjuration to the stars recited by the Castilian sorceresses as early as the sixteenth century. Isabel added a brief and surprising ritual difficult for us to interpret. She measured the door jamb and door of her house with a cord, threw salt into one of the door jambs and placed a broom in the other, conjured the nine stars just as the other sorceress did, and then specified her desire that the man not forget her:

Tres varas de mimbre me traeréis
por las muelas de Barrabás las afiléis
por las calderas de Pedro Botero las pasaréis
una la hincareis por el sentido
que no me eche en olvido
otra por el coraçón
que vaya a mi afición
otra por las espaldas
que venga por mis palabras[32]

[Bring me three willow rods
Sharpen them on Barabbas's molars
Carry them through hell
Drive one into his mind
So that he won't forget me
Another into the heart
So he will come when I desire
Another into his back
So he will answer my call]

The conjurations that employ the stars, the sun, and the moon as the magical motifs, as well as others we will examine below, are basically all the same. The sorceress varied the invocation to the evil spirits, increased or reduced the form of the cant, but always concluded by supplicating the same thing: the recovery of lost love.

We can observe this wish clearly in the cants invoking the sun and the moon, which are usually quite brief: ". . . so that [man's name] cannot live without me" [que Fulano no pueda estar sin mí], or simply, "so that [man's name] loves me" [que Fulano me quiera]. The cant to the moon recited by doña Juana de la Paz, tried in Valencia in 1655, demonstrates the features of these conjurations, actually the laments of abandoned women expressed aloud:

Luna clara
bella y hermosa
tan clara y tan bella
como me paresces a mí
tan bella y hermosa
paresca yo a mi galán
como la estrella que está cerca de ti[33]

[Bright moon
Lovely, beautiful
As bright and beautiful
As you appear to me
So bright and beautiful
May I appear to my man,
As the star which is near to you]

To express simultaneously their frustration and attempt to recover lost love, the sorceresses not only resorted to profane elements like the stars; their repertory also included the Church's intercessors, certain saints, whose relation to the golden legend associated them with the basic purpose of the sorceresses' love magic. The sacred figures most frequently invoked include the "Lonely Soul" [Ánima Sola], who requires prayers because of her destitution; San Silvestre, magical because of the date of his feast day; and Santa Elena and San Onofre.

The prayer to the Lonely Soul, generally quite beautiful, nonetheless sheds very little light on the situation of these enamored women. After the ritual invocation, the woman simply repeats a wish very similar to that which we have already seen. Doña Juana de la Paz recited thirty-three Our Fathers, Hail Marys, and the accompanying Glorias, standing by her window, and enumerated the conditions of her plea to the spirit:

> Esto que he rezado os ofrezco
> os encomiendo
> ánima sola
> para que me traigas y me déis
> buena señal desto que os pido[34]

> [I offer you this prayer
> I commend you
> Lonely soul
> To bring me and give me
> A hopeful sign of what I ask of you]

In other cases, the prayer is even more similar to previous conjurations. The preambles employed to conjure the Lonely Soul are not prayers but rather diabolical entreaties to such various elements as "Lucano's blood" [la sangre de Lucano], "the heart of the man who was stabbed in cold blood" [el corazón del hombre muerto a hierro frío], and the "twelve tribes of Israel" [las doce tribus de Israel] to cut nine wicker staffs:

> Tres me las clavaredes a Fulano por el corazón
> que no pierda mi amor
> tres por el sentido
> que no me eche en olvido[35]

> [You thrust three of them into (man's name)'s heart
> So he won't forget my love
> Three of them into his consciousness
> So he won't forget me]

Still less original are the invocations in the prayers to Santa Marta, San Onofre, San Silvestre, and Santa Elena, yet they are beautiful compositions that would naturally impress a woman in need of help. As in the former case, all of these cants are simply assorted preambles followed by familiar refrains employed on other occasions. In the case of the prayer to San Onofre, the sorceress limits herself to entreating:

Como atastéis y encontrastéis
a todos estos—la Draga y el Dragón—
así venga Fulano
tan humilde,
tan rendido, tan prostrado
tan atado y tan encortado
como todos estos se rindieron
y prostraron a vuestros santísimos pies . . .

[As you bound and encountered
All of these—the lady Dragon and the Dragon—
Thus will (man's name) come
So humble
So surrendered, so prostrated
So bound and tied
Like all of those who surrendered themselves
And prostrated themselves at your holy feet]

The conjuration ends with the refrain, "May he not eat, or drink, or rest," and so on [Que no pueda comer, ni beber, ni reposar, etc.].[36]

All the petitions to San Onofre are very similar. First, the sorceress evoked his harsh penitence in the following manner:

Así como estas palabras son verdad
santo glorioso
me cumpláis esto que os pido
de traerme a mi marido[37]

[Just as these words are true,
Glorious saint
Do what I ask of you
And bring me my husband]

The prayers to Santa Marta, Marta "the Wicked" [La Mala], and Santa Elena usually repeat familiar refrains ("May he not eat or drink . . ." [Que no pueda comer, ni beber . . .]) and various entreaties to make the man appear or to "resuscitate" his heart.

THE EROTIC BOND AS WEAPON

Once the enamored woman had exhausted all the possibilities of the above magical cants, she was then obliged to employ the most powerful weapon in this type of magic. She had to bind her lover so tightly through intimate relations that he would be unable to leave her for another woman. The "binding" or "impotency spell" thus consists of rendering the man impotent, except when in the presence of the woman who bound him either through the conjuration or some other magic practice.

Men and women of the sixteenth and seventeenth centuries literally believed in the possibility of producing this kind of spell, ironically justifying the double meaning of the term "sorceress" as pronounced by the male lover. Frequently we find men who appear before the Inquisition, afraid that they have fallen victim to this embarrassing spell and hoping that the imprisonment and sentencing of their domestic Circe will release them from it. Women were at once perpetrators and victims of an attitude that helped them to achieve their goals, but that also brought them to the attention of the Inquisition. Although these details cannot be described here, the repertory of conjurations itself reveals sufficient information to help us understand their circumstances. "Love magic" also contains the appropriate cants for "binding" a man to prevent him from approaching anyone other than the woman who loves him.

The conjuration of "the shadow-broom" appears in multiple versions throughout Castile, Valencia, and other regions. According to the documents, it renewed "illicit relations," its essentially erotic content recited by a woman generally completely naked and with her hair down. The shadow-broom came to symbolize an entreaty to both a demonic spirit and to the man whose return was desired. Actually, each sorceress added the touches from her personal repertory which seemed most opportune or which most openly suggested the possibility of inducing the absent lover to desire the woman once again. In one case the woman simply swept her own shadow with the broom, saying, "Come, husband, for I am alone."[38] The beata from Huete, however, added a conjuration allowing us to appreciate the symbolic value of the scene:

Sombra
cabeça tenéis como yo
cuerpo tenéis como yo
yo te mando que ansí como tienes
mi sombra verdadera
que tu vayas a Fulano
e lo traigas a mí[39]

[Shadow,
You have a head like mine
You have a body like mine

I command that, just as you have
My true shadow,
You go to (man's name)
And bring him to me]

María de Santarem, tried in Cuenca in 1538, employed a cant that
seems to apply sorcery of the beans to her specific case. She would pitch
several black chickpeas as she mentioned them (calling them beans in
the invocation), finishing the spell by positioning herself to await the
conjured man:

Sombra señora
con vos me vengo a enamorar
sombra señora
con vos me vengo a consolar
ava, que me habéis de ir por Fulano
y me le avéis de traer
ava, que quiero echar las suertes
ava, que si en vos cayere
ava, que me lo avéis de traer . . .
¡ah! en vos cayó la sombra
presto, presto
traédmelo preso y atado
y presto en un crédito
y no me lo dexéys a la puerta
sino traédmelo a mi cama[40]

[Madame shadow
I come to fall in love with you
Madame shadow
I come to console myself with you
Bean, you must fetch (man's name)
And bring him to me
Bean, I want to cast lots
Bean, I want to cast them
Bean, if it falls to you
Bean, you must fetch him to me.

(Here, she pitched the chickpeas, letting the last one fall in her shadow.)

Ah! The shadow fell on you
Quickly, quickly
Bring him captured and tied
And quickly on your word
And don't leave him at my door
But bring him to my bed]

Sexual relations constituted the real weapon which the sorceresses and their clients relied upon in order to retain a man. The woman's physical surrender, however, guaranteed neither his constancy nor his good humor, the two fundamental goals that were desired. Consequently, sorceresses cast spells obliging the man to seek out only one woman, who became the heroine of these occult narratives. Our enamored women counted on a wide range of methods for their purposes. They may have bewitched the man by using his semen to cast various "impotency spells." Similarly, he may have been bound to the woman by means of some love potion composed of her sexual fluids. The following are examples of several practices which, while not always poetic, were indeed quite expressive.

Throughout Spain, sorceresses frequently performed the "conjuration of the oil lamp's wick," which utilized semen. The woman would collect it after having had "contact with her friend"—called illicit in the documents. The cotton or linen with which the woman cleaned herself after intercourse was twisted into a "wick," then placed in an oil lamp and ignited. For several nights she would leave it burning while she recited:

Así come arde esta torcida
arda el corazón de Fulano

[As this wick burns
So shall (man's name)'s heart burn]

Doña Juana de la Paz performed this conjuration in Valencia,[41] while in Castile we find a similar procedure where the woman recited a more complex and explicit cant:

Vida de la vida
de la carne y de la sangre
de Fulano
que me ames . . .
y te conjuro Fulano con Barrabás
y assí como estas torcidas arden en este candil
assí me quieras[42]

[Life of life
Of the flesh and blood
Of (man's name)
You must love me
. . . And I conjure you, (man's name), with
Barabbas

And just as these wicks burn in these lamps
You will love me]

Another curious ceremony with wicks had to be performed collectively. The women all sat in a circle and called upon the man to perform "lewd acts." Lighting nine wicks, they would pass around three grains of salt, three lumps of coal, nine nails, nine beans, and a wax candle. They would throw the salt, beans, and other objects into the circle and then pick them up again; if the two beans indented with teeth marks landed together in the circle, it was a sign that the absent man would return.

Women's menstrual blood also contained magical powers that could be channeled to the same ends as semen. In this case, the sorceresses generally did not utilize this ingredient alone, but would add the brains of an ass and pubic hairs. Once the dish containing the impotency spell had been prepared, the man would have to eat it for the desired effect. Laura Garrigues, for example, added a little pepper; doña Juana de la Cruz simply dried the blood and mixed it with wine; other women spread it on a meat dish. The conjuration recited by doña Juana de la Paz adds a poetic touch:

Yo te conjuro
sangre de la fuente—o de mi fuente—la vermeja
que vaya Fulano tras de Fulana
como el cordero tras la oveja[43]

[I conjure you,
Blood from the crimson fountain—or my fountain—
Make (man's name) follow (woman's name)
Like the lamb after the sheep]

The inclusion of menstrual blood, pubic hair, and semen guaranteed these rites the most obvious and astonishing sexual content. Yet the "conjuration of the sexual member" probably originated because some women dared to venture even further in their desire to cause their lovers' impotency with other women. Laura Garrigues held her lover's penis and, making several crosses, recited: "I repeat, the cross enters" [Hago coro, entra cruz].[44] María Antonia de Neroña made the sign of the cross on her lover's back—presumably in bed, although the document does not specify where—and said:

Hasta que esta cruz te veas
tú me ames y me quieras[45]

[Until you see this cross
May you love and desire me]

Besides these "love potions" and magical concoctions, sorceresses resorted to less complicated rites also aimed at rendering the undecided lover impotent. The Valencian sorceresses would take a ribbon touched by the man, and at the stroke of six, they would make nine knots, tying and untying them nine times; the woman would then wear the belt for nine days. Variations of the "spell of the knots" with cloths or similar objects appeared in Castile and other areas.

These rituals thus describe clearly women's anxieties regarding love, but a more profound analysis reveals that, although they wished to be accompanied and loved by men, material support was an equally desired goal, a fact evinced orally through the conjurations.

SENTIMENTAL PRAGMATISM AND LOVE MAGIC

Despite the essential constant in love magic of winning over and keeping a man, the institution of matrimony appears only in an occasional conjuration. Marriage, the official bond par excellence, is scarcely ever mentioned; in most cases the magical rites were directed toward a purely sexual conquest. "Love magic" was also extramarital magic, one in which erotic relations always carried a sinful, condemnable connotation for the zealous priests and inquisitors. The inquisitorial proceedings refer to physical relations in such unequivocal terms, in spite of the fact that no lack of married women resorted to the sorceresses to recover husbands distracted by other women. In the terminology appearing in the inquisitorial documents, the sorceresses and their clients sought "illicit contact" and "lewd acts," they used fluids from "private parts," and they were interested in "dishonest relations"; in effect, the words "husband" and "wife" were rarely mentioned, nor were marriages reclaimed.

While the term "husband" does not always mean a spouse officially recognized by the Church, but can also refer to a stable couple, only Isabel María de Mendoza, tried in Valencia, employed the term in her prayer to San Onofre:

Assí como estas palabras son verdad
santo glorioso,
me cumpláis esto que os pido
de traerme a mi marido[46]

[. . . Just as these words are true,
Glorious saint
You will do what I ask of you
And bring me my husband]

Very few of the experts whose practices I have collected in this basic repertory of love magic make any reference to marriage or to legal husbands. Nor is the conjugal bond mentioned with any frequency in the proceedings and causas de relaciones in other peninsular trials I have studied. This does not mean that married women were not involved in this type of magic, but they generally resorted to it in secret when they suspected their husbands of leaving them for some rival. It was undoubtedly better to try to recover a husband's love through spontaneous means such as physical relations than to suffer in silence and resign oneself, following the confessor's advice. In any case, love magic became an unorthodox method, not only for the religious reasons adduced by the theologians and judges of the Holy Office, but because the Church Fathers condemned and marginalized sexual relations. For these women, carnal pleasure thus assumed a significance that is more characteristic of the classical world than of Christianity.

Of course, the term "husband" is not completely absent from the basic repertory, a term whose distinct resonances compare with the variant "friend," according to Cirac Estopañán.[47] Significantly most of these women were either prostitutes, the lovers of friars or married men, or simply women who had no qualms about having sexual relations with whomever they chose. One of the advocates they appealed to most frequently was "Marta the Wicked," whose description illustrates the extramarital nature of these relations:

Marta, Marta
no la digna ni la santa
la que descasa casadas
la que junta los amancebados
la que anda de noche por las encrucijadas
yo te conjuro con tal y tal demonio
y con el de la carnicería
que me traiga a Fulano más ayna
o de hombre que hable
o de perro que ladre[48]

[Marta, Marta,
Neither decent nor a saint
She who separates married women

She who unites lovers
She who travels the crossroads by night
I conjure you with such-and-such a demon
And with the demon of the slaughterhouse
That you bring (man's name) to me more quickly
Than a man speaking
Or a dog barking]

In truth, the women who practiced such rites were rather importu-
nate, taking advantage of their male friends' sexual desires to benefit
themselves. Requests for gifts are an essential part of the conjurations
and rites that attempt to recover and maintain carnal relations with
scornful suitors. Many of the more poetically structured compositions
usually end with the pragmatic refrain: "Let [man's name] come, and
give me all he has and tell me all he knows" [Venga Fulano y me dé lo
que tuviere y me diga lo que supiere].

Although one of the most erotic, the following conjuration of the
wicks recorded by Paz y Melia ends on a pragmatic note:

Que me ames
me estimes y me regales
que me des cuanto tuvieres
y me digas lo que supieres[49]

[. . . So that you love
And esteem me and give me gifts,
So that you give me all you have
And tell me what you know]

The lengthy and poetic invocation to the stars also contains the same
line:

Que venga con ansias y pena en su corazón
por verme y hallarme
dándome lo que tuviere
y diciéndome lo que supiere[50]

[So that he come with anguish and pain in his heart
To see me and find me
Giving me all he has
And telling me what he knows]

The same phrase appears in Laura Garrigues's invocations of the
street:

Ansias le daréis
que no le dejaréis reposas
hasta que me venga a buscar
dándome lo que tuviere y diciéndome lo que supiere[51]

[. . . You will provoke his anguish
And you won't let him rest
Until he seeks me out
Giving me all he has and telling me what he knows]

As the reader may guess, this phrase appears in the conjurations and phrases that conclude the ceremonies with explicitly erotic content, and in the superstitious cants:

La gloriosa santa Elena
de la cruz los tres clavos sacó
el uno en el mar echó
el otro a su hijo Constantino dió
para que en las batallas entrase
no fuese vencido sino vencedor
así, santa bienaventurada,
sea yo la vencedora con Fulano
que no pueda estar . . .
hasta que me venga a buscar.
Que venga volando
que you le estoy esperando
véngame dándome quanto tuviere
y me diga quanto supiere[52]

[Glorious Santa Elena
Took the three nails from the cross
She threw one into the sea
She gave one to Constantine her son
So that in battle
He would be victor instead of conquered
In like manner, blessed saint
Let me be the victor over (man's name)
So that he cannot . . .

(The sorceress adds the refrain conjuring the anxiety wished upon the man)

Until he comes to find me
May he arrive as fast as possible
As I am waiting for him
Let him come to me, giving me all he has
And telling me all he knows]

This new leitmotiv reveals facets that were unimagined until now. What conclusion can we reach regarding these women and their practices after having analyzed the material? Were they, in effect, basically concerned with love, or were they unprotected and self-centered women? They seem to include elements of both, no doubt, but what is most essential is that their rituals created an authentic popular poetry that allows us a view of a previously unknown world.

NOTES

1. The documents in the Archivo Histórico Nacional (hereafter AHN) in Madrid dealing with cases of superstitious practices include sixty-six men and two hundred women. They are incomplete as to the sentences, and in some instances the case record consists merely of a denunciation. According to the investigation that I have carried out—which includes files 82–89 with a total of 113 proceedings, from A through L—the cases can be grouped under the following headings: twenty-eight men were accused of practices related mainly to the search for enchanted treasures which they tried to recuperate through a more or less extensive knowledge of the cabala, derived from "learned magic," although there are also spell-casters (ensalmadores) and curanderos; nineteen women testified before the inquisitors regarding their superstitious practices for healing sick people, generally employing cants and similar ceremonies; another thirty-one women were also accused, however, of performing the evil eye (*mal de ojo*) or curses (*maleficios*), that is, of attempting to make their neighbors ill by means of magical practices; finally, thirty-eight women were tried for performing superstitious practices related to amorous ends, what I have called "love magic" in this essay. To complete the picture, we need to keep in mind the four women considered witches by their neighbors, accused before the Holy Office of this supposed crime. This makes a total of ninety-two women versus the twenty-eight men I have mentioned. According to the previous classification, the four types of superstitious practices in Castile and the rest of Spain are evident: masculine magic, approximating "learned magic" in most of the cases and generally dedicated to the search for enchanted treasures; feminine magic, which emphasizes the woman's connection to evil or to curses (maleficio); the male and female spell-casters (ensalmadores); and the enamored women spoken of in this essay.

2. When I wrote the first version of this study, "love magic" spontaneously suggested itself as a title for these typically feminine manipulations, since I had already employed it in previous lectures. At the time, I was unfamiliar with Professor Noemí Quezada's interesting work, *Amor y magia amorosa entre los aztecas* (Mexico City: Universidad Nacional Autónoma de México, 1984), an ethnological investigation of cants and techniques similar to the Spanish ones. This significant coincidence of titles demonstrates, from my point of view, the pressing need to identify the rich repertory of magical practices accumulated by women

in Europe and the Americas during various centuries. It is important to remember Covarrubias's definition of *hechizar*: "a type of incantation which controls the bewitched person in such a way that his judgment is distorted and he desires what would normally repel him. This occurs through an express or tacit pact with the Devil; and sometimes, or concurrently, he rejects what he rightly desired before, as in the case of enchanting a man so that he rejects his wife and pursues another woman." Sebastián de Covarrubias, *Tesoro de la lengua española*, ed. Martín de Riquer (Barcelona: Editorial Alta Fulla, 1987). Covarrubias believes that the term derives from the Latin *fascinum: fachizar-hechizar-hechizería*.

3. The discussions in which the theory of the "diabolical pact" was formulated by theologians from the Sorbonne, as well as the evolution of ecclesiastical legislation, are found in Henry Charles Lea, *A History of the Inquisition of Spain*, 4 vols. (New York: Macmillan, 1906; reprint, New York: AMS Press, 1966). Refer to vol. 4, chap. 8, "Sorcery and Occult Arts." On the evolution of beliefs surrounding the problem of relations with the devil, see Jeffrey B. Russell, *Witchcraft in the Middle Ages* (Ithaca, N.Y.: Cornell University Press, 1972).

4. In order to understand the evolution of the Spanish Inquisition on these issues, refer to the indispensable works by Julio Caro Baroja, *Las brujas y su mundo* (Madrid: Revista de Occidente, 1961) (Eng. trans., *The World of the Witches* [London: Weidenfeld and Nicolson, 1964]), and Gustav Henningsen, *The Witch's Advocate* (Toronto: Toronto University Press, 1982).

5. For a more complete approximation from a formal perspective on the practices of these women, see my *La Inquisición y los gitanos* (Madrid: Taurus, 1988).

6. The complete versions of these conjurations and cants which I will analyze below are found in *La Inquisición y los gitanos*. The rites I examine in this essay represent, from my point of view, the "fundamental repertory" familiar to and employed by most of the women dedicated to these practices throughout Spain. The common store or "basic recipe book" deserves to be examined carefully in its entirety.

7. In this essay, I focus only on the phrases and gestures that are erotically or amorously significant. As I pointed out previously, the complete versions are in my book, *La Inquisición y los gitanos*. The sorceries used to identify a husband or male friend are, in effect, very frequently employed by single women and can be traced to very recent times; see R. Salillas, *La fascinación en España* (Madrid: E. Arias, 1905), and Julio Caro Baroja, *La estación de amor* (Madrid: Taurus, 1980). This does not mean, however, that this essay does not comply with its own basic suppositions. The "honest" woman could use love magic during the early stages and reserve the rest of the ritual for more serious situations which we will examine below. We must add to the rites of the beans and the cards that of the egg floating in water taken from a urinal or a wash bowl, which reveals, according to the way the egg floats, whether or not the boyfriend (*novio*) will arrive. This rite usually took place on the night of San Juan, and Caro Baroja has beautifully depicted the almost immediate repercussion of these rites.

In any case, the theses I have arrived at in this essay seem to be confirmed by the admired late José Antonio Maravall's study in *El mundo social de "La Celestina,"* 3d ed. (Madrid: Gredos, 1972), and by the theories of the Swiss philosopher Denis de Rougemont in *L'amour et l'occident* (Paris: Plon, 1939).

8. As noted earlier, I am concerned in this essay with what I have denominated the "fundamental repertory." It is necessary to emphasize however, that this "basic recipe book" coincides almost completely with the one compiled by Sebastián Cirac Estopañán in his book *Los procesos de hechicerías en la inquisición de Castilla la Nueva (tribunales de Toledo y Cuenca)* (Madrid, 1942). The reasons for this'"coincidence" are explained in my book *La Inquisición.* Quoted by Cirac Estopañán, *Los procesos,* chap. 8, p. 150.

9. The Valencian sorceresses I have alluded to in this essay were tried in 1655 in an auto de fe condemning forty women for the same crime. For the complete study of this auto, see my *La Inquisición.*

10. AHN, Inquisición, libro 942, fol. 230v. Laura Garrigues's version includes the word *martelaço,* augmentative of *martelo,* jealousy or amorous anguish brought on by jealousy. Covarrubias does not record the term, which appears for the first time in the *Diccionario de autoridades.* It is interesting to note that the word appears to have a learned origin. The dictionary of the Royal Spanish Academy (1980 ed.) states that it is derived from the Latin *martillus.* The Espasa encyclopedia attributes an Italian origin, since the same term appears with the same meaning in that language as well (*Enciclopedia universal ilustrada europeoamericana,* vol. 33, [Barcelona: Espasa, n.d.]). This dictionary notes the meaning of *dar martelo* as equivalent to "to provoke jealousy."

The sorceresses, therefore, employ a learned term which Covarrubias did not consider to be worth recording; it has survived in modern Spanish in the term *estar amartelado* as synonymous with "to be in love." Laura Garrigues spoke of *martelaço* in the conjuration of the wicks and said *martillaço* in the conjuration of the palms because of its relation to the nail, which also desired the lover: "[Man's name], I send you this nail, I strike you with this hammer" [Fulano, te envío este clavo, te doy este martillaço], AHN, Inq., lib. 942, fol. 230v.

11. Doña Juana de la Paz, from the group of sorceresses tried in 1655, said, "[Man's name], I send you this shooting pain / I extend your life / and I shorten your steps" [Fulano, yo te envío este ramalaço / y te alargo la vida / y te acorto el paso]. She made the sign of the cross and said, *ergo sum.* At the end of the conjuration one should swallow saliva and strike the left palm three times with a closed fist. Esperanza Badía, also from the same group, recalled the conjurations utilizing fire with her formulas: "May the fire of love burn you, let the fire of love be consumed as Christ was crucified" [Fuego de amor te abrase, fuego de amor sea abrasado así como el Cristo fue crucificado]. There are many variations that depend on the sorceresses' imaginations, as they try to expand and enrich a frequently repeated augury.

12. Quoted in Cirac Estopañán, *Los procesos,* chap. 8, p. 126.

13. AHN, Inq., lib. 942, fol. 27v.

14. Ibid., fol. 60v.

15. Ibid., fol. 282.

16. Quoted in Cirac Estopañán, *Los procesos*, chap. 8.

17. The exclusive use of the spoken word in this group of cants and conjurations led me to denominate this group "the power of the word" in my aforementioned book as a means of emphasizing the persuasive power of these women.

18. Prudencia Grillos's trial can be found in the AHN, Inq., legajo 87, numero 20 (1571). I referred to this woman in my essay "La mujer en el Antiguo Régimen: Tipos históricos y arquetipos literarios," in *La mujer y la inquisición en la perspectiva inquisitorial* (Madrid: Universidad Nacional de Educación a Distancia, 1988).

19. This was the case with María Ruiz, processed for bigamy, who fled from her husband for this reason. See my essay, "La mujer en el Antiguo Régimen."

20. AHN, Inq., lib. 942, fol. 55r.

21. Quoted in Cirac Estopañán, *Los procesos*, chap. 8.

22. AHN, Inq., lib. 942, fol. 56v.

23. Quoted in Cirac Estopañán, *Los procesos*, chap. 8.

24. AHN, Inq., lib. 942, fol. 233v.

25. Ibid., fol. 59v.

26. Ibid., fol. 59v.

27. Ibid., fol. 27r.

28. Ibid., fol. 56v.

29. Ibid., fol. 54v.

30. Quoted in Cirac Estopañán, *Los Procesos*, chap. 8.

31. Ibid.

32. Ibid.

33. AHN, Inq., lib. 942, fol. 16r.

34. Ibid., fol. 16v.

35. Ibid., fol. 62v.

36. Quoted in Cirac Estopañán, *Los procesos*, chap. 8.

37. Ibid.

38. Love magic experts do not frequently employ the term *marido*—I will return to this point below—and seem to prefer *galán*; it is interesting to recall Covarrubias's definition: "An elegantly dressed man who appears to be a gentleman, and because enamored men usually appear very smartly dressed in order to capture a woman's interest, the women call them their *galanes*" (*Tesoro de la lengua española*).

39. Quoted in Cirac Estopañán, *Los procesos*, chap. 8.

40. Ibid.

41. AHN, Inq., lib. 942, fol. 178r.

42. Quoted in Cirac Estopañán, *Los procesos*, chap. 8, p. 42.

43. AHN, Inq., lib. 942, fol. 180r.

44. Ibid., fol. 230v.

45. Ibid., fol. 62v.

46. Ibid., fol. 8or.

47. *Galán* (suitor) is the word most frequently used by these women, but the term *marido* (husband) is not entirely absent. It is important to remember, however, that in terms of rhythm it is interchangeable with *amigo* (friend) and it is not essential to refer to a marriage that is legal from the civil or ecclesiastical point of view. The only conjurations from this "fundamental repertory" that refer to a husband are Catalina Gómez, condemned in Toledo in 1535. The versions collected by Cirac Estopañán, who adds the word amigo as variant, mention the arrows that must be thrust into the husband's heart in the conjuration of the "star maiden."

48. Quoted in Paz y Melia, *Papeles de Inquisición, Catálogo y extractos* (Madrid: Patrimonio del Archivo Histórico Nacional, 1947), p. 240. Professor Noemí Sánchez has collected the American versions of devotions to this permissive saint. See her "Santa Marta en la tradición popular," in *Anales de Antropología* 10 (Mexico, 1973): 221–240.

49. Paz y Melia also cites another version of the prayer to St. Marta that confirms the designs of this saint, protectress of enamored women in need of special aid according to the nature of their loves:

Marta, Marta
a la mala digo, no que no a la santa
a la que por los aires anda
a la que se encadenó, y por ella nuestro padre Adán pecó
y todos pecamos, al demonio del polo
al del repolo
al del repeso
y al que suelta al preso, al que acompaña al ahorcado,
diablo cojuelo, al del rastro, y al de la carnicería,
que todos juntos os juntéis,
y en el corazón de (man's name) entréis
a guerra, a sangre y fuego le deis, que no pueda parar,
traédmelo luego
demonio del peso,
traédmelo preso. (Paz y Melia, p. 239)

Marta, Marta
I speak to the evil one, not the saint
to the one who goes through the air
to the one who chained herself, and for whom our father Adam sinned
and we all sin, to the devil of the pole
to the one of the double pole
to the one of the double weight,
and to the one who frees the prisoner, to the one who accompanies the hanged man,
to the Lame Devil, to the one from the flea market, and the meat market,
that you all may come together,
and enter in (man's name)'s heart
and war, blood, and fire give him, so that he cannot stop

until he comes to find me,
bring him to me soon,
devil of the weight,
bring him to me a prisoner.

50. Paz y Melia, p. 241.
51. AHN, Inq., lib. 942, fol. 59v.
52. Ibid.
53. Ibid., fol. 56v.

FIVE

Visionaries and Affective Spirituality during the First Half of the Sixteenth Century

Geraldine McKendrick and Angus MacKay

Shortly before his death on 25 January 1516, Ferdinand the Catholic received a message from God, passed on to him by Sor María de Santo Domingo, the celebrated visionary and Dominican tertiary who was also known as the Beata de Barco de Avila or the Beata de Piedrahita:[1]

> And while His Highness was in this place (Madrigalejo), his illness became much worse, and he was made to understand that he was very close to death. But he could hardly believe this because the truth is that he was much tempted by the enemy who, in order to prevent him from confessing himself or receiving the sacraments, persuaded him to believe that he would not die so soon. And the reason for this was that, when he was in Plasencia, one of the royal councilors who had come from the Beata de Barco de Avila told him that the Beata was sending to tell him on behalf of God that he would not die until he had taken Jerusalem. And for this reason he would not see or send for Fray Martín de Matienzo, of the Order of Preachers, his confessor, even though the confessor himself tried to see him several times.[2]

Although in this particular case Sor María's prophetic powers proved ineffective, she had for many years been a cult figure. In love with God, with whom she talked intimately, embracing his body, Sor María delivered sermons-in-trance, underwent ecstatic crucifixions, and even claimed that she was Christ. She enthralled the royal court with her ecstasies and celestial dances, Cardinal Ximénez de Cisneros consulted her on important matters such as the conquest of Oran, and the duke of Alba built a magnificent convent for her in Aldenueva, near Avila.[3] Of course, not everyone believed in her, and the Dominicans in particular were hostilely skeptical.[4] Nevertheless she had protectors in high places, and when a special ecclesiastical commission was set up to investigate her, she emerged from the investigation with her reputation for saintliness intact. The Italian Pietro Martire d'Anghiera particularly commented on Cisneros's devotion to Sor María, and indeed the cardinal, who was himself a Franciscan, gave the beata a Franciscan girdle to wear under the Dominican habit, thus emphasizing both his attachment to her and a symbolic process of "Franciscanization."[5]

A large number of visionaries like Sor María de Santo Domingo, as well as other practitioners of an emotional, intensive, and affective spirituality, figure in one way or another in the Inquisition records, and in terms of culture and control, they raise some very interesting problems. In the first place, the degree to which some visionaries of the first half of the sixteenth century were left undisturbed by the Inquisition is quite remarkable. Perhaps the most astonishing case is that of the millenarian friars of Escalona.[6] In 1524 the Franciscan church in Escalona witnessed some bizarre scenes. Fray Olmillos, for example, improved on his public visionary performances by moving the altar to the middle of the church so that more people could witness his ecstasies,[7] and Fray Ocaña unfolded a millennial program for the reform of the Church. Preaching on the text, "Behold we go up to Jerusalem, and all things that are written by the prophets concerning the Son of man shall be accomplished" (Luke 18:31), Ocaña told his audience that the people of Escalona were the most blessed in the world. In another sermon he called for those in power in the Church to be "thrown out like pigs"; the messianic program revealed to him and Fray Olmillos stipulated that Charles V would defeat the king of France and take over his kingdom, the pope would be deposed by the Marquis of Villena, Ocaña himself would be installed as the new reforming pope, and the illiterate visionary Francisca Hernández would reform and revise the Holy Scriptures.[8] Here surely was an open challenge to establish authority within the Church that could hardly be ignored. Yet the Inquisition never moved against these friars, or indeed against the group to which they belonged that practiced *recogimiento,* an interiorized religious state, but concentrated instead on the *dejados,* who practiced spiritual abandonment to God and actually considered the visions, ecstatic fits, convulsions, and excesses to which recogimiento gave rise to be delusions induced by the Devil. Moreover, even when the Inquisition did condemn individual visionaries, it frequently did so after a considerable delay, during which the visionary enjoyed fame and prestige. In this sense the career of Magdalena de la Cruz, the celebrated visionary of Córdoba, constitutes a good example. During the early decades of the sixteenth century she was considered saintly and was in constant and intimate communication with God, and her devotees included the general of the Franciscan Order, Fray Francisco de los Ángeles Quiñones; Fray Francisco de Osuna, the mystic whose writings were so appreciated by Santa Teresa; and the archbishop of Seville and inquisitor general, Alonso Manrique. Indeed, on the birth of the future Philip II in 1527, "the *hábitos* of this nun were sent off as a sacred object so that the *infante* could be wrapped up in them and thus apparently be shielded and protected from the attacks of the Devil." In 1533 Magdalena was elected abbess of her convent and was at the height of her power and popularity. But only in 1546, and after many prophecies, visions, and miracles, including even a pregnancy by the Holy Spirit, did the Cordoban Inquisition finally try her and sentence her to life imprisonment in a convent in Andújar.[9]

The second point of interest is the fact that so many of the visionaries and practitioners of intense affective spirituality were women. In addition to the Beata de Piedrahita and Magdalena de la Cruz, already mentioned, a list of only a few outstanding examples would include Francisca Hernández, whose powers and marvels were well known in Salamanca and Valladolid, and whose reputation for sanctity spread to New Castile; Isabel de la Cruz, leader and idealogue of the dejados; Isabel de Texeda, whose visionary excesses were notorious in Guadalajara; the ecstatic Mother Marta, a miracle-working Benedictine nun in Toledo who was visited by the king, courtiers, and prelates; and Juana de la Cruz, the visionary abbess of Cubas.[10] Nor were these isolated cases, as incidental references in the Inquisition records demonstrate. In Guadalajara, for example, a widow went into a trance in a public square and claimed that she had seen more visions than St. Bridget of Sweden, and elsewhere in the same town another widow fell into a rapturous ecstasy and saw all the blessed souls in heaven.[11]

The object of this essay, therefore, is to place affective spirituality and the visionary phenomenon into context. Why were some "excesses" controlled and others condoned? What assumptions and beliefs lay behind María de Santo Domingo's assertion, and Ferdinand's apparent acceptance of this assertion, that the king would not die until he had conquered Jerusalem? Why did women play such a relatively prominent role in the visionary phenomenon?

In pondering why the inquisitors failed to take any action after they had learned of the revolutionary reform program of the Franciscans of Escalona, Nieto comments: "The solution which comes readily to one's mind is that in some way, somehow, they themselves believed the ideas contained in this ideology of religious-political reformation."[12] He is surely right; the fact is that in the drive to define and protect orthodoxy the policies of both the monarchy and the Inquisition are of interest not only because of the war waged on "heresy" but also because of what was accepted or tolerated within the confines of orthodoxy.

Christian eschatological doctrines or beliefs concerning "the last days" enjoyed a particularly flourishing tradition in the Iberian world: rooted in the appropriate biblical texts and producing Spanish and Portuguese variants, its last important manifestation occurred as late as 1896 in the famous Brazilian rebellion, inspired by Sebastianism, of Antonio the Councilor.[13] But its most outstanding feature was that it was based on a mutation of the apocalyptic legend of *The Last Roman Emperor*. The source of this West European legend was the Greek apocalypse of Pseudo-Methodius, written in the seventh or early eighth century, although the Greek text was itself a translation of a seventh-century Syriac original, also attributed to a Methodius, but composed in Mesopotamia. This apocalyptic legend was translated into Latin in the late seventh or eighth century in Merovingian Gaul, thus introducing into the West the belief that at the end of days a king of the Greeks or Romans would defeat the Muslims, conquer Jerusalem, and renounce his empire directly to God at the hill of the skull, Golgotha. Subsequently a tenth-century monk, Adso, rewrote the legend to fit an eschatological French king, and between the thirteenth and fifteenth centuries Germanic variations developed, so that by the fifteenth century it was believed that Emperor Frederick II, who died in Apulia in 1250, was still alive and hidden on Mount Kyffhauser, awaiting to return and fulfil the millennial prophesy.[14] But, in addition to the last World Emperor, the figure of the Angelic Pope emerged toward the end of the thirteenth century and came to reflect the aspirations of the spiritual Franciscans. For the Spirituals Rome was identified with the carnal Church, to be rejected by Christ at the end of the sixth age. Rome was Babylon *meretrix et impudica; illa Babylon meretrix magna*. At the end of days, therefore, the World Emperor would be helped by the Angelic Pope.[15]

In Spain the legend of *The Last World Emperor*, suitably influenced by Joachimite ideas and prophesies attributed to St. Isidore of Seville, produced a messianic king and world emperor, known variously as the *Encubierto* (the Hidden One), the *Murciélago* (the Bat), and the New David.[16] Moreover, as was amply demonstrated in the highly influential apocalyptic treatise of the Franciscan Fray Alemán, the eschatological "events" underwent a marked process of Hispanicization, for in Alemán's treatise the Antichrist appears in Seville, the messianic armies disembark "near Antioch, which is the port of Cádiz," and a titanic battle ensues in Seville near the present-day cathedral. Victorious, the messianic forces proceed to take Granada; thereafter Jerusalem and the rest of the world are conquered, and of course an Angelic Pope is installed in Rome.[17]

Although the eschatological tradition was a long-standing one, it was only from about 1470 onward that reality began to match messianic expectations; as Milhou has demonstrated, an avalanche of prophetic texts, commentaries, and ballads, and even a letter of revelation which the Marquis of Cádiz, don Rodrigo Ponce de León, circulated to the great nobles of Castile in 1486, identified Ferdinand the Catholic as the Encubierto or Bat who would conquer the Holy House of Jerusalem and the whole world.[18] Nor was Ferdinand averse to believing all this. Pietro Martire thought in 1510 that Ferdinand was obsessed with the conquest of Africa, and in February of that year Ferdinand himself wrote in one of his letters that "the conquest of Jerusalem belongs to Us and We have the title of that kingdom."[19] Is it a coincidence that Sor María de Santo Domingo's rise to fame dated from 1509, or that from 1510 onward *rey de Jerusalén* came to be included by Ferdinand among his other royal titles?[20] In any case the dying Ferdinand would certainly have understood all the implications of the divine message which Sor María had sent him.

Of course, such messianic ideas could be projected onto others or be assumed by others. Within months of the conquest of Granada, for example, Columbus had received royal backing for his *empresa de las Indias,* which was designed to establish contact with the pro-Christian Mongol grand khan in the East in order that a combined offensive to recover the Holy House of Jerusalem might be undertaken. Subsequently Columbus continued to regard the lands he discovered as a stepping-stone toward this objective, and on the basis of a purported Joachimite prophecy that the conqueror of Jerusalem would come from Spain, he eventually came to believe that he himself was the messianic figure.[21] Messianic ideals were similarly projected onto Cardinal Ximénez[22] and, after his death, onto Charles V. Thus, for example, the famous apocalyptic prophecies contained in Manuscript 1779 of the Biblioteca Nacional (Madrid) identify Charles V as the messianic ruler who will be lord of Spain, France, and Germany, and who, after being crowned emperor of Rome, will cross the seas, become the ruler of all the world, conquer the Holy House of Jerusalem, and finally surrender his crown, presumably to God, on the Mount of Olives.[23] When, therefore, the Franciscans of Escalona prophesied that Charles V would depose Francis I in 1523 and that Clement VII would be replaced by the equivalent of an Angelic Pope, were they not simply confirming messianic notions already in circulation? As far as the inquisitors were concerned, it would appear that visionaries who identified Ferdinand the Catholic or Charles V as the world emperor should be tolerated and left alone. Matters would be quite different when a visionary like Lucrecia de León would identify someone like Miguel de Piedrola as the New David or the Encubierto destined to rule over the whole world.[24]

Yet few visionaries conformed to this precise eschatological tradition, and the phenomenon needs to be placed within a broader context—particularly, but not exclusively, within the context of the nature and influence of Franciscan spirituality.[25] Above all, the anti-intellectual and affective thought espoused by the Franciscans made them favorably disposed to certain aspects of female spirituality.[26] The dejados' opposition to "men of letters," for example, was a motif running through evidence given by witnesses in Inquisition trials. "In order to know God, the study of letters is not necessary," declared Pedro de Baeza, repeating what he had heard in Escalona about the teachings of the dejados;[27] and Isabel de la Cruz, a Franciscan tertiary from Guadalajara, believed that "learning killed the spirit," a sentiment echoing the old Franciscan dictum that "Paris has destroyed Assisi."[28] The Franciscans' attachment to an intuitive and emotional religiosity also led them to value the gift of prophecy. By the fourteenth century the Franciscan Nicolás de Lyra already referred to prophetesses as *illuminatae mentis,* made lucid by special grace.[29] Thus as the example of Francisca Hernández demonstrated, studying theology of the Scriptures at university was not essential—and was indeed inferior to knowledge obtained through faith and above all by an intimate experience of God. For when Francisca, responding to the request of her Franciscan devotee Fray Francisco Ortiz, offered her own interpretations of passages of Scripture, such as the Sermon on the Mount, The Song of Solomon, and Revelation, the friar had been astounded by her grasp of the essential truths of these writings; what Francisca had discussed in three short words would have been endlessly debated by theologians in long and arid treatises.[30] Similarly, those who listened to the sermons-in-trance of Sor María de Santo Domingo marveled at her insight into difficult theological problems:

> Sometimes in her raptures Sor María is accustomed to answering difficult questions about theology, profound problems, matters concerning the Holy Scriptures, things pertaining to our Holy Catholic faith or to good customs, the glory of Paradise, the pains of Hell, Purgatory, and the Holy Sacraments . . . Thus all who see her and hear her respond think that it

is a marvelous thing that a poor, ignorant little woman like Sor María, who was brought up in a village, should respond so well and sometimes better than a Master of Theology or a man of great learning.[31]

"A poor, ignorant little woman": being a "fragile" female without any formal education and from a suitably humble background was in itself a guarantee that only God (or the Devil) could work such a miracle.[32] And so Cardinal Ximénez would consult Sor María as to whether he should cross the Straits of Gibraltar, and Fray Francisco de los Ángeles Quiñones, the General of the Franciscan Order, would ask Francisca Hernández for advice about a proposed journey to Italy.[33] Even the clothes of these women transmitted spiritual graces and healing powers as if they were relics. Contact with the girdle of Francisca Hernández, for example, cured Fray Francisco Ortiz of sexual temptation; Cardinal Ximénez gave Sor María a Franciscan girdle, requesting that she should always wear it and, through it, continually remember him in her divine prayers;[34] and, as has been seen, the habits of Magdalena de la Cruz were wrapped round the infante Philip to protect him from the Devil.

In fact, women were positively encouraged to develop an affective and intense spirituality. For example, Pedro Ruiz de Alcaraz, the devoted disciple of the Franciscan tertiary Isabel de la Cruz, spent long hours persuading women to practice *dejamiento,* or abandonment to the love of God, and Inquisition witnesses claimed that he had targeted three particular types of women—widows, beatas, and *doncellas.*[35] In Escalona he had considerable success among the maidservants and ladies-in-waiting in the palace of the Marquis of Villena. After mass in the local Franciscan church, the women would kneel at his feet, with their hands on their breasts, and listen in adoration as he discussed dejamiento. In Pastrana and Madrid, likewise, he would lodge in the houses of widowed devotees and hold private spiritual consultations for women, particularly those who were not married.[36] Alcaraz, of course, was a "heretic," but Ignatius Loyola was to operate in a similar fashion amongst the widows and beatas of Alcalá in 1526–1527.[37]

Moreover, the great Cardinal Ximénez de Cisneros himself helped to promote a visionary spirituality characterized by such mental states as trances, swoons, visions, dreams, and fits. It was not simply that Mother Marta, Juana de la Cruz, and Sor María de Santo Domingo were all his spiritual mentors; Cisneros also exerted a powerful influence over the type of material that issued from the printing presses at Toledo and Alcalá, and this included numerous works by such mystical authors as Vincent Ferrer, Catherine of Siena, and Angela of Foligno.[38] Indeed, just as Cardinal Ximénez protected Sor María from her Dominican detractors who thought her trances were the work of the Devil, so the passage in which the Dominican Vincent Ferrer condemned such mystical excesses as revelations and visions was deliberately omitted from the 1510 printed edition of his *Tract of Spiritual Life*.[39] Such mystical works were primarily intended for friars and nuns, but, as Bataillon rightly pointed out,[40] Cisneros almost certainly wished them to be distributed among the laity as well. The works of Catherine of Siena and Angela of Foligno must have been of particular interest to nuns and beatas, for both these women were tertiaries whose mystical experiences took the form of visions and raptures. Angela of Foligno, for example, was devoted to contemplation of the minutiae of Christ's suffering on the Cross, and her most profound mystical experiences took place during this spiritual contemplation. Thus in the Franciscan church in Assisi, Christ appeared to her dripping in blood, whereupon she herself, like Sor María, experienced the agony and pain of the Crucifixion.[41] And, like many Spanish female visionaries, Angela in her raptures suffered from temporary loss of speech or lost the use of her limbs.

But, although they did not enjoy the educational opportunities that were available to men, it should not be imagined that women who practiced an affective spirituality or were visionaries were either ignorant or simply reacting in a slavish manner to the encouragement or promptings provided by the male establishment. The medieval Church, following Pauline injunctions, had silenced women; but the language and behavior of the female spirituality that emerged during the early sixteenth century circumvented this silence, and some women seized the opportunity. Besides, the testimony of Inquisition witnesses provides ample evidence that women were actively interested in the religious education of their own sex. The town of Guadalajara provides an example. There María de Cazalla, who was arrested by the Inquisition in 1532 on a variety of charges ranging from Lutheranism to *alumbradismo*, or illuminism, did not confine herself merely to educating her two daughters and encouraging them to read the many spiritual tracts emanating from the Alcalá press, but she also gave catechism classes to rural women[42] and preached in urban households. In Advent, 1522, for example, she visited her widow friend Catalina Hernández Calvete and read one of the Epistles of St. Paul aloud, discussing its meaning in front of a female audience gathered together in the kitchen. As Catalina Alonso recalled:

> ... there were a lot of people there, and it seemed as if they were all women. . . . I think that there were more than twenty women because the kitchen was big and it was full. María de Cazalla read from a book, and then spoke, and everyone was silent as if they were listening to a sermon.[43]

Nor was María de Cazalla unique or exceptional. In the same town of Guadalajara a woman recalled seeing Isabel de la Cruz reading a book in a public square, a cleric affirmed that he had seen many women reading books aloud in the vernacular in front of other people, and the aristocratic Doña Mencía de Mendoza categorically stated that "it is a well-known fact that literate women read aloud to illiterate women books such as the Scriptures and Lives of Saints."[44] Although such examples could be multiplied, it is also important to note that female literacy was also assuming an even more active role, with women either writing books themselves or having their books written for them. Isabel de la Cruz and Alcaraz, for example, were rumored to have composed a book on contemplation,[45] María de Cazalla's written correspondence on spiritual matters was bound together like a book and circulated among sympathizers and acquaintances,[46] the visionary Isabel de Texeda enlisted the services of a cleric to commit her revelations and prophecies to paper,[47] Juana de la Cruz had her sermons-in-trance written down by three of her fellow nuns,[48] and Sor María de Santo Domingo's *Oración y contemplación* was published by the press of Jorge Coci in Aragoza in 1520.[49] This was the same Sor María whose celestial ecstasies had so enthralled the royal court, who had been protected by the great Cisneros himself, and who had relayed God's personal message to the ailing Encubierto, promising that the Bat would not die until he had taken Jerusalem. During the first half of the sixteenth century God moved in mysterious ways.

NOTES

1. This study draws much of its inspiration from G. McKendrick, *Franciscan Spirituality in Early Modern Castile* (in preparation for Cambridge University Press).

2. See Lorenzo Galíndez de Carvajal, *Anales breves de reinado de los Reyes Católicos D. Fernando y Doña Isabel, de gloriosa memoria*, in *Crónicas de los reyes de Castilla*, ed. Cayetano Rosell, vol. 3, Biblioteca de autores españoles, vol. 70 (Madrid: Real Academia Española, 1953), 562–563; and, with minor differences, the same account in Alonso de Santa Cruz, *Crónica de los Reyes Católicos*, 2 vols., ed. Juan de Mata Carriazo (Seville: Escuela de Estudios Hispano-Americanos de Sevilla, 1951), 2:331–332.

3. On Sor María de Santo Domingo, see B. Llorca, *La Inquisición española y los alumbrados (1509–1669)* (Salamanca: Universidad Pontificia, 1980), 37–64, 259–271; V. Beltrán de Heredia, *Las corrientes de espiritualidad entre los Dominicos de Castilla durante la primera mitad del siglo XVI* (Salamanca: Convento de San Esteban, 1941), 9–17; Pietro Martire d'Anghiera, *Epistolario*, ed. J. López de Toro,

4 vols., Documentos inéditos para la historia de España, vols. 9–12 (Madrid: Real Academia de la Historia, 1953–1957), 3:41–42; Alonso de Santa Cruz, *Crónica* 2:125.

4. There was a profound split within the Dominican Order between the "irrational" group at Piedrahita and the "rational hierarchy." On the hostility of the latter, see V. Beltrán de Heredia, *Historia de la reforma de la provincia de España, 1450–1550* (Rome: Institutum historicum F. F. Praedicatorum, 1939), 78–142. On the mixed reaction of some at the royal court, see Anghiera, *Epistolario* 2:300–302.

5. Llorca, *La Inquisición,* 267; Anghiera, *Epistolario* 2:300–302; Beltrán de Heredia, *Las corrientes de espiritualidad,* 10.

6. For a short account of this affair, see José C. Nieto, "The Franciscan *Alumbrados* and the Prophetic-Apocalyptic Tradition," *Sixteenth-Century Journal* 8 (1977): 3–16. For subsequent changes in inquisitorial attitudes to female visionaries, see the excellent chapter by Claire Guilhem in B. Bennassar, *Inquisición española: Poder político y control social* (Barcelona: Editorial Crítica, 1981), 171–207.

7. *Proceso* of Pedro Ruiz de Alcaraz, Archivo Histórico Nacional (hereafter AHN), Inquisición, legajo 106, n. 5, fol. 9v. It should be emphasized that although much of the information about the excesses of the Escalona Franciscans derives from Alcaraz himself, there is other evidence which makes it virtually impossible to dismiss his allegations. See, for example, the testimony of the visionary wavers from Pastrana in C. Carrete Parrondo, *Movimiento alumbrado y renacimiento español: Proceso inquisitorial contra Luis de Beteta* (Madrid: Centro de Estudios Judeo-Cristianos, 1980), 70.

8. AHN, Inq., leg. 106, no. 5, fols. 7r, 8v, 281r–282v.

9. See the documents on Magdalena de la Cruz in J. Imirizaldu, *Monjas y beatas embaucadoras* (Madrid: Editora Nacional, 1977), 33–62.

10. For a succinct discussion of most of these women, see M. Bataillon, *Erasmo y España: Estudios sobre la historia espiritual del siglo XVI* (Mexico City and Buenos Aires: Fondo de Cultura Económica, 1966), 69–71.

11. AHN, Inq., leg. 106, no. 5, fols. 47v, 49r.

12. Nieto, "The Franciscan *Alumbrados,*" 9.

13. On Iberian eschatology see the excellent studies by Alain Milhou, *Colón y su mentalidad mesiánica en el ambiente franciscanista español* (Valladolid: Universidad de Valladolid, 1983) and "La chauve-souris, le Nouveau David et le roi caché: Trois images de l'empereur des derniers temps dans le monde iberique, XII–XVIIe siècles," *Mélanges de la Casa de Velásquez* 18 (1982): 61–78. Although discussion here is confined to Christian eschatology, it should be noted that the Jewish and Muslim apocalyptic ideas enjoyed vigorous traditions as well. On Antonio the councilor and his millennial movement, see the fundamental and contemporary account by Euclides de Cunha, *Os sertoes* (Rio de Janeiro: Laemmert, 1902).

14. See P. Alexander, *Religious and Political Thought in the Byzantine Empire* (London: Variorum Reprints, 1978), study XII: "Byzantium and the Migration

of Literary Works and Motifs: The Legend of the Last Emperor," 54–55, 57, 61–62; M. Reeves, *Joachim of Fiore and the Prophetic Future* (London: SPCK, 1976), 59–64, 66–72.

15. Reeves, *Joachim*, 38–48.

16. Milhou, "La chauve-souris."

17. The Spanish version of the treatise by Fray Alemán or Alemany is published in R. Alba, *Acerca de algunas particularidades de las Comunidades de Castilla tal vez relacionadas con el supuesto acaecer terreno del Milenio Igualitario* (Madrid: Editora Nacional, 1975), 180–197. On the importance of the treatise and of the mysterious Fray Alemán, who originally wrote his work in Latin, see the excellent discussion by Milhou, "La chauve-souris," 61–78.

18. Milhou, *Colón*, 391–394. For the text of the letter by Rodrigo Ponce de León, see *Historia de los hechos de don Rodrigo Ponce de León, Marqués de Cádiz (1443–1448)*, Colección de documentos inéditos para la historia de España, vol. 106 (Madrid: Real Academia de la Historia, 1893), 247–251. And of course the chroniclers saw the hand of God aiding Ferdinand and Isabella in all their triumphs.

19. J. N. Hillgarth, *The Spanish Kingdoms, 1250–1516,* 2 vols. (Oxford: Oxford University Press, 1976–1978), 2:571.

20. Milhou, *Colón*, 397–398.

21. See Abbas Hamdani, "Columbus and the Recovery of Jerusalem," *Journal of the American Oriental Society* 99 (1979): 39–48.

22. See in particular the strange case of Charles de Bovelles and also the penetrating remarks about Cisneros's reactions to all the messianic expectations in Bataillon, *Erasmo y España*, 53–58, 70–71.

23. See Alba, *Acerca*, 204–205.

24. See Milhou, "La chauve-souris," and Richard Kagan's contribution to the present volume as well as his book *Lucrecia's Dreams: Politics and Prophesy in Sixteenth Century Spain* (Berkeley, Los Angeles, Oxford: University of California Press, 1990).

25. On Franciscan spirituality see the forthcoming book by G. McKendrick cited above, n. 1.

26. There were of course other factors at work: see in particular A. Vauchez, *La sainteté en occident aux derniers siècles du moyen âge* (Rome: École Française de Rome, 1981).

27. AHN, Inq., leg. 106, no. 5, fol. 72v.

28. J. E. Longhurst, "La beata Isabel de la Cruz ante la Inquisición," *Cuadernos de Historia de España* 25–26 (1957): 288.

29. I. Maclean, *The Renaissance Notion of Woman* (Cambridge: Cambridge University Press, 1980), 21.

30. See A. Selke, *El Santo Oficio de la Inquisición: Proceso de Fr. Francisco Ortiz* (Madrid: Ediciones Guadarrama, 1968), 98–99.

31. Llorca, *La Inquisición*, 262–263.

32. María de Santo Domingo was the daughter of farm laborers, and both Francisca Hernández and Magdalena de la Cruz were of humble backgrounds:

see Llorca, *La Inquisición,* 263; Selke, *El Santo Oficio,* 45, Imirizaldu, *Monjas y beatas,* 46.

33. See, for example, Selke, *El Santo Oficio,* 112 n. 26.

34. Ibid., 100, and Llorca, *La Inquisición,* 266–267.

35. Some caution is needed here, however, because the leading question asked of witnesses was formulated in such a way as to encourage them to identify these types of women.

36. AHN, Inq., leg. 106, no. 5, fols. 75r, 97v; Carrete Parrondo, *Movimento alumbrado,* 70.

37. F. Fita, "Los tres procesos de San Ignacio de Loyola en Alcalá de Henares: Estudio crítico," *Boletín de la Real Academia de la Historia* 33 (1898): 431–432, 442, 520–521.

38. See Bataillon, *Erasmo y España,* 49.

39. Ibid., 170.

40. Ibid., 49.

41. *The Book of Divine Consolations of the Blessed Angela of Foligno,* trans. M. G. Steegman (London and New York: Chatto and Windus, 1909), 210. Catherine's mysticism centered round a detailed meditation on Christ's Passion which was accompanied by extreme asceticism: *Obra de las epistolas y oraciones de la bienaventurada virgen sancta Catherine de sena de la orden de predicadores* (Alcalá, 1512), fols. 38v–39r, 144v, 225r–v, 318v.

42. See M. Ortega Costa, *Proceso de la Inquisición contra María de Cazalla* (Madrid: Fundación Universitaria Española, 1975), 329–335.

43. Ibid., 252–253.

44. AHN, Inq., leg. 106, no. 5, fol. 41r; Ortega Costa, *Proceso,* 281, 327.

45. AHN, Inq., leg. 106, fol. 45v.

46. Ortega Costa, *Proceso,* 258–259.

47. Hamilton, *Proceso de Rodrigo de Bivar,* 123.

48. A. Daza, *Historia, vida, y milagros, extasis, y revelaciones de la bienaventurada virgen Santa Juana de la Cruz* (Zaragoza, 1611), fols. 61v–62r. That this is not simply a pious legend can be seen by consulting Bataillon, *Erasmo y España,* 70 n. 29.

49. See F. J. Norton, *A Descriptive Catalogue of Printing in Spain and Portugal, 1501–1520* (Cambridge: Cambridge University Press, 1978), 268; J. M. Blecua, *Libro de la oración de Sor María de Santo Domingo (Beata de Piedrahita)* (Madrid: Hauser y Menet, 1948).

SIX

Politics, Prophecy, and the Inquisition in Late Sixteenth-Century Spain

Richard L. Kagan

The aim of this essay is to explore a triad of Inquisition trials, from the late 1580s, that centered on the issue of prophecy. The trials are those of Miguel de Piedrola, a seer nominated by the Castilian Cortes for the position of Spain's national prophet; that of Sor María de la Visitación, a Dominican nun in Lisbon famous for her stigmata; and that of Lucrecia de León, a young woman from Madrid known for her millennial dreams of Spain's future. Together these trials provide an opportunity to examine the Inquisition's attitudes towards seers, and, in a wider sense, the relationship between prophecy and politics in late sixteenth-century Spain.

Prophecy—which can be understood as a spiritually-inspired teaching or warning—is a complex subject that has been extensively studied by anthropologists, sociologists, historians, and literary scholars. Generally speaking, research on the history of European prophecy has followed one of two tracks. The first considers prophecy as a literary genre; its principal concern is to classify various types of prophecy as well as to establish what might be called a "thematic genealogy," tracing individual prophecies back to their source, either biblical or medieval, and then explaining the changes and permutations that occurred along the way. In this guise prophecy serves as an available language, a discourse always available for use and one that is constantly being adapted and reformulated to fit particular purposes and needs. An excellent example of this type of inquiry is Robert Lerner's study of the Cedar of Lebanon prophecy from the Middle Ages until the Enlightenment.[1] The other track, pioneered by social scientists, considers prophecy primarily from a structural-functional perspective and views it principally as the product of a particular set of social circumstances, usually of moments of crisis and/or unusually rapid social and economic change. Scholars as diverse as Norman Cohn and Michael Adas thus seek to explain the role prophecy played in society and to understand the specific purposes to which prophecy was put.[2] Although these tracks are sometimes viewed as running in opposite directions, in this essay I shall attempt to make the two intersect, paying particular attention to the motivations of Piedrola, Lucrecia, and Sor María, one aspect of prophecy that scholars have frequently ignored.

Prophecy is essentially a public endeavor, though its origin is quintessentially a private experience, such as a vision or dream. Prophecy is also a social act. Often allied with a particular cause, the prophet is a mediator between the supporters of that cause and the general public as well as a transmitter of messages received through a miraculous medium: a mysterious voice, an angel, a heavenly vision. The prophet usually addresses a concrete, well-defined audience and intends to achieve specific, well-articulated ends such as the reform of the Church, a perennial theme in medieval prophecies. Prophecy is also a collective phenomenon; prophets rarely speak for themselves but rather serve as the mouthpieces for ignored, neglected, or marginal groups seeking to obtain legitimacy for a particular cause. Prophecy in this guise becomes a legitimating device, or, if you will, a cloak, a disguise; it represents a bid both for legitimacy and power. From this proposition it follows that ruling authorities almost invariably view prophets with considerable suspicion.[3]

Yet prophecy need not necessarily serve as a vehicle for protest. In early modern Europe prophecies were commonly announced to consolidate support for a new monarch or regime, and in Spain royal births were regularly accompanied by the circulation of "fulfillment prophecies" which avowed that the future monarch was destined to complete the work of the Reconquest.[4]

The "gift of prophecy" was also considered a sign of divine favor, and hagiographers regularly took pains to establish the clairvoyance of the individual whose sainthood they sought to promote. Thus Fray Pedro Navarro's 1616 biography of Juana de la Cruz, the beata associated with the foundation of the miracle working shrine in Illescas, included a chapter on Juana's prophetic powers.[5]

Yet most prophets were not candidates for canonization. Many, like the peasant girls studied by William Christian, were ordinary individuals who claimed to have seen into the future as a result of a dream, a vision, or some other form of supernatural experience.[6] Others had a political agenda, especially those seers who Ottavia Niccoli has called "plaza prophets," that is, individuals, both clerical and lay, who used prophecy to establish religious standards by which to judge a secular regime.[7] Prophecy thus often became an ideological weapon wielded by opposition movements and radical groups. Among those who turned prophecy toward political protest, the best known are Savonarola, the radical Dominican preacher whose followers gained control of Florence in 1491, and Thomas Müntzer, the Anabaptist leader who attempted to establish a millennial kingdom at Allstedt and later at Mühlhausen before being defeated by imperial forces in 1525. William Hackett, the former serving man who warned of plague unless Queen Elizabeth reformed her government, was somewhat less successful; he was arrested for sedition and executed in a London square in 1590.[8]

The history of plaza prophets in Spain has yet to be written, but there is ample evidence of their activity. At the start of the fifteenth century, for example, the fiery Dominican preacher Vicente Ferrer (1350–1419) cited Jeremiah 23:16 to warn against the horde of prophets inundating Spanish streets: "Do not listen to the words of the prophets who prophesy and deceive you. What they tell you are their visions; it does not come from the mouth of God."[9] Despite this admonition, a Savonarola-like street prophet known popularly as "el bachiller Marquillos" claimed to have been inspired by the Holy Spirit and collected a sizeable following during the anti-converso riots that erupted in Toledo in 1449. Other prophets surfaced in Valladolid during the tumultuous years immediately preceding the outbreak of the Comunero revolt in 1520, among them Fray Juan de San Vicente, a Franciscan who made public pronouncements about the "bad government" of Spain.[10] Two years later, during the Germanía revolt in the Valencian town of Játiva, there appeared a hermit who described himself as *el rey encubierto* (The Hidden King), evoking the medieval idea of the pastor angelicus or blessed redeemer who would come from the east, rescue the kingdom from its enemies, and forever defeat the Moors. Dressed in animal skins, possibly to identify himself with the biblical David, the hermit claimed to have been sent by the Holy Spirit to destroy "the swamp of this kingdom." Promising riches for all his followers and rewarding some with noble titles, this "king" was soon assassinated by agents hired by the royal viceroy.[11]

The decade of the 1580s was another period in Spanish history when street prophets suddenly proliferated, in part prompted by international events of the day. In 1580, for example, there surfaced in Albuquerque, a small town near the Portuguese border, a widow who claimed to have experienced a vision which revealed that Philip II's endeavor to become king of Portugal would not succeed unless he first vowed to follow in the late King Sebastian of Portugal's footsteps and embark on a North African crusade.[12] There was also Isabel de Jesús, a Dominican nun in the small town of Huete, who first became known around 1583 for her stigmata, various miracles, and her "prophetic gift." Gradually, Isabel's reputation for saintliness grew and by 1587 her supporters compared her with the then famous Nun of Lisbon, Sor María de la Visitación (see below). Yet Isabel's prophecies were not strictly religious and among the "secret and future things" she told Hernando de Toledo, one of Philip's councilors of state, were events related to "the war with England."[13]

Most of this decade's prophetic activity was centered in Madrid and was linked to the monarchy's mounting economic and political difficulties, both at home and abroad. Another cloud on the horizon was the health of Philip II. The king suffered a serious illness in 1585 and the slow pace of his recovery fueled speculation that Philip was no longer capable of personal rule nor of protecting his kingdom against its enemies. The depth and extent of this crisis of confidence in Philip's ability to rule remains to be determined, yet it is clear that by the late 1580s many Spaniards feared that Philip's reign was nearing its end. Remarkably, the monarch ruled another ten years despite his age and ill health, but they were years marked by the spread of apocalyptic ideas and various doomsday scenarios. In Madrid, Fray Alonso de Orozco, a prominent Augustinian preacher widely revered for his saintliness and prophetic gift, publicly expressed concern that the Armada would end in defeat because "our sins are great." Millenarian ideas were also fomented by the discovery, in a tower in Granada in March 1588, of the *plomos de Granada,* lead boxes holding a series of parchments written in Arabic and Greek. Among these documents was an Arabic version of John the Evangelist's prophecies about the end of the world, as well as others that scheduled the millennium for "the years just short of 1600." Although the parchments were later proven to be forgeries, the interest they aroused indicates that the current of millennialism had spread well beyond the royal court.

Astrological forecasts added yet another dimension to these alarms about Spain's future. In 1566 Michel Nostradamus announced that "in the year five hundred fourscore more or less, there shall be a strange age." Other astrologers were more precise, predicting that 1588 would be a year of cataclysm because of one solar eclipse, two lunar eclipses, and a grand conjunction, namely a rare astronomical alignment of Saturn, Jupiter, and Mars. Since biblical times, these conjunctions had been associated with wars, revolutions, deaths of important persons, and other momentous events. In sixteenth-century Europe printed almanacs and popular *prognostica* helped to spread these astrological ideas among street prophets and soothsayers. Throughout the continent, 1588 was anticipated as the "wonder year," a time of great changes, perhaps even the end of the world.[14] In Spain these ideas could be found in the prophecies of Isabel de Jesús as well as in those of Miguel de Piedrola.

The first Spanish street prophet who actually voiced dissatisfaction with the monarchy itself was probably Juan de Dios, a faith healer by trade and still a somewhat mysterious personage previously connected to a group of Toledan visionaries arrested by the Inquisition in 1574. By the mid-1580s Juan de Dios turned up in Madrid, where he spent half of his time in the mental ward of the Hospital of Anton Martín, and the rest on the streets uttering prophecies about the coming destruction of Spain. Allied to members of the Mendoza family and the court faction associated with Antonio Pérez, the once popular royal secretary who had been arrested on suspicion of murder in 1579, Juan de Dios identified himself with St. John the Baptist and publicly announced that Spain's sins would soon lead to her destruction by her enemies.[15] More directly critical of the monarchy was Guillén de Casaos, a royal official from Seville who, after a stint in the Yucatan, returned to Madrid in search of a royal gift and expressed his frustration at failing to obtain this prize through a series of dream visions that pertained to the bad government (*mal gobierno*) of Spain and attacked the corruption of Philip's court.[16] In these two examples at least, prophecy served political purposes, and its heralds were individuals who used it to proclaim in public what could otherwise only be whispered behind closed doors.

The attitude of the Spanish Church toward prophets was somewhat ambivalent. On the one hand, the church could not deny the proposition that God had the power to communicate prophetic messages through ordinary individuals; to do so would be to refute Scripture itself. On the other hand, it was skeptical of anyone, particularly of "unlettered" men and "weak" women, who claimed to have received divine communications. This skepticism was first articulated by Aquinas in the thirteenth century, although it was left to the famous fifteenth-century theologian, Jean Gerson, to develop the investigative formulae required to separate the true prophet from the false.[17] In *De Probatione Spirituum and De Distinctione Verarum Visionum A Falsis,* two treatises prepared for the Council of Constance in 1415, Gerson argued that the only sure way to dispel uncertainty about prophetic visions and dreams was, quoting John the Evangelist (1 John 4:11), to "test the spirits to see whether they are of God." He therefore recommended that both the contents of the vision and the personality of the alleged visionary or prophet be subjected to a series of rigorous tests, which he memorialized in a famous couplet:

> *Tu, quis, quid, quare,*
> *Cui, qualiter, under, requiere.*
>
> [You should seek who, what, why,
> to whom, what kind, whence.][18]

In the course of the fifteenth century, Gerson's *De Probatione Spirituum* and its companion treatise became a vademecum no confessor could afford to be without. Gerson influenced Jakob Sprenger, the German inquisitor responsible for the *Malleus Maleficarum,* first published in 1493. Gerson also had a profound effect on the Fifth Lateran Council, which in 1516 ordered bishops to investigate anyone who claimed prophetic knowledge on the basis of divine revelation.[19] In Spain, Gerson's influence can first be detected in Sánchez de Vercial's *Book of Examples,* written circa 1420, a treatise which warned "not to believe in visions," particularly those of women.[20] Gerson's skepticism toward prophetic visions later appears to have influenced Diego de Simancas, author of the much reprinted *Institutiones catholicae* (first ed., Valladolid, 1552), a handbook widely used by Spain's inquisitors.[21] In the seventeenth century Gerson's rules for distinguishing true visions from false appeared in the "Interrogatorio para e examen de revelaciones, visiones, y sueños," a set of instructions distributed to judges by the Inquisition.[22]

Still, the criteria for distinguishing true prophets from false remained somewhat vague, and this perhaps explains why inquisitorial persecution of would-be prophets was haphazard and generally limited to those whose prognostications constituted a direct political threat to the monarchy.[23] In this sense it was politics, rather than religion, that occasioned the prosecution of prophets. What this suggests is that historians from Henry C. Lea to Henry Kamen may be wrong in concluding that the Holy Office did not serve as an instrument of royal absolutism.[24] As we shall now see with Piedrola, Lucrecia, and Sor María, the Inquisition only became involved in these cases after having been prodded to do so by the Crown.

PIEDROLA

The first of the three case studies to be discussed here is that of Miguel de Piedrola Beamonte, the so-called soldier-prophet.²⁵ Originally from Navarre where he had worked as an itinerant tinker (*ollero*), Piedrola later joined the army and became a foot soldier, serving first in Italy where, by his own account, he was captured by (and ransomed from) the Turks on two separate occasions. After having served briefly in the campaign to suppress the morisco revolt in Granada (1568–69), Piedrola drifted into Madrid in about 1570, hoping to secure a royal pension. Shortly thereafter he began writing a series of *arbitrios* (memorials) to the king, offering advice about the "conservation of his kingdoms," and suggestions for ending the war in Flanders. Such missives were a commonplace means of communicating with the monarch, but Piedrola's messages had a macabre twist: he warned that Philip's children would die unless the monarch heeded his advice. For a while Piedrola was evidently considered harmless, and he was left alone. Official attitudes changed, however, some time late in 1578, when Piedrola began to deliver similar messages in the streets of Madrid. Identifying himself with the biblical prophets Elijah and Malachi, Piedrola publicly asserted that the advice he was offering the monarch had a divine source. Soon after, one of Philip's secretaries advised Piedrola to abandon Madrid. This he did, sometime in 1579. Piedrola's precise movements over the next few years are difficult to trace. He seems to have rejoined the army, arriving in Naples some time before January 1580. By 1584 he had returned to Madrid and resumed his career as the soldier-prophet. Piedrola's reputation as a seer rested on the (mistaken) belief that he was an illiterate soldier who had miraculously memorized the entire Bible with divine assistance. He further claimed that his knowledge of the future derived from a series of dreams—seventy-two in all—which he attributed to God. No records of these dreams survive, but evidently they dealt with contemporary political events and openly criticized the king and his ministers. Some spoke of the "greatest events of the year 1588," which would result in the "imminent destruction of Spain." The soldier-prophet also proclaimed that at the moment this destruction began, his supporters were to seek refuge in a cave called la Espelunça. There, like a latter-day Pelayo, the mythical eighth-century king said to have planned the Reconquest, Piedrola would deliver Spain from her enemies. He envisioned a new Spain governed by a limited monarchy under a constitution—ideas that represented an open challenge to the absolutist principles of Habsburg rule.

The source of Piedrola's radical ideas remains unknown, although it may be traced to the constitutionalist traditions (fueros) of his native Navarre which limited the powers of that kingdom's monarch. Piedrola's adopted second surname of Beamonte—or Beaumont—further identifies him with old Navarrese traditions of resistence to monarchs perceived to be unjust. The Beamontes were an aristocratic faction that surfaced in the mid-fifteenth century in opposition to Juan II, an Aragonese monarch who had deposed his son Carlos, Prince of Viana, as ruler of Navarre. The leader of this faction, Luis de Beamonte, claimed that Juan deserved to be overthrown since he violated the kingdom's fueros. Piedrola's position on this particular moment in Navarrese history remains unknown, but his identification with the Beamonte faction suggests that he might have considered Philip II as the Castilian equivalent a Juan II—a tyrant who ruled without popular consent.

Very little is known about the extent of Piedrola's following. In 1588 the papal nuncio in Madrid reported to the Vatican that Piedrola "was esteemed by many persons of great and small estate" along with other "wise persons of quality" who compared his prophetic powers with those of Isaiah and Jerome.[26] No list of these supporters has survived, and Piedrola himself referred to his friends only by a series of mysterious aliases such as "Dr. Silence, the Strong Knight of the Golden Key, Pastor Anastasio, and Lady Obstinate."[27] Other sources indicate that Piedrola was closely allied with the supporters of Antonio Pérez as well as other individuals directly associated with the royal court.[28] Alonso de Orozco, for example, alleged that Piedrola deceived "many honorable letrados," a group which seems to have included Juan de Herrera, the royal architect, and even Gaspar de Quiroga, the inquisitor general.[29] The royal chronicler, Jerónimo de Sepúlveda, also attested that Piedrola "fooled and deceived . . . not just anyone but very important people," among them the dukes of Medina Sidonia, Nájera, and Pastrana, the marquis of Carpio, as well as Lady Jane Dormer, an English Catholic and widow of the duke of Feria, who frequently meddled in the politics of the Spanish court.[30] In sum, Piedrola successfully gathered a small but influential band of followers, many of whom were evidently prepared to enter the Espelunça once the millennium began.[31]

Piedrola's followers appear to have had several agendas, including the prompt release of Antonio Pérez. In this respect the apocalyptic message of Piedrola's prophecies and the demand for governmental reform can be interpreted as part of an attempt to rally popular support for the imprisoned royal secretary. Another aim was to have Piedrola officially designated as Spain's national prophet, a new and previously unfilled post. Oddly enough, this scheme almost succeeded, owing to worries about the worsening economy and increasing dissatisfaction with Philip's government. At the prompting of Piedrola's well-placed allies, the Castilian Cortes appointed a special commission to investigate Piedrola's prophetic credentials and the implications of his dire prognostications for Spain's future.

Thus during the summer of 1587, at a moment when Piedrola's reputation as a prophet and seer reached its height,[32] the national assembly sent the head of a parliamentary commission, a certain Gaspar Gómez, to meet with Piedrola. Apparently, the two engaged in a learned discussion about Holy Scripture. In a report delivered to a plenary session of the Cortes on 22 August 1587, the commission acknowledged that many "important churchmen and preachers ... consider him [Piedrola] a prophet, as in times past" and recommended that the king establish his own royal commission to determine "if Piedrola justly deserves the title of Prophet and if the prophecies he publicizes are sincere and true." During the subsequent debate in the Cortes on the merits of this proposal, Dr. Guillén, a representative of Seville, maintained that "one of the most important issues facing the kingdom is to determine whether Piedrola is a prophet."[33]

Yet Piedrola also had powerful detractors, among them, Fray Alonso de Orozco, a rival prophet, and Fray Juan Baptista, an Italian Franciscan then resident in Madrid.[34] Beginning in June 1587, Fray Juan denounced the soldier-prophet as an "evil spirit" and an "agent of Lucifer"; in one sermon the friar claimed that Piedrola "was possessed by a demon that was responsible for everything he said and did."[35] Within a matter of weeks the controversy sparked by these denunciations spread to the royal court and apparently led Philip II to name a commission to investigate Piedrola's prophetic career.

The three commissioners—Quiroga, the inquisitor general; Fray Diego de Chaves, the royal confessor; and García de Loaysa, the royal almoner—met in late July and gathered a series of reports concerning Piedrola. Fray Luis de León, the famed Augustinian theologian and expert in prophetic discourse, advised that Piedrola's "spirit of prophecy" should not be doubted. But the vicar of Madrid accused the soldier-prophet of speaking only to those "a quien tocar" (that is, his friends) and of treating many important people with "poca modestía" (little respect).[36] The commission also heard testimony that Piedrola's prophecies included ideas that "our Holy Catholic Faith cannot tolerate," and it was apparently this allegation that persuaded its members to recommend that the proper venue for a detailed inquiry into Piedrola's prophetic credentials was not the Cortes but the Inquisition. Thus, on 18 September 1587, precisely at the moment when the Cortes was publicly debating the merits of Piedrola's prophecies, the Holy Office ordered the soldier-prophet's arrest and spirited him off the following day to Toledo for trial. The arrest, the secretary of the Florentine ambassador in Madrid noted, caused "great murmurings" at the royal court.[37]

In the weeks that followed, Piedrola's supporters worked diligently to secure their prophet's release. On 19 September 1587, only a day after the arrest, Dr. Alonso de Mendoza, canon of Toledo, appealed to Cardinal Ascanio Colonna in Rome, comparing Piedrola's arrest and imprisonment to Darius's order to cast Daniel into the lions' den.[38] In the meanwhile, Piedrola saw to his own defense with a claim of insanity as well as a confession, offered in May 1588, in which he asserted that his visions were nothing more than "illusion and deceit." Later that year the Holy Office decided that Piedrola was indeed a "false prophet" and on 18 December 1588, at an auto de fe staged in Toledo, sentenced him to two years' seclusion followed by perpetual exile from Madrid.[39]

Piedrola's case illustrates several points relevant to our understanding of the relationship between prophecy and politics in late sixteenth-century Spain. The Spanish Inquisition, it appears, treated false prophecy as a relatively minor offense. In Elizabeth's England, by way of comparison, William Hackett's prophecies and public criticisms of the queen's government led him directly to the scaffold. In theory the Inquisition, following the general tenets of the Counter-Reformation, took a dim view of any lay person who claimed to have the "prophetic gift." Yet in practice most seers were tolerated so long as they did not openly espouse heretical concepts or ideas.

The Spanish Crown also tolerated the vitriol of self-proclaimed street prophets—for years the monarchy did not acknowledge Piedrola's presence in Madrid—as long as the prophet had only a scattered following. In part, such tolerance derived from Philip II's own skepticism about the importance of prophecy. Thus when discussion of the "public abuses" emanating from various "prodigies and divinations" arose in a meeting with the papal legate in March 1588, Philip reportedly said, "It was the practice of the emperor [Charles V], my father, not to believe in or to act upon such things."[40] But once a prophet seemed to pose a political threat to the power of the throne, once the Cortes started to transform Piedrola into a national figure, even Philip's tolerance ceased. To deny Piedrola a public pulpit for further criticisms of the monarchy, Philip decided to have him arrested by the Holy Office rather than by civil authorities, since the Inquisition was the sole tribunal that could guarantee a secret trial. The essentially political, rather than religious, nature of Piedrola's arrest was evident to his supporters, one of whom wrote to another that the political implications of the case required the Inquisition to handle the trial in an "extraordinary" fashion.[41]

Even then the Crown went to extraordinary lengths to ensure that Piedrola be kept in strict isolation, a policy it enforced long after his sentence was announced. Ordinarily, the Holy Office sent those condemned to a period of seclusion to any convent or monastery willing to take them. In this case, however, the Crown instructed the *Suprema*, the Supreme Council of the Inquisition, to undertake a thorough investigation of a number of sites in order to make certain that security for this seditious prisoner was adequate. After considerable deliberation it was decided that Piedrola would be confined to the fortress of Guadamur, situated in a small and relatively isolated village six miles west of Toledo.

LUCRECIA DE LEÓN

Lucrecia de León was a young madrileña directly inspired by Piedrola's bleak vision of Spain's future.[42] Born in 1568, Lucrecia was the semi-literate daughter of a Madrid solicitor, Alonso Franco de León. Beginning when she was twelve, Lucrecia experienced a series of dream-visions about the future of the Spanish monarchy. By 1587 these dreams focused on the defeat of the Armada and the subsequent destruction of Spain, a "loss" which Lucrecia attributed to the "bad government" and personal sins of Philip II. Lucrecia also envisioned the monarch as a tyrant who levied unjust taxes and failed to provide either charity or justice. Some of the dreams even portrayed him as a new Roderic, the Visigothic monarch believed to have been singly responsible for the Muslim conquest of Spain in 711.

Knowledge of these dreams was initially limited to Lucrecia's family, but in September 1587, immediately following Piedrola's arrest by the Inquisition, Lucrecia began speaking freely about these dreams in public. Lucrecia's father, afraid of the Inquisition, urged her to remain silent, but her mother, eager for the notoriety the dreams brought, encouraged her daughter's dreaming. Lucrecia's own aspirations are vague, but clearly she relished being a clairvoyant, once comparing herself to "the sun in the window." She also appreciated the attention her dreams inspired, particularly the suitors they brought to her door. She in fact secretly "married" a certain Diego de Vitores, the amanuensis of her confessor, although the two agreed to keep their union a secret so as not to jeopardize Lucrecia's prophetic career—prophets, particularly female prophets, were supposed to be chaste. The dreams also suggest that Lucrecia had a political "agenda" roughly akin to that of Piedrola and his followers. Both she and her father were supporters of Antonio Pérez; they were also critical of Philip II and his ministers, and in the dreams the monarch regularly appears as a tyrant and his beloved Escorial as a building constructed with "the blood of the poor." Lucrecia, a former serving girl at court, also had personal reasons for being angry with the king; he had once promised her a dowry which he had failed to deliver.

As with Piedrola, Lucrecia succeeded in establishing a small but enthusiastic following that promoted her as a prophet whose dreams were divinely inspired. Her most ardent supporters were Alonso de Mendoza, previously a supporter of Piedrola, and Fray Lucas de Allende, the influential head of Madrid's Franciscan convent. Against her father's wishes, Lucrecia agreed to dictate her dreams to these two churchmen on a daily basis. They in turn prepared copies of the alleged dream texts and circulated them for wider distribution to their friends and allies at court. By February 1588, rumors of the seer who dreamed of Spain's impending "loss" led the Vicar of Madrid to place Lucrecia under house arrest for a brief period. Allende and Mendoza protested and managed to convince the archbishop of Toledo to order Lucrecia's release, thus allowing for the continuation of her prophetic career.

Lucrecia went on to experience over four hundred dreams, nearly all of which warned of Spain's impending loss unless Philip reformed his government, altered his economic policies, and publicly repented his sins. Gradually, Lucrecia's prophetic reputation grew, particularly after her prediction about the loss of the Armada came true. She even inspired a small cult, similar to Piedrola's Espelunça, whose members formed a brotherhood (gremio) and even hoped to establish a new military order—the Holy Cross of the Restoration—dedicated to the defense of Spain from its enemies, both Muslim and Protestant. By 1590, Lucrecia's reputation was such that she was featured at fashionable gatherings where she recited what she claimed were her dreams to groups of courtiers. Some of these onlookers viewed her as a mere curiosity, one of "the ignorant and rustic who dream marvelous things, including predictions about future events." But others considered her a prophet and expressed their belief in her prophetic powers by wearing a scapular similar to the one she had envisioned in her dreams. According to Lucrecia, those who wore this garment would survive the disasters her dreams presaged and subsequently establish a new regime which, unlike Philip's, would be dedicated to charity, justice, and the defense of the Church.

In the end Lucrecia's undoing was directly related to her fame. In the weeks following Antonio Pérez's escape from prison in April 1590— an escape known to have been aided by some of Lucrecia's supporters— Chaves, the royal confessor, initiated an investigation into the source of Lucrecia's dreams and by late May gathered evidence suggesting that Lucrecia and her followers were engaged in some sort of seditious plot. He subsequently convinced the monarch to put a stop to their activities and on 25 May 1590, the Inquisition, acting on Philip's orders, arrested Lucrecia together with five of her most ardent supporters. The following day, the Florentine ambassador in Madrid reported:

> Here, and in Toledo, the Inquisition has arrested some important noblemen, among them is the brother of Don Bernardino de Mendoza, ambassador to France, and the prior of the [convent of] San Francisco [in Madrid]. The reason is a woman who some call a beata and who is said to have had divine revelations in her dreams and to have predicted the defeat of the Armada and now says that the king will soon die.[43]

Lucrecia's trial began within a week, with the judge noting briefly that she was "six or seven months pregnant." Lucrecia later gave birth to a girl who was still alive when her *proceso* was finally over, in July 1595. The trial itself was a tumultuous one, marked by a series of scandals that involved a notable lack of secrecy in the proceedings, a series of late night parties that disrupted life in the supposedly "secret prisons" of the tribunal, and even the attempt of one inquisitor, Licenciado Lope de Mendoza, to seduce Lucrecia. Mendoza and several other members of the tribunal were subsequently suspended and fined, but disruptions caused by these scandals help to explain why Lucrecia's trial lasted so long.

In any event, the Inquisition repeatedly attempted to get Lucrecia to confess that she had purposely invented her dreams for political ends. This was something which, even in the torture chamber, she steadfastly refused to do. Her dreams, Lucrecia claimed, were dreams whose message she, as an ignorant *doncella*, did not understand. Finally, in July 1595, her case was voted "en diferencias," an admission that her inquisitors were unable to determine if Lucrecia was truly responsible for her dreams. But they did agree that the dreams contained some false and heretical ideas as well as statements critical of the monarchy. Castilian law defined as *alevoso* or seditious, "anyone who speaks badly of the king and his family." The minimum penalty for such statements was the confiscation of one half of one's goods. But if it was determined that the accused had advised or counseled anyone to rebel against or refuse to obey the king's law, the penalty was death.[44] In this instance, however, the Inquisition only punished Lucrecia—as she herself had predicted—with an *abjuración ad levi*, a relatively light sentence which called for one hundred (lightly delivered) lashes, two years confinement in a convent, and life exile from Madrid.[45]

The parallels between Lucrecia and Piedrola are many, and it is worth emphasizing that their arrests were prompted primarily by political as opposed to religious or spiritual considerations. The same applies to the arrest of the third of our prophets, Sor María de la Visitación, prioress of the Dominican Convento de la Anunciata in Lisbon.

THE "NUN OF LISBON"

Beginning in 1575, the Nun of Lisbon, as Sor María was called, experienced a series of ecstasies, raptures, visions, and miraculous levitations. She was far better known, however, for her stigmata or *"llagas,"* five wounds in her side that dripped blood in the shape of a cross. These were publicized by her confessor, Fray Luis de Granada, the famous author of *Guía de pecadores* and a number of other widely read devotional books. Beginning in 1584, Fray Luis wrote letters to various Church authorities, including Carlo Borromeo, archbishop of Milan, and Juan de Ribera, patriarch of Valencia, describing Sor María as "another Saint Catherine of Siena."[46] He also wrote a short, hagiographic treatise, *Relación de la vida y milagros de la priora de la Anunciata,* published in Paris in 1586.[47] Adding further to Sor María's notoriety was a painting of her and her miraculous llagas by Hernán Gómez Román, a late Mannerist Spanish artist employed at the Portuguese court. The original is now lost, but it was reproduced (as a woodcut) in Alonso de Villegas's best-selling (but soon censored) *Flos sanctorum*. Reports of Sor María's miracles were also included in the correspondence of the Fuggers, the famous German banking house.[48] By 1588 Sor María was known throughout Europe for her saintliness. It was also said that no visitor to Lisbon failed to stop by la Anunciata convent in order to catch a glimpse of the famous nun.

In addition to her visions and ecstasies, Sor María also had worldly concerns. Following the annexation of Portugal by Philip II in 1582, she emerged as a supporter of the exiled Portuguese pretender, Antonio, Prior of Crato and nephew of the late King Sebastian. Antonio had taken refuge in England where he endeavored to persuade Queen Elizabeth to organize an invasion designed to restore him to the Portuguese throne. Expectations for such an expedition ran high in the months following the Armada's defeat in August 1588, and at this time Sor María stirred up the political ashes by making several public, anti-Spanish statements on Antonio's behalf. According to one source she boldly announced that "The Kingdom of Portugal does not belong to Philip II, but to the Braganza family," and prophesied that "if the king of Spain does not restore the throne that he unjustly usurped, then God will punish him severely." Sor María also presented herself as the living incarnation of Portugal and her wounds as the symbol of Portuguese sufferings under the Spanish yoke.[49]

As with Piedrola and Lucrecia, it was these overtly political statements that led to Sor María's downfall. Cardinal-Archduke Albert, the royal governor in Lisbon, feared that Sor María's prestige would strengthen the Portuguese nationalist cause at a time when Antonio was known to be actively planning an invasion, and in October 1588 he ordered the Holy Office to investigate Sor María's many miracles. The inquisitors soon reported that her famous stigmata were self-induced pinpricks, that her levitations were faked with the aid of sticks, and that her halos had been craftily created by mirrors and lamps. Sor María confessed her wrongdoing; on 6 December 1588 the Inquisition announced that she was guilty of "trickery and deceit" and sentenced her to life exile to Brazil, although this was later changed to Abrantes, a small town north of Lisbon.[50]

More needs to be learned about Sor María's case, but her trial resembles those of Piedrola and Lucrecia to the extent that they were all causes célèbres, widely reported throughout Europe. These cases are also alike to the extent that each of three prophets considered here drew from a common wellspring of apocalyptic imagery and thought. On the one hand, the apocalyptic tradition provided these prophets with a grammar of political protest as well as a way of expressing various criticisms of the monarch and his regime. On the other hand, this grammar was not immutable, and each of these prophets shaped it to suit particular needs and purposes. In this sense, prophecy cannot be fully understood unless it is examined within its historical context and directly related to the aspirations of the individuals involved.

As for the Inquisition, the fact that the Holy Office did not immediately muzzle plaza prophets like Piedrola but waited for instructions from the king suggests that this institution, despite its celebrated role as a censor, was generally prepared to allow seers considerable room to maneuver. This is not to say that freedom of political expression in Habsburg Spain was any greater or lesser than in other sixteenth-century states—an important issue yet to be adequately studied—but that the Inquisition's ambivalent attitude toward prophecy, together with its reluctance to involve itself in cases where the religious issues were not necessarily clear-cut, offered Philip's vassals a political voice along with a political language that modern scholarship has overlooked.[51] To be sure, the political use of prophecy in Spain generally surfaced in times of political and economic crisis, moments when the future looked especially bleak or uncertain. But in a regime which offered few other modes of political expression, prophecy ensured discontents a means of being heard. Beyond the three cases discussed in this paper, however, much still needs to be learned about this particular strain of Spanish political life.

NOTES

The following abbreviations are used in the notes:

AGS Est   Archivo General de Simancas, Sección de Estado (followed by *legajo* number)

AHN Inq   Archivo Histórico Nacional (Madrid), Sección de Inquisición (followed by number of *legajo, expediente,* and *pieza*).

ASF   Archivio di Stato di Firenze

ASV NS   Archivio Segreto Vaticano (Rome), Nunziatura spagnola

BL Eg.   British Library, Egerton Mss.

BN   Biblioteca Nacional (Madrid)

IVDJ   Instituto de Valencia de Don Juan (Madrid)

1. Robert Lerner, *The Cedar of Lebanon Prophecy from the Middle Ages until the Enlightenment* (Berkeley, Los Angeles, London: University of California Press, 1983).

2. I refer to Norman Cohn, *Pursuit of the Millennium* (New York: Harper & Row, 1961), and Michael Adas, *Prophets of Rebellion* (Cambridge: Cambridge University Press, 1979).

3. This discussion of prophecy follows that of Keith Thomas, *Religion and the Decline of Magic* (London: Penguin Books, 1971), Thomas Kselman, *Miracles and Prophecies in Nineteenth-Century France* (New Brunswick: Rutgers University Press, 1983), and Adas, *Prophets of Rebellion*.

4. See, for example, the prophecies that accompanied the birth of Philip IV's children in Cristóbal López de Cañete, *Compendio de los pronosticos y baticinios antiguos y modernos* . . . (Madrid, 1630).

5. Pedro Navarro, *Favores del rey del cielo* (Madrid, 1622). See also Antonio Daça, *Historia vida y milagros, extasis y revelaciones de Sor Juana de la Cruz* (Madrid, 1613).

6. William A. Christian, Jr., *Apparitions in Late Medieval and Renaissance Spain* (Princeton: Princeton University Press, 1981).

7. Ottavia Niccoli, "Profezie in piazza. Note sul profetismo populare nell'Italia del primo cinquecento," *Quaderni Storici* 41 (1979): 500–539. See also her *Profeti e popolo nell'Italia del Rinascimento* (Bari: Laterza, 1987).

8. See Thomas, *Religion*, 154.

9. "Tratado del Cisma Moderno," in José M. de Garganta y Vicente Forcada, *Biografía y escritos de San Vicente Ferrer* (Madrid: Editorial Católica, 1956), 448.

10. Another was Fray Polanco, also a Franciscan; he preached against the Flemings in the court of Charles V and prognosticated disaster unless the new monarch reformed his government. See Joseph Pérez, "Moines frondeurs et sermons subversifs en Castille pendant le premier séjour de Charles-Quint en Espagne," *Bulletin Hispanique*, lxvii (1965): 5–24, and Ramón Alba, *Acerca de algunas particularidades de las comunidades de Castilla* (Madrid: Editora Nacional, 1975).

11. See Gaspar Escolano, *Decada primera de la historia de la insigne y coronada ciudad y reyno de Valencia. Segunda parte* (Valencia, 1611), 1610–1621. The incident is also discussed in Ricardo García Carcel, *Las germanías de Valencia* (Barcelona, 1981), 132–138. According to Escolano, a second "rey encubierto" caused an "alboroto" in the city of Valencia in 1523 when his followers sacked parts of the city on Holy Thursday.

12. Gregorio de Andrés, "Las revelaciones de una visionaria de Albuquerque sobre Felipe II," *Homenaje a Luis Morales Oliver* (Madrid, 1986), 419–427.

13. AHN, Inq., leg. 496, no. 1. Isabel was investigated by the Holy Office in October 1590.

14. An excellent introduction to this astrological literature may be found in Robin B. Barnes, *Prophecy and Gnosis: Apocalypticism in the Wake of the Lutheran Reformation* (Stanford: Stanford University Press, 1988), esp. 120–121, 158–164.

15. For a brief discussion of Juan de Dios, see Juan Blázquez Miguel, *Hechicería y superstición en Castilla la Nueva-La Mancha* (Toledo: Servicio de Publicaciones de la Junta de Comunidades de Castilla-La Mancha, 1986), 114–115.

16. AHN, Inq., leg. 2105. Casaos is also mentioned in Maria Zambrano, Edison Simons, and Juan Blázques Miguel, *El proceso y sueños de Lucrecia de León* (Madrid: Ternos, 1987), 46–47.

17. Gerson's position on dreams is examined by Paschal Boland, *The Concept of Discretio Spirituum in Johannes Gerson's "De Probatione Spirituum" and "De Distinctione Verarum Visionum A Falsis"* (Washington, D.C.: Catholic University of America Press, 1959).

18. Ibid., 30.

19. Karl-Joseph Hefele, *Histoire des conciles*, trans. H. Leclerq (Paris, 1917), viii, 526.

20. Clemente Sánchez de Vercial, *Libro de los exemplos por A.B.C.*, ed. John Easton Keller (Madrid: CSIC, 1961), 235, 329. The Spanish texts read: "Del engaño de muger te deves bien guardar . . ." and "Tu deves de saber a todas visiones non es de creer."

21. See Chap. 20, pp. lxix–lxxii, *De divinatoribus*.

22. AHN, Inq., leg. 1226, fols. 787–812v.

23. Other than the *alumbrados*, the heretical sect that first surfaced in Guadalajara, Toledo, and other towns of New Castile during the 1520s, cases involving *ilusos*, *videntes*, and other types of prophets were relatively few. See Juan Blázquez Miguel, *La inquisición en Castilla-La Mancha* (Madrid: Librería Anticuaria Jeroz, 1986), 132.

24. See Henry Kamen, *The Spanish Inquisition* (London: Weidenfeld & Nicolson, 1965), 235. Recently, however, Kamen has suggested that the Holy Office did occasionally serve as an instrument of royal power; see his *Inquisition and Society in Spain* (Bloomington: Indiana University Press, 1985), 242. Bartolomé Bennassr, *L'inquisition espagnole* (Paris: Hachette, 1979), 373–388 offers a similar interpretation.

25. The best introduction to Piedrola remains Vicente Beltrán de Heredia, "Un grupo de visionarios y pseudoprofetas durante los últimos años de Felipe II," *Revista Española de Teología*, vii (1947): 373–397. Heredia, however, does not utilize the "traza de la vida" Piedrola prepared for the Inquisition; BN: Ms. 10,470. Further information about Piedrola may be obtained in AHN, Inq., leg. 3712, no. 2, fol. 6.

26. ASV NS: filza 34, fols. 352–354, dispatch of 20 May 1588.

27. BN: Ms. 10,470, fols. 96v–97.

28. AHN, Inq., leg. 3712, no. 2, fol. 6, n. 8, letter of Mendoza to Gerónimo de Mendoza Manrique, 19 Sept. 1587, in which he refers to Piedrola as a "true prophet."

29. Orozco, *Obras*, 3:47–48. On Piedrola's ties with Herrera and Quiroga, see AHN, Inq., leg. 3712, no. 2, fol. 5, Agustín Parra to Juan de Herrera, 22 June 1588. Referring to Herrera's inquiry about Piedrola, Parra reports that Piedrola, at least prior to his arrest in Sept. 1587, was Quiroga's *familiar*, a term which connotes that he had received financial and possibly political support from the cardinal.

30. Jerónimo de Sepúlveda, "Historia de varios sucesos del reino de Felipe II," *Ciudad de Dios*, 115 (1918): 304. See also IVDJ: Envío 189, fol. 176, which contains a series of letters pertaining to his case. AGS Estado 165, fol. 340 contains a copy of the Inquisition's *sentencia* of 10 Dec. 1588 against Piedrola. Further reference to Piedrola occurs in BL Eg. 1506, fols. 59–60, 93–95v; Eg. 2058, fols. 205–206v.

31. Also in this group were Dr. Mantilla, a court physician, and the alchemist Agustín Parra, a friend of both Juan de Herrera and Alonso de Mendoza.

32. ASV NS, filza 33, fol. 33, letter of Juan Baptista de Pesaro, 5 June 1587.

33. *Actas de las Cortes de Castilla y León*, 9:119.

34. For Orozco's comments see his *Obras*, 3:48; it is reported that Piedrola and Orozco had an "odio mortal" for one another. Little is known about Juan Baptista except that he had studied theology in Spain at the University of Alcalá de Henares. His campaign against Piedrola apparently began in Barcelona during the spring of 1587; AHN, Inq., leg. 3712, no. 2, fol. 6, n. 8.

35. AHN, Inq., leg. 3712, no. 2, fol. 6, Papel contra García de Loaysa por Alonso de Mendoza, 7 Aug. 1587. According to Piedrola, Fray Juan's sermons began on 11 June 1587 and prompted what he described as an "alboroto" (uproar, riot) in Madrid.

36. IVDJ: Envío 89, n. 176, report of the vicar of Madrid, 9 Aug. 1587. Fray Luis's testimony reads: "que no se podria poner en duda sin que el tenia spiritu de profecia." For Fray Luis on prophecy, see Colin P. Thompson, *The Strife of Tongues. Fray Luis de León and the Golden Age of Spain* (Cambridge: Cambridge University Press, 1988), 94–101.

37. ASF Mediceo, filza 5103, fol. 430.

38. AHN, Inq., leg. 3712, no. 2, fol. 6, n. 8. Mendoza had written to Cardinal Colonna the previous August complaining about a letter in which García de Loaysa had attacked Piedrola.

39. Piedrola's *sentencia* is noted in Gerónimo Román de la Higuera, "Historia eclesiástica de Toledo," BN: Ms. 1293, vol. 7, fol. 239. Higuera refers to him as a "false prophet."

40. ASV NS 34, fol. 197.

41. AHN, Inq., leg. 3712, no. 2, fol. 5, n. 5, letter of Agustín Parra to Juan de Herrera, 22 June 1588. Parra also noted that the underlying reason for Piedrola's arrest was Quiroga's decision to distance himself from the soldier-prophet.

42. For Lucrecia, see Beltrán de Heredia, "Un grupo de visionarios"; Simons, Blázquez Miguel, *Sueños y procesos*; Alain Milhou, *Colón y su mentalidad mesiánica* (Valladolid: Casa-Museo de Colón, 1983), 245, 316; and my monograph, *Lucrecia's Dreams: Politics and Prophecy in Sixteenth-Century Spain* (Berkeley: University of California Press, 1990).

43. ASF Mediceo, filza 4920, fol. 515v (copy 535v), Cammillo Guidi to the Grand Duke of Tuscany, 30 May 1590.

44. *Nueva recopilación de todas las leyes* . . . (Alcalá de Henares, 1569), Libro 8, título 18, ley 1, and título 26, ley 11.

45. The full text of her *sentencia* is published in Jesús Imirizaldu, *Monjas y beatas embaucadoras* (Madrid: Editora Nacional, 1977), 65–69. For Lucrecia's trial record; AHN, Inq., legs. 2105; 2085; 3712–3713.

46. Cited in Ramón Robres, "La Monja de Lisboa según nuevos documentos romanos con una carta de Fray Luis de Granada," *Boletín de la Sociedad Castellonense de Cultura*, 28 (1952): 523.

47. Fray Luís de Granada, *Historia de Sor Maria de la Visitación y sermón de las caídas públicas*, ed. Bernardo Velado García (Barcelona: Juan Flors, 1962).

48. *The Fugger News Letters. A Selection 1566–1605,* ed. Victor von Klarwill, trans. Pauline de Chary (London: John Lane, 1924), 265.

49. Daniel A. Mortier, *Histoire de maîtres généraux de l'ordre des frères prêcheurs* (Paris: A. Picard, 1911), v. 646. Sor María's political interests are confirmed by her contemporary, the astrologer Guillén de Casaos. Writing shortly after her arrest in October 1588, he noted that "it is certain that all [i.e., Sor María's miracles] was faked and designed to favor the party of don Antonio"; AHN, Inq., leg. 312, no. 2, fol. 5, Casaos to Alonso de Mendoza, Madrid, 19 Nov. 1588.

50. For Sor María, see Ramón Robres Lluch, "La monja de Lisboa. Sus fingidos estigmas. Fray Luis de Granada y el Patriarca Ribera," *Boletín de la Sociedad Castellonense de Cultura* 83 (1947): 182–214, 230–278. See also Álvaro Huerga, "La vida seudomística y el proceso inquisitorial de Sor María de la Visitación," and his "La Monja de Lisboa y Fray Luis de Granada," *Hispania Sacra* xii (1959): 35–96, 333–356. For a contemporary Protestant assessment of her "false miracles," see Cipriano de Valera, *Two Treatises* (London, 1599). Sor María's case is also discussed in José Sebastiao da Silva Dias, *Correntes de sentimento religioso em Portugal* (Coimbra, 1960) 1:317–318.

51. See Henry Kamen, "Toleration and Dissent in Sixteenth-Century Spain," *Sixteenth-Century Journal* xix (1988): 3–23.

PART TWO

Persecution and Persistence

SEVEN

Family and Patronage: The Judeo-Converso Minority in Spain

Jaime Contreras

In 1983, Professor Heim Beinart, who has studied the crypto-Jewish community of Ciudad Real in great detail, called attention to the importance attached in that community to family ties and kinship relations. Searching for formulas to explain the cultural community which the Judaizing conversos of La Mancha had apparently established, Beinart concluded that endogamous matrimony was the essential cause behind the "manifestations of a common destiny"; manifestations which the entire cryptic community expressed openly with the violent eruption of the Tribunal of Faith in the final years of the fifteenth century."[1]

Indeed, it was Julio Caro Baroja who, thirty years ago, spoke of the need to elaborate a "cohesive and organic" history of the Spanish crypto-Jews from a more ethnohistoric perspective. Don Julio recommended that, for such an arduous task, it would be necessary to study "a couple of thousand Inquisition trials," which would eventually lead to the "history of a few hundred families united by a system of lineages." Caro Baroja thus defined a very precise operative method.[2]

As of today, neither the methodology proposed by Caro, nor the attention of H. Beinart, has elicited much enthusiasm among historians of the Hispanic crypto-Jews. It must be recognized that within specialized historiography, the judeoconverso families and their systems of lineage and kinship have hardly attracted much attention. Nonetheless, there is an obvious need to understand the mechanisms that develop within the limits imposed by blood ties, kinship, or relation through marriage. Today, our historiography demands this knowledge. To strike off on that barely intuited path, to delimit its contours, to specify its destiny, and to draw up its outline, are the principal objectives we propose for ourselves as a team of investigators.

Our goal is, without a doubt, ambitious, because tackling the problems presented by the judeoconverso minority from a multidisciplinary perspective is a very involved and complicated procedure. Initially, we are obliged to study previous works in order to construct the first basic levels of study. Obviously, neither the original manuscripts, nor the printed sources, and certainly not the topic's enormous bibliography were conceived of or elaborated in terms of our own original focus. But whatever the methods of study, the questions posed were always similar in both structure and form from the very origins of the converso problem. All historical periods have dealt with the same protagonists, clothed at times in similar garb and at other times in contrasting dress. We are familiar with all the characters: they are the Old Christians and the New Christians; they are the Jews, the Judaizers and the "marranos"; they are also the Inquisition, the Crown, the Church, and the rabbinical authorities of the Jewish communities of the Iberian Diaspora.

The questions ordinarily posed by historians to these protagonists stem from the fact that two religious communities existed—the one a majority and the other a minority—who lived out their relationships in an especially dramatic manner. This much is true, but the issue of the degree to which the members of one community identified themselves vis-à-vis the members of the other, and the degree to which orthodoxy defined itself as such in an antinomian relationship with heresy has produced an inevitably simplistic and excessively rigid methodological framework.

Religious overtones shaded questions formulated from the two sides. Did marranismo exist as a religious phenomenon, or, to the contrary, was it "invented" by the inquisitors? What is the significance of the term Judaizer? Did all the New Christians Judaize? These questions were posed repeatedly, and always from either side of the problem. Not surprisingly, the answers were also inevitably polemical, and always elicited rich and subtle interpretations.

As a result, the issue, always complex and always unfinished, has remained, in my judgment, without precise horizons. Inordinate and at times intentional attempts to establish one sole perspective as a means of targeting and understanding the problem have blocked other interpretations. In this case, the historian must understand his own limitations. Is it possible to render comprehensible and objective a phenomenon which, because of its nature, resists focus?[3] Secrecy and clandestinity, both inherent aspects of crypto-Jewish sociology, complicate any attempt to understand its nature. The cryptic nature of the Judaizing communities was concomitant with the unstable grounding of their very existence. Heretics in the eyes of the Catholic majority, they also experienced extreme difficulties in being acknowledged as Jews by the Hebrew communities abroad. This lack of adaptation to either system created a constant and permanent tension in the daily existence of the cryptic community; there was no alternative but to accept the situation and to make of it a customary form of internal coexistence. Nevertheless, and in spite of the relative guarantee of institutional security, this state of constant anxiety inevitably generated multiple responses from both individuals and groups. Both the actual situations and the social rejection that caused them resulted in a voluminous documentation from both the Catholic authorities and their Jewish counterparts which, while extremely interesting, is profoundly biased as well. The conversos who Judaized did not bequeath to posterity their own testimony; on the contrary, they were obliged to accept the fact that this task would be undertaken by others: at times, by their bitterest enemies, the inquisitors, and at others, by the Jews of the Diaspora, who frequently demonstrated a manifest unwillingness to integrate them into their communities.

As a result of all this, it is an incontrovertible fact that many historians, of whatever leaning, have found themselves unfailingly "trapped" by the seduction of the documents they have studied, documents not necessarily objective. Partly because of the documental bias and mainly because of the unilateral methodology applied, historiography on Iberian marranismo has turned out to be oversimplified and dualistic. There are two principal positions: (1) that marranismo is clandestine Judaism and (2) that marranismo existed only in the minds of the inquisitors and those who supported them.

These two entrenched conclusions have made it difficult to distinguish the diverse variations existing between one position and the other. More relativized positions need to be adopted: neither do all the trials begun by the Holy Office convey the image of a conscious and orthodox Judaism, nor can we assume from the rabbinical response that many conversos did not wish to Judaize. Liturgical obligations or traditional religious observances do not in themselves define the religion of the marranos. We are not in the presence of a religious creed that conforms to fixed or stable concepts. Clandestinity and secrecy reduced the religious socialization and allowed for a varied religious individuality; the trials of the Holy Office provide an extensive collection of examples in this regard.

Consequently, marranismo resulted less in a ritualistic and observant practice than in a consciously motivated integration within Mosaic law,[4] undertaken individually or socially. There are many paths that lead to such a level of consciousness, but the ethnic bonds of a community are the first basic step toward initiating the process of social and religious integration. In other words, the term so commonly used in the documents of the times defining the converso ethnically as a "New Christian of Jewish origin" is merely the starting point. From this there developed a more or less singular religious practice—crypto-Jewish religiosity— which, under favorable circumstances, may have culminated in the complete acceptance of actual Judaism. This usually occurred when the individual, having to flee from the Iberian peninsula, arrived at a Jewish community in one of the other European countries.

This process may explain the existence of the cryptic communities of Iberian marranismo and their logical migratory patterns toward the diverse Jewish communities of Europe.[5] This produces, in turn, a "natural" evolution that begins with the New Christian and concludes with the Jew; the marrano is the intermediary stage.[6] There do not appear to be many doubts in this respect. Therefore, ethnic issues were mainly responsible for social segregation and juridical-administrative differentiation. To be marginalized in sixteenth- and seventeenth-century Spain, it was not necessary to have been tried as a Judaizer by the Tribunal of Faith; all that was necessary was to have a few drops of Hebrew blood. Only by concealing the presence of these drops could the individual begin to aspire to an accepted social status that conferred both respect and honor. A vast amount has been written on these issues,[7] and it also has been pointed out quite clearly that money could expunge dubious ancestry and create ancient and time-honored lineages. Through these means, one purchased the required reputation; yet one error, one small, barely perceptible but intentional indiscretion was sufficient to destroy the entire achievement. When this occurred, the affected individual suffered immediate exclusion. While such a thing rarely happened, the important fact is that it did happen, and this revealed the extent to which lineage, belonging to a clan line, and ethnic origin were the central issues in the drama of coexistence between the majority and the minority. Race and lineage, both separately and barely differentiated from each other, represented the primary characteristics of social exclusion.[8]

The statutes on purity of blood, that neurotic obsession to "stir up entombed bones," as Quevedo wrote,[9] functioned as a means of attacking the social and juridical rights of the New Christians, but what is particularly interesting is that they also made more selective the social mechanisms that led to marriage. The "quality of the blood" was transmitted through lineage and could be purchased with money; yet, like wine that must age with time, only marriage guaranteed it. For this reason the politics of marriage were of vital importance.

The letters patent of nobility and the certificates of purity, results of tedious and complex secret investigations, were superimposed onto the inexorable and selective economic process and provoked a sharply defined and strengthened reaffirmation of the traditional social groups and estates. The social expansion timidly carried out in the first forty years of the sixteenth century was aborted after the generalization of the statutes. Lineages were once more reaffirmed, family ranks closed ever more tightly among themselves, and clans and kinships were consolidated. Very few possibilities remained for persons of questionable background who had not succeeded in establishing themselves within respected and highly regarded lineages.

If, as we know, the Edicts of Faith published by the Holy Office occasionally served as propaganda through which many crypto-Jews, heretofore ignorant of the religion they wished to practice, reaffirmed their faith,[10] the statutes also allowed many New Christians, isolated within the vast expanse of the majority, to discover their unique identity. It was obviously a cultural identity that consequently reinforced the bonds defining them—both social bonds and ethnic ties.[11]

In examining the wide range of implications which these premises suggest, my principal objective is to unravel the complex familial structures developed internally within the ever unstable cryptic communities; such an objective demands as well that we focus carefully on the relations between these judeoconverso groups and the surrounding environment, that is, the Old Christian majority.

We must therefore adopt a rigorously selective criterion with regard to the "diverse messages" transmitted by the documentation of the period. As is well known, the documentation of the time exhibits a virulent anti-Semitism, sometimes latent and at other times quite explicit. The image presented in this vast quantity of paper is stereotypical, but no less real for this reason. The Judaizer is a permanent protagonist in daily reality. His presence is constant—always necessary but always uncomfortable. He embodies adverse stereotypes; he is the typified enemy, the opposing archetype who permits self-affirmation by means of negation. The Judaizer is the expiatory victim, the most hated antisocial agent because he is the heretic par excellence and, affirming the magic aspect of collective existence, he is the cause of all the evils that afflict the realm.

The image, most definitely stereotypical, that emerges from these mountains of books, documents, and treatises reveals a rarefied cultural atmosphere that logically corresponds to the collective parameters of the Catholic majority. Constant references to this stereotype have slowly formed a strategy of exclusion silencing all divergent manifestations. Uniformity has been imposed and thought has become monolithic.

The polemic over the statutes of purity, described in meticulous and detailed form by Albert A. Sicroff, exemplifies the inexorable tendency to suppress all differences. Sicroff demonstrates how certain positions that emerged triumphant at the end of the process had been very weak at the start. The supporters of the statutes increased in number over time, suggesting the existence of two "periods" of diverse evolution, at the end of which social coexistence fossilized. The various options were polarized into two essential positions: the dominant groups and the excluded ones. The former defined themselves through racial purity, noble lineage, virtuous reputation, and orthodox religion. Wealth was also an attribute. The excluded groups, in contrast, were so defined by the absence of all of these factors.[12]

There were many New Christians, crypto-Jews who accepted their marginalized condition and used it to cement their identities; they viewed their isolation as the feature that most defined them. Thus, in the face of religious persecution, they reconfirmed their desire to Judaize; in the face of social rejection, they reaffirmed their clandestine relations; in the face of the contempt and political neglect of their king, they collaborated with his enemies;[13] and finally, in the face of the baroque exaltation of "the lineage of the peasants," they defined a premeditated familial strategy, distinctly endogamous, as an essential means of ensuring the survival of their ethnic lineage.

Obviously, we cannot deduce a monolithic uniformity in either social structure, belief, or behavior. The attitudes learned in the bosom of the community, as well as those acquired in the contacts with foreign synagogues (aljamas), blended with difficulty within the limited and asphyxiating boundaries of clandestinity. There, the pressure from the majority was felt as an oppressive burden. It was not easy to resist, and on many occasions the weakness of the cryptic system was unable to withstand it. It was therefore necessary to maintain, among individual tendencies and general requirements, a certain degree of laxity that would guarantee coexistence, minimizing the risk of flight and the profound estrangement which, tragically and irreversibly, resulted in the Holy Office.

Of all the elements that assured the cohesion of the cryptic group, two stand out: the unity of faith and the solidarity of blood ties. Américo

Castro, with remarkable intuition, discovered the enormous importance that the Hebrew community of the Hispanic kingdoms gave to the issue of "blood." When Castro studied the emergence of the statutes, he saw in them the triumph of the Christian "caste" over the Hebrew "caste," a triumph based precisely on a particularly Jewish characteristic: the interest in maintaining at all costs their own specific singularity. Castro's thesis, bold and original, provoked angry and, at times, bitter reactions. This is not the occasion to repeat past dissensions that can only be understood within their social and intellectual context; yet today, when many historians, whether they are Jewish or not, investigate these themes, they arrive at hypotheses quite similar to those formulated earlier by Américo Castro. The topic of blood and lineage is one of these overworked themes.

The Hebrews, argued don Américo, boasted of possessing pure and ancient blood; they thus displayed pride in having an ancestry at least as long and ancient as that of the Old Christians. They considered themselves descendants of a superior ancestry that conferred attributes of nobility upon them. In their theories, the Hebrew minority followed the same arguments as the Old Christians. They explained, for example, that the exaltation of blood and lineage was not, in and of itself, strictly a racist formulation. This was not a mechanistically physiological or biological racism but rather the nourishing of a collective sentiment that inherits the consciousness of a past tradition, culture, and collective family. In the same way that they operated for the Old Christians, the laws of heredity—biological laws—did not alone transmit the blessing of a Jewish ancestry; moral and cultural values acquired in the mythical and courageous past were what determined the quality of blood. Lineage was the end of this process. Lesser nobility, nobility, and purity of blood formed the essential triumvirate of the Iberian Jews' social ethic, which they defended with the same energy as the Christian apologists: "Do not try to shame me by calling my parents Hebrews. Certainly that is what they are, and I desire it so: if near-antiquity is nobility, then who is more ancient?" Alonso de Cartagena eloquently defended his Hebrew ancestry.[14]

The antiquity of those mythical lineages lost in the past was what transmitted the honor, respect, and reputation which the Old Christians claimed exclusively for themselves. The Iberian Jews and New Christians developed an imitative strategy as anti-Semitism was unleashed and, encouraged by popular hatred, the justice system, with its Christian bias, penetrated the synagogues. The contempt of the masses extended everywhere, the Jews' protectors lost power, and the Crown acceded to the cries for extermination. During those years of violence, Jewish Spain and the newly converted proudly exhibited the antiquity of their lineages. This was a tardily awakened consciousness, since the ghetto had already been formed and its violent siege presaged terrible fatalities. That "historical" consciousness which rejected exclusion was deeply resented by the Christian majority. The palace priest exemplifies this attitude: "They [the Jews] pretended to supreme excellence, presuming that in the entire world there were no better people, neither more discreet nor more respected than they, being of the lineage of the tribes of Israel."[15]

The lineages of Israel, therefore, were ancient. Nobility, virtue, and pure and respected blood: these were the parameters Castro considered fundamental to the Hispanic Hebrews. They are not, in principle, new arguments, but nevertheless it is interesting to see how other historians, with another focus and different documentation, have emphasized the same themes that obsessed Castro.

A recent study by Swetschinski on the Jewish communities of Amsterdam during the seventeenth century stresses the social differentiation of the Sephardic Jews as compared with the Ashkenazi branch. In the city of Amstel, the Jews who had emigrated from the Iberian peninsula acted as if they were superior to natives of other areas. Swetschinski, studying the apologetic writings of the founders of the "Portuguese" community, notes the constantly brandished argument: "the superiority of the Hebrews originally from Sefarad."[16] Mosés Aron ha Leví, chronicler of the recently established community, argued that the Iberian Jews who settled in Amsterdam had brought with them the ancestry of their blazoned lineages. Daniel Levi de Barrios, the most prolific of all the Jewish writers who wrote in Castilian in Amsterdam, referring to the origin of his brothers, could not find more authoritative terms than "purity of blood" and "superior lineage." Daniel Levi de Barrios was so "Hispanicized" that Scholberg, his principal scholar, generalizes that "the Sephardic Jews of Amsterdam seem very Spanish in this respect."[17]

Thus, the bourgeois and "tolerant" Amsterdam of the mid-seventeenth century hosted a Jewish community of Iberian origin which, having fled from the Holy Office, was as much obsessed with lineage as were the Old Christians. This obsession was their governing feature and was what distinguished them most clearly from Jews who were emigrants from other areas. Escaping from a closed and secret situation, those Jews who in former days had survived the persecution of the Tribunal of Faith knew better than anyone else that only through blood alliances could they preserve their religious beliefs.

In this as in many other issues, Revah, when studying the "Bocarro-Francés" Jewish clan, understood the interests of family ties and, consequently, the singular importance of marriage for the community.[18] It was therefore essential to employ the appropriate strategy. Only those unions which faced the future with the weight and the duty—ultimately, the heritage—of the past could sustain the magic of the lineage, and with it, tradition, honor, and esteem.

Here we have the Jewish family or the Judaizing family constituting itself as a basic element of social and cultural cohesion. The classical endogamy of the Judeo-Christians was ultimately necessary, because it alone allowed religious affirmation, facilitated the process of socialization, and also assured the reproduction and subsequent development of economic structures. The judeoconverso family thus fulfilled three principal functions: it ensured faith, preserved the entity of lineage, and made possible the attainment of wealth.

Historians of the conversos have scarcely questioned this triple familial function. In this regard, the partial and myopic vision of the historian has portrayed a false and incomplete image of the conversos. We do not know them as forming part of a social group, or within their familial organization, or as participating in their own specific cultural world; nor do we know them, with rare exceptions, as individuals, persons in and of themselves. Our knowledge is limited to an image conveyed by the literature of the period and the documents of the Holy Office, and that image is particularly biased. In the inquisitorial documents, their predominant role is that of victims, and they are recognized as such in the formal and often tragic language of the penal trials. We have rarely sought any meanings beyond this image; we must therefore find and decipher the documents. Histories of the family, lineages, and kinships are, in themselves, suggestive and novel vantage points which the historian cannot ignore.

Caro Baroja has shown us this path. As indicated above, he believed it necessary to write the history of those "hundreds of lineages." But when striking off on that path, we discover that the methodology is unknown to us and that our lack of precision forcefully limits our steps.

Nevertheless, as we know, research on the history of the family has increased since the decade of the 1960s. This growth is due to the qualitative evolution occurring in historical demographic studies.[19] Through the analysis and the quantification of natural factors of population, this discipline has shifted toward the study of the social aspects that develop around the family structure such as types of marriages, transmission of belongings, access to property, and localization and analysis of patronage. The history of the family is thus an immense field where the interdisciplinary nature of the social sciences may well demonstrate its effectiveness. Whatever the future directions may be, some thoughts have already been firmly established: the family is the key institution sustaining the social system, and this occurs through two opposing yet complementary functions: on the one hand, the transmission of socio-cultural values through the biological laws of heredity, and on the other hand, the "control" of any dysfunctional element that might arise within the family.[20] In summary, contemporary cultural anthropology reminds us that the family in the Habsburg period reproduces itself, thus making "commercial strategies" possible, regulating the relations among its members, and perpetuating the force of authority by sacralizing its effects.

Nonetheless, such conclusions result from theoretical speculation, since concrete empirical analysis as applied to past eras is in the initial stages. Moreover, the scarcity of this type of research on minority groups is overwhelming. With such a limited background, to investigate the systems of familial organization of an ethnoreligious minority that also lives cryptically and whose real existence is not legally recognized by the majority implies an effort that remains to be carried out in all its aspects.[21]

The history of the crypto-Jewish family must be patiently reconstructed. Such an objective requires an initial premise on the part of the investigator: in the crypto-Jewish community, the family was always a component of internal solidarity. Let us begin, then, at the beginning.

During the fifteenth century, when the intensity of the conversion process paralleled institutional violence, the converts from Judaism, the New Christians, developed an entire strategy in order to reach the highest levels of the urban aristocracy. Thirty years ago, Francisco Márquez Villanueva explained that the objective was to control many municipal offices.[22]

Essential and complementary elements intervene in that historical process of social and political ascent; one is the economic level attained and the other, the bonds of solidarity woven by family and lineage. The second element is conditional upon the first, as the essential means that assured the marginalized minority's economic success was the harmonious, supportive, and operative inclusion of the individual within the family clan. Only when this had been accomplished could the individual ascend socially and politically, obtaining municipal offices, positions that ensured a certain immunity. This was surely the social direction of the recently converted minority, whose specific marginality halfway between the two religions gravely endangered their existence as a group.

The propensity toward sociopolitical ascent originating in familial solidarity does not suggest a behavior unique to the crypto-Jews, but their only possible strategy. The dominant sociopolitical system was based not upon the individual but rather upon the larger kinship system. Today, it is obvious to everyone that the group's definitive component was to be found in the hierarchical relations of loyalty, and that such loyalty, a primary characteristic of private family relationships, constituted the fundamental public feature of political relationships as well. For this reason there was no possibility of promotion or of any kind of social recognition not based a priori in these primary structures. The converso, like any other individual, ascended socially and politically through channels attained by the clan and the "family" to which he belonged. The political importance of groups as defined by blood and lineage tainted public life with a sordid and, on occasion, unabashed struggle for higher levels of power. The conversos were not strangers to such conflicts. Márquez Villanueva writes very lucidly on this point: "The clan spirit of the converso cliques impelled the ascent, in the face of all opposition, of their diverse members through tactics as efficacious as they were rancorous and, in the long run, prejudicial against those who employed them."[23]

The "clan spirit" dominated political relations, and all pertinent obligations were derived from it. Given that the attained occupation or post was not an individual achievement but rather a triumph in which the clan played the main role, this same clan could also impose its own internal needs, the two most important being the "cession" by the individual of the office to a third party and the establishment of new ties or obligations of patronage. The degree of kinship relations was a well-known leverage, in the cession of sinecures or municipal offices and in the persistent interest in seeking the "protection" of a powerful house.[24]

Let us summarize: blood ties and kinship bonds, whatever their extent and degree of intensity, wove a tight network of interests and solidarities throughout Iberian society with hardly any individual exceptions. Such were the basic principles of social structures. The conversos followed the same system as the majority group, but their circumstances obliged them to reinforce it. The mere fact of belonging to an ethnic minority was in itself a segregating factor, aggravated besides by harsh religious repression; all of this thrust the conversos to the margins of the system. Internal cohesion thus became the sole essential condition for survival. At the end of the fifteenth century, when the recently created Inquisition penetrated straight to the heart of the cryptic communities, they had still not found a better solution in their defense than to practice a closed endogamy. Mixed marriages (between Judaizing conversos and Old Christians) were not very frequent, and although there were exceptions, nuptials within the Judaizing group were always the norm.

This endogamous practice established networks of solidarity among most members of a community, and, by extension, it created connections with other small local communities to the point where, at the end of the fifteenth century, almost all communities were affected. The constant references to relatives and friends which abound in the procedural documents of the Holy Office indicate the extent to which the bonds of solidarity were extended far beyond the more precise limits of blood ties. Ethnic ties, family connections, and religious fellowship formed the defenses that guaranteed survival. Heim Beinart discovered a similar situation in Ciudad Real around 1480, which he describes in these terms: "At the end of two or three generations, [the conversos of Ciudad Real] had become one big family whose members were as powerful as ever."[25]

Obviously, a system structured in such a way could not be perfect. Its coherence was not totally guaranteed because it ultimately depended upon the degree of individual and social adhesion. Blind loyalty could not be counted upon, and the existing adhesions are explained by the subtle results and the dialectical play that were developed internally in consequence of the group's needs, expectations, and gratifications. The complexity of these relationships inevitably created frustrations— implicit or explicit—affecting either the individual or the group and constituting the breaches through which the repressive mechanisms of the majority were able to penetrate the interior of the community. The principal mission of the cryptic authorities was to prevent this from happening, giving warning and appealing urgently and anxiously to the community's internal solidarity. Their principal task was to avert the destructive effect of the talebearer. The Judaizers of many small communities had already experienced the devastating consequences brought about by the tribunal. The same thing always took place: the inquisitors penetrated through the breaches left open by private dissatisfactions. When this misfortune occurred, solidarity, which had been attained with such difficulty, was destroyed.[26]

The danger of intrusion was difficult to avoid given the constant fear one lived in: "They always live uneasily and in fear of the harsh Inquisition," wrote Levi de Barrios.[27] Even during the periods of minor repression, security was not guaranteed. Clandestinity and secrecy imposed a tense and harsh way of life. The crypto-Jew not only had to protect himself from the "raids" of the tribunal but was also severely censured by many former compatriots who, now safely practicing Judaism in some foreign community, bitterly criticized the crypto-Jew's reluctance to flee, as they themselves had, in search of a safe port. Abandoning home and business, they had fled from idolatry in order to live the religious tenets of their faith.[28] The effects of their criticism on the crypto-Jew were thus very important, given the moral authority that such criticism wielded.

It was difficult to live in a state of permanent internal exile; the need to leave the ghetto and participate in some way in the public arena was urgently felt, even when it entailed adopting a false identity. While dangerous, crossing into the hostile exterior of the majority could also alleviate the seriously conflictive tensions that accumulated within the interior. Permanently forced to live a double life, the cryptic community paid dearly for its inherently deficient structure. A progressive loss of cultural patrimony, an increasing weakening of religious devotion,[29] and also the overwhelming presence of the majority weighing down forcefully upon any minority cultural spirit were to blame for the grave deterioration which the community inevitably suffered.[30]

It was necessary to counteract these deficiencies through compensatory means, which were not only helpful to the individual but provided bonds of solidarity for the group. One of these means was the economic influence held by the community as a whole, especially during the sixteenth and seventeenth centuries.

We should, however, first consider some specific issues regarding the Jew's so-called aptitude for accumulating wealth. Like all generalizations, this is a simplistic distortion of historical reality. It is no longer possible to maintain that economic prosperity prevailed in all the Judaizing communities on the peninsula; examples proving the opposite abound everywhere, in Iberia as elsewhere. Need it be stated that neither the Jews nor the conversos constitute, in themselves, a specific social group in the production of capital of the period? One can easily demonstrate the presence of Hebrew blood, Jewish or converted, on each and every one of the rungs of the social ladder. Wealth is not a patrimony derived from ethnicity or beliefs. To affirm the opposite is to assume as true the classic typical anti-Semitic argument which endeavors to make a totality out of what can be no more than a partial reflection of reality. The strategy of stereotyping,[31] as we already know, consists of assimilating a partial reality (some conversos were wealthy) into a fictitious totality (all conversos were wealthy).

By affirming these basic principles, the historian does not obscure

reality: a minority of judeoconversos had amassed substantial patrimo-
nies and risen to the highest levels of social prestige. Jewish men played
crucial roles in the world of commerce, in business, and in government.[32]
Although their participation in such activities assumes far more importance if we compare it with their numerical insignificance, it is also true
that their contemporaries' view of this problem was biased, because of
the perpetually distorting effects of official propaganda. But when it was
said, for example, that "the pulse of commerce is sustained only by the
merchants of the Hebrew caste,"[33] we should understand that such a
judgment, while not totally accurate, did not convey a completely distorted image of reality. The so-called "businessmen" of the seventeenth
century were made up of a contained group of wealthy conversos principally in Portugal.

The people were not too misguided when, humiliated by their poverty, they observed, in contrast, how wealth overflowed the homes of
some New Christians. While it would be absurd to deny this fact, it has
not been possible to measure its entire extent and significance, nor is
this the moment to do so.

Nonetheless, we must ask what the reasons were for this acknowledged economic success. There is no single or direct answer, but an
objective reading of Inquisition documents discloses several basic causes,
one of which is the organic solidity of the kinship ties. This relation was
pointed out above, as was the fact that even though research is scarce,
some has been carried out.

In his study of the Bocarro-Francés family,[34] Revah furnished proof
of the connections between its kinship ties and the commercial enterprises the family sustained. This is not the only example; in his investigation of the Sephardic communities of Hamburg and Altona,
Kellembez[35] patiently worked out the complex networks of commercial
contracts uniting them among themselves and with the conversos from
the interior of the Iberian peninsula. This splendid work outlines a
complex variety of commercial formulas structured and guided by the
imperatives of kinship. Kellembez demonstrated with precise genealogical data that these well-known commercial ventures, expanded across
oceans and characterizing the rise of early capitalism in the seventeenth
century, were built upon the permanence of blood and kinship through
marriage. Located throughout the commercial routes that linked other
continents to Europe, many Jewish families maintained permanent commercial ties made possible only through kinship or affinity.

New Christians from Portugal and Castilian crypto-Jews who traded
wool, for example, maintained close relations that merged together fam-

ily and business. The Judaizing conversos of the interior and Jews who had fled to the exterior organized commercial societies that at times extended to the coastal boundaries under family protection. Neither dispersion nor distance presented any kind of obstacle to families and businesses; on the contrary, the strength of the blood ties conferred fundamental advantages on such risky ventures.[36]

Commerce, whether domestic or destined for the great overseas routes, was the speculative activity par excellence. The most prosperous fortunes were based not on production, but on trade. The secret of a successful business lay in knowing how to exploit the price differential which a particular commodity could generate on its round through diverse markets. The merchant in charge of buying or selling required specialized agents, located in each and every one of the markets on the circuit. He needed to gain the trust of these agents. For this reason, the most suitable partner or employee either was a relative or belonged to the same lineage. Commerce functioned through strong ties of internal solidarity, and such "securities" constituted an essential condition for its development. This is not very difficult to document; we need only list the great fortunes originating in the Portuguese community of Amsterdam. The commercial emporia of Abraham Pereira, of Duarte Fernández, and of Jerónimo Nunes da Costa reveal a hierarchical family organization, with each member of the family assigned a specific task.

Let us summarize: there is no doubt that the history of the crypto-Jews of the Iberian peninsula demands new approaches in order to reveal the fundamental components of the life of this minority interiorized by their own clandestinity. We need to ask how cryptic families functioned. Yet this is only part of the problem. It would be too simplistic to convey the impression of a strong, solid, socially and culturally cohesive minority deriving those characteristics solely from its secret religion, without mentioning that, together with its integrating tendencies, the minority also experienced disintegrative factors and opposing tendencies.

If the study of the interiority of the crypto-Jews is suggestive and attractive, their external profile, their social life, is as much if not more so. In public the judeoconverso was an ordinary sort with no distinguishing characteristics. Like any other individual, he formed part of the complex mesh of social relations; he acted within the framework of duties and privileges inherent in a hierarchical society. He also shared in the consciousness that defined, socially, economically, and ideologically, the social group to which he belonged. The judeoconverso, upon leaving the "ghetto," could not avoid entering the corporate structures that regulated everyday life. He belonged to guilds and confraternities and participated as well in the factions so frequent at the time. In each and every one of these, the importance of dual loyalty systems (bonds between two people which provide protection and benefit) took precedence over every other form of horizontal relationship. This primary system functioned throughout the entire social pyramid, weaving dense social networks, made hierarchical and vertical according to a set of rights and obligations that were unwritten but were always effective. The society as a whole was formed by a complex graded network of dual relationships that ascended to the apex of the pyramid, the position held by the nobility, the great protector and recipient of diverse loyalties.[37]

The patronage system thus defines relations of dependence whose essential cohesive elements are kinship and lineage. The crypto-Jew was no exception to the "patron-client" relationship. When, from the secret recess of his private life, the Judaizer went out into the world, he did so in obeisance to his noble patron and, like so many others, expected his protection in return. Whatever vantage point on the social pyramid we assume, the spectacle of a society "under patronage" is the same. The judeoconverso behaved the same way as any other individual. At court they depended upon this or that patron; Rodrigo Méndez Silva, for example, belonged to the Cortizo clan, which was very close to the Conde-Duque de Olivares.[38] The great physician and philosopher who fled from the Venetian ghetto, Fernando Cardoso, found himself "protected" by another illustrious Spanish personage: don Juan Alonso Enríquez de Cabrera, duke of Medina de Rioseco and admiral of Castile.[39] These are two examples of very well-known people, but there are many other unknown participants in the same system. To learn about these social mechanisms and to study the intricate network of interests is, ultimately, our essential objective.

NOTES

1. Heim Beinart, *Los conversos ante el Tribunal de la Inquisición* (Madrid: Riopiedras, 1983), 268.

2. Julio Caro Baroja, *Los judíos en la España moderna y contemporánea*, 2d ed., (Madrid: Istmo, 1978), 1:453.

3. Y. H. Yerushalmi, *From Spanish Court to Italian Ghetto: Isaac Cardoso: A Study in Seventeenth-Century Marranism and Jewish Apologetics* (New York: Columbia University Press, 1971; reprint, Seattle and London: University of Washington Press, 1981), 23: "Let us recognize at the outset that few phenomena can be more elusive of historical scrutiny than a secret religion whose subterranean life has been documented largely by its antagonists."

4. I. Revah, "Les marranes," *Revue des études juives* 118 (1959–60): 30–77. P. 55: "In reality, as the great Portuguese writer Joao de Barros would have seen, in 1531–1532 the 'Judaism' of the marranos was in essence a potential Judaism which the entrance into a Jewish community most frequently transformed into real Judaism."

5. On immigration, see C. Roth, *Los judíos secretos. Historia de los marranos* (Madrid: Altalena, 1979), chaps. 8 and 9. H. C. Lea, *Historia de la Inquisición Española* (Madrid: Fundación Universitaria Española, 1983), see vol. 3, chap. 1.

6. "Paraphrasing Professor Revah's statement, it is perhaps even more fundamental to recognize that, even before he began to Judaize, every New Christian was a potential marrano." Yerushalmi, *From Spanish Court to Italian Ghetto*, 39.

7. On these issues, see Américo Castro, *De la edad conflictiva: Crisis de la cultura española en el s. XVII* (Madrid: Taurus, 1976), 47–137; J. A. Maravall, *Poder, honor y élites en el s. XVII* (Madrid, 1979); J. A. Maravall, "La función del honor en la sociedad tradicional," *Ideologies and Literature* 7 (1979): 9–27; C. Chauchadis, *Honneur, morale et société dans l'Espagne de Philippe II* (Paris: CNRS, 1984): 163–182.

8. Maravall, *Poder*, 41–61.

9. Quevedo, *Obra poética*, ed. J. M. Blecua (Madrid: Castalia, 1969), 1:213, quoted in Castro, *De la edad conflictiva*, 25.

10. Solange Alberro, "La gran conspiración judeo-conversos en México, 1642–1650" (Thése d'Etat, Université Toulouse-Le Mirail, 1985).

11. Albert A. Sicroff, *Los estatutos de limpieza de sangre. Controversias entre los siglos XV y XVII* (Madrid: Taurus, 1979), 26: "Oppressed by the Purity of Blood statutes, the judeocristianos discovered with more intensity their identity as an equivocal element of Spanish life."

12. Chauchadis, *Honneur, morale et société*, 219.

13. H. Mechoulan, *Hispanidad y judaísmo en tiempos de Espinoza: Estudio y edición anotada de "La Certeza del Camino" de Abraham Pereyra, Amsterdam, 1666* (Salamanca, Universidad de Salamanca, 1987), 33: "There is no doubt that the Jews who had recently arrived in Amsterdam took thorough advantage of the fact that the Republic of the United Provinces accepted them with open arms, against Spain's commercial interests."

14. Quoted in Castro, *De la edad conflictiva*, 143.

15. A Bernáldez, *Memorias del reinado de los Reyes Católicos*, ed. M. Gómez-Moreno and M. Carriazo (Madrid: Casa, 1962).

16. D. Swetschinski, "The Portuguese Jewish Merchants of Seventeenth-Century Amsterdam: A Social Profile" (Ph.D. diss., Brandeis University, 1979), 334–336.

17. K. R. Scholberg, "Miguel de Barrios and the Sephardic Community," *Jewish Quarterly Review* 53, no. 2 (1962).

18. I. Revah, "Une famille de 'nouveaux-crétiens': Les Bocarro-Francés," *Revue des études juives*, n.s. 16 (116) (1957): 73–87.

19. V. Pérez Moreda, "Matrimonio y familia: Algunas consideraciones sobre el modelo matrimonial español en la edad moderna," *Boletín de la Asociación de Demografía Histórica* (Madrid) 4, no. 1 (March 1985): 3–51.

20. J. Casey et al., *La familia en la España mediterránea (siglos XV–XIX)* (Barcelona: Centre d'etudis d'Historia Moderna "Pierre Vilar," 1987), 13–35.

21. Although the scarcity of studies on the internal components of the cryptic organizations is evident, an exception such as the works of B. Vincent, which are especially relevant, deserves mention. Of particular interest is his essay "Los elementos de solidaridad en el seno de la minoría morisca" in his *Andalucía en la edad moderna* (Granada: Ediciones de la Universidad de Granada, 1985), 203–214.

22. F. Márquez Villanueva, "Conversos y Cargos Consejiles en el siglo XV," *Revista de Archivos, Bibliotecas y Museos* 7, LXIII (1957): 506.

23. Márquez Villanueva, "Conversos y cargos," 506.

24. J. Contreras, "Criptojudaismo en la España moderna: Clientelismo y linaje," *Areas* (Universidad de Murcia, 1989): 46–89.

25. Beinart, *Los conversos ante el Tribunal*, 268.

26. In this respect the study which I am carrying out at the present time of two Judaizing communities in Extremadura (Albuquerque) and Murcia, which were dispersed during the decade of the 1560s, is particularly interesting.

27. D. Levi de Barrios, *Triunfo del Gobierno Popular en la Casa Jacob* (Amsterdam, 1684), 25, quoted in H. Méchoulan, *Hispanidad y judaismo*, 35.

28. Abraham Pereyra, *La Certeza del Camino* (Amsterdam, 1666), in Méchoulan, *Hispanidad*, 286. The author mercilessly criticizes the Judaizer who, carried away by his avarice, does not flee Spain to go abroad: "The other, wrapped up in his honors and misfortunes and unhappinesses, the greatness in which he found himself did not guide him to the love of the Blessed Father whom he should know, nor to the fear of the Inquisition because, being nothing but an idolater, committing major offenses before God, he judged himself free."

29. Revah, "Les marranes," 54–56.

30. On this issue, see I. Revah, *Spinoza et le Dr. Juan de Prado* (Paris and The Hague: Mouton, 1959), 13–205 and Uriel da Costa, *Espejo de una vida humana (exemplar humanae vitae)*, ed. Gabriel Albiac (Madrid: Editorial Hiperion, 1985), 37–40.

31. J. M. Monsalvo Anton, *Teoría y evolución de un conflicto social. El antisemitismo en la corona de Castilla en la baja edad media* (Madrid: Siglo XXI, 1985), 107–134.

32. A. Domínguez Ortiz, *Política y hacienda de Felipe IV* (Madrid: Derecho Financiero, 1960), 127–141.

33. D. Gómez Solís, *Discursos sobre los comercios de las dos Indias*, [1622], ed. Moïse Bensabat Amzalak (Lisbon, 1943), 20.

34. I. Revah, "Une famille de 'nouveaux-chretiens': Les Bocarro-Francés," *Révue des études juives*, no. 5, 16 (1957): 73–87.

35. H. Kellembez, *Sephardim an der Unteren Elbe: Ihre wirtschaftliche und poli-

tische Bedeutung von Ende des 16. bis zum Beginn des *18.* Jahrhunderts (Wiesbaden, 1958), cited in Yerushalmi, *From Spanish Court to Italian Ghetto,* 17, n. 24.

36. D. Swetschinski, *The Portuguese Jewish Merchants of Seventeenth Century Amsterdam: A Social Profile* (London University Microfilms International: 1979) 135–326, describes commercial societies "which integrated them within a vast network which included the Philippines, the European countries, the American colonies, and the African coasts . . ."

37. On this issue, see W. S. Maltby, *El gran duque de Alba (un siglo de España y de Europa, 1507–1582)* (Madrid: Turner, 1985), 36 and 595.

38. B. Loupias, "Recherche sur la vie, la culture et les oeuvres de Rodrigo Méndez Silva" (Thèse d'Etat, Paris, 1969).

39. "By 1632, as we shall see, he was enjoying the patronage of the most august of the Spanish grandees, D. Juan Alonso Enríquez de Cabrera, the Admiral of Castille." Yerushalmi, *From Spanish Court to Italian Ghetto,* 95.

EIGHT

The Jew as Witch: Displaced Aggression and the Myth of the Santo Niño de La Guardia

Stephen Haliczer

From the perspective of the social historian, one of the greatest successes achieved by Habsburg Spain was its ability to avoid, in large measure, the massive witch-hunts that swept over most of the rest of Christian Europe during the sixteenth and seventeenth centuries. Historians have generally ascribed to the Inquisition much of the credit for this achievement. As a highly respected institution with well-established jurisdiction over matters of heresy or other threats to the Catholic faith, the Inquisition was in a position to set the tone for the entire Spanish legal system regarding such offenses. Although the Holy Office never attained complete control over crimes involving witchcraft, its skeptical attitude toward much of the evidence produced in these trials, and its well-advertised role in ending the Navarre witch panic of 1609–1612 profoundly influenced the entire climate of public and learned opinion in ways that tended to discourage witch-hunting on a massive scale.

In most respects, however, early modern Spain was little different from other contemporary societies since it housed the same kind and degree of social and economic pressures that engendered witchcraft accusations elsewhere. Spain shared with other countries, for example, the stereotypical image of women as being morally and intellectually weaker than men and, as a result, more likely to be vulnerable to the temptations of the Devil.[1] Moreover, apart from the reassurance in matters of religion offered by the fact of the Inquisition's existence, early modern Spaniards experienced the same anxieties and insecurities as their contemporaries in France or Germany and were, therefore, equally concerned about the threat from supernatural forces to their everyday life.

For its part, the Inquisition's attitude toward witchcraft accusations can hardly be attributed to any enlightened rationalist negation of the power of the Devil. As late as 1631, seventeen years after Alonso de Salazar Frías's celebrated Seventh Report to the Inquisitor General, Gaspar Navarro published his *Tribunal de la superstición ladina*, in which he explicitly accepted the reality of diabolical pacts, maleficia and the witch's sabbath and called for exemplary punishment of witches. The work frequently quoted from the famous *Malleus Maleficarum* in support of its arguments and carried with it the warm endorsement of Dr. Baltasar de Cisneros, inquisitorial *cualificador* of the Zaragoza tribunal.[2]

The Spanish rulers of the period were themselves haunted by the threat of foreign aggression and internal subversion, an atmosphere hardly conducive to calm in the face of the witch craze. One of these rulers, Charles II, was himself the reputed victim of witchcraft perpetrated by the royal confessor Froilán Díaz. In the Franche-Comté, Luxembourg, and other parts of the Spanish Netherlands, the governments of Philip II, III, and IV strongly encouraged the persecution of witches and in Luxembourg alone there were 355 executions between 1606 and 1650.[3]

Given the fact that the Inquisition never had complete control over these cases, its increasing concern for the niceties of legal procedure alone could hardly have prevented a witch craze. Indeed this is amply demonstrated by the situation in Navarre in 1610–1612 where local justices aided by certain parish priests carried out the initial arrests, tortured suspects unmercifully, and extorted confessions which were then eagerly and uncritically accepted by the inquisitors on the spot.[4]

Under sixteenth- and seventeenth-century social conditions, therefore, the only thing that could account for Spain's relative inactivity in the face of the European witch craze was the presence in that country of another target of displaced aggression, a target so firmly identified in the public mind with all that was evil and pernicious that it could readily substitute for the witch as the ultimate source of social evil.

During the fourteenth century, with the breakdown of the old toleration that had permitted Christian, Jew, and Moslem to live side by side in relative harmony, the Jew became more and more identified as the chief enemy of Christianity. By the time of the Cortes of Toro in 1371, the Jews were described as "rash and evil men, who sow corruption with impunity so that the greater part of our kingdom is ruined by them in contempt of Christians and the Catholic faith."[5] Ironically, this description came at a time when the Jewish communities had suffered grievously during the recently concluded civil war between Pedro I and his half brother Henry of Trastámara.

By the 1380s the weakened condition of the Jewish communities and the relativistic philosophy then popular among Jewish intellectuals were producing numerous conversions.[6] After the rioting of 1391, Jews converted en masse, led by their rabbis, and from then on Spain's Jewish communities became smaller and more impoverished while the converted Jews grew in numbers, wealth, and political importance. By the middle of the fifteenth century, however, resentment of the conversos was giving rise to a polemical literature that rejected the possibility of their true conversion to Christianity and blamed them for all the crimes normally attributed to Jews. The most interesting and important of these writings was the *Fortalitium Fidei* (Fortress of the Faith) by the Franciscan Alonso de Espina, first published in 1460. The work is divided into four volumes, each dedicated to describing the iniquity of one of the four chief enemies of the Catholic faith: heretics, Muslims, Jews, and demons. For Espina, Jews and converts did not exist as a separate category; there were only "public Jews and secret Jews." Since conversos were secret Jews, they were naturally guilty of all the offenses traditionally attributed to Jews by European folk tradition, including profanation of Hosts and the murder of Christian children and the use of their blood or body parts in religious rituals. According to Espina, Jewish law, which is equally binding on both Jews and converts, commands the destruction of Christians and Christianity, which they actively strive to accomplish by starting fires, poisoning wells, and doing other evil deeds.[7]

It was left to the Spanish Inquisition, however, to officialize medieval demonological myths about Jews and apply them to Jewish converts to Christianity in such a way as to keep alive the flames of Spanish anti-Semitism long after the expulsion of the Jews themselves. This process began with the case of the so-called Holy Child (Santo Niño) of La Guardia when both Jews and converts were accused of working together to commit a crime of unimaginable horror which threatened the very existence of Christian Spain. So successful were the inquisitors in this that the La Guardia case served to create in the public imagination a kind of bogyman, a larger-than-life image of the Jew/converso who was at once child murderer, blood sucker, rebel, and demonic sorcerer who sought to reverse the divinely established order of things by destroying Christianity so that, according to Licenciado Vegas, the Holy Child's first chronicler, the Jews "would become the absolute lords of the earth."[8] It was this bogyman who provided the Spanish masses with an ideal object of displaced aggression capable of absorbing the sadomasochistic fantasies and infanticidal impulses that provided the psychological force behind the witchcraft panics in other parts of Europe.

The complexity and sophistication of the Santo Niño legend stands out remarkably when it is compared to the closest contemporary ritual murder accusation of which we have a record: the case of Simon of Trent. This case, which began before Trent's podestá in 1475 and concluded in 1478, involved two elements that were traditionally a part of such accusations: extraction of blood for use in Jewish Passover rituals and the grotesque reenactment of the crucifixion of Christ in order to mock Christianity itself.[9]

Of these two elements, however, it was the use of the child's blood for ritual purposes that clearly predominated while the elements related to the mockery of the Passion and of Christians in general were weaker and clearly of secondary importance. Again and again, the podestá, whose earlier prejudices had been confirmed when a convert assured him that his own father had quaffed glasses of wine mixed with blood on Passover, forced his Jewish victims to enumerate the various ways in which they and their coreligionists used the blood of Christian children. Faithful to the traditions of the medieval ritual murder accusation, Samuel and Tobia, two of the most important defendants, admitted after repeated torture that they drank wine mixed with blood at Passover and they also sprinkled blood on the dough used to make the ritual matzos.[10] The court was also told that Christian blood was routinely fed to pregnant Jewesses so that their babies would be born fat and healthy.[11] In a clear reference to Christian fears about the use by Jews of Calamus Draco, the dark or blood-red gum of a species of palm, to relieve pain after circumcision, the Trent Jews were also forced to admit that they applied wine mixed with blood to the circumcision wound.[12]

Of course the truth, the fact that Judaism categorically prohibits its adherents from consuming blood as in Leviticus 17:11–13, did have a way of coming out in proceedings of this nature, and the case of Simon of Trent was no exception. At one point, the podestá asked Mose, one of the defendants, very directly why Jews drank Christian blood when their own law prohibits the consumption of blood in any form. Mose's reply neatly disposed of this issue, however, when he declared that the law applied only to the blood of animals and not to the blood of Christian children, which is consumed to show disdain for Christianity. After another session in the torture chamber, Mose even stated that leading rabbinical authorities had openly declared that it was no sin to consume the blood of Christians. In this way, through careful stage-management and the liberal application of torture, the podestá's potentially embarrassing question was turned into yet another way of adding to the trial record more "evidence" of the Jews' insatiable thirst for blood.[13]

Consistent with the emphasis placed on the ritual use of blood by Jews rather than the reenactment of Christ's Passion, the wounds allegedly inflicted on the hapless Simon seem almost haphazard rather than designed to imitate those inflicted on Christ. Simon's cheeks were torn with pincers, his body stuck with pins in many places and then the pincers were used to inflict a wound on his shins from which blood was collected.[14]

In contrast with the vivid imagery invoked to describe the collection and ritual use of Christian blood, the testimony that was forced out of the accused relating to their mockery of Christ's Passion seems strained and unnatural, almost as though the judges themselves were less than convinced of its centrality to the case. In the first place, although Simon was allegedly crucified, this was almost an afterthought since he received most of his wounds before his arms were extended to form a cross and he died shortly thereafter.[15] Furthermore, the description of the actual mockery of Simon's body is clumsy and childlike; the Jews were even made to testify that they had stuck their tongues out and shown their bare buttocks to the corpse.[16]

The case of the Santo Niño de La Guardia involved six Jews and five conversos from the villages of La Guardia and Tembleque near Toledo and was tried between December 1490 and 16 November 1491, when the accused were burned at the stake. From its very inception, the trial unfolded in an atmosphere of intense anti-Semitism stirred up by the Inquisition's tremendous wave of prosecution against the converted Jews of the Toledo region beginning in 1486. Surprisingly enough, however, the case was not brought before the Toledo tribunal. Instead, it was heard by a special inquisitorial court convened under the watchful eye of Inquisitor General Tomás de Torquemada in the monastery which he himself had founded with money confiscated from the converted Jewish victims of the Holy Office: Santo Tomás of Avila.[17]

In the trial record, the blood libel itself represents only a minor chord in a complex variety of charges. Of course blood was allegedly drawn from the child's body and collected in an earthenware jug, but it was removed by Lope Franco, one of the accused, after the child was brought out for burial. Apart from this, the case omits any mention of the elements that normally comprised the blood libel and which figure so prominently in the Simon of Trent legend. Rather than concentrating on the ritual use of Christian blood by Jews, the case of the Santo Niño brings together a series of charges that are most often separated in medieval anti-Semitic folk tradition. The affair of the Santo Niño was alleged to have begun as a Jewish plot to use black magic in order to destroy first the inquisitors and then all Christians. According to the confused and often contradictory testimony that was extorted from Yuce Franco, one of the tribunals' Jewish prisoners, this plot started as early as 1487 and involved the employment of Rabbi Abenamias, a master magician, living in Zamora.[18] Abenamias was to be responsible for casting an evil spell using a heart torn from the body of a Christian child and a consecrated Host, both of which would be obtained for him by the accused.[19]

Furthermore, the plotters were alleged to have gone to great lengths in order to imitate Christ's Passion down to the smallest detail. On 24 September 1491, Benito García, one of the hapless conversos, was accused of having carried the child to a cave near La Guardia where he had been nailed to a wooden cross, lashed repeatedly, and a crown of thorns placed on his head.[20] While the child was being beaten, his supposed torturers recited curses designed to mock Christ for whom the child was a substitute. Among other things, Christ was called a "traitor and deceiver who had preached lies against the Jewish faith," an "evil sorcerer who had sought to destroy the Jews and Judaism," and the "bastard son of a perverse and adulterous woman."[21] In this way, out of the pain and torment inflicted on their Jewish and converso victims, Avila's special inquisitors had managed to concoct an extraordinarily suggestive myth which lent itself easily to being further elaborated and made more horrifying by later authors.

We can see how this process began in the very first known account of the case, the *Memoria muy verdadera de la pasion y martirio, que el glorioso martir, inocente niño llamado Cristobal, padescio . . . en esta villa de la guardia,* written in 1544 by Licenciado Vegas, the apostolic notary of the village. In the *Memoria verdadera* the vague plot to destroy Christians through enchantment is assimilated to the tradition of Jewish poisoners that had cost so many innocent lives during the Black Death and other periods of unexplained epidemics. Drawing upon a French folktale from some time after the Black Death, Vegas makes the story of the Santo Niño begin in France with the frustrated attempt by several of the individuals involved in the case or their ancestors to poison the wells there with a magic powder made from the heart of a Christian child and a consecrated Host. They were successful in obtaining the Host but were thwarted in their efforts to secure the heart of a Christian child and were tricked into accepting a pig's heart instead.[22] Of course the maleficia that they were planning failed, but somehow these Jews or their descendants found their way down to Castile, converted nominally to Christianity, and chose La Guardia as the ideal spot to try their enchantment because of its allegedly close resemblance to Jerusalem. But this time, instead of relying on the impoverished parents of the child to murder him and supply his heart as they had done in France, they determined to kidnap a child (whose name turned out to be Christobalico) and cut his heart out themselves after carrying out a mock crucifixion.[23]

It is in describing this crucifixion that Vegas gives free reign to his imagination, transforming the meager details contained in the tribunal's final sentence into a richly detailed imitation of Christ's entire Passion as suffered by the child martyr. According to Vegas's perfervid account, little Christobalico was first forced to carry a heavy cross up the hill to the cave where he was to be crucified. Before he was crucified he was given no less than 6,200 lashes, although we are told that the child informed his tormentors that only the last one thousand really hurt because they were more than Christ himself received.[24]

Vegas's account, which must have circulated widely in Toledo since it was copied by the converso Sebastián de Horozco (1510–1581), was incorporated into Licenciado Sebastián de Nieva Calvos's *El niño inocente; hijo de Toledo y martyr en La Guardia*. It is in this work, published in 1628, where the Jew/witch connection is made quite explicit. Jews and conversos involved in the Santo Niño affair are depicted as fiendish, physically repellent creatures acting with the support of the devil to carry out his purposes in the world. Benito García de las Mesuras, for example, is described as having an appearance so horrible as to "menace with destruction not only some poor innocent but even the most resolutely defended kingdom." His close associate, Garci Franco, had a "depraved expression" and was so ugly that "it would not be strange if he were to be the executioner of the wrath of heaven." Franco had such an evil reputation in La Guardia that mothers would frighten their noisy or disobedient children by threatening them with his appearance. For his part, Franco is said to have gloried in the hatred and abhorrence of his neighbors, which helped to keep his "vindictive rage against Catholics" at a fever pitch.[25] Like the witches described by Sprenger and Kramer in the *Malleus Maleficarum*, Benito García, Garci Franco, and their companions had made an explicit pact with the Devil, who sought their perdition by convincing them that they could destroy using the very things with which God gave life to the body and the spirit: the human heart and the consecrated Host.[26]

After Vegas's account was published, the myth of the Santo Niño took hold of the popular imagination and became the subject of plays by Lope de Vega and José de Cañizares and sermons by such popular preachers as Fray Damián López de Haro (Toledo Cathedral, 1614). Little Christobalico became a patron saint of La Guardia and his shrine received visits from such luminaries as Ferdinand the Catholic, Charles V, and Philip II.[27] The case also figured prominently in the anti-Semitic writings of the period, including Fray Francisco de Torrejoncillo's fanatical *Centenella contra los judios,* where it served to demonstrate the "intense hatred" felt by Jews for Christianity.[28]

By the mid-sixteenth century, however, the story of the Santo Niño had become just one element in a pervasive anti-Semitism that was directed first against the Spanish conversos and later against the Portuguese New Christians who came to Spain after the union of the two crowns in 1580. Thus, in Spain and Portugal anti-Semitism was not just a social atavism but had real potential victims who were persecuted and discriminated against as much for their racial origins as for their religious practices. The infamous *limpieza de sangre* statutes that required genealogical investigations designed to prevent the descendants of Jews from entering honorable corporations only really took hold after the major centers of Spanish crypto-Judaism had been exterminated.[29] For its part, the Inquisition kept popular anti-Semitism at a fever pitch with spectacular show trials directed at prominent New Christian financiers like Joao Nunes Saraiva and his brother Henrique, who appeared at the auto de fe of 1636 in spite of their staunch protestations of fervent Roman Catholic belief.[30] Spain's Old Christian ruling elite was quick to see the hand of the Jew behind any threat to the faith. As early as 1556 Philip II expressed the view that "all the heresies which have existed in Germany and France . . . have been sown by the descendants of Jews."[31]

Interestingly enough, at around the same time that anti-Semitic ordinances were being passed by more and more Spanish institutions, the Spanish Inquisition began staking out a moderate position for itself on the witchcraft issue. In 1526, just one year after the Franciscan Order adopted a limpieza statute, the Inquisition held an important meeting in Granada to discuss its policy toward the witchcraft trials that were beginning to take place with increasing frequency in northern Spain. After careful deliberation, four of the ten inquisitors present, including future Inquisitor General Hernando de Valdés, voted that witches only went to the Sabbath "in their imagination." Those present at the meeting also decided that henceforth witches should be tried by the Holy Office because the murders that witches confessed might be mere illusions.[32]

In spite of the lack of unanimity on the issue of the Sabbath, the 1526 meeting set the tone for the Inquisition's attitude toward witchcraft

cases. In 1538, when witches were accused of having caused harvest fail-
ures and other evils, the local inquisitor was instructed to explain that
these things are "either sent by God for our sins or are a result of bad
weather, and that witches should not be suspected." In August 1614, in
reaction to the Logroño auto de fe of 1610 at which six persons accused
of witchcraft were burned, the Suprema officially adopted a skeptical
attitude toward the crimes supposedly committed by witches and em-
bodied that attitude in a set of instructions meant to guide local inquisitorial tribunals.[33] In fact, the 1614 instructions changed little because,
with the sole exception of the inquisitors of Logroño in 1609–1610, local
inquisitors tended to be extremely unwilling to hand down harsh sentences in cases that would have earned the death penalty in France or
the Holy Roman Empire during the same period.[34]

By officializing medieval anti-Semitic folk traditions and extending
them from the Jews to the conversos through a well-publicized show
trial, the Spanish Inquisition made sure that anti-Semitism and not Scho-
lastic witch theory would answer the early modern Spaniards' craving
for an object of social aggression. Moreover, even though France and
the Holy Roman Empire shared many of the same folk beliefs about
Jewish iniquity and diabolism, Jews could not provide them with an effective object for collective anxiety and frustrations. The Jews of France
had been expelled in 1394 and, even though the decree was repeated
in 1615, the sight of Jews was so rare in France that they were regarded
as an exotic sight when Frenchmen met them while traveling abroad.[35]
In sixteenth- and seventeenth-century France witches and Huguenots
assumed a "Jewish" role and were widely accused of many of the same
things of which the Jews had been accused in former times.[36] In the Holy
Roman Empire most Jews were expelled during the sixteenth century
and both Catholic and Protestant focused on the witch as an ideal
scapegoat for social ills.[37] Only Spain and Portugal among the great
European states of the early modern period could combine theories of
Jewish diabolism and implacable hatred of the true faith with the actual
presence on their territories of large numbers of persons of Jewish origin. Significantly, serious witch persecution in Spain was mainly confined to the Basque region, precisely the area that had had least contact
with Jews in the Middle Ages. For the rest of the country the converted
Jew substituted for the witch as a pariah, reflecting through antithesis
and projection society's most ingrained fears and repressed longings.

Perpetuated in plays, paintings, and histories down to 1955 when
Ramón Saravia published his *El Santo Niño de La Guardia* through a
Catholic press specializing in children's books, the myth of Jewish in-

iquity represented by the Santo Niño legend has contributed powerfully to that curious Spanish phenomenon: anti-Semitism without Jews. Even today, in a Spain increasingly secular, pragmatic, and cosmopolitan, the legend of the holy child prowls around like the ghost of past intolerance. Christobalico, the holy martyr, remains the patron Saint of La Guardia, and the Church, which in the mid-1960s disavowed the Simon of Trent blood libel, continues to support and profit financially from the annual celebrations that commemorate the creation of the far more dangerous anti-Semitic myth of the Santo Niño de La Guardia.

NOTES

1. Brian Levak, *The Witch-Hunt in Early Modern Europe* (New York: Longman, 1987), 126. Women who attempt to make themselves sexually attractive are called "ministers of the devil" in Pedro Galindo, *Parte segunda del directorio de penitentes y practica de una buena y prudente confesion* (Madrid: Antonio de Zafra, 1686), 518.

2. Gaspar Navarro, *Tribunal de la superticion ladina* (Huesca: Pedro Bluson, 1631) ffs. 52–55v, 56v–57.

3. Levak, *The Witch-Hunt*, 180.

4. Gustav Henningsen, *The Witches' Advocate: Basque Witchcraft and the Spanish Inquisition* (Reno: University of Nevada Press, 1980), 62–70, 108–117, 217–220.

5. Leon Poliakov, *The History of Anti-Semitism*, 4 vols. (New York: The Vanguard Press, 1973), 2:151.

6. Ibid., 154.

7. Henry Charles Lea, *A History of the Inquisition of Spain*, 4 vols. (New York: Macmillan, 1906), 1:149–150.

8. Fidel Fita, "La verdad sobre el martirio del santo niño de la Guardia, o sea el proceso y quema (16 noviembre1491) del judio Juce Franco en Avila," *Boletin de la Real Academia de la Historia*, XI (julio-setiembre, 1887): 135.

9. Joshua Trachtenberg, *The Devil and the Jews* (Philadelphia: Jewish Publication Society of America, 1983), 130–131.

10. Guiseppe Divina, *Storia del beato Simone de Trento*, 2 vols. (Trento: Artigianelli, 1902), 1:286–287.

11. Ibid., 302.

12. Trachtenberg, *The Devil*, 151; Divina, *Storia*, 301.

13. Divina, *Storia*, 302–303.

14. Ibid., 231–233.

15. Ibid., 234.

16. Ibid., 372, 380.

17. Fray Juan López, *Tercera parte de la historia general del Santo Domingo y de su orden de predicadores* (Valladolid: Francisco Fernández de Córdoba, 1613), 276–277.

18. Fita, "La verdad," 52.

19. Ibid., 65.

20. Ibid., 55.

21. Ibid., 104.

22. Trachtenberg, *The Devil*, 145.

23. Fita, "La verdad," 139.

24. Ibid., 141.

25. Sebastián de Nieva Calvo, *El niño inocente; hijo de Toledo y martyr en La Guardia* (Toledo: Juan Ruiz de Pareda, 1628), 78–79, 83v.

26. Ibid., 126v–128.

27. Antonio de Guzmán, *Historia del inocente trinatario el Santo Niño de la Guardia* (Madrid: Diego López Abad, 1720), 186–188.

28. Fray Francisco de Torrejoncillo, *Centenella contra judios*, Fray Diego Gavilán Vela, trans. (Madrid: Vda. Melchor Alegre, 1680), 132.

29. Henry Kamen, *Inquisition and Society in Spain* (Bloomington: Indiana University Press, 1985), 118–120.

30. James Boyajain, *Portuguese Bankers at the Court of Spain 1626–1650* (New Brunswick: Rutgers University Press, 1983), 118.

31. Geoffrey Parker, *Philip II* (London: Hutchinson, 1978), 193.

32. Kamen, *Inquisition and Society*, 211.

33. Ibid., 213–214.

34. Archivo Histórico Nacional, Inquisition, 19 June 1588, libro 937, 74–75v.

35. Leon Poliakov, *The History of Anti-Semitism From the Time of Christ to the Court Jews*, Richard Howard, trans. (New York: The Vanguard Press, 1976), 174.

36. Ibid., 189.

37. H. C. Erik Midelfort, *Witch Hunting in Southwestern Germany, 1562–1684* (Stanford: Stanford University Press, 1972).

NINE

On Knowing Other People's Lives, Inquisitorially and Artistically

Joseph H. Silverman

The epigraph for my essay comes from the play by Lope de Vega, *El niño inocente de La Guardia*. Its words—spoken by a Jew—are a dramatic summation of many significant aspects of this conference:

> What King and Queen are these [Ferdinand and
> Isabella] who
> through such chimeric schemes
> —based on secret counsel—
> would send into exile those
> who scarcely offend them?
> What flames are these, rekindled
> from ash by Dominican hordes?
> What new Cross is this, black and white,
> that delights the Catholics so?
> What new mode of scrutiny and
> legal system have we here?
> Why are trials now held in secret?
> Oh, if only Spain had never known such rulers!
> Woe unto us, exiled from our own
> fatherland in such misery!
> The suffering that so long ago was foretold
> has not yet ceased and our
> punishment is unending.
>
> (Pp. 59–60)

In an unforgettable moment of epiphanic self-revelation, the squire in the anonymous sixteenth-century novel *Lazarillo de Tormes* confesses to his young servant that, if he had a chance to serve a noble master, he

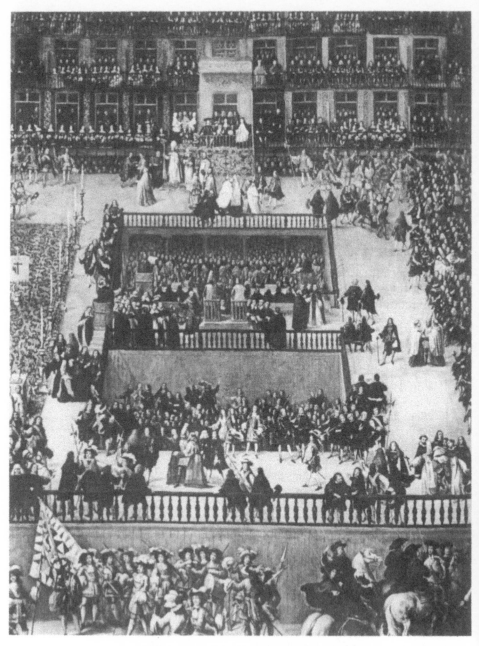

Fig. 6. Auto de fe by Pedro Berruguete.

would—among other virtuous (!) acts—"be malicious, mocking, and a trouble-maker, a *malsín,* among those of the house and outsiders; [he'd] go prying and trying *to know other people's lives* so [he] could tell his master about them. And [he'd] do all kinds of other things of this sort which are the vogue in palaces today and please the nobility well" (p. 57). As Covarrubias informs us in his *Tesoro de la lengua,* the malsín, a word of Hebraic derivation, is "that individual who secretly warns the authorities of the transgressions of others with evil intention and self-interest, and to perform this function is called malsinar" (p. 781b).

The phrase *to know other people's lives* in this context, closely allied with the activities of the malsín, persuaded me to offer, in 1961, a very negative appraisal of the squire, in contrast with Azorín's judgment of him as the most noble and worthy in Spanish history. But, more importantly, the words *saber vidas ajenas,* "to know other people's lives" were to become a signpost in my reading and teaching, which in the early 1950s were influenced by the irresistible imperative dimension of the writings and person of Américo Castro. And so, over the years, I collected examples of the phrase, in its exact form or in words that suggested its meaning, which inevitably led me to see the aspects of Golden Age literature I now want to evoke, basing myself on Mordecai M. Kaplan's premise that the full meaning of any text cannot be derived from the contemplation of the text itself, apart from the social, economic, psychological, and intellectual setting to which it belongs.

Antonio de Guevara, who always seems to be saying more than his words denote, even in those commonplace truths and fabulous lies that he manipulates between the remote past and his own moment, writes:

> Among the inhabitants of Crete it was customary, even obligatory, not to dare ask any visitor from a foreign land who he was, what he wanted, and from where he had come, under penalty of being whipped or sent into exile. And the purpose involved in promulgating such laws was to rid men of the temptation to be curious, that is to say, to want *to know other people's lives* and not pay attention to their own. . . . For what men seem to devote most of their time to is asking and investigating what their neighbors are doing; what they're involved in, how they support themselves, with whom they have dealings, where they go, what places they enter and even what they're thinking; because it is not enough that they insist on asking, they even presume to guess . . . For this reason Plato said: "Know thou, if thou knowest not . . . , that the sum of all our philosophizing is to persuade and counsel men that each one should be the judge of his own life and not be concerned *to scrutinize the lives of others.*" (*Menosprecio,* 30–36)

It goes without saying—though I'll say it anyway—that despite his reference to Plato's "Know thyself" and the realm of philosophy, Guevara is really talking about what Francisco Márquez termed "el problema del rigor inquisitorial" (p. 350). Elsewhere, becoming more specific about the potential danger and destructiveness involved in knowing other people's lives, that is, saber vidas ajenas as a weapon of an Inquisition-crazed society, he observes that "I have never seen a man insult another without prying into the life he was leading, without scrutinizing his blood line, [every branch and twig of his genealogical tree] . . . or without disinterring his ancestors" (pp. 375–382). These last remarks appear in a letter addressed to a friend who had called recent converts to Christianity "dogs, Moors, Jews, and pigs." With even greater force and specificity, Guevara writes that

> one solitary blemish will dishonor an entire generation. A stain on the lineage of some country bumpkin affects no one beyond him, but a stain on an hildalgo's blood affects his entire family, because it sullies the reputation of his forebears, it serves to disinter his ancestors, it leads to the investigation of his living relatives, and it corrupts the blood of those yet to be born. (Pp. 441–442)

Now, Guevara is writing these last words in answer to an Italian gentleman who had sought to implicate Fray Antonio in the disappearance of a vial of perfume. But we can hardly believe that this is the kind of offense that would destroy a family's reputation retrospectively and proleptically. Guevara's broader and deeper meaning—his condemnation of irrational intolerance—is more apparent against the background of an earlier remark to his Italian accuser: "I, sir, am determined to pay no attention to your insult, nor to respond with anger to your letter, for I take much more pride in the religious order I belong to than in the pure blood of my ancestors . . ." (p. 440).

Alonzo de Orozco, in his *Victory of Death,* proclaims:

> O sinner, you who go lost and wandering through the sea of life! Do you want to know why every passion stirs you and draws you after it? The reason is that you forget death, because it seems to you that you are immortal . . . In the dead man's house there is the only true philosophy . . . , but in the gatherings of the living they speak of other people's lives, and not being content to speak ill of the living, they engage in a greater cruelty: they disinter the dead, with great offense to God and infamy to those who died. (P. 136 n. 7)

It is scarcely necessary to mention that the dead alluded to here are the ancestors of New Christians, or that the disinterring of the dead is an analogue of the inquisitorial practice of exhuming and burning the mortal remains of discovered secret Jews. In 1580—as C. R. Boxer has noted—the remains of the great pioneer of tropical medicine, Garcia d'Orta, "were exhumed and solemnly burned in an auto de fe held at Goa, in accordance with the posthumous punishment inflicted on crypto-Jews who had escaped the stake in their lifetime" (p. 11). For the Judeo-Christian Mateo Alemán, those who dug for this kind of information were like hyenas "who nourish themselves on the dead bodies they disinter" (1:48). Through the animal imagery Alemán communicated what Stephen Gilman called the full horror of inquisitorial dehumanization (p. 179). Juan de Zabaleta observed that "the malicious curiosity of men is so penetrating that it perceives blemishes in the bones of those who lie buried" (p. 247). And Gracián—writing with aphoristic density—recommends that "one should not be in life a book of vital statistics, an archive of genealogies and family traditions, for to concern oneself with the infamy in other people's lives is usually an indication of one's own tainted reputation. . . ." "In such matters," he concludes, "the one who digs the deepest will be most covered with mud," for which reason one must avoid at all costs "the effort to be a walking registry of others' ignominy, which is to be, though alive, like a soulless and despised public record of the Inquisition's trials and convictions" (p. 85 no. 125). In Quevedo's *Buscón*, don Pablillos's mother is imprisoned by the Inquisition of Toledo "because she disinterred corpses," but not because she did it in order to know other people's lives or to destroy a reputation by discovering some trace of Jewish blood, as an inquisitor in her own right, but because, as a witch with tainted blood no less, she literally disinterred freshly buried bodies, so that "in her house were found more legs, arms, and heads than in a shrine for miracles" (p. 94). The meaning of "to know other people's lives," then, in all these contexts and any number of others that could be cited, tells us something about the inquisitorial bent of the world in which Cervantes lived while writing *Don Quixote*, a world in which these words from *La Celestina* had disastrous validity: "When you tell someone your secret, your freedom is gone" (p. 57). In Cervantes's *Colloquy of the Dogs*, Cipión suggests to his friend Berganza that they should take turns relating their lives, "because it will be better to spend the time in telling their own lives than in *delving into the lives of others.*" At another point, while discussing police officers and notaries, Cipión observes that not all notaries are corrupt, "for there are many notaries who are good, faithful, law-abiding, and eager to please without harming anybody; for not all of them extend lawsuits, or advise both parties, or pocket more than what they're entitled to; nor do they go searching and *prying into other people's lives* to put them under suspicion with the law [or the Inquisition]."

In another vein, but even closer to my subject, are these words spoken yet again by Cipión, who knows something about the difficulties of finding a decent job:

> The lords of the earth are very different from the Lord of Heaven. The former, before they accept a servant, first examine his lineage as if they were looking for fleas, then they scrutinize his qualifications and even wish to know what clothes he has. But to enter God's service the poorest is the richest, the humblest is the man of most exalted lineage, and so long as he sets out to serve him with purity of heart [not of blood], God orders his name to be written in his wage-book and assigns him such rich rewards that in number and excellence they surpass all his desires.

"All this, friend Cipión, is preaching," says Berganza, and of course it is. But it was a sermon that Moorish dogs (*perros moros*) barked and Jewish pigs (*marranos judíos*) squealed, that New Christians and even some Old Christians preached, with the hope of achieving in Spain an open society, that kind of society which—in the words of the spiritual New Christian Henri Bergson—"is deemed in principle to embrace all humanity. A dream dreamt, now and again, by chosen souls, it embodies on every occasion something of itself in creations, each of which, through a more or less far-reaching transformation of man, conquers difficulties hitherto unconquerable" (p. 251).

In Hispanic terms it was a utopian dream that a neutral society might awake from the nightmare of history, offering neutral spaces and public places where the descendants of Moors, Christians, and Jews might mingle civilly and socially, a social system in which differences in culture made no difference in society, so that different peoples could survive and flourish in and through their differences. But what was to prevail in its place was the messianic dream of the Hispano-Christians expressed in the words of Hernando de Acuña: "una grey y un pastor, solo en el suelo," "*One* flock and *one* shepherd, *alone* on earth."

Before looking at the positive aspects of knowing other people's lives as portrayed in *Don Quixote,* let me provide a few more examples of the oppressive aspects of the phenomenon. Let us hear a brief anecdote that appears in two Lope de Vega plays and in the *Segunda parte de la vida de Lazarillo de Tormes* by Juan de Luna.

In Lope's *Mirad a quién alabáis* (Look at Whom You're Praising), we read:

A Jewish swindler and cheat,
one of those that abound in the world,
had a pear tree whose fruit
he praised to one and all.
Its renown spread so far and wide
that an official of the Inquisition
sent a page of his to request
a bowl of the pears that he had grown.
The Jew became greatly alarmed
for, though it was cold weather at the time,
the slightest fear seemed to set him ablaze
[recalling, of course, the flames of the
Inquisition]. So, he put an ax to its trunk
and when at last he saw it fall,
in order to have no further cause for fear,
he sent the tree itself to the Inquisitor.

(Pp. 42b–43a)

Juan de Luna wrote:

> About this point (even though it lies outside of what I am dealing with
> now) I will tell of something that occurred to a farmer from my region.
> It happened that an inquisitor sent for him, to ask for some of his pears,
> which he had been told were absolutely delicious. The poor country fellow
> didn't know what his lordship wanted of him, and it weighed so heavily
> on him that he fell ill until a friend of his told him what was wanted. He
> jumped out of bed, ran to his garden, pulled up the tree by the roots, and
> sent it along with the fruit, saying that he didn't want anything at his house
> that would make his lordship send for him again. People are so afraid
> of them—and not only laborers and the lower classes, but lords and
> grandees—that they all tremble more than leaves on trees when a soft,
> gentle breeze is blowing, when they hear these names: Inquisitor, Inqui-
> sition. (P. 693)

Finally, in a play of doubtful authenticity, *En los indicios la culpa* (Evidence Confirms Guilt), attributed to Lope de Vega, we find the following version of the anecdote:

There was once an *hidalgo*
who had a most fragrant
orange tree. One day it
occurred to someone to send
a messenger to him for
a sprig of orange blossom.
The one who was to deliver the message

did not find the *hidalgo* at home.
So, in order not to remain there,
since the dinner hour was at hand
and he was already tired of waiting,
he left word with the *hidalgo*'s wife
on behalf of Mr. So-and-So,
the inquisitor, that an employee of
the Holy Office had come to see him.
Scarcely had the *hidalgo* been
informed of the message
when he became so violently ill
that he could not even swallow a morsel of food.
He mulled over and over again in his mind
with prolix detail all that
he had ever said and done from his birth
to the present moment.
And learning finally what the messenger
had come for and that he would probably
return for more, if the whim were
to strike the inquisitor again,
the *hidalgo* exclaimed:
"By God, I swear that he'll have
no further reason to return to this house!"
And he sent the orange tree to him.

(P. 288a)

Let us examine the major difference in the elaboration of the three
texts in order to grasp its implications for a more meaningful apprecia-
tion of each version. The central figure in *Mirad a quién alabáis* is a Jew.
In *En los indicios la culpa*, the brunt of the joke is an *hidalgo*. In Luna's
sequel to *Lazarillo de Tormes*, however, the victim of the Inquisitor's un-
intentional, unconscious threat to his very existence is a *labrador*, a *pobre
villano*, "a farmer, a pitiful peasant."

We have, then, three different levels of Spanish society represented
in the texts at hand: (1) a Jew, (2) a member of the lesser nobility,
undoubtedly an *hidalgo cansado*, a convert of recent vintage, and (3) a
farmer, a representative of that mythical group of quintessential Old
Christians, the last vestige of pure blood on Hispanic soil. In these three
figures we have the basic components, the fratricidal antagonists, of the
civil war that raged on in Spain throughout the sixteenth and seventeenth centuries. By the time that Lope was writing for the theater the
Jew was only a phantasmagorical presence in his land, an imaginary

threat to the catholic unity of the Spanish faith. The *hidalgo*, however, was a daily irritant to the average Spaniard, a stimulant for envy and resentment, an ideal scapegoat for pent-up frustrations and unfulfilled ambitions; he was the inevitable victim, the perfect object of scorn and derision, whose tainted blood was an ineradicable stigma.

Now, why would Juan de Luna change the main character of the anecdote from a Jew or an *hidalgo* to a peasant? It is not difficult to suggest a reasonable justification for the change. That a Jew or convert should fear the proximity of an inquisitor or the interest of some Inquisition authority in his possessions, however innocuous that interest might seem, is hardly novel or unexpected. The aesthetic delight provided by the incident derives precisely from the reinforcement of a shared truth. However, that a peasant, a farmer, should fear the mere presence of an inquisitor is an overwhelming indictment of an institution whose supposed function was to assure the religious purity and orthodoxy of an entire nation. Thus, the psychic pleasure afforded by Juan de Luna's text is of a very different order. He was a violent enemy of the Inquisition, perhaps a *converso* himself, and he wrote from bitterly resented exile in France. He must have found it enormously satisfying to present a peasant—not a Jew or even someone of mixed blood—as a quaking coward, for it enabled him to demonstrate with insidious subtlety that no one in Spain was beyond the reach of the arbitrary and unpredictable injustice of the Holy Office.

In the conclusion to his interlude *El retablo de las maravillas* (The Wonder Show), Cervantes showed the lunacy of a peasant community that assumed an army quartermaster had to be a coward simply because, as they all mistakenly believed, he was of Jewish ancestry, *ex illis*, "one of them" (p. 123). With vengeful genius Juan de Luna chose to make a peasant, the very symbol of Old Christianity, a coward. In the process, he revealed how all people in Spain—even lords and grandees—tremble when they hear the words *inquisitor* and *Inquisition*. Lope de Vega, faithful to the stereotypical presentation of the cowardly Jew and tainted hidalgo, made now one, now the other, the victim of a joke meant to amuse the Old Christian majority in his audience. And yet, his great gift for artistic empathy enabled him to present, even within the skeletal frame of an anecdote, the sense of anguish experienced by the hidalgo as he rehearsed in his mind a life's words and deeds—words and deeds, even a blemished birth, that might be considered heretical and could soon be the raw materials of a prolonged and painful inquisitional trial.

From three versions of a simple anecdote I have teased a series of details that help us to experience yet again how the Inquisition—that bastion of un-Christlike Christianity—destroyed the pluralist paradise that Spain might have been.

And now let us look at the theme of knowing other people's lives in *Don Quixote,* surely one of those creations alluded to by Bergson, which, "through a more or less far-reaching transformation of man, conquers difficulties hitherto unconquerable." That the subject is present in *Don Quixote* as a kind of commonplace of the period is immediately apparent from the following references. In the opening verses of Part 1, humorously attributed to "Urganda the unknown," we find this advice:

> Keep to the business at hand
> and don't stick your nose into other people's
> lives.

Sancho insists that he is not "one to pry into other people's lives" (p. 201) and Don Diego de Miranda, the Gentleman in the Green Coat, asserts: "I do not enjoy scandal and do not allow any in my presence. I do not pry into my neighbors' lives, nor do I spy on other men's actions" (p. 567). Finally, Doña Rodríguez informs Sancho that "squires are our enemies; for seeing that they are imps of the antechambers and watch us at every turn, such times as they are not praying—and those are many—they spend in gossiping about us, disinterring our bones and interring our good names" (p. 712).

What now remains to be done is to show the unique and genial utilization of the concept in *Don Quixote,* the way in which the shopworn maxim about *knowing other people's lives* was infused with a new and revolutionary force, to contrast with the ominously inquisitional overtones that echoed in the texts I have just been citing.

If Américo Castro impressed anything on readers of *Don Quixote,* it was his position that Cervantes conceived of literary creation as the re-creation of a creative process of life, of life in the making, life unencumbered by what might be called hereditary determinism. Avalle-Arce brilliantly exemplified Castro's view in his analysis of the novel's opening paragraph, which he compared to the initial pages of *Lazarillo de Tormes* and *Amadís de Gaula,* in order to demonstrate the extraordinary freedom of the Cervantine hero. But whereas both Castro and Avalle stressed the reasons for Don Quixote's freedom and the open, undetermined nature of his future, I should like to examine what he was freed *from,* and how it prepares us for the attitude toward other people's lives that will prevail throughout the work, though more prominently in Part 1.

In a sense, the first paragraph of *Don Quixote* is more important for what it does not tell us than for the paradigmatic, illusorily specific, yet ultimately deindividualizing details about the hidalgo's life that it does present; for the narrator has *chosen* to omit precisely those details that were most crucial to that scrutiny of other people's lives I have just been describing. Let us consider the novel's first two paragraphs:

> In a certain village in La Mancha, which I do not wish to name, there lived not long ago a gentleman—one of those who have always a lance in the rack, an ancient shield, a lean hack and a greyhound for coursing. His habitual diet consisted of a stew, more beef than mutton, of hash most nights, bacon and eggs on Saturdays, lentils on Fridays, and a young pigeon as a Sunday treat; and on this he spent three-quarters of his income. The rest of it went on a fine cloth doublet, velvet breeches and slippers for holidays, and a homespun suit of the best in which he decked himself on weekdays. His household consisted of a housekeeper of rather more than forty, a niece not yet twenty, and a lad for the field and market, who saddled his horse and wielded the pruninghook.
>
> Our gentleman was verging on fifty, of tough constitution, lean-bodied, thin-faced, a great early riser, and a lover of hunting. They say that his surname was Quixada or Quesada—for there is some difference of opinion amongst authors on this point. However, by very reasonable conjecture we may take it that he was called Quexana. But *this does not much concern our story*; enough that we do not depart by so much as an inch from the truth in the telling of it. (P. 31)

Where was he born, what was his lineage, who are the ancestors we can investigate, inform on, scrutinize, disinter; what, even, was his family name? And we are told that these details, the indispensable material *to know other people's lives*, the central concern of generations of Spaniards in their literature and lives, is *not* of much importance to our story. And so Don Quixote is not only free in the Castronian sense to become himself, to realize his full being, but he has been freed of the fear and inhibitions provoked by that infamy that endures forever, the infamy of tainted blood that Fray Luis de León railed against in *The Names of Christ*, when he wrote: "A noble kingdom is one in which no vassal is considered of vile lineage, nor humiliated for his background, nor considered less well born than another. How can there be justice if some are despised and humiliated from generation to generation and the stigma is unending?" (p. 935). It is this freedom from inquisitional pressures that allows the vision of a Spain that might have been to emerge, a Spain in which the departure of Ricote's daughter from her village is depicted in the following manner by Sancho Panza:

> I can tell you that your daughter looked so beautiful when she went that everyone in the place came out to see her, and they all said she was the loveliest creature in the world. She departed weeping, and embraced all her friends and acquaintances and all who came to see her, begging everyone to commend her to Our Lord and Our Lady His Mother; and all this with such feeling that it brought tears to my eyes, and I'm not generally much of a weeper. There were many in fact who wanted to go out and capture her on the road and hide her away, but fear of breaking the king's decree prevented them. (P. 822)

Need I remind you that Ricote was a Morisco and that his daughter was leaving their village for exile? We have the feeling, though, that the Old Christian villagers loved her as much as the inhabitants of Burgos loved the Cid and feared to disobey King Alfonso's orders. Unlike the informers don Diego Coronel of the *Buscón* and Guzmán de Alfarache, Sancho will not betray his friend Ricote. "I will not betray you," says the authentic Christian to his Morisco friend. But he will not do treason against the King either, "to favor his enemies" (p. 821). "*His* enemies," says Sancho, not *mine*, but he does not dare to help Ricote, since he shares the villagers' fear of breaking the king's decree. And the happy ending of the episode of Ricote and his daughter is the wish-fulfilling dream of a Spain that—as Francisco Márquez has written—"instead of shedding their blood in sterile fratricidal strife, fused the blood of all Spain's children, laying aside the absurd and anti-Christian division between the pure and the tainted" (p. 335).

In this way, Don Quixote is free to face the future on his own terms, precisely because he has been freed of the unending threat involved in having a past. The specifics of his genealogy "are of little importance to our story" for the same reasons that Aldonza Lorenzo, alias Dulcinea, is lovely and virtuous, and her lineage does not matter a bit; "for no one will investigate it for the purpose of investing her with any [religious] order and, for my part"—says Don Quixote—"I think of her as the greatest princess in the world" (p. 210). For similar reasons Sancho could become a count, even if he were not an Old Christian. "I'm an Old Christian," affirms Sancho, "and that is enough ancestry for a count." This remark has been cited over and over again, when what really matters is Don Quixote's answer, in which he minimizes the significance of Sancho's Old Christian background: "And more than enough," responds Don Quixote, "but even if you were not [an Old

Christian] it would not matter, for if I am King I can easily make you noble . . ." (pp. 169–170). For Don Quixote, Sancho's Old Christian stock was as important for his becoming a count as—in Cervantes's interlude *The Wonder Show*—is a musician's being identified as "a very fine Christian and a well-bred hidalgo," in order to enhance his musicianship. The ironic reply is that "such qualities are essential indeed in a first-rate musician!" (p. 117). In the dream world of Don Quixote, lineage, purity of blood, Jewish or Moorish ancestry, meant nothing. There was no Inquisition and there were no relentless investigations.

Once Cervantes has insulated his novelistic world against the real and ever-present danger of an Inquisition-style scrutiny of other people's lives, it becomes possible for the work to be comic in the Bergsonian sense: "The comic comes into being [within a neutral zone in which man simply exposes himself to man's curiosity] . . . when society and the individual, freed from the worry of self-preservation, begin to regard themselves as works of art" (p. 73).

Unamuno was right when he noted that "Don Quixote was extremely curious and given *to prying into other people's lives*" (p. 90), but so were almost all the other characters in the work! What matters, of course, is what was behind the curiosity. From the moment of Don Quixote's encounter with the prostitutes, transformed through his persuasive will and art into Doña Tolosa and Doña Molinera, we are embarked on a seemingly endless number of encounters with people who will give up the secrets of their lives—or who will create marvelous fictional existences that resemble their own—with more or less artistry to satisfy the insatiable and beneficent curiosity of their listeners. Over and over again we come to recognize the special quality of knowing other people's lives in *Don Quixote,* the overwhelming delight that derives from entering into the lives of others and thereby living in another dimension. A few examples must suffice.

Having heard some of the details of Grisóstomo's tragic death, recounted by a young villager named Pedro, Don Quixote interrupts to observe that "it is a very good story, and you, my good Peter, are telling it with a fine grace" (p. 93). When Pedro concludes his remarks with an invitation to attend Grisóstomo's funeral, Don Quixote responds: "I will certainly be there, and I thank you for the pleasure you have given me by telling me such a delightful story" (p. 95).

When Zoraida and the Captain arrive at the inn—one of those Hispanic inns described by Angel Sánchez Rivero as "the crossroads of life . . . , more intimate than a modern hotel because of the primitive installations, the hazards of the road, the infrequency of travel, the generous cordiality of a group of people aware of danger and sensitive to adventure, all obliged to come together in a cramped and poorly lit space to tell one another their lives" (p. 13)—people can scarcely keep from asking them to tell their life story, "but no one cared to ask just then, for at that time it was clearly better to help them get some rest than to ask them for the story of their lives" (p. 338). After they have rested, "Don Fernando asked the Captain to tell them his life's story, for from what they had gathered by his coming in Zoraida's company, it could not fail to be strange and enjoyable" (p. 345). As in so many other cases throughout the work, we are made to feel the importance of the artistry involved, the histrionics in relating a life story as a source of pleasure and edification:

> Listen then, gentlemen, and you will hear a true story, and I doubt whether you will find its equal in the most detailed and careful fiction ever written.
> At these words they all sat down in perfect silence; and when he saw them quiet and waiting for him to speak, he began in a smooth and pleasant voice. (P. 345)

At the conclusion of the Captain's tale, Don Fernando gives voice to the audience's reaction:

> I assure you, Captain, that the way in which you have told your strange adventure has been as remarkable as the strangeness and novelty of the events themselves. It is a curious tale and full of astonishing incidents. In fact we have enjoyed listening so much that we should be glad to hear it all over again, even if it took till tomorrow morning to tell it. (P. 381)

Naturally the content of the narrated life is important; tragic events are to be lamented and joyous reunions celebrated, but what matters most is the willing suspension of belief in the Spain that really was, so as to enjoy to its fullest the parenthetical paradise of Art, offered up to us in these numerous portraits of characters as artists.

When the irresistible Dorotea completes her tale of woe, she is asked to provide some additional details:

> She told him, briefly and sensibly, all that she had previously told Cardenio; and Don Ferdinand and his companions were so delighted with her story that they would have liked it to last longer, so charmingly did she tell the tale of her misfortunes. (PP. 331–332)

As if to remind us of that other world where the scrutiny of people's lives is a sinister and venomous pursuit, there are chapters like the "Scrutiny of Don Quixote's Library," a small-scale model of an Inquisition trial, rich in the lexicon of such investigations, which ends with the heartless destruction of innocent victims. The text reads:

> Some [books] that were burnt deserved to be treasured up among the eternal archives, but fate and the laziness of the inquisitor forbade it. And so in them was fulfilled the saying that the saint sometimes pays for the sinner. (P. 64)

Unamuno, blind to the possible meanings of this chapter, refused to examine it, because "it deals with books and not with life" (p. 46). But however much the discussion of the books is conducted in aesthetic terms, ultimately we are forced to believe that these books, constantly described in human terms, are the Anne Franks of Cervantes's day, the innocent victims of whose beauty and genius we have been deprived through the indifference, the cruelty, if not the "laziness of the inquisitor": "The priest was too tired to look at any more books, and therefore proposed that the rest should be burned without further inspection" (p. 63). It is indeed ironic that an *escrutinio,* a scrutiny, an inquisition, should end on such a note, when Covarrubias tells us that *escudriñar* means "to look for something with excessive meticulousness, care and curiosity"; *escudriñador* "he who is curious to know secret things." He concludes, cryptically, that "there are men who are tempted to find out what others have locked up in their breasts and at times what God has concealed in his own" (p. 543a).

In direct contrast with the Inquisition-like proceedings of the scrutiny made in Don Quixote's library is the knight's encounter with the galley slaves and his insistence—due to the infinite care and humanity in his notion of justice—that each galley slave be discreetly and sympathetically examined, since it is "better for ninety-nine guilty to escape than for one innocent person to be wrongfully condemned." Ginés de Pasamonte, a galley slave who knows the dangers that lurk behind the scrutiny of other people's lives—Lope de Vega's "new mode of scrutiny"—and has learned to be wary of such interrogations, tells Don Quixote "you annoy me with all your *prying into other people's lives*" (p. 176). And these words, which—in the interpretation of Ginés and the intention of Don Quixote—exemplify the collusion of the real world with a utopian Spain, suggest yet another dimension to Don Quixote, one more way to enjoy and appreciate the genius of Cervantes.

In 1973 the Nobel Prize-winning German novelist Heinrich Böll was asked: "How do you think a novel about Germany in the 1930s would differ from the idea that most people have of it?" His reply was:

It would be at the same time both worse and better than the propaganda was. If you imagine that children would really give the names of their parents to the police for political offenses, it is terrible. There's really a Shakespearean tragedy behind such a small fact. Reading it as a note in the press, you wouldn't get that. It would be a terrible fact, but you would forget about it. Yet out of that fact a writer can make a very informative and true novel, one that is much more important than nonfiction. What is behind it is up to me, my imagination and my experience of the time.

And, paradoxically, literature makes it possible for us to enjoy, to derive pleasure as well as information and edification from reading and experiencing in an imaginatively insulated setting—the protective privacy of a book, the communal comfort of a theater, the womb-like intimacy of a darkened movie house—the suffering and persecution of others as well as their joys and satisfactions.

Having mentioned suffering and persecution, I should like to close with some general observations, particularly since a distinguished Hispanist claimed some years ago that "as many as ninety-nine out of every hundred conversos lived unmolested by the Inquisition," as if in some paradisiacal sanctuary. (Can one live "unmolested"—even psychically unmolested—with the potential threat of persecution always at hand?) Sister Marie Despina recently wrote in a moving essay entitled "The Accusations of Ritual Crime in Spain" that one is amazed by the similarities between the procedures of the Spanish Inquisition and those of the Russian Gulag, the similar treatment of the accused, overwhelmed by terror, torture, and utter despair (pp. 61–62). In a statement characteristic of any number of references to the oppressively negative effects of the Inquisition on Hispanic life, the great Argentine statesman and author Domingo F. Sarmiento declared that

> the crime of the Inquisition is to have destroyed in daily practice and in one's intimate feelings the notion of human rights, the sense of security of life before the law, the awareness of justice, the limits of public power ... Since crimes of the mind cannot be determined by a law or code, the Spaniard and the Hispanic American lived [because of the Inquisition] under the fear of possibly committing a crime by thinking. (P. 184)

In her book on *The Conversos of Majorca*, Angela Selke reminds us that

> in stressing the terrible injustice which the Holy Office committed by persecuting and punishing *innocent* people, there is an implicit justification of such persecutions provided they are based on true accusations and verified

evidence. Yet such an attitude tends to obscure what today [we recognize and accept]—that is, the fundamental injustice of all persecutions for dissident beliefs, be the charges true or false. . . . [We] must reject as contrary to Christian ethics not only the abuses of the Inquisition or its proceedings, but, above all, the radical injustice inherent in any institution whose business—whatever its professed purpose may have been—[is] the systematic organization of such persecutions. (P. 19)

Like many New Christians, Cervantes dreamed of a Spain that might have been, recognizing that its fulfillment was impossible. The visionary religious syncretism that the Moriscos of Granada strove to achieve, certain that every individual could be saved under the law of Christ, under that of the Jew, and that of the Moor, if he kept the precepts of his religion faithfully; the unified kingdom of heaven on earth which the New Christians struggled vainly to establish in Spain; the mythical Golden Age of ideal justice which Don Quixote imagined he could restore, can best be summed up in these words of Wallace Stevens:

> He had to choose. But it was not a choice
> Between excluding things. It was not a choice
> Between, but of. He chose to include the things
> That in each other are included, the whole,
> The complicate, the amassing harmony.
>
> (P. 124)

The majority of Spaniards in the retrospectively halcyon years of Spain's artistic Golden Age chose, through the Inquisition, to renounce the opportunities for "amassing harmony," and to this day Spain has endured the consequences of that tragic choice.

* This essay is for Robert Silverman, who taught me to appreciate the beauty and power of words.

Unforeseen circumstances have made it impossible for me to provide the footnotes I had planned to include. Unless otherwise indicated in the list of works cited, the translations are my own.

WORKS CITED

Alemán, Mateo. *Guzmán de Alfarache,* edited by Samuel Gili y Gaya. 5 vols. *Clásicos castellanos,* vols. 73, 83, 90, 93, 114. Madrid: Espasa-Calpe, 1942–1950.

Anonymous. *The Life of Lazarillo de Tormes,* translated by Harriet de Onís. Great Neck, N.Y.: Barron's Educational Series, 1959.

Avalle-Arce, Juan Bautista. "Tres comienzos de novela." In *Nuevos deslindes cervantinos.* Barcelona: Ariel, 1975.

Bergson, Henri. "Laughter." In *Comedy,* edited by Wylie Sypher. Garden City, N.Y.: Doubleday, 1956.

Boxer, C. R. *Two Pioneers of Tropical Medicine: Garcia d'Orta and Nicolás Monardes. Diamante,* vol. 14. London: The Hispanic and Luso-Brazilian Councils, 1963.

Cervantes, Miguel de. *The Adventures of Don Quixote,* translated by J. M. Cohen. Harmondsworth: Penguin Books, 1950. Translation slightly revised.

———. *The Colloquy of the Dogs.* In *Six Exemplary Novels,* translated by Harriet de Onís, 3:12–13. Great Neck, N.Y.: Barron's Educational Series, 1961. Translations slightly revised.

———. ———. In *The Deceitful Marriage and Other Exemplary Novels,* translated by Walter Starkie, 249, 258, 276. New York: New American Library, 1963. Translations slightly revised.

———. ———. In *Exemplary Stories,* translated by C. A. Jones, 197, 204–205, 220. Harmondsworth: Penguin Books, 1972. Translations slightly revised.

———. *El retablo de las maravillas.* In *Interludes,* translated by Edwin Honig. New York: New American Library, 1964. Translation slightly revised.

Covarrubias, Sebastián de. *Tesoro de la lengua castellana o española,* edited by Martín de Riquer. Barcelona: Horta, 1943.

Despina, Sor Marie. "Las acusaciones de crimen ritual en España." *El olivo* (Madrid) 3, no. 9 (1979): 48–70.

Gilman, Stephen. "The Sequel to *El villano del Danubio.*" *Revista Hispánica Moderna* 31 (1965): 175–185.

Gracián, Baltasar. *Oráculo manual y arte de prudencia,* edited by Arturo del Hoyo. Madrid: Castilla, 1948.

Guevara, Fray Antonio de. *Menosprecio de corte y alabanza de aldea,* edited by M. Martínez de Burgos. *Clásicos castellanos,* vol. 29. Madrid: Ediciones de "La Lectura," 1928.

———. *Libro primero de las Epístolas familiares,* edited by José María de Cossío. Vol. 2. Madrid: Aldus, 1952.

León, Fray Luis de. *De los nombres de Cristo,* edited by Federico de Onís. Vol. 2. Madrid: Espasa-Calpe, 1917. Material adapted and reduced.

Luna, Juan de. *Segunda parte de la vida de Lazarillo de Tormes.* In *La Celestina y Lazarillos,* edited by Martín de Riquer. Barcelona: Vergara, 1959.

Márquez Villanueva, Francisco. *Personajes y temas del Quijote.* Madrid: Taurus, 1975.

———. "Crítica guevariana." *Nueva Revista de Filología Hispánica,* 28 (1979): 334–352.

Orozco, Alonso de. *Victoria de la muerte.* Cited in Américo Castro, *An Idea of History,* edited by Stephen Gilman and Edmund L. King. Columbus: Ohio State University Press, 1977. The translation by Carroll Johnson is slightly revised.

Quevedo, Francisco de. *El buscón,* edited by Américo Castro. *Clásicos castellanos,* vol. 5. Madrid: Ediciones de "La Lectura," 1927.

Rojas, Fernando de. *The Spanish Bawd: La Celestina*, translated by J. M. Cohen. Baltimore: Penguin Books, 1964.

Sánchez Rivero, Angel. "Las ventas del Quijote." *Revista de Occidente*, año 5, vol. 17, no. 46 (1927): 1–22.

Sarmiento, Domingo F. *Conflicto y armonías de las razas en América*. Buenos Aires: "La Cultura Argentina," 1915. Cited by Daniel E. Zalazar, "Las ideas de D. F. Sarmiento sobre la influencia de la religión en la democracia americana." *Discurso Literario*, 2 (1985): 541–548.

Selke, Angela S. *The Conversos of Majorca: Life and Death in a Crypto-Jewish Community in XVII Century Spain*, translated by Henry J. Maxwell. Hispania Judaica, vol. 5. Jerusalem: Magnes Press, Hebrew University, 1986.

Stevens, Wallace. "Notes toward a Supreme Fiction." In *Selected Poems*. London: Faber and Faber, 1960.

Unamuno, Miguel de. *Vida de Don Quijote y Sancho*. Colección Austral, vol. 33. Madrid: Espasa-Calpe, 1949.

Vega, Lope de. *En los indicios la culpa*. In *Obras de Lope de Vega, publicadas por la Real Academia Española* (nueva edición), vol. 5. Madrid: Tipografía de la "Revista de Archeologia, Bibliografia y Museos," 1918.

———. *Mirad a quién alabáis*. In *Obras de Lope de Vega, publicadas por la Real Academia Española* (nueva edición), vol. 13. Madrid: Imprenta de Galo Saez, 1930.

———. *El niño inocente de La Guardia*, edited by Anthony J. Farrell. London: Tamesis Books, 1985.

Zabaleta, Juan de. *El día de fiesta por la mañana*, edited by María Antonia Sanz Cuadrado. Madrid: Castilla, 1948.

TEN

Scorched Parchments and Tortured Memories: The "Jewishness" of the Anussim (Crypto-Jews)

Moshe Lazar

If a man abide not in me, he is cast forth as a branch and is withered; and men gather them and cast them into the fire, and they are burned. [JOHN 15:6]

I enter this house [i.e., church], I will worship neither wood nor stone, but only God who governs the universe.
[*Converso's* silent act of faith]

Inquisitors and inquisitorial institutions initiate their pious enterprise with the burning of manuscripts and books to forcibly halt the dissemination of beliefs contrary to their own dogmas. Failing to eradicate the faith and ritual practices of the "non-believers," stigmatized as heretics, they then resort to mental and physical torture most often leading to conversion. Those accused of being "false converts," stubborn and secret adherents to their earlier beliefs, are destined to burn at the stake, ironically qualified as an auto de fe, an "act of faith." The burning of books is often therefore a classical prelude to the burning of people.

The road that leads from the burning of more than twelve thousand volumes of the Talmud (Paris, 1243), and innumerable Hebrew biblical and parabiblical manuscripts during the subsequent centuries, and to the lighting of the autos de fe is the *via dolorosa* of medieval European Jewry and its descendants, the Anussim in Spain, Portugal, Brazil, Peru, Mexico, and elsewhere.[1] In the thousands of trial records, which the Holy Office of the Inquisition has left as its enduring legacy, lay buried nightmarish chapters in the lives of men and women among the Anussim, from whose memories the torturers have extracted and transcribed religious practices and utterances as evidence of their secret Judaizing. These carefully elaborated minutes of the trial proceedings endlessly record what sort of rituals the Anussim were accused of practicing (mainly presented in the depositions of the prosecution's witnesses) and the kind of prayers they were reciting daily or on certain Jewish holidays (particularly recorded in the confessions of the accused). It is possible therefore, even from the partially published trial records as well as from other sources, to present a synthetic overview on the continuity of "Jewishness" and Jewish religious devotion among a large number of Anussim over a period of several centuries.

This very continuity of retaining a hidden religious Jewish life, based on a set of customs and rituals, and strengthened by prayers, by biblical and postbiblical reminiscences, and by yearnings for a messianic deliverance has been questioned by some scholars[2] in a manner that is contradicted by the historical evidence of various sources.

Communities of Anussim in Spain, between 1391 (a year of widespread assaults on the juderías and of mass conversions) and 1492 (the year of Expulsion), living amidst or beside those Jews who did not convert, certainly had different opportunities to preserve their hidden "Jewishness" in comparison with the Anussim of Portugal after 1497 (where all the Jews were forcibly converted)—even more so after the horrible massacre in Lisbon (1506)[3]—and in comparison with those of Spain after 1492. While the Anussim of Spain between 1391 and 1492 maintained close contacts with those who lived openly as Jews and had no major difficulties in obtaining prayer books, biblical, rabbinical, and Jewish-philosophical texts,[4] special ritual objects, and kosher food products, the Anussim of Portugal were more dependent on their memory and oral transmission, on symbolic observance of traditional rituals, and on occasional contacts during business trips with former Anussim now living as Jews in Italy and the Netherlands.[5] These latter Anussim, many of them educated now in convents and monasteries, submitted to the teaching and the preaching of the friars, and had the opportunity to learn a great deal about Judaism, Jewish history, biblical prophecy, and theology excerpted in the literature of the Fathers of the Church and in the anti-Jewish polemical treatises; they could read in the missals, psalms, and other hymns derived from ancient synagogal liturgy; for generations they learned about their patriarchs from Villegas's *Flos Sanctorum*; and whatever details they ignored concerning specific Jewish customs, they were introduced to them in the cellars of the Inquisition, learning from both the inquisitors and the confessions of the "Judaizers" the traditional list of Judaizing practices.[6] Beinart's statement concerning the conversos of Ciudad Real during the fifteenth century is appropriate also to the Anussim of later periods:

And though the memory and knowledge of mitzvoth [religious commandments] became increasingly blurred as the generations went by, and Mosaic laws were the first to be forgotten, customs and traditions nevertheless remained in the Conversos' memory and were handed down for centuries from generation to generation. Furthermore, for as long as the Inquisition courts existed, the inquisitors were always there to remind the Conversos of what Jewish tradition was, and to revive their memories of Judaism.[7]

In the Inquisition's cellars in Lima for some twelve years (1627–1639), Francisco Maldonado de Silva, shortly before his death at the stake, composed a letter destined for the Jewish community in Rome, writing that he had a solid knowledge of the Prophets,

> . . . et memoriter teneo omnes praedictiones promissionum Dei nostri per ipsos et deprecationes illorum pro populo suo Israel omnesque psalmos David absque nulla exceptione, proverbia multa Salomonis et [eius] filii Sirach, et plurimas orationes tam idiomate Hispano quam Latino a me compositas, sed horum maiorem partem in hoc lacu inclusus didisci, quae omnia (scilicet orationes prophetarum et laudes et psalmos) singulis sabbatis absque libro repeto flexis genibus in conspectu Dei mei depraecans illum pro peccatis meis et populi sui si forte possim (licet indignus) placare furorem suum, ut salvet et congreget eum sicut per suos prophetas promisit. Ego quidem a die qua captus fui devovi illi mori pugnans argumentis viribus et posse propter veritatem eius et observare legem eius usque ad aras ignis qui mihi paratur in brevi (ut colligo) utque me in holocaustum pro peccatis nostris Deus suscipiat . . .[8]

[. . . and I know by heart all the predictions related to the promises of our God, revealed through them, and His deprecations in favor of his people Israel, as well as all the Psalms of David without exception, many Proverbs of Salomon and of his son Sirach, and many prayers in both Spanish and Latin versifications composed by me; but most of all these I have learned while confined in this [lion's] den; all these [i.e., the Prophets' prayers, the hymns and the psalms], without any book, I recite every Saturday, kneeling in the presence of God, supplicating Him for my own and His people's sins, in the hope I could (though unworthy) placate His wrath so that He may save and ingather his people as He has promised through his prophets. Verily, from the day I was arrested I vowed to fight to death, with my power and arguments, against the adversaries of His truth and to uphold His Law until the altar of fire being now (I think) prepared for me, so that God may accept me as a holocaust for our sins . . .]

While in prison, Francisco Maldonado de Silva held fourteen disputations with theologians and wrote a great number of essays and two longer works, signing them "Heli Judio, indigno del Dios de Israel, por otro nombre Silva." He was led to his auto de fe in Lima (January 1639) at the age of forty-nine; a friar describes his last moments as follows:

frail, gray-haired, long-bearded, and with the books he had written tied around his neck, when led to the fire the wind had ripped off the curtain behind the podium; seeing this, he exclaimed: "This has been so arranged by the Lord of Israel as to see me face to face from heaven!"[9]

Martyrs such as Luis de Carvajal (el Mozo), Maldonado de Silva, and José de Silva, like hundreds before them during the Middle Ages, went to the stake sanctifying their monotheistic faith (*qiddush ha-Shem*), and imitating the martyrology of the ten celebrated rabbis (*'asarah harugey malkhuth*) which occupies a special place in ancient Jewish lore and in the traditional prayer books. One of these sages, Hanina ben Teradyon, we are told, had been draped in a Torah scroll by his persecutors and thrown into the fire. Seeing his daughter distressed, he said to her: "Were I to be burning alone, it would be dreadful to me; now that I am in the fire with the Torah around me, whoever will avenge the honor of the Torah will at the same time avenge mine." His disciples asked: "Rabbi, what do you see?" And he replied: "Burning scrolls, I see, and letters rising in the air."

Contrary to those scholars who doubt the degree of "Jewishness" of the Anussim, the source materials and the sprouting of new communities of former Anussim in Italy, the Netherlands, and the Ottoman Empire present a reality which shows that their "Jewishness" was more than a bundle of vague memories. Yerushalmi rightly therefore states that

> the yearning which impelled them to seek the God of Israel in Amsterdam, Venice, or Constantinople remains difficult to understand unless there existed a continuing crypto-Jewish tradition in the Peninsula itself. If, between one hundred and two hundred years after the extinction of the last vestiges of organized Jewish life in Spain and Portugal, this force was still strong enough to graft these withered branches back onto the trunk of the Jewish people, it must have been considerable.[10]

Concerning the oral transmission among the Portuguese Anussim and, in particular, the important role played by the women, Revah writes:

> In this continuous or discontinuous transmission of marranism two social groups performed a decisive role: the family milieu and the professional or university milieu. The women have greatly contributed to the perpetuation of marranism, often behind the back of their husbands: they figure also in greater numbers than men in the autos de fe. Marranism was a simplified religion which ignored hierarchy. Its articles of faith and its essential practices were perpetuated not only through the clandestine oral

transmission but also through the constant harassment by the inquisitorial persecution.[11]

A confirmation of this role played by women in the preservation of "Jewishness" among the Anussim is already clearly articulated in a letter written (1481?) by Fernando del Pulgar (of converso origin himself): "In Andalusia there are at least ten thousand young women who have never left their parents' home. They observe the ways of their fathers and learn from them. To burn them all is an extremely cruel and difficult act and will force them to flee to places where their correction will be impossible."[12] During his trial in the Canary Islands, Antonio Correa Núñez relates how his grandmother had initiated him at age thirteen to Judaism:

> In this book [Psalms?], he will be able to see all what God did to David and to those who kept the Law God gave to Moses. Through guarding this Law and its ceremonies he will attain the merits King David and all the other attained. By fulfilling the commandments he will receive God's blessing; not keeping them he will be cursed by God.[13]

The women's role as activists in the dissemination of Jewish customs and prayers,[14] and their outstanding courage in proclaiming their faith and accepting martyrdom at the stake,[15] are corroborated during the centuries by the trial records from Portugal, the Canary Islands, Mexico, Peru, and Brazil,[16] as well as by the testimonies from a community of "New Christians" rediscovered in this century by S. Schwartz in Belmonte, Portugal.[17] Even at the time that Anussim came out from their schizophrenic existence and returned to open Jewish life, Rabbi Yom Tob Zahalon (in a *responsa*) expressed his admiration for the stature and quality, among the Portuguese Anussim, of the women amidst them, "from whom Torah and Judaism shall yet go forth!"[18]

The knowledge of traditions and rituals was also preserved through smuggling in from abroad books printed in Italy and the Netherlands, especially during the sixteenth and seventeenth centuries.[19] But even before that time, information was available from books hidden in wells, buried in gardens, secretly kept inside walls, or acquired from Christians who had snatched them from the flames.[20]

To put this in its proper historical context, let us follow Rabbi Abraham Saba's description of his flight from his hometown during the tragic events of 1497 in Portugal:

> Then the anger of the Lord burnt against his people, so that all the Jews who were in Portugal were ordered by King Emmanuel (God blot out his

name and memory!) to leave the land. Nor was this enough; but after the king had commanded that boys and girls should be torn [from their parents for baptism and Christian education], and then we should be deprived of our synagogues, he ordered that all our books should be seized. So I brought all my books into the city of Porto in obedience to the royal decree; but yet I took my life in my hands by carrying with me to Lisbon the Commentary on the Law which I had composed, as well as a commentary on the treatise Ethics of the Fathers, and one on the Five Scrolls . . . . But when I reached Lisbon all the Jews came to me and told me that it had been proclaimed to the community that every Jew who might be found with a book or with philacteries in his possession would be put to death. So straightaway, before I entered the quarter outside the city, I took these books in my hand; two brothers went with me and dug a grave among the roots of a blossoming olive tree; there we buried them. . . . Tree of Sorrow, for I had buried there all that was pleasant in my sight—the Commentary on the Laws and the Commandments, more precious than gold. . . . For in them I had found consolation for the loss of my two little ones, torn from me by force to become unwilling converts. And I had said: these [books] are the inheritance of those who worship God; therefore must they be better for me than even sons and daughters.[21]

Commenting upon this rabbi's dramatic description of losing his children to forced baptism and endangering his life in trying to save his own manuscripts, W. Popper writes: "Hidden in wells, buried among the roots of trees, snatched from the very flames, there were always some volumes saved. And as soon as the watchfulness of enemies became a little relaxed, these treasures were brought from their hiding-places; others were smuggled into the city from distant lands by various devices; and still others perhaps were bought from neighbors."[22] At the end of the fifteenth century, in Soria, a mason working in the home of Juan de Salzedo (formerly Rabbi Yantó [Yom Tob?]) discovered inside a hidden niche in a wall some scrolls in Hebrew which, according to his testimony at a trial, he refused to hand over to their owner, instead taking them home and burning them in his stove.[23] Several centuries later, in 1848, during the dismantling of an old house in the former *call* (Jewish Quarter) of Barcelona, three late-fifteenth-century manuscript prayer books in Catalan were discovered inside one of the walls, including one complete traditional Jewish Ritual of daily and holidays prayers, the two others being of a hybrid type (personalized prayers, somewhat spiritually Christianized), having belonged probably to a converso originally from Valencia.[24] The historian Caro Baroja remembers having seen in his childhood a leather-covered desk whose owner, while doing some repair work, uncovered two scrolls of Hebrew prayers hidden by some crypto-Jew.[25] One could multiply these cases to show that in spite of the burning of thousands of biblical and parabiblical manuscripts and books, the Anussim were able to procure for themselves over the centuries copies of Bibles, prayer books, commentaries on the Law, essays on Jewish history, and cabalistic and other mystical treatises to maintain their faith; and wherever those books were not available, they memorized a portable Judaism often transferred from scorched parchments and from inquisitorial sessions to their tortured souls.

Accusations against the Anussim, as well as their confessions, in Spain and Portugal and the New World, used customs and rituals to define them as Judaizers, or "Jews on all four sides" (judeus dos quatro costados) as some of them were called in Portugal. The collection of bits and pieces in the already published trial documents[26] corresponds to the thirty or more specific "Judaic" beliefs, practices, and customs by which a Judaizing converso could be detected (observance of one of them being sufficient to be brought before the Tribunal of the Holy Office). The list of these practices and customs was published time and again, the edict issued by the Seville inquisitors Morillo and San Martin in 1481 serving as the basic model for all subsequent promulgations. One may sum them up in the following groups:

1. sweep the house clean Friday afternoon; wear clean clothing and festive garments that evening and Saturday; bring out fresh linen and a white tablecloth for the occasion; cook the necessary meals for the Sabbath on Friday, keeping in the oven overnight a special dish [adafina, calyente, hamin];[27] abstain from work on Saturday;

2. light newly prepared candles on Friday before sunset; at dinner, make a blessing over a cup of wine (baraha, or baraha del vino) and have each family member drink from the same cup;

3. fast from sunset to sunset, particularly on the Day of Atonement (çinqepur, çonqipur [= tzom qippur: Fast of Yom Kippur]), on the eve of Purim (Ayuno de la Reina Esther [Ta'anith Esther: "Fast of Queen Esther"]);[28] and fast on Mondays and Thursdays;

4. ritual bathing of women on Friday afternoon, on the eve of fasting days, possibly in a special bathhouse [batibila, bet tebilah];

5. observance of special holidays, such as Passover (pascua del pan çençeño [hag ha-matzoth = "feast of the unleavened bread"]), which occurs at the time of "semana santa"; the feast of the Tabernacles (pascua de las cabañuelas), which occurs in the Fall;

6. reciting certain Jewish prayers such as Shema Yisrael Adonay

Elohenu, Adonay, Ehad ("Hear, o Israel, God our Lord, God is one"), or specific prayers when washing the hands,[29] when partaking at a meal, and so on;

7. praying in a "Jewish" fashion: facing the wall, standing rather than sitting or kneeling [related to prayers like the *amida*], cabdis [= *qaddish*], moving head, limbs, and body in a rhythmic manner (*sabadear*);[30]

8. bury or burn nail clippings, rather than throw them away;[31]

9. ritual slaughter of cattle and fowl, reciting some specific prayer during the process; covering the spilled blood with earth or ashes;

10. purifying the meat by cleansing it from any blood, salting and rinsing it; removing all fat, and the sinew from the animal's leg;[32]

11. abstaining from eating certain animals, birds, or fish considered as impure by the Mosaic law; eating therefore *manjares caseres* ("kosher food");[33]

12. observance of special funerary rites when mourning the dead (sitting on the ground, eating hard-boiled eggs and olives); pouring out the water from the jars [*cohuerco*], for fear that the soul of the departed might bathe in it);

13. when kneading bread, throw a piece of dough [*hala*] into the fire (a custom that was still preserved among the Anussim in Belmonte in this century);[34]

14. celebrating, on the eve of the eighth day following the birth of a male child (the night before the prescribed circumcision), with dancing and music [*hazer hadas*];[35]

15. when baptizing their children, rubbing off immediately the *crisma* (baptism);

16. read in books of prayers [*çidur, rezar en hebrayco, meldar como judio*][36] or other books on Jewish matters in Hebrew or in the vernacular [*libros judiegos*]; possess amulets with Hebrew inscriptions [*nomina escripta en hebrayco*],[37] and the like;

17. in church, acting hypocritically (not looking at the elevation of the Host, at the Cross; kneeling imperfectly; changing the Pater Noster; etc.).[38]

All these, and some others,[39] amply documented in all trials, testify to the permanence and widespread preservation of essential and symbolic rituals among the Anussim over many centuries. It is in the context of the accusations and confessions that one finds the greatest number of Hebrew words, particularly frequent in fifteenth- and sixteenth-century documents, such as: *baraha, varaha* (blessing); *baraha del vino* (blessing on wine); *baraha de la mesa* (blessing after meal); *Dio barohu* (for *barukh hu,* "blessed be He"); *trefa, trefe* ("non-kosher food"); *caser, caxer* ("kosher food"); *maror* ("bitter herbs"); *çedaca* ("alms, charity");[40] *çidur* ("prayer book" in Hebrew or vernacular); *çilhod, zelahod* (for *selihoth,* "penitential prayers"); *targun* (for *targum,* Aramaic translation of Pentateuch); *quidux* (blessing on the wine); *cabdis* (for *qaddish,* "mourner's prayer"); *guezera* ("edict" of Expulsion); *tafelines* (for *thefillin,* "phylacteries"); *çeçit* (generally for *talith,* "prayer shawl"); *çefer, çefer tora* ("parchment scroll of the Law"); *humas* ("Pentateuch"); *hevel, vanidad* ("vanity, Christian dogmas"); *çara* ("trouble, tribulation"); *quinyan* ("property"); *midras* (for *beth midrash,* "synagogue, school");[41] *tibila* ("ritual bath"), and *bitibila* ("house of the ritual bath"); and so on. Concerning the frequent use of euphemisms one may note: wood (for "cross"); bread ("Holy Host"); house ("church"); stone ("statue of Christ or saint"); stick ("wooden cross");[42] very good man ("practicing Judaizer"); servant of God ("of the Jewish faith"). Finally, it should also be noted that *Adonay* (rather than *Señor*), *Dio* (instead of *Dios*), and *meldar* (more than *leer*) are frequently used in fifteenth- and sixteenth-century documents as they are in parallel Judeo-Spanish texts after the Expulsion.

The depth and continuity of "Jewishness" of many Anussim may best be grasped through a comparison beween two testaments, written centuries apart, couched in a language that testifies to the profound roots of religiosity in both tortured souls. They reflect in content and in style a cleaving devotion to the faith and practices of Judaism. Don Juda (from Alba de Tormes) in 1410, two decades after the forced conversions of 1391, writes a long will from which I quote the following excerpt:

> I give thanks to the almighty Lord God who created the universe and governs us, who did not make me an animal and has kept me to this day in his commandments, for pious and noble is the man who in his last years and old age dies to start a new life—God willing—for I have always placed my hope in His love. And as I am dust and will return to dust, I desire not to be moaned and mourned; nor should you, doña Sol, act despondently, for I hold you in such esteem that should I give you a letter of divorce you would not accept it, as you have stated: "Were you to give me the letter [of divorce] I would refuse it, for your shoe is a firm warrant . . . of my heart";[43] and I would respond: "May it be God's will!" . . . Let my body be buried in the golden field where our parents are resting—God grant them everlasting peace . . . placed in the grave with my eyes and face looking eastward . . . At learning about my death in the Jewish quarters of Segovia

and Alba, where I was well loved by all my relatives, hoping for the same in the next world, let them say: "Alas, alas, the one who did good deeds has passed away!"[44]

Luis de Carvajal el Mozo, after some ten years in the Inquisition's cellars of New Spain, having changed his name to Joseph Lumbroso,[45] writes his final testament a short time before his anticipated auto de fe (December 1596), in which he states the ten principles of his mono-theistic creed, partly modeled after the "Thirteen Principles of Faith" of Maimonides (quoted by Luis in his discussion with two doctors of theology during his incarceration):

> I believe in the one and only God, almighty and true, Creator of heaven, earth, and sea . . . I believe that God our Lord and universal Creator is one and no more . . . I believe that the law of God our Lord, which the Christians call the dead law of Moses, is alive and everlasting, as recorded in the holy Pentateuch . . . The fourth belief of mine is that it is a sin to worship idols and images;[46] I believe that the Sacred Sacrament of Circumcision is eternal . . . I believe that Christ [literally "the anointed," as in Hebrew mashiah] the true Father of the future son, Prince of Peace, real son of David, possessor of the scepter of Judah has not arrived . . . I believe in what relates to the mysterious vision of the holy Daniel . . . Tenth:[47] I believe that King Antiochus, whom the Holy Scriptures called root of sin, because he was the persecutor of God's people and of His holy law, represents the kings of Spain and Portugal . . . from which originate the branches of the inquisitions and the persecutions of the blessed martyrs . . . true Jews [whom they call] Judaizing heretics. However, Judaizing is not heresy but is living according to the Commandments of God our Lord.

Luis de Carvajal concludes with a confession that sounds like a prayer recited on the Day of Atonement:

> I again swear, in the name of the Almighty, to live and die for His faith. May it please Him, so that, imitating the zeal of Hananiah, Azariah, Mishael,[48] and Matathias,[49] I shall joyfully give away my soul for the faith of the Holy Testament for which they died . . . I hope for strength from the Lord. I do not trust myself, since I am only flesh and of frail nature; and just as I have placed a mother and five sisters in danger for this faith,[50] I would give away a thousand, if I had them, for the faith of each of His holy Commandments . . . My Lord, look upon me with grace, so that it may be known and seen in this kingdom and upon all the earth that Thou art our God and that Thine almighty and holy name, Adonay, is invoked with truth in Israel and among Israel's descendants. I commit this soul that Thou gavest me to Thy holy hands, promising with Thy help not to change my faith till death nor after it.

I end happily the narrative of my present life, having lively faith in Thy divine hope of saving me through Thine infinite mercy and of resurrecting me, when Thy holy will is accomplished, together with our fathers Abraham, Isaac, and Jacob and his faithful sons, for whose holy love I beg Thee humbly to confirm this and not to forsake me. May it please Thee to send the angel Michael, our prince, to defend and help me. . . . O Lord, have mercy on the glory of Thy name, Thy law, and Thy people, and the world which Thou Thyself didst create; fill it with Thy light and the truthful knowledge of Thy name, so that heaven and earth will be filled with Thy glory and praise, amen, amen.[51]

In the spaces between the multiple autos de fe over three centuries, and in the shadow of celebrated martyrs, thousands of humble Anussim led a life filled with shame and fear, guilt and despair, hoping for some Moses to deliver them from the Christian Pharaoh, or some new Esther who would defeat the Hamans of the Inquisition. Asked if he were not a New Christian, a certain Gonçalo, who was suspected of avoiding crossing himself in church, replied: "No, I am not; but I am a converso." Commenting on this seemingly paradoxical statement, Carrete Parrondo writes: "This sentence, if it is correct, is quite surprising as New Christian and Converso are synonyms."[52] They might certainly have been synonymous in the common language and in the minds of the Christians, but this Gonçalo was resisting being identified as a Christian, New or Old, stressing the fact that he had been converted against his will. Elvira García declared that "in the faith she was born in she wishes to die;" and to the question why she had converted, she replied: "for the sake of my children."[53] Pedro Núñez de Santa Fe, formerly don Yuça of Valladolid, confessed that if not for all the debts owed to him he would not have converted [in 1492] nor returned from Portugal [in 1494].[54] Ruy Dias confided to a witness[55] that "if not for his children, he would leave for the land of Judaea."

Guilt feelings for having converted, or for going on to live as Anussim, dreaming of leaving Christian kingdoms for Jerusalem or Constantinople, and keeping alive the hope of messianic redemption are some of the most frequent themes in the confessions of the Anussim as well as in the most memorized traditional prayers among them and in the personalized poetic versions of certain Psalms transmitted from one generation to the next. Don Yuça, who would send a barrel of wine to his Jewish parents every year for Purim and Passover, confessed that "he repented of having become a Christian, that he would give his wife all their common property, have her return to her father's home, because he wished to leave for Jerusalem."[56] In Tras-os-Montes, Portugal, the following fragmentary prayer has survived the centuries:

O meus Deus, quem ja se vira
N'aquela santa cidade
Chamada Jerusalem.
Jerusalem está esperando
cada hora e cada dia . . .
O alto Deus d'Israel,
Cumpri vossas profecias . . .

[O my God, pray one would be so fortunate / to reside in that holy city / called Jerusalem. / Waiting for Jerusalem, / every hour and every day . . . / O exalted God of Israel, / accomplish your prophecies . . .]

From a crypto-Jewish physician living in Guarda, Portugal, who had been denounced in 1582 to the Inquisition in Lisbon, we possess a poetic expression of the deep-seated yearnings for messianic redemption and the ingathering of the captives and exiles in the Holy Land:[57]

O SONHO

O Sonho que eu sonhava
Se o ouzasse a dizer,
Mas eu ey grande vergonha
Que mo não quizessem crer.

Que sonhava com prazer
Que os mortos se erguião
E tornavam a viver
E que todos [se sahião];[58]

Os que estavão nas prisões
Traz dos montes escondidos,
Sonhava que erão sahidos
Da dura e forte prisão.

Vi a tribu de Adão
Com as dentes apreganhados
E muito espedaçados
Da serpente do dragão.

E assi vi a Ruben
Co hua voz de muita gente.
O qual vira mui contente
Cantando em Jerusalem.

O quem vira a Belem
E os montes de Syon
E a esse bom Jurdão
Para se lavar mui bem . . .

[THE DREAM. The dream I have dreamed, / if I dared to tell it; /but I feel so ashamed / for fear of not being believed.

For I dreamed with joy / that the dead were resurrected / and returned to live, / that all of them left their graves.

Those who were in the prisons / beyond the mountains hidden, / I dreamed that they went free / from the harsh and cruel prison.

I saw the tribe of Adam / caught in the gnashing teeth / and bitten to pieces / by the serpent, the dragon.

And I also saw Ruben / with the noise of a multitude / coming in great happiness, / singing in Jerusalem.

Fortunate who would see Bethlehem / and the mountains of Zion, / and reach the good river Jordan / to completely wash oneself, etc.][59]

To give expression to their guilt feelings and yearning for a prompt divine redemption, the Anussim made the Psalms the most important vehicle to convey their innermost emotions, projecting in the texts they often learned by heart personal variations and allusions to their own situation. We find therefore in the surviving documents of the Inquisition a great number of paraphrased Psalms, particularly those dealing with contrition and repentance, with yearning for messianic deliverance and dreams of returning to Zion. Thus, the book of Psalms, available to them in Jewish or Christian translations in Spanish, became for the Anussim the most continuous source of hope and consolation, prayer and meditation, personal devotion and mystical spirituality. From Christian apocalyptic literature, in particular from the commentaries on Daniel brought by the preachers as persuasive arguments for converting to Christianity, the Anussim appropriated the same texts to deepen their faith in the messianic redemption yet to come. Juan de Salzedo,[60] when asked one day about how he felt, replied "that he was feeling fine, but that it was said in the Scriptures of the Jews that happy the man who will be found as a Jew after the passing of these [troubled] times," referring probably to Daniel 12:2–3: "And many of them that sleep in the dust of the earth shall awake, some to everlasting life, and some to shame and everlasting contempt. And then they that be wise shall shine as the brightness of the firmament, and they that turn many to righteousness as the stars for ever and ever."[61]

A typical poetic paraphrase and personal adaptation of a psalm, frequently alluded to in inquisitorial confessions, has been preserved in two complete versions (in Portuguese and Spanish), with slight variations between them, and recorded during two different trials.[62] The Portuguese version of 1596 opens as follows:

> Alto Dio de Abraham,
> Rey forte de Israel,
> tu que ouuiste a Ismael,
> ouue a minha orazón;
> tu que en las grandes alturas
> te aposentas Señor,
> ouue a esta pecadora
> que te chama das bajuras;[63]

The Spanish version of 1643 reads:

> Oh, Alto Dios de Abraham,
> Dios fuerte, Dios de Israel,
> tu que oíste a Daniel,
> oye mi oraçion;
> tu que en las grandes alturas
> te pusiste, mi Señor,
> oye aquesta pecadora[64]
> que te llama de las basuras;
> tú que a toda criatura
> abres caminos y fuentes;
> alce mis ojos a los montes,
> donde vendrá mi ayuda.[65]
> Yo bien sé que en mi se encierra
> gran pecado que en mi hay.
> Mi ayuda de Adonay,
> que hizo cielos y tierra;
> Santo(s) Dios, fuerte Dios,
> misericordioso Dios immortal,
> Habed misericordia de mi, Señor.

[O exalted God of Abraham, / almighty God, God of Israel, / you who hearkened to Daniel, / listen to my prayer; / you, who in the high spheres / have residence, O my Lord, / listen to this sinning woman / who calls upon you from the abyss; / you who open for every creature / pathways and water sources; / I lifted up my eyes unto the hills / whence my help will come. / I confess that in me enclosed / a great sin is hidden.[66] / My help comes from Adonay / who created heaven and earth. / Holy God, almighty God, / merciful and immortal God, / have mercy on me, O Lord.]

Manuel de Morales, an active Judaizer in Portugal, who had arrived
in New Spain with the Carvajals and played a major part among the
Anussim there, wrote many poetic prayers (some erroneously attributed
to Luis de Carvajal, el Mozo)[67] which were recited on the High Holidays
during several generations. One of them opens as follows:

Recibe mi ayuno en penitencia,
Señor, de todo mal que te he cometido;
no permites me falte tu clemencia
pues ves con cuanta angustia te la pido;
ensalzaré tu suma omnipotencia,
será de mí tu nombre engrandecido
y no me des, Señor, lo que merezco,
pues ves que aún en pensarlo estremezco.

Si te he ofendido gravemente,
era por falta de entendimieto . . . (P. 307)

[Accept, O Lord, my fast as penitence for any evil I have done to Thee;
do not withhold Thy clemency from me, seeing how anxiously I beg
Thee for it; I will extol Thy almightiness, Thy name will be exalted by
me; do not retribute to me, Lord, according to my merits, seeing how I
tremble only at this thought. / If I have gravely sinned in Thy eyes, it was
for lack of understanding; etc.]

His disciple, Luis de Carvajal (el Mozo), destined to become the
charismatic martyr of sixteenth-century New Spain, wrote a sonnet that
might well be considered as one of the most outstanding mystical and
penitential texts ever written, in the style of the traditional piyyutim (sacred hymns) recited in the synagogue on the High Holidays. This composition, in fact, was composed for Yom Kippur and was still known
among the Anussim in the mid-seventeenth century:

I have sinned, my Lord; but not because I have sinned
Do I abandon plaint and hope for Thy mercy;
I fear that my punishment will equal my guilt,
But I still hope for forgiveness through Thy kindness.

I suspect that, as Thou hast awaited my return,
Thou hast held me in contempt for my ingratitude;
My sin is made still greater
Because Thou art so worthy of being loved.

If it were not for Thee, what would become of me?
And who, except Thee, would free me from myself?
Who would free me if Thy hand did not shower Thy grace on me?

And except for me, my God, who would not love Thee?
And, except for Thee, my God, who would bear with me?
And, without Thee, my God, to Thee who would take me?[68]

From single sentences, fragments of psalms and hymns, and poetic paraphrases preserved in both inquisitorial documents and other sources, one can ascertain that the Anussim had at their disposal more than just memorized bits and pieces of traditional prayers. However, the mixture of Portuguese and Spanish, or Catalan and Spanish (in Majorca), in earlier phases illustrates the new presence of books of prayers and other texts in the Spanish language, smuggled in from Ferrara and Amsterdam in the sixteenth century. From the surviving quotations and fragmentary texts it is possible to state without equivocation that the Anussim knew the most important prayers of the Sephardic ritual, the daily prayers as well as those used for the Sabbath, the holidays, and for special occasions (blessings before and after meal, before sleeping and after awakening, before leaving on a journey by land or sea; rules and precepts for certain ceremonial customs; etc.), including some texts of cabbalistic origin which were not in use among non-Sephardic worshipers. We will illustrate these points with a select number of samples from various sources and different periods.

In spite of the mass conversion of the Jewish community in Majorca in 1435, almost fifty years before the official establishment of the Inquisition in the Spanish kingdom, and their seeming insulation from the Jewish and crypto-Jewish communities on the mainland, these Anussim denigratingly known as xuetes, chuetas (the Majorcan equivalent of marranos), who 250 years later were still branded as "New Christians" and excluded from the "Old Christian" society, seem to have preserved important fragments of prayers from the Sephardic ritual.[69] Isabel Martí y Cortés, noted for her disparaging remarks to her torturers, brings up in her complaints verses from Psalms among Jewish articles of faith:

> Christians believe in a God made by the hands of man, who has eyes and does not see, ears and does not hear, mouth and does not speak, hands and does not touch, feet and does not walk; and they have invented a law adapted for their needs which gives them sustenance, and the inquisitors and their secretaries obtain a good salary which sustains them, but the Christians know very well that the Law given by the Lord of Israel to Moses is the true one, and that at the hour of death they believe in the Law of Moses, and so are saved, and that if they would read the Bible without distortions they would all become Jews, but they have mixed up everything, including all the commandments, for the third commandment of the Mosaic Law says to observe the Sabbath . . .

The following text, for example, recorded at her trial in 1678 and transcribed by Braunstein as one unit, represents in reality three different segments of the introductory portion of the morning service (the order being II, I, III; segment II is recited when entering the synagogue):

> I. Bendito tu Adonay, nuestro Dios, Rey del mundo, que formó el hombre con sabiduría, y crió en el orados orados, huecos huecos. Descubierto(s) y sabi[d]o delante çilla de tu trono, que si serasse uno dellos, o si se abriesse uno dellos, no [seria] possible sustenarse [por] una hora. Bendito tu Adonay, mel[e]ci[n]an toda criatura, y maravilha(s) para hazer.
>
> II. Yo [1] / con muchedumbre [2] / de tu merced [3] / vendre [4] / a tu cassa [5] / a humillarme [6] / a [7] / Palacio(s) [8] / de tu santidat [9] / (y) con temor [10]
>
> III. Todos criados de arriba [y] abaxo . . .'[70]

Segment II, recited when one enters the synagogue, comprises in the Hebrew original ten words from Psalm 5:8, representing the number of persons necessary (a *minyan*) for a regular full service. Segment III here constitutes just the opening line of a special prayer (see next example) of cabbalistic origin, composed by Shelomoh Mosheh Alsaqar, and only incorporated in the Sephardic ritual of prayers.[71] This composition (which starts in Hebrew, *Kol beruey ma'alah u-matah ye-'idun yagidun*, etc.), accompanying the other two segments, is already present in an early sixteenth-century Catalan version of the Book of Prayers (Brit. Museum, MS Bodl. Or. 9):[72]

> II. Beneyt tu A[donay], nostre Deu, rey del mon. que crjha l'home ab sabiesa, y cria en ell forats forats, buyts, buyts; descubert y sabut davan cadira de ta honra, que si [sera obert un d'ells, o] sis tancha un d'ells no li es posible per se sostenerse sols hora una. Beneyt tu A[donay], medecinant tota criatura y maravelha[n] per far.
>
> I. Y io en multitud de ta merçe vindre en ta casa, encorbarme a palau de ta santedad, en ta temor.
>
> III. Tot criat alt y baix testificaran y recontaran tots ells [com uno] que A[donay] 1, y son nom 1; 30 y 2 çenderos, y tot entene[n]t sa puritat recontara[n] sa grandeza . . .
>
> [Blessed be Thee Adonay, our God, King of the universe, who createth man with wisdom, and createth in him openings, holes; it is clear and known before the throne of Thy glory, that if one of them would be obstructed, or one of them would burst open, he could not possibly sur-

vive even for a short time. Blessed be Thee Adonay, who careth for all creatures, and createth with marvel.

But as for me, I will come into Thy house in the multitude of Thy mercy, and in Thy fear will I worship toward Thy holy temple.

All the creatures in heaven and on earth will testify and proclaim unanimously that God is one and His name is one. Thirty-two pathways, for those who understand their secret, will proclaim Thy greatness . . .]

The following prayer, equally from among those preserved in the community of Chuetas, was used particularly during the Sabbath service, and is found with more elements in most Hebrew Rituals of Prayer as well as with some variations in the surviving prayers of several communities of Anussim (the original in Hebrew [starting *Barukh she-amar we-hayah ha-'olam* comprises eighty-seven words, a number which has some esoteric connotations):[73]

Bendito tu Adonay, nuestro Dios, Rey del mundo, y Rey el grande, el Santo Padre ["santo" not in Hebr. text], el Piadoso, lloado en boca de su Pueblo; afermo[z]icado en lengua de todos sus buenos, y sus siervos . . . y con cánticos de David tu siervo. Te lloa[re]mos, engrandeceremos, te alabaremos, te glorificaremos, te enaltezeremos, y nombraremos tu nombre, nuestro Rey, nuestro Dios, unico vivo de los mundos. Alabado y glorificado sea tu nombre sienpre de sienpre. Bendito tu Adonay, nuestro Dios, Rey alabado con alabamiento.

[Blessed be Thee Adonay, our God, King of the universe, exalted King, holy Father ["holy" not in Hebr. text], the merciful, praised on the lips of His nation; extolled in the tongue of His pious followers and servants, . . . and with the psalms of David Thy servant. We will praise Thee, exalt Thee, extol Thee, glorify Thee, magnify Thee, and we will mention Thy name, our King, our God, uniquely alive in all eternity. Praised and glorified be Thy name for ever and ever. Blessed be Thee, Adonay, our God, King exalted with hymns of praise.]

Another prayer, paraphrasing Psalm 91 with additions from other psalms, known as Oração da Formosura ("Prayer of Exaltation"), is found with slight variations in a great number of specimens preserved for centuries among the Anussim of Portugal, Spain, Brazil, Mexico, and elsewhere.[74] I present here the opening sequence of various versions, among many others, in Portuguese. It was recorded at the trial of Brites Henriques between 1674 and 1683. Arrested at the age of twenty-two and tortured over a period of eight years, this young woman recited a great number of prayers, some very extensive, including the Oração da Formosura [notice the use of first person singular in this version (as in the original psalm) contrary to first person plural in the next examples]:

A honra e louvor do Senhor dos altos Ceos: Seja a santa formosura de Adonay, nuestro Dios, perfeita a obra das minhas mãos compõe, perfeita a obra das minhas mãos comporá. Sobre my cobertura do alto, que me lembre do abastador. Digo Adonay é meu Deus, meu abrigo, meu catelo, e meu Senhor, que vos Senhor dos altos Ceus me livreis e me guardeis do laço do encampamento, de mortandade, de quebranto. Não temo o pavor da noite . . .

In a different version recorded in Belmonte half a century ago the prayer reads as follows:

Em honra e louvor dos 73 [in Hebrew text: 72] nomes[75] do Senhor seja! A Formosura santa do meu Deus de Adonai sobre nós seja. O Senhor dos Ceus compõe as obras das nossas mãos, o Senhor dos Ceus as comporá. Estamos encobertos no alto, á sombra do abastador nos adormecemos. Viva Adonai, meu brio, meu rei, meu Senhor, meu castelo, meu edifico. Elle nos guardará e nos livrara do mau laço, tortura, mortandade, castimento da sua santidade. Debaixo da sua santa Saquiné [for Hebrew *shekhinah*, "divine presence"] não temeremos o pavor da noite . . .

And at the trial of Diogo Teixeira, the inquisitors recorded the following version:

Em formosura de ti Adonai, nosso Deos, exalçado sobre nos e sobre os feitos de nossas mãos, Adonai Sabaho, sobre nos a conta do alto, a sombra do Abastado, maris (? meu?) rei, Adonai meu grande abriguo, minha penha, meu castello, o Senhor me livrará de laço encampado, de mortandade arrebatosa; debaixo de suas asas me estaziarei . . .

Another hymn of praise, paraphrasing Psalm 148 with personal interpolations, has been recorded in many trial documents or simply alluded to. Recorded in the 1920s in Belmonte, Portugal, the traditional example starts as follows:

Louvai o Senhor, os moradores dos Ceos,
Louvai-o nas alturas;
Louvai-o todos os seus anjos,
Louvai-o todas as suas virtudes.
Louvai-o o sol, a lua, as estrellas e a luz,
Louvai-o todos . . .

A Spanish variation on the same Psalm 148, recorded at the trial of Juan López de Armenia in 1590, starts as follows (showing clearly some individual interpolations):[76]

A. a S. [Alabad al Señor] todos los arcangeles y los profetas,

A. a S. todos los patriarcas,
A. a S. todos los martires,
A. a S. de dia y de noche,
A. a S. de ynvierno y en verano y en frio y en calor,
A. a S. la luz y las tinieblas,
A. a S. las alturas,
A. a S. las baxeças de la tierra,
A. a S. que no come ni beue, y juzga y ue . . .

In Belmonte, the same psalm has been elaborated in a short song, easy to learn, following the structure and the style of the popular cantigas de amigo of the Gallego-Portuguese tradition, and adapted to a female congregation as a morning prayer:[77]

Levantai-vos meninas cedo,
Ja quere amanhecer;
Louvaremos ão altissimo senhor
Que nos ha de fortalecer.
Louvai o Senhor ão som da viola
Ele è tudo som e tudo gloria.
Louvai o Senhor meninas
Louvai-o com vozes finas.
Louvai o Senhor donzelas
Louvai-o com vozes belas.
Louvai o Senhor casadas
Louvai-o com vozes claras.
Louvai o Senhor viuvas
Louvai-o com vozes puras.
O Senhor de todos os amores,
Louvai meninas e flores.

Amén, Senhor, que fizeste o dia.

[Awake and rise, O maidens, hastily, / the time of dawn is near; / we will praise the almighty Lord / who will give us strength. / Praise the Lord with the lute / for He is sound and glory. / Praise the Lord, O maiden, / Praise Him with noble voices. / Praise the Lord, O damsels, / Praise Him with beautiful voices. / Praise the Lord, O spouses, / Praise Him with clear voices. / Praise the Lord, O widows, / Praise Him with pure voices. / The Lord of all the loves, / Praise ye maiden and flowers. / Amen, O Lord, who maketh the new day.]

Among the poetic adaptations of the prayer to be recited before retiring to bed at night, we quote one recorded in *Idanha-a-Nova*:

Na minha cama me deitei,
As minhas portas fechei

Com as chaves de Abrahão;
Os bons entrarão,
Os maus sahirão;
Os anjos do Senhor
Comigo estão.
            Amén, Senhor . . .

[I lay down in my bed, / I have closed my doors / with the keys of Abraham; / the pious will come in, / the evil ones will leave; / the angels of the Lord / are here with me. Amen, Lord, etc.]

As the women in Portugal were particularly active among the Anussim and served in a way as lay "cantors" or "priests" (*sacerdotisas*) in conducting the secret religious services and educating their children, many prayers for all the various occasions were adapted in song form, including allusions to their own tragic situation. These could then be memorized with ease and preserved as popular songs for generations. A good example is such an adaptation for the Day of Atonement (Oração que se diz no "Dia Puro do Senhor"), possibly composed in 1500 or 1543 (depending on the interpretation of line five in the fragment quoted here; the allusion could be to D. Manuel or Don Juan III):

. . . .
Quebrai, Senhor, este jugo
Que nos peza deshumano;
Livrai-nos, Senhor, livrai-nos
Das garras d'este tirano.

Ha trez annos que o teu povo
Em ferros geme e suspira,
Bastem os males passados,
Aplaque-se a tua ira!

Livraste-o de hum pharãó;
Por santo prodigio novo
De outro pharãó mais duro
Outra vez livra o teu povo.

A tua voz formidavel
Quebrem-se os duros grielhões,
Hoje, porque he o teu dia
Deve ser o dos perdões.

Para nos he a ventura,
Para ti, Senhor, a gloria;
O teu dia sacro santo
Seja o dia da victoria.
            Amèn, Senhor . . .

[Break, O Lord, this yoke / of inhumane oppression; / deliver us, O Lord, deliver us / from this tyrant's claws. / For three years already your people / in chains cry and complain; / suffice the past evils, / placate now your anger. / You delivered him from a Pharaoh; / with a new sacred miracle, / from another Pharaoh more cruel, / free once more your nation. / At the sound of your tremendous voice, / let the harsh chains be smashed; / this day, for it is your day, / has to be the day of forgiving. / It should be good fortune to us, / and glory to you, O Lord; / let your sacred holy day / be the day of victory. / Amen, O Lord . . .]

From a series of Passover songs that have survived among the Anussim, I selected the following examples (the first two from Belmonte):

Caminhamos e andamos
Louvaremos ão Deus d'Abrahão,
Que nos livrou do Egypto
De terra da escravidão.

[Let us go forth and march, / praising the Lord of Abraham, / who has freed us from Egypt, / the land of slavery.]

Caminhamos e andamos
Louvaremos ão Deus d'Israel
Que nos livrou do Egypto
Da quelle Rei tão cruel (bis).

[Let us go forth and march, / praising the Lord of Israel, / who has freed us from Egypt, / from that very cruel king.]

The traditional and popular song ("Who knows One? / I know One. / One is God. / Who knows two?" etc.) was preserved among the Chuetas in Majorca in the seventeenth century (with the typical opening part common to the Sephardim: "Qui sabes y entregues; qui es Deu alt en cel? Alabat sie el seu santo nom. Amen. Amen."):

El Uno: El gran Dios de Israel; / Los Dos: Moysen y Aarón; / Los Tres: Abram, Isach y Jacób; / Los Quatro: Maridos de Israel; / Los Cinco: Libros de la Lei; / Los Seis: Dias del Sábado (Misna); / Los Siete: Dias de la Semana; / . . . Los Doze: Tribus de Israel; / Las Treze: Palabras que dijo Dios omnipotente a Moyses. Amen. Amen.

Compare this with a later version sung among the Sephardim in the Ottoman Empire, recorded in two versions by Camhy and Samuelson.[78]

And, finally, let us quote here a poetic adaptation of the Ten Commandments, originating in Belmonte, which the mother recites to her son as an initiation to their secret monotheistic faith. In this song form, the youngsters could learn with ease the basic tenets of Judaism:

Eu sou teu Deus e Senhor,
Deus dúm poder infinito
Que, piedoso, te salvei
Do captiveiro do Egypto.

Não terás alheios Deuses—,
Que em mim tens o sumo bem;
Ama-me, como a ti mesmo,
E ão teu próximo tambem.

Não tomarás do teu Deus
O seu santo nome em vão—;
E nem por Elle, debalde,
Jures na mais leve acção.

Ao sabbado não trabalhes,
Nem tu, nem filho, ou criado—,
Santificando este dia,
So para mim reservado.

Honrarás teu pãe e mãe—,
Com particular dever;
São pessoas respeitaveis,
Porque te dérão o ser.

Irado, não matarás
O teu proprio semelhante—,
E não conserves jamais
O odio, nem por um instante.

Com castidade serás—,
Modesto em tuas acções,
Sem manchares a tua alma
Com obscenas corrupções.

Não furtarás—, porque o furto,
De propósito e vontade,
E' um crime abominavel,
Que revolta a sociedade.

Contra o próximo não falles,
De todos dizendo bem;
Nem com falso testemunho
Jamais insultes alguem.

Nem por leve pensamiento,
Desejarás a mulher,
Que não seja a tua propria—,
Intentando-a corromper.

Não cubiçarás, emfim,
Aquillo que não for teu—,
Contenta-te com os bens,
Que a Providencia te deu.

Aqui tens, querido filho,
Do bom Deus a lei primeira,
Que devemos observar
Com a fé mais verdadeira.

[I am thy God and Lord, / God of infinite power, / who mercifully delivered thee / from captivity in Egypt. // Thou shalt not have alien gods, / for in me is your supreme good; / thou shalt love me as thyself, / and also thy neighbor. // Thou shalt not use for naught / the holy name of thy God; / and, in His name, never swear / in vain even for a trifling sum. // Thou shalt not labor on the Sabbath day, / neither thy son nor thy servant; / sanctify this day, / set aside only for me. // Thou shalt honor thy father and mother / with particular devotion; / they are respectable people / having given thee thy being. // Irate, thou shalt not kill / any creature in thy likeness; / and never harbor in thy heart / hatred, not even for an instant. // In chastity thou shalt dwell, / modest in thy deeds, / not tarnishing thy soul / with obscene corruptions. // Thou shalt not steal, for theft / done with purpose and intention / is an abominable crime / that subverts society. // Thou shalt not malign thy neighbor; / say good things about all people; / never cause harm to anybody / by false testimony. // Thou shalt not desire, / not even in furtive thought, / a woman which is not thine, / causing her to be defiled. // Lastly, thou shalt not covet / whatever is not thine; / be happy with thy lot / which Providence has given thee. // This is, my beloved son, / the good Lord's First Law; / and we have to observe it / with perfectly sincere faith.]

On 8 December 1596, Luis de Carvajal the Younger was led to his auto de fe. All the way to the *quemadero,* Father Alonso de Contreras was begging him to kiss the cross—to save his soul, and thus deserve being garroted before burning instead of being burned alive—but in vain. He wanted to die, writes Father Contreras, as the "great zealot, grand teacher and restorer of the forgotten Law":

He was always such a good Jew and he reconciled his understanding, which was very profound and sensitive, with his highly inspired divine determination to defend the Law of God—the Mosaic—and fight for it. I have no doubt that if he had lived before the Incarnation of Our Redeemer, he would have been a heroic Hebrew, and his name would have been as famous in the Bible as are the names of those who died in defense of their Law when it was necessary.[79]

These words of Father Alonso de Contreras, which sum up the life and martyrdom of Luis de Carvajal, could well serve as an epitaph to thousands of known and anonymous Anussim as well as a conclusion to our inquiry on the degree and continuity of their "Jewishness."*

NOTES

*The forcibly converted Jews in Spain and Portugal, many of whom went on leading double lives for generations or even centuries, were called conversos and New Christians but, when suspected of clinging to the Mosaic faith, were branded most often as Judaizers, and more denigratingly as Marranos (pigs). Since they were the victims of physical and mental violence in the torture cellars of the Inquisition, and were martyrs at the stake, the insulting anti-Jewish name coined by the victimizers will be avoided in this essay. The term crypto-Jews (secret Jews) is certainly appropriate and neutral enough but expresses only in part their real existential condition. In Hebrew literature they are called Anussim (singular Anuss: "coerced, raped"), signifying that they were converted under duress, mentally and physically raped, in opposition to *meshumadim* ("apostates, willingly converted"). I therefore advocate the use of Anussim instead of marranos. It is worthwhile noting that the late Francisco Cantera Burgos in his *Chebet Jehuda [La Vara de Juda] de Salomon Ibn Verga* (Granada, 1927) consciously made a similar choice when writing: "la terrible matanza de los *annusim* o judaizantes del año 1506." Note: All translations are mine, except where otherwise indicated.

1. For some examples, see below, n. 25.

2. Contrary to the view of most scholars dealing with the Anussim (Y. Baer, C. Roth, H. Beinart, Y. H. Yerushalmi, I. S. Revah, Gerson D. Cohen), who assert the continuity of a fundamental "Jewishness" among the so-called "Judaizers," some others (notably B. Netanyahu, followed by E. Rivkin, and A. Domínguez Ortiz) have tried to argue that it was a fiction fabricated by the inquisitors in their persecution of the New Christians, a political and economic weapon against them, and that therefore the inquisitorial trial records constitute an unreliable source. For a summary presentation of this controversy and a rejection of the latter thesis, see Y. H. Yerushalmi, *From Spanish Court to Italian Ghetto: Isaac Cardoso. A Study in Seventeenth-Century Marranism and Jewish Apologetics* (New York: Columbia University Press, 1971; reprint, Seattle and London: Washington University Press, 1981), 21–42.

3. See Y. H. Yerushalmi, *The Lisbon Massacre of 1506 and the Royal Image in the "Shebet Yehudah,"* Hebrew Union College Annual, Supplements, vol. 1 (Cincinnati: Hebrew Union College-Jewish Institute of Religion, 1976).

4. See, for instance, even in Spanish translation, Maimonides's *Guide for the Perplexed* and Yehudah Halevi's *Book of the Kuzari*, preserved in fifteenth-century manuscripts, edited by Moshe Lazar (Los Angeles: Labyrinthos [The Sephardic Classical Library, 1989, 1990], vols. 2 & 4); some surviving rituals of prayers in Spanish and Catalan; and so on. Traveling Judaizers were guests in homes of relatives or in "trustworthy converso homes"; see H. Beinart, *Conversos on Trial,*

The Inquisition in Ciudad Real (Jerusalem: Magnes Press, 1981), 246–247: "When a Jew came to a Converso home, crypto-Jews came to see him, listening attentively as he instructed them in the Torah and the observance of the mitzvoth . . . Reading from the Bible and the Sidur, the Jews acted as a stimulus to their crypto-Jewish brethren."

5. Contacts were also maintained through correspondence, using a variety of cryptograms. For some examples, see British Museum, MS Add. 29, 868–1677/8; and a reproduction in S. Liebman, *Jews in New Spain* (Coral Gables, Fla.: University of Miami Press, 1970), 213.

6. See below, a summary of the basic Jewish customs serving the interrogators in Spain, Portugal, and the New World.

7. Beinart, *Conversos on Trial*, 241.

8. Archivo Histórico Nacional (hereafter AHN), Inquisición, libro 1031, fols. 119v–126v. See the complete dossier of Maldonado de Silva published by José Toribio Medina, and also L. García de Proodian, *Los judíos en América: Sus actividades en los Virreinatos de Nueva Castilla y Nueva Granada, s XVII* (Madrid: Consejo Superior de Investigaciones Científicas, 1966).

9. A hundred years later, deported from Rio de Janeiro to Lisbon, another gifted young writer, Antonio José da Silva, was led to the stake at the age of thirty-four along with his wife (October 1739). His surviving dramatic works are known as *Operas do Judeu*.

10. Yerushalmi, *From Spanish Court to Italian Ghetto*, 32.

11. See I. S. Revah, "Les Marranes portugais et l'Inquisition au XVIe siècle," in *The Sephardic Heritage*, ed. R. D. Barnett (London: Vallentine, Mitchell, 1971), 1:520.

12. Quoted by Beinart, *Conversos on Trial*, 38.

13. See L. Wolf, *Jews in the Canary Islands* (London: Spottiswoode, Ballantyne, 1926), 466.

14. See H. Beinart, *Records of the Trials of the Spanish Inquisition in Ciudad Real*, 4 vols. (Jerusalem: The Israel National Academy of Sciences and Humanities, 1974–1985). María Díaz, leading figure among a group of conversos who had fled from Ciudad Real in 1474, is described by Fernando de Trujillo as follows: "Her knowledge [of the laws] was no less than his own, for he himself could not instruct [the conversos] in the Law of Moses [better than she could]." Fernando de Trujillo had acted as a rabbi in Palma and Ecija before his conversion.

15. See, for example, Liebman, *Jews in New Spain*, 263: Isabel Núñez Duarte, exclaiming at the stake: "Look, Mother of the Maccabees, how you are being revived to be the mother of so many who are going to the stake [for their faith]."

16. See, among others, Liebman, *Jews in New Spain*; A. Toro, *La Familia Carvajal* (Mexico City, 1944), 2 vols; M. A. Cohen, *The Martyr: The Story of a Secret Jew and the Mexican Inquisition in the Sixteenth Century* (Philadelphia: Jewish Publication Society of America, 1973); Wolf, *Jews in the Canary Islands*; B. Lewin, *El Santo Oficio en América* (Buenos Aires: Sociedad Hebraica Argentina, 1950); B. Braunstein, *The Chuetas of Majorca: Conversos and the Inquisition of Majorca*, Columbia University Oriental Studies, vol. 28 (Scottsdale, Pa.: Mennonite Pub-

lishing House, 1936; reprint, New York: Ktav Publishing House, 1972); Lucía García de Proodian, *Los judíos en América*.

17. See S. Schwarz, "Os cristãos-novos em Portugal no seculo XX," *Arqueologia e história* [6th ser.], 4 (1925): 5–114; also published separately (Lisbon, 1925). References below are to page(s) of the article followed in parentheses by corresponding page(s) of the separate publication.

18. Quoted by Yerushalmi, *From Spanish Court to Italian Ghetto*, 24 n. 37.

19. See AHN, Inq., lib. 1021, fols. 240v–241, cited in García de Proodian, *Los judíos en América*, 478–479, a fragmentary list of books confiscated from Luis Méndez Chaves, including some seven prayer books in Spanish published in Amsterdam between 1617 and 1641.

20. Yosef ha-Kohen, *Emeq ha-bakha*, ed. M. Letteris (Crakow: J. Fischer, 1895), 8: "I, Yosef ha-Kohen, saw a book which was in bad shape, one of those which had been hidden for a long while during those evil days [1391] inside wells." See also Beinart, *Records* 1:322.

21. See W. Popper, *The Censorship of Hebrew Books* (New York: Knickerbocker Press, 1899; reprint, New York: Ktav Publishing House, 1969), 20.

22. See W. Popper, *Censorship*, 11–12; and n. 32, quoting Yehudah Lerma: "Then I found one book in the possession of Christians who had snatched it from the flames, and I secured it at great cost."

23. See C. Carrete Parrondo, *Fontes Iudaeorum Regni Castellae, II: El Tribunal de la Inquisición en el Obispado de Soria (1486–1502)* (Salamanca: Universidad Pontificia de Salamanca, 1985), 119.

24. See J. Riera i Sans, "Un recull d'oracions en català dels conversos jueus (segle XV)," *Estudis Romànics* 16 (1971–1975): 49–97.

25. J. Caro Baroja, *Los judíos en la España moderna y contemporánea* (Madrid, 1961), 1:388; see also p. 119, a mention by Andrés Pacheco, inquisitor general, in 1623, concerning the most celebrated burning of books in Salamanca after the establishment of the Inquisition: "cuantos libros hallaron sobre vanas artes, ciencias ilícitas, supersticiones de magia y encantamientos que encontraron, sobre todo, en poder de los judíos y de los conversos, y que en auto (que se celebró junto al monasterio de San Esteban) ardieron unos sesenta mil libros." Quoted by C. Carrete Parrondo, *Fontes Iudaeorum Regni Castellae, I: Provincia de Salamanca* (Salamanca: Universidad Pontificia de Salamanca, 1981), 140.

26. See, in particular, Beinart, *Records*; Wolf, *Jews in the Canary Islands*; Braunstein, *Chuetas*; Schwarz, "Os cristãos-novos"; Lewin, *El Santo Oficio*; and Carrete Parrondo, *Fontes Iudaeorum*.

27. See, for example, Carrete Parrondo, *Fontes*, I, nos. 3, 20, 68, 87, 111, 122, 419, 423. *Hamin* ("warm," in Aramaic) and *calyente* ("warm"), called in Yiddish among Ashkenazi Jews cholent (from Old French, chalent, "warm").

28. See Wolf, *Jews in the Canary Islands*, xxiii: the Canariote New Christians compiled a special ritual "in which the apocryphal prayer of Queen Esther with its pathetic avowal of crypto-Judaism and its fierce denunciation of the persecution and the heathen, prominently figured." Esther and Joseph are central figures in the life and the prayers of the Anussim in general.

29. See Braunstein, *Chuetas*, 298: "Bendito tu Adonay, nuestro Dios, rey del mundo, que nos santifico en sus mandamientos y nos encomendo sobre limpieza de manos"; Schwarz, "Os cristãos-novos," 53 (49): "Louvado seja o Senhor que nos deu agua para nos lavarmos"; see Liebman, *Jews in New Spain*, 241: Tomás Treviño de Sobremonte, at his trial in 1649, confesses that he had learned from his mother to recite: "Blessed be the Almighty God who in his lessons has taught me the washing of the hands, mouth, and eyes, in order to bless, serve, praise, and honor Thee, O God, according to the Law of Moses."

30. See, among others, Carrete Parrondo, *Fontes*, II, no. 108: "la vio que se levantava de la cama, e come se ovo vestido e lavado, que começo de resar una oraçion en abrayco estando en pie e vuelta a la pared, e sabadeava e fasia los abtos en el desir de la oraçion, como judia"; no. 107: "que nosotros nos confesamos a hombre e los judios a la pared"; E. Lipiner, *Os judaizantes nas capitanias de cima: Estudos sobre os cristãos-novos do Brazil nos séculos XVI e XVII* (Sao Paulo: Editora Brasilense, 1969), 101: "dando saltos para cima dizendo: *Cadox, Cadox, Cadox*, que queria dizer Sanctus, Sanctus, Sanctus Dominus Deus Sabaoth." This quotation from Isaiah, incorporated among the eighteen blessings of the *Amidah*, is also quoted by Tomás Treviño de Sobremonte during his trial in 1649 (see Liebman, *Jews in New Spain*, 241; and above n. 27).

31. According to a custom based on a talmudic dictum: "three things are told about nails: he who burns them is virtuous; he who buries them is righteous; he who throws them away is wicked."

32. See Gen. 32:33.

33. See, for example, Carrete Parrondo, *Fontes*, I, nos. 6, 11, 19, 20, 42, 59, 336, 392, and so on.

34. See, Num. 15:20; Schwarz, "Os cristãos-novos," 83 (79) "Quando se dizima a amassadura: Bemdito meu Senhor, Meu Deus, meu Adonai, que nos encomendou com as suas encomendas bemditas e bem-santas que dizimassemos este pão, para a boca do leão, como fizeram os nossos irmãos na Santa Terra da Promissão. Amen, Senhor, etc."

35. See Beinart, *Records* 1:241, 456–457: "Hadas, hadas, hadas buenas que te vengan"; 2:10; and *Conversos*, 279–280.

36. See Carrete Parrondo, *Fontes*, II, no. 96: "Juan Sanchez meldaba en un libro en abrayco en la forma que los judios suelen meldar"; no. 110: Diego Ferrando and others going to an orchard, taking with them "su çidur [prayer book] e el humas [Pentateuch], que son libros de la ley judayca"; no. 111: Diego Ferrando would go early morning to an orchard, "llevava su çidur, e los sabados que llevava el humas"; no. 134: "calla, que digo çilhod [penitential prayers], por que Dios me escape de esta çara; çilhod es unos maytines que dizen los judios de media noche avaxo"; no. 277: "quando resava las dichas oraçiones tenia vestido un abitillo que se llamava çeçit e tenia puesta en la cabeça los tafelines de la misma forma que lo tenian los judios"; and so on.

37. See Carrete Parrondo, *Fontes*, II, nos. 13, 146.

38. Ibid., no. 347: Guiomar López, wife of Juan García, when going to church: "A ti, Dio [notice the common use among Sephardic Jews of Dio rather

than Dios!] de mi padre, me encomiendo, Dio de Abraham, Dio de Ysaque, Dio de Jaco, y en ti fio, que todo lo otro es nada y vanidad [Hebrew *hevel wa-riq*]"; Lipiner, *Os judaizantes*, 47: a converso, at the elevation of the holy Host, mumbles "eu creio o que creio" (I believe in what I believe); 154–155: Alvaro Pacheco, instructing his cousin Antonia de Oliveira, "taught her to save her soul as did their ancestors; fasting on Mondays and Thursdays, not to recite on those days the Pater Noster, nor Ave Maria, nor any other Christian prayers; to keep the Sabbath [the true "Sunday"]; to believe in One God, not to adore icons"; Amilcar Paulo, "Os marranos nas Beiras" in *Revista Beira Alta*, 1960:631–676: "Eu não adoro o pão, nem a pedra, mas o grande Deu que todo governa" (I don't worship the wood [the cross; and/or (pão = bread? = holy Host)] nor the stone, but only the Great God who governs everything); "nesta igreja entro, mas não adoro [pão? pau?] nem pedra, tambien não adoro pão nem vinho; venho unicamente adorar ão Deus de Moises vivo" (I enter this church, but I don't worship [wood] and stone, nor worship bread or wine; I come only to worship the living God of Moses); Schwarz, "Os cristãos-novos," 83 (79), no. 70: "Nesta casa [using "house" rather than "church"] entro, não adoro nem o pau nem a pedra; só a Deus que em tudo governa."

39. See Beinart, *Conversos*, 259–283.

40. See Carrete Parrondo, *Fontes*, II, no. 80: "demando la çedaca con una bolsa abierta en la mano."

41. Ibid., I, 113: "que fue midras e casa de oracion de los judios."

42. See Liebman, *Jews in New Spain*, 282: Diego Díaz, 80 years old, at the stake in 1659, refuses to kiss the cross to save his soul: "Stop, padre, that stick can't save anybody."

43. See Deut. 2:7–10; Ruth 4:6–7.

44. Carrete Parrondo, *Fontes*, I, 26–27.

45. See S. B. Liebman, *The Enlightened: The Writings of Luis de Carvajal, el Mozo* (Coral Gables, Fla.: University of Miami Press, 1967). The choice of Joseph is obvious, he and Esther being the most revered heroes among the Anussim; Lumbroso, a well-known name among sixteenth-century Sephardic people, might be a translation of Meir (also spelled Mehir, Mayr, Mair, etc., in medieval Spanish documents), meaning "the enlightener" rather than "the enlightened," as used by Liebman. Luis de Carvajal saw himself as a new Joseph, a suffering messianic prophet, destined to awaken and free his fellow Anussim from the Inquisition's bondage. His youngest brother, Miguel, who with another brother escaped to Salonica, became a celebrated rabbi under the name of Jacob Lumbroso.

46. The fifth article of faith seems to have been omitted, unless the paragraph dealing with the observance of the Sabbath and the dietary laws was meant to be the fifth. See Liebman, *The Enlightened*, 128.

47. No. 9 is missing.

48. See Daniel 1:6–7; 3:8–25.

49. See 1 Maccabees, chap. 2.

50. In secret messages he was circulating among them from cell to cell, written on scraps of paper, banana peels, avocado nuts, and eggshells, Luis addressed them with biblical names (calling his mother Rachel, whose son was Joseph); to his sisters he wrote: "Be consoled, and have consolation in [the ultimate] victory. Be suffused with high spirits and gladness, like Annas and Esthers; be like beautiful Rachels, faithful Sarahs, strong Jaels and Judiths. Sing a song of victory with Deborah and Miriam."

51. For the complete translation of Luis de Carvajal's testament, see Liebman, *The Enlightened*, 125–133.

52. Carrete Parrondo, *Fontes*, II, no. 312, and note 3.

53. Ibid., no. 34.

54. Ibid., no. 231.

55. Ibid., no. 114.

56. Ibid., no. 9.

57. Trovas Do Licenciado Antonio Vaz; see Schwarz, "Os cristãos-novos," 91 (87).

58. Text: erão sahidos; scribal error: see next stanza.

59. Possibly alluding to a "baptism" (ritual bath) that would wash off the baptism of forced conversion.

60. The same Salzedo, as in Carrete Parrondo, *Fontes*, II, no. 134, who in prison prayed in Hebrew every night, reciting penitential psalms at midnight so that "God may deliver him from the present tribulations."

61. Carrete Parrondo, *Fontes*, no. 286; see also no. 347; and Carrete Parrondo's article "Mesianismo e Inquisición en las juderías de Castilla la Nueva," *Helmantica* 31 (1980): 251–256.

62. See, Liebman, *Jews in New Spain*, 155–156; trial of Diego Díaz Nieto in 1596 (Archivo General de la Nación [Mexico], tomo 159, expediente 2); and trial of Catalina Henríquez in 1643 (Huntington Library).

63. The following lines are absent from the Spanish text: "pues que somes os teuuos seyes / de adorar ed Dioses alleihos / coissa en que tanto ho me encerra . . ."; these lines are corruptly transcribed. This is proved by a three-line fragment preserved in Tras-os-Montes. See Schwarz, "Os cristãos-novos," 88 (84): "Saimos do vosso seio / A adorar ao *deus alheio,* / Coisa que tanto nos erra," which makes perfect sense: "We went forth from your bosom / to worship an alien god, / thus leading us into error . . ."

64. Notice that "sinner" is in feminine (as in many other preserved prayers), because of the central role played by women in the oral transmission of customs and prayers.

65. See, Psalms 121:1–2: "I will lift up mine eyes unto the hills, from whence cometh my help. My help cometh from the Lord, which made heaven and earth."

66. Alluding, as always, to the capital sin of conversion.

67. See Cohen, *The Martyr*, 308.

68. Translation in Liebman, *The Enlightened*, 49.

69. For the history of the "Chuetas" (shamefully discriminated against by their neighbors well into the twentieth century) and fragmentary prayers recorded in the seventeenth century, see Braunstein, *Chuetas*, appendix VI.

70. I have corrected some misreadings by both the scribe and Braunstein.

71. See *Siddur Otzar ha-Thefilloth, Nosah Sefarad*, with commentaries, 2 vols. (New York: A. Y. Friedman Publishers, n.d.), 1:103. The prayer in question is not discussed in A. Z. Idelsohn, *Jewish Liturgy and its Development* (New York: Schocken Books, 1960), otherwise a very useful reference guide.

72. See M. Lazar, "La traduction Hébraico-Provençale du Rituel," in *Mélanges offerts à Jean Frappier* (Geneva: Droz, 1970), 579–580.

73. See *Otzar ha-Thefilloth*, 1:184–185; Idelsohn, *Jewish Liturgy*, 80–81.

74. See, for example, Schwarz, "Os cristãos-novos," 79 (75)m 108 (104); José Gonçalves Salvador, *Cristãos-novos: Jesuitas e Inquisição* (Sao Paulo: Livraria Pioneira Editora, 1969), 181; J. Riera i Sans, "Un recull d'oracions," Catalan version, starting: "*Aquests son los LXXII vessors del psaltiri los quals devets dir tots dies,*" and so on.

75. Of cabalistic origin (see Abraham Ibn Ezra's *Sefer ha-shem*), this hymn comprising seventy-two verses is based on a mystical interpretation of the *tetragramaton* (YHWH: the abstract, symbolic and unpronounceable name of God) and the numerical value of its letters in Hebrew (10, 5, 6, 5). Adding the value of the first with that of the two first, then with the three first, and with all the four, the sum is 72 [10 + (10 + 5) + (10 + 5 + 6) + (10 + 5 + 6 +5)]. Finally, the number 72 corresponds to the numerical value of the Hebrew letters ḤSD (*Ḥesed*: "divine mercy"). Cf. Schwarz, "Os cristãos-novos," 27.

76. See Beinart, "Converso community," 469.

77. This and the following examples have been transcribed by Schwarz, "Os cristãos-novos," 51 ff. (47ff.).

78. O. Camhy, "Le Judeo-Espagnol—facteur de conservation pendant quatre siècles," in *Sephardic Heritage*, ed. Barnett, 1:565 and 546 respectively.

79. Quoted and translated in Liebman, *Jews in New Spain*, 182.

ELEVEN

The Inquisition and the Crypto-Jewish Community in Colonial New Spain and New Mexico

Stanley M. Hordes

Within the scope of Mexican history, the subjects of the Inquisition and crypto-Jews have long been the focus of heated controversy and misplaced value judgments.[1] The unfortunate result of this has been, and still remains today, a lack of understanding of the Inquisition, particularly in its relation to the crypto-Jewish community. The polemical nature of the historiography reflects the same Black Legend-versus-White Legend debate that has plagued colonial Latin American historiography continuously since the Spanish conquest. Because the theme of inquisitorial persecution strikes at the very nerve center of this debate between assailants and defenders of the Spanish colonial system, that is, the rigid enforcement of Catholic orthodoxy and exclusivity, historians of both schools have demonstrated a great deal of emotion and self-righteousness in the pursuit of their respective causes. Many authors have placed a heavy emphasis on the role that the Holy Office of the Inquisition played in the persecution of crypto-Jews, despite the fact that the inquisitors concerned themselves far more with more mundane breaches of faith and morals such as blasphemy, bigamy, witchcraft, impersonation of priests and solicitation of women in the confessional. One of the great barriers to gaining an understanding of the Inquisition and the crypto-Jews in New Spain has been the inappropriate imposition of current value-judgments on people and events in the past. The stress placed by certain historians on the persecution of crypto-Jews reflects an implicit and explicit application of twentieth-century values to an institution and a society of an earlier age.

It will be the purpose of this essay to examine in a more critical and dispassionate manner the experiences of the crypto-Jewish community of New Spain in the colonial era, not only their treatment at the hands of the Holy Office of the Inquisition but their role in the economy and society of the viceroyalty. I will conclude by offering some preliminary observations concerning a new project, just under way, to study a living remnant of the Mexican crypto-Jewish community only now emerging from the shadows in *New* Mexico.

With the conquest of New Spain by Hernando Cortés in 1521, the long arm of the Inquisition extended across the Atlantic Ocean from Spain to Mexico. The small number of Judaizing cases tried by the Mexican Inquisition during the first half-century of Spanish colonization in New Spain indicates that crypto-Jews were able to practice their faith in an atmosphere of relative toleration.[2] This situation began to change in the 1580s, when crypto-Jewish immigration to New Spain increased dramatically. The establishment of Spanish hegemony over Portugal in 1580 motivated Portuguese conversos to move in unprecedented numbers to other areas of the world, including the Indies. The new arrivals were considerably more educated and better versed in Jewish doctrine than were their predecessors, and their presence resulted in a new infusion of religiosity in the viceroyalty.[3]

The increase in the number and activity of the crypto-Jews in New Spain did not go unnoticed by the Mexican Inquisition, only a few years earlier strengthened by elevation to the status of Tribunal del Santo Oficio. Between 1589 and 1596 almost two hundred persons were tried for the crime of *judaizante*. During this period, the most notable and celebrated campaign by the Holy Office was directed toward Luis de Carvajal, el Mozo, his family and associates.[4] The vigorous activity of the Mexican Inquisition against the crypto-Jews at the end of the sixteenth century was short-lived, however. After the auto de fe of 1601 the prosecution of those accused of judaizing declined, and the tribunal concentrated on other breaches of Catholic orthodoxy. The nucleus of Portuguese crypto-Jewish settlement formed in the late sixteenth century served to attract ever-increasing numbers of their countrymen in Spain and Portugal to New Spain in the early seventeenth century.

Indeed, the climate in New Spain was favorable for the settlement of crypto-Jewish immigrants in the early 1600s. The Mexican economy was experiencing a boom period at the end of the sixteenth century that carried over into the early decades of the seventeenth century. The mining sector enjoyed unprecedented expansion from the 1590s through 1620. Agriculture, stock raising, and textiles kept pace with the demand produced by the mining boom, and the level of trade between

New Spain and Europe reached new heights. In the succeeding decades the Mexican economy grew more autonomous, and, despite the decline in trans-Atlantic trade, it continued to grow.[5] In this atmosphere of economic expansion, enterprising crypto-Jewish merchants found themselves ready and able to participate actively in all levels of commerce throughout the viceroyalty.

While crypto-Jews were to be found in almost every region of New Spain in the mid-seventeenth century, Mexico City served as the focal point for converso society just as it did for the larger Spanish economy and society. With few exceptions, crypto-Jewish immigrants from Spain and Portugal traveled directly to the capital after landing at Veracruz.[6] Of the majority who initially settled in Mexico City only a little over half remained there after two or three years. The rest dispersed to more remote regions of the viceroyalty in search of greater economic opportunities. Many left to take advantage of the lucrative trade in the mining areas of Pachuca or northern New Spain; others established themselves in the ports of Acapulco, Veracruz, or Campeche, where they had direct access to the fleets arriving from Spain or in the Philippines. Still others continued westward in search of greater opportunities in the Philippines themselves.

The crypto-Jews who arrived in Mexico City from their distant homelands in Spain and Portugal were quickly absorbed into the mainstream of economic and social life. The established converso community in the capital was a closely knit group with a well-developed system of extended family and patron-client relationships. Several extended family units operated in Mexico City from the 1610s through the 1640s, the most notable of which was the family of Simon Váez Sevilla, without question the wealthiest crypto-Jewish merchant in the viceroyalty. At the head of each such clan there generally appeared a wealthy patron who, like Váez, not only directed the commercial activities of his family but also supervised such mundane functions as the housing, relocation, marriage, burial, and religious ceremonies of those in his charge. Often the passage of a nephew or cousin from Spain or Portugal was financed by the head of one particular clan, arranged through contacts with a relative in Seville or Lisbon.

In their role as merchants, the crypto-Jews blended very well into the mainstream of Mexican society, not distinguishing themselves as a distinct element apart from the general community, except, perhaps, by their particular orientation toward mercantile careers. In a sense it is proper to see the converso experience in this perspective. Crypto-Jews were, after all, first and foremost Iberians, maintaining the language and customs of their forebears in Spain and Portugal. Many had the opportunity to leave the Spanish dominions in favor of lands where they were free to practice Judaism openly and in peace, but most opted to remain in familiar cultural surroundings.

Mexican crypto-Jews were not singled out as a separate group until 1642, when for a variety of reasons to be examined below, the Inquisition embarked on a campaign against the community. It must be emphasized that from 1610 until 1642 there was very little attention paid by the Inquisition, or by any other body, to the crypto-Jewish element in New Spain. Nevertheless, to judge from the testimony offered by the conversos in the trials of the 1640s, it is evident that in certain respects Mexican conversos did conduct themselves in a manner that reflected a consciousness of their ethnic identity.

The patterns demonstrated by crypto-Jews living in Mexico City strongly suggest the presence of a certain degree of ethnocentrism. The Mexican conversos exhibited a strong tendency to live in close proximity to one another, clustered mostly in a three-block area between the cathedral and the Church of Santo Domingo, ironically within a stone's throw of the palace of the Inquisition. Converso traders tended to concentrate their commercial associations within the ethnic community. In almost every area of trade, crypto-Jewish merchants relied upon one another as sources of supply and credit, as agents in remote regions, as fiadores, and as bondsmen in business ventures.

A further demonstration of ethnocentrism may be seen in the propensity of Mexican crypto-Jews to marry within the faith. The practice of endogamy was almost universal. In over ninety-five percent of the marriages, conversos chose partners from within the community. In certain instances efforts were made to "convert" a prospective bridegroom to Judaism in order to gain the approval of the bride's family. In 1638 Isabel Tinoco, niece of Simon Váez Sevilla, found herself being courted by Manuel de Acosta, a young man recently arrived from Lisbon. Relations between Acosta and Isabel's family were cordial throughout the courtship, and eventually Acosta asked her grandfather, Antonio Rodríguez Arias, for her hand in marriage. On the day that Rodríguez's response was to be delivered, Acosta visited him at his house on Calle Tacuba. During a stroll around the nearby Alameda, Rodríguez offered his consent to the marriage, but only on the condition that Acosta abandon the Law of Jesus Christ in favor of the Law of Moses. Acosta agreed, proceeded to learn the practice of Judaism from Rodríguez's wife, and married Isabel Tinoco shortly thereafter.[7]

Perhaps more than any other factor, religious observances served as a vehicle for achieving and maintaining a sense of religious identity within the Mexican crypto-Jewish community. Fast days, especially that of Yom Kippur (referred to as *el día grande*), provided an opportunity for families to stop their normal routine and gather together in the home of one of the worshipers. Inquisition procesos are filled with the detailed accounts of Yom Kippur observances, identifying the location of the service and the names of the worshipers, and vividly describing the manner in which the fasts were broken. Not all conversos were able to meet the stoic test of the fast. Pedro de Espinosa, a traveling merchant in the mining region of Tierra Adentro, stole away from the service at about three o'clock in the afternoon to relieve his hunger.[8] The Sabbath was also generally observed by Mexican conversos. Men refrained from working, and women bathed, changed clothes, and put out clean bed linen on Friday in preparation for the day of rest. Upon the death of a member of the community, the body was prepared for burial in the traditional manner whereby it was bathed, dressed in a shroud, and then placed in virgin soil.[9] Another Jewish rite that was almost universally practiced among Mexican conversos was that of male circumcision. Inspections by Inquisition surgeons revealed that almost ninety-one percent of male conversos were circumcised. When confronted with this evidence, one crypto-Jew made an effort to exonerate himself, explaining that the scar was due to "an earlier infirmity that I had in those parts." Another dismissed it as the result of "the mischief of women." Still another admitted that he subjected himself to the circumcision, but protested that it was only to please a Jewish lover in Italy.[10]

These expressions of ethnic identity manifested by the crypto-Jewish community of New Spain passed virtually unnoticed from 1610 to 1642 by the Holy Office, the body entrusted with the enforcement of religious orthodoxy in the viceroyalty. With few exceptions, Mexican conversos lived their lives, pursued their careers, and discreetly practiced their observances in relative obscurity. In the early 1640s, however, a complex series of developments took place that would dramatically shatter the calm that had prevailed in the converso community for the previous three decades.

In 1640 the Portuguese Duque de Bragança led a successful movement for independence from Philip IV of Spain, thus ending a sixty-year period of Spanish domination. Fear on the part of royal officials in Mexico City that a Portuguese invasion of New Spain was imminent stimulated a series of anti-Portuguese measures aimed at potential subversives.[11] The viceroy suspected of harboring pro-Portuguese sympathies was deposed in 1642 and replaced by the strongly anti-Portuguese archbishop of Mexico, Juan de Palafox y Mendoza.[12] It is no coincidence that within days of Palafox's assumption of viceregal power, the Holy Office issued orders for the arrest of nearly one hundred persons, most of Portuguese descent, on suspicion of being *judaizantes*. Letters sent by Mexican inquisitors to the Supreme Council of the Inquisition in Madrid after the mass arrests shed a good deal of light on the motivation for their actions. The letters clearly place the arrests in the context of the widespread fear of invasion by the Portuguese armada that gripped Mexico in June and July of 1642. Constant reference was made to the threat posed to New Spain by these *"portugueses,"* not so much because of their Judaizing activities as on account of their allegiance to the leaders of the Portuguese revolt. The inquisitors felt that it was their duty as zealous defenders of the kingdom to lend whatever assistance was necessary to counter the threat posed by these perceived subversives within their midst.[13]

On Saturday night, 12 July 1642, agents of the Inquisition arrested seven persons for Judaizing. The next night thirty more were apprehended. Within a year, over seventy-five conversos had entered the secret prisons of the Holy Office, charged with the criminal offense of observing the Law of Moses. By 1647, over 130 had been taken. The Holy Office issued warrants for the arrest of many more but could not follow through on them because the suspects had either died or successfully evaded the Inquisition's agents.[14] Only a small percentage of those convicted were relaxed and burned at the stake (and only one person burned alive). Most were reconciled by the Holy Office, suffering confiscation of their goods and exile from the Indies. In many cases, this sentence of exile was never enforced, and certain crypto-Jews were found to be living in New Spain years after leaving the Inquisition prisons.[15]

Following the *Gran Auto de Fe* of 1649, little attention was paid to the crypto-Jewish community of New Spain by the Inquisition. The period of vigorous activity against judaizantes from 1642 to 1649, like that of 1585–1601, stands as an aberration in the context of three centuries of colonial Mexican history. What happened to those crypto-Jews who left the secret prisons of the Holy Office, or to those countless others who successfully evaded the suspicions of the Inquisition? One can only assume that most melded into the mainstream of Mexican society, some gradually losing all ethnic identity, others passing on vestiges of their Sephardic heritage from generation to generation.

Today, in the former Spanish frontier province of Nuevo México, it appears that a small remnant of these crypto-Jews is just beginning to emerge from the shroud of secrecy that has protected it for two dozen generations. Stories of Hispanic Catholic residents in diverse parts of the state refraining from eating pork, lighting candles on Friday nights, and marrying only within certain families who performed the same customs, have appeared with such regularity that they cannot be dismissed out of hand as anomalies.

There appears to be some strong historical evidence to substantiate the hypothesis that New Mexico was the locus of converso settlement. The period of the expansion of New Spain's northern frontier into New Mexico coincided directly with the most significant crypto-Jewish immigration to New Spain, as well as with the conversos' difficulties with the Inquisition in the late sixteenth and early seventeenth centuries. Following the disappointing search for the mythical Seven Cities of Cíbola and the Kingdom of Quivira undertaken by Francisco Vázquez de Coronado in 1540–1542, Spanish officials and entrepreneurs turned their attention toward exploiting the lucrative silver mines on northern New Spain closer to central Mexico. But in the 1580s and 1590s several *entradas*, both official and unsanctioned, were initiated northward into New Mexico. There are indications that at least three of these expeditions might have been designed to allow crypto-Jews from central Mexico and Nuevo León to escape from the inquisitorial persecutions that centered on the Carvajals and their coreligionists.

In 1582, Governor Carvajal commissioned the expedition of Antonio de Espejo, ostensibly for the purpose of rescuing three Franciscan friars who had been left behind by the Rodríguez-Sánchez Chamuscado mission the year before.[16] The timing of this expedition, coinciding with the arrival of growing numbers of secret Jews into Nuevo León, however, suggests that Carvajal may have had another motive. Perhaps he sought to undertake a discreet search for a refuge on the northern frontier of New Spain for crypto-Jews, should the need arise. Such a need did indeed arise after the crackdown by the Holy Office of the Inquisition against the governor's nephew and his associates in 1589. The following year, Carvajal's lieutenant governor, Gaspar Castaño de Sosa, led a hastily organized and unauthorized expedition of some 170 men, women, and children northwestward out of Nuevo León, to the Pecos River, and upriver into northern New Mexico. Castaño's mission did not receive the authorization of the royal officials in Mexico City, and thus was considered to be illegal.[17]

The close ties maintained by Castaño to Governor Carvajal, and the allegations that he might have been a practicing crypto-Jew in Nuevo León,[18] suggest strongly that he might have initiated the dangerous expedition for the purpose of leading other secret Jews to a secure haven on the far northern frontier. This hypothesis is strengthened by a comparison of names of the expedition with those found in contemporary Inquisition records, accused of the crime of judaizante. Others possessed family names identical to those tried by the Holy Office in Mexico City, such as Rodríguez, Nieto, Carvajal, Díaz, Hernández, and Pérez, and may well have been practicing crypto-Jews themselves.[19]

In 1598, after several years of preparation, Governor and Adelantado Juan de Oñate led some 135 colonists and soldiers northward to establish the first permanent colony in New Mexico. Substantially more is known about the makeup of this expedition than that of Castaño de Sosa. As in the case of the earlier expedition, several indicators point to a crypto-Jewish presence among the founding settlers of New Mexico. The names of several individuals listed on the 8 January 1598 Muster Roll recruited for the enterprise also appear in the records of the Inquisition. Juan Rodríguez, Francisco Hernández, Miguel Rodríguez, and Antonio Rodríguez were cited by the Holy Office as "fugitives"; three of them were burned in effigy in the autos de fe of 1596 and 1601. Sebastián Rodríguez, another member of the Oñate expedition, was possibly one of two individuals by that name taken by the Inquisition. One was reconciled in the auto de fe of 1596, and the other denounced by another judaizante in 1601 as a crypto-Jew. Several other soldiers and colonists maintained either family names associated with conversos, or demographic profiles similar to others known to be practicing crypto-Jews.[20]

Because the Great Pueblo Revolt of 1680 resulted in the destruction of almost all of the locally generated documentation from New Mexico, very little is understood about life in the new colony during the seventeenth century. On the basis of material unearthed in the archives of Spain and Mexico by pioneer scholars such as France V. Scholes, it is known that the Inquisition was administered by the Franciscan missionaries from their base in the Salinas Province. The inquisitorial powers vested in the friars, however, appeared to have been used selectively for political purposes in their struggle for power with governors and other civil officials. The most notorious case during this period was initiated against Governor Bernardo López de Mendizábal, his wife, Teresa de Aguirre y Roche, and certain members of his entourage in 1661–1662 for the crime of judaizante. Most of those charged were ultimately acquitted, including Francisco Gómez Robledo, against whom the inquisitors had amassed the most compelling evidence.[21] Regardless of the official outcomes of these and other trials, the evidence presented raises provocative questions concerning the extent of the crypto-Jewish presence in New Mexico in the seventeenth century.

In the wake of the Reconquest of New Mexico by Governor Diego de Vargas in 1692–1693, thirteen years after the Pueblo Revolt came a new wave of settlers to recolonize New Mexico. By this time the Inquisition was no longer actively prosecuting judaizante cases anywhere in the viceroyalty, and consequently there are no contemporary lists of prisoners against which to compare. Nevertheless, the account of new colonists who accompanied Vargas in 1693, and of those recruited by Juan Páez Hurtado two years later, reveal some familiar names and demographic profiles, strongly suggesting a renewed crypto-Jewish presence.[22] Vargas's secretary, for example, was named Alfonso Rael de Aguilar. A persistent family legend repeated by the present-day descendants of Rael holds that the name derives from "Israel." This story is validated by an examination of baptismal records from the mission of Isleta, where two entries from the year 1756 include references to María Manuela Israel de Aguilar, the granddaughter of Alfonso.[23] Several of Rael's descendants have come forward and acknowledged the presence of Judaic practices among the family's customs.

The families that persevered in this remote province for the next three hundred years left behind few clues to explain their ethnic identity and origins. Many of the descendants of the converso families who settled here apparently assimilated, to a greater or lesser extent, into the mainstream. On the basis of preliminary ethnographic evidence, however, it appears that others continued to practice vestiges of their ancestral faith, some with no consciousness of their ethnic identity, and others maintaining a strong sense of Jewish identity.

NOTES

1. The term *crypto-Jew* refers to those baptized as Catholic Christians and living outwardly as such, but secretly practicing Judaic rites and customs. While the terms converso and New Christian strictly should refer to those Jews who actually converted to Catholicism, it will be extended for the purposes of this paper to the descendants of the original conversos, who lived as crypto-Jews.

2. Richard E. Greenleaf, *The Mexican Inquisition of the Sixteenth Century* (Albuquerque: University of New Mexico Press, 1969), 81; Seymour B. Liebman, *The Jews in New Spain: Faith, Flame and the Inquisition* (Coral Gables, Fla.: University of Miami Press, 1970), 123, 130.

3. Liebman, *The Jews in New Spain,* 135, 151, 184.

4. No attempt is made here to detail the events surrounding the campaign of the Mexican Inquisition against the Carvajals. For an elaboration on this

period see: Liebman, *The Jews in New Spain*, chaps. 7 and 8; Martin Cohen, *The Martyr* (Philadelphia: Jewish Publication Society of America, 1973); Alfonso Toro, *La familia Carvajal* (Mexico City: Editorial Patria, 1944); Seymour B. Liebman, *The Enlightened: The Writings of Luis de Carvajal, El Mozo* (Coral Gables, Fla.: University of Miami Press, 1967); Greenleaf, *Mexican Inquisition*, 169–171.

5. Jonathan Israel, *Race, Class and Politics in Colonial Mexico* (Oxford: Oxford University Press, 1975), 20–30.

6. Based on the *discursos de la vida* of those crypto-Jews arrested by the Inquisition in the 1640s, 82 percent of the converso immigrants settled initially in Mexico City, 11 percent in Veracruz, and the remaining 7 percent scattered about the viceroyalty.

7. Archivo General de la Nación (Mexico) (hereafter AGN), Inquisición, tomo 418, expediente 1, "Proceso y causa criminal contra Manuel de Acosta" (1643), 156–170.

8. AGN, Inq., tomo 403, exp. 1, "Proceso y causa criminal contra Pedro de Espinosa" (1642), 81–85.

9. AGN, Inq., tomo 381, exp. 5, "Borrador de la relación de las causas que se han despachado desde principio de año de 1634 hasta fin del año de 1635." The *relación de causa* of Simón Montero describes the burial of Francisca Núñez.

10. AGN, Inq., tomo 497, exp. 8, "Proceso y causa criminal contra Duarte Castaño," 133–138; AGN, Inq., tomo 395, exp. 3, "Proceso y causa criminal contra Melchor Rodríguez López" (1642); AGN, Inq., tomo 409, exp. 1, "Proceso y causa criminal contra Pedro Fernández de Castro" (1642), 521v; Liebman, *The Jews in New Spain*, 76.

11. AGN, Inq., tomo 489, 84–85, "Traslado del papel que remitió a este Santo Oficio el Sr. Obispo Don Juan de Palafox y Mendoza . . ."; AGN, Inq., tomo 489, 97, Cédula of Philip IV, issued 7 January 1641; AGN, Inq., tomo 489, 114, "Papeles del Sr. Virrey Conde de Salvatierra acerca del donativo de los Portugueses . . ." (1643). This document contains a partial accounting of the *donativo* collected from crypto-Jews in New Spain; AGN, "Reales Cédulas expedidas en relación a los Portugueses . . ." (1642); Archivo General de Indias (Sevilla), Contratación, legajo 102B, "Ante los oidores de la Contratación . . . en Cádiz y Sevilla para embargar perteneciente a portugueses que venia en los galeones y flotas del aquel año; varios autos y diligencias" (1641–42). A total of 332,629 pesos worth of goods sent from New Spain to Portuguese merchants in Seville was embargoed in compliance with a royal order of 17 June 1641.

12. Biblioteca Nacional (Mexico), MSS. 12054, 281, 287v.

13. Archivo Histórico Nacional (Madrid), Inquisición, legajo 1054, "Cartas originales del Tribunal de Mexico para el Consejo."

14. AGN, Inq., Lote Riva Palacio, tomo 48, exp. 2, "Libro donde se sientan todos los presos . . . desde trece de julio de 1642 . . ."(1647?). Data are also extracted from the procesos of judaizantes contained in the AGN.

15. It is difficult to estimate how many of the judaizantes reconciled by the Inquisition remained in New Spain, as the records pertaining to the compliance

of the sentences of exile are unavailable and only those *reconciliados* who relapsed into Judaizing were recorded by the Holy Office. An examination of civil and criminal records for Mexico City revealed several reconciliados picking up their businesses where they had left off years earlier, apparently suffering neither full confiscation of their estates nor exile.

16. John Francis Bannon, *The Spanish Borderlands Frontier, 1513–1821* (Norman: University of Oklahoma Press, 1970), 32–33; Cohen, *The Martyr,* 104.

17. George P. Hammond and Agapito Rey, *The Rediscovery of New Mexico, 1580–1594: The Explorations of Chamuscado, Espejo, Castaño de Sosa, Morlete, and Leyva de Bonilla and Humaña* (Albuquerque: University of New Mexico Press, 1966), 28–39.

18. Cohen, *The Martyr,* 103–104.

19. Hammond and Rey, *Rediscovery,* 245–320; Liebman, *The Inquisitors and the Jews in the New World: Summaries of Procesos, 1500–1810, and Bibliographical Guide* (Coral Gables, Fla.: University of Miami Press, 1974).

20. Hammond and Rey, *Oñate, Colonizer of New Mexico* (Albuquerque: University of New Mexico Press, 1953), 1:286–301; Liebman, *The Inquisitors and the Jews.*

21. France Scholes, *Troublous Times in New Mexico, 1659–1670* (Albuquerque: Historical Society of New Mexico, 1942); AGN, Inquisición, tomo 583, exp. 3, "Proceso y causa criminal contra El Sargento Mayor Francisco Gómez . . . por sospechoso de delitos del judaismo . . ." (1661).

22. Clevy Lloyd Strout, "The Resettlement of Santa Fe, 1695: The Newly Found Muster Roll," *New Mexico Historical Review,* 53, no. 3 (July 1978): 261–270.

23. Archives of the Archdiocese of Santa Fe, Baptisms, Mission of Isleta, Reel 5, frames 227 and 229.

Bibliographical Essays

PART THREE

Biographical Essays

Recent Historiography of the Spanish Inquisition (1977–1988): Balance and Perspective

Jesús M. De Bujanda

The commemoration ten years ago of the fifth century of the establishment of the Spanish Inquisition with Sixtus IV's papal bull dated 1 November 1478 coincided with a veritable explosion of inquisitorial studies. The relative scarcity of studies on the Spanish Inquisition in previous decades contrasts sharply with the awakening in the 1970s and 1980s of an interest manifested in numerous conferences and symposia as well as in the large number of publications that have completely revised our knowledge of the Inquisition and its fundamental influence upon the shape of modern Spain.

It is worth noting that the March 1988 meeting in Los Angeles is chronologically the tenth important scientific congress to deal directly with the theme of the Spanish Inquisition. The previous congresses were: Santander (1976), Copenhagen (1978), Cuenca (1978), Rome-Naples (1981), Santander (1982), Madrid (exposition and conferences, 1982), New York (1983), Madrid-Segovia-Palma (1985), and Chicago (1986).

The Los Angeles congress, investigating the Inquisition's impact on Spain and the New World, provides an appropriate occasion for examining the present state of inquisitorial studies since the reevaluation that took place ten years ago as well as the orientations and perspectives we can discern on the horizon.

It is not our intention to review here the numerous publications on the Inquisition of the past decade. At the end of this essay is a list of the main publications between 1977 and 1988 which serves as a base for the following considerations and focuses our attention on the issues characterizing the evolution of inquisitorial studies. The reader interested in studies prior to 1977 can consult the recent edition in two volumes of the *Bibliography of the Inquisition* by Emil van der Vekene, published in 1982–1983.

It is interesting to note that inquisitorial studies have become popular at the moment when Spanish society is becoming increasingly democratic. If history is a teacher, then the critical and unbiased examination of an organism that institutionalized intolerance for three and a half centuries of present-day Spain's gestation may provide us with a point of reference and reflection for an open, pluralistic society.

From the professional point of view, it is necessary to look beyond the present polemical juncture and become aware of the new orientations of historical studies regarding social history and the history of mentalities. The inquisitorial sources offer the new generations of historians diverse possibilities for the practice of new history.

A BETTER KNOWLEDGE OF THE INQUISITORIAL SOURCES

The historian investigating the Spanish Inquisition is much better equipped in 1988 than the historian who began his studies in 1977. Many valuable publications orient the investigator's steps and put him in direct contact with inquisitorial documents. The content and organization of the *Fondo Inquisición* of the Archivo Histórico Nacional were described in 1978 by M. Avilés, J. Martínez Millán, and V. Pinto in the *Revista de Archivos, Bibliotecas y Museos,* as well as in V. Pinto and M. Vergara Doncel's subsequent publications. Other extremely useful publications include that of the archivist Natividad Moreno Garbajo, *Catálogo de alegaciones fiscales* and the *Inventario de los libros 1225–1281,* both containing valuable indexes of people, places, and material.

Regarding the inquisitorial documents in the Simancas Archive, A. Represa Rodríguez's work can be consulted. Of great value for those who frequent the Diocese Archive of Cuenca, where the most important inquisitorial source outside the AHN is kept, is the second volume of the *Catálogo del Archivo de la Inquisición de Cuenca,* published in 1982 by the present director, Dimas Pérez Ramírez, containing the reproduction of the first volume published in 1965 by S. Cirac Estopañán. A third volume dedicated to the remaining papers will complete the series.

We also have a more complete knowledge of the inquisitorial sources conserved in the libraries and archives outside of Spain, thanks to G. Henningsen's publication describing the Moldenhauer collection of Copenhagen and M. Avilés's contribution that not only records the sources from the British Museum described by E. Llamas Martínez[1]; but also notes the principal European and North American sources where documents related to the Spanish Inquisition can be found.[2]

Investigators interested in the Tribunal of the Holy Office of Portugal will find Charles Amiel's presentation at the Copenhagen congress extremely valuable; it contains a description of the vast resources on the Portuguese Inquisition which have been preserved but poorly cataloged. An important cataloging project on the Lisbon Inquisition trials, subsidized by the Gulbenkian Foundation, began in 1982 under Robert Rowland's direction. This is not simply a catalog or summary of data, but rather a bank of data which the investigator can consult interactively. Professor Amiel has compiled a bank of data based on the proceedings of thirty-eight hundred trials of the Goa Inquisition which reveal the unimagined wealth of the inquisitorial documents for ethnographic and social-historical studies. There is no doubt that the Portuguese archives will orient new projects in the Spanish Inquisition archives.

Beside the catalogs and investigative tools guiding our archival consultations, we must note the publication of specific inquisitorial sources, among which the importance of the collections of autos de fe and *relaciones de causas* must be emphasized. We have partial knowledge of the activity of the Granada Inquisition, whose archives were almost completely destroyed, thanks to the publication of the sixteenth-century autos de fe conserved in the AHN by José María García Fuentes. Antonio Domínguez Ortiz has utilized the seventeenth-century autos de fe to describe the activity of the Seville Inquisition. In his two volumes, *Colección de documentos* and *Autos de fe de la Inquisición de Córdoba*, Rafael Gracia Boix has partially reconstructed the Córdoba Inquisition documentation; these archives were sacked and burned in 1808 and 1812 by order of the central powers at the time of the first suppression of the Inquisition. Llorenc Pérez, Lleonard Muntaner, and Mateu Colom have recently published the first volume of a documentary corpus that will comprise half a dozen volumes compiled from the Majorca Inquisition's *relaciones de causas de fe* from the period 1578–1806, which have been scattered in various archives. The authors are analyzing the causas de fe using an informative procedure.

J. Angel Sesma has published documents from the years 1489–1886 concerning the establishment of the Aragon Inquisition. Miguel Jiménez Monteserín's *Documentos básicos para el estudio del Santo Oficio* offers an anthology of various types of inquisitorial texts.

The publications of texts like the deliberations of the Valladolid Council of 1538 regarding Erasmus by M. Avilés, María de Cazalla's trials by M. Ortega Costa, and Rodrigo de Bivar's trials by A. Hamilton extend the studies undertaken in previous decades by M. Bataillon, J. E. Longhurst, and A. Selke[3] among others, regarding the Inquisition's interventions with respect to Erasmism and illuminism. J. I. Tellechea's monumental edition of the trial of Bartolomé Carranza de Miranda, the archbishop of Toledo, has been published by the Academia de la Historia[4]; Tellechea continues publishing numerous monographs and documents of great interest regarding the Inquisition's repression of the Reformation and Molinism.

A MORE SERENE, COMPLETE, AND CRITICAL HISTORY

Thanks to a renovated methodological approach to the sources, the historical production on the Inquisition of recent years is generally of high quality. Not only has a great deal more been written than previously, but it is novel and generally more solid than previous investigations.

Until recently, it was difficult to approach a topic as polemical as the Inquisition without provoking strong reactions of disapproval or assent. While many of the Inquisition historians were members of the secular clergy or of religious orders studying the tribunal of the faith from the Catholic perspective and with a Tridentine mentality (or at least a mentality predating that of Vatican II), others studied from a political, social, or cultural angle, guided by the ideals of open-mindedness and progress in human rights. We can thus comprehend how the outstanding work by the historian Henry C. Lea, *History of the Inquisition of Spain*, and above all its polemical conclusion entitled "Retrospect," has provoked such extremely negative reactions from the Jesuit historian Bernardino Llorca. The apologists' and detractors' aprioristic positions have impeded the progress of historical knowledge of the Holy Office. We can contrast this traditional historiography on the Inquisition with the position of present-day historians, whose goals of objectivity and impartiality reflect an ideal which we cannot attain, but can indeed approach.

This does not mean that ideologies, religious creeds, political and social options, or natural sentiments do not continue to orient investigative projects or to be reflected in historical production. Thus for example, in the meritorious collective work *Historia de la Inquisición en España y América*, published by the Centro de Estudios Inquisitoriales and the Biblioteca de Autores Cristianos, the first criterion established, which determines the elaboration of the entire work, is "the *españolidad* of the authors invited to collaborate" (vol. 1, p. xxii). While we cannot but lament this completely obsolete position, we must recognize that this statement contrasts strongly with the spirit of collaboration of which the work itself is proof. The first published volume presents the work of thirty specialists on the subjects of "the bases of historical knowledge of the Holy Office" and "the stages of its historical process." This concerns, without a doubt, a great realization that acts as a reference point for everyone interested in the study of the Spanish Inquisition.

Among the other notable anthologies of the past ten years is *L'Inquisition espagnole, XVe–XIXe siècles* by Bartolomé Bennassar and various collaborators including Jean-Pierre Dedieu, whose firsthand investigations have completely reorganized the problematics of the Holy Office. Nor should we forget Henry Kamen's contribution, *The History of the Inquisition of Spain,* which twenty years after publication has recently been followed by *Inquisition and Society in Spain,* a text incorporating many of the most interesting investigations of recent years.

We have also recently been witness to the revalorization of historical works of great breadth which stimulated the polemic for many years. José Antonio Llorente's works have elicited various studies viewing them from a new perspective, principally the *Historia crítica de la Inquisición,* which has come out in a new edition. For the first time, and seventy years after the appearance of the original version, Lea's monumental history has been published in Spanish as *Historia de la Inquisición Española.* Edited by Angel Alcalá, this version has the advantage of giving the references to the inquisitorial documentation as they are currently indexed in the AHN, while the original English version as well as the translations give the catalog numbers of the previous location in the Simancas archive, before the documents were transferred in 1914 to the AHN in Madrid.

Among the studies published in the last ten years, there are various important contributions that have completely renewed previous historiography, upon which we have based our synthesis of what the Spanish Inquisition was.

At the same time, we are conscious that our study omits areas in which important progress has been made. For example, there has been a great step forward in our knowledge of the organization and activity of the local tribunals. Besides the article by J. Contreras and J. P. Dedieu on the formation of local districts, there are a number of impressive monographic studies on most of the provincial tribunals. Much could also be said of the various monographic studies dedicated to investigating the catalogs of persecuted groups such as the Judaizers, moriscos, Protestants, Illuminati, spiritualists, *brujos*, masons, and Gypsies. I hope that the reader wishing to expand his knowledge on a particular theme will be guided by the bibliography included at the end of this paper.

A POLITICO-RELIGIOUS TRIBUNAL

The Spanish Inquisition, a politico-religious institution of the Habsburg regime, cannot be understood without a knowledge of the latter and its evolution during three centuries of modern history.

In the first place, we cannot forget that the Spanish monarchy of the Austrians and the Bourbons was a religious state whose very foundations were based upon Catholic faith. The union between Church and state produced a mixture, and frequently a confusion, of the political and religious spheres. The Catholic monarchy established its political, social, economic, and cultural program on the basis of religion, and constructed national unity upon the solid foundation of religious unity. It is not necessary to show here how the "Christian republic" and its corresponding institutions were born and developed from the time of the emperor Constantine and throughout the millennium of the Middle Ages. We must recall that the medieval Inquisition, and to an even greater extent the Inquisition established by the popes in response to the Catholic Monarchs' pleas, is a hybrid institution at the service of both the altar and the throne, controlled by the religious state and the political Church.

The Inquisition defines itself as the tribunal of the faith whose duty is not only to pass judgment following a denunciation or accusation but also to inquire into the prisoner's orthodoxy. If we wish to know what the very essence of the Inquisition is, the most fundamental question we must pose concerns "the juridical nature of the institution." We are not concerned, as Francisco Tomás y Valiente indicated at the Cuenca symposium, with entering into old polemics about whether the Tribunal of the Holy Office is a political organism or essentially an ecclesiastical institution. We must approach its examination without preconceived notions, studying its standards and examining its function with respect to political and juridical state institutions on the one hand, and to the ecclesiastical authorities and tribunals on the other.

Various investigative projects and publications are contributing elements essential for an understanding of the Holy Office as a juridical institution. According to María Palacios Alcalde's presentation at the Lisbon congress in February 1987, the Department of Modern History at the University of Córdoba is working on the elaboration of a "legislative corpus of the Spanish Inquisition which attempts to record exhaustively the Inquisition's entire regulatory standard, that is, the demand for temporal power (royal letters patent, decrees, consultations, pragmatics, etc.) as well as pontifical power (bulls, briefs, motuproprios, etc.) and the normative demand of the Inquisition itself (council decrees, orders of the inquisitor general, instructions, edicts, etc.)."[5]

Knowledge of instruments utilized by the inquisitors, such as *abecedarios de textos legales* that Francisco de Borja Luque Muriel works with[6] and the *manual de inquisidores* like the famous manual of the medieval inquisitor Eymeric which was discovered in the mid-sixteenth century by Francisco Peña and which Sala Molins has studied,[7] provides information about the normative bases guiding the inquisitorial process. The *instrucciones* issued by the first inquisitors, Torquemada and Deza, and the recasting carried out by Fernando de Valdés in 1561 regulating the Holy Office's procedures until the moment of its suppression, are equally deserving of our attention.[8] At the Burdeos symposium in October 1987, Henningsen presented a data base of the Spanish Inquisition's secret legislation compiled in the *Codex Moldenhawerianus* in Copenhagen. There is no doubt that the sources listed here will greatly facilitate our understanding of the Inquisition Council and its connections to the institutions of the monarchy and the Church.

AN INSTITUTION WITH RELIGIOUS AND SOCIAL CONTROL

As indicated in the founding bull of the Spanish Inquisition, *Exigit sincerae devotionis affectus,* and repeated in subsequent documents, the Holy Office functioned as a coercive instrument of defense of the Catholic faith against heretical depravity. It is an exact mandate, restricting itself to cases concerning faith, and referring solely to the fundamental articles of the Catholic faith. It is, in reality, an extremely long mandate. Everything depends upon what is understood by *faith* and what is considered a transgression against the faith. Faith is a fluid concept, specified over time by the ecclesiastical magistrate as he defines dogma and delimits the true content and consequences of the evangelical message. As the Roman Church considers itself repository of the revelation as well as legitimate and authorized interpreter of divine and natural law, it may pass judgment on morality and all human acts. The coercive power received by the Holy Office from the Church and the state varies according to how Catholic faith is understood. Foundation and pillar of the Habsburg society, Christianity is not interpreted and experienced uniformly during the three and a half centuries of the Inquisition's exis-

tence. Both Church and state must modify their institutions according
to the needs of a continually evolving society. We can thus understand
how the Inquisition, acting as an instrument of religious and social control throughout its entire existence, modifies the object of its activities
and its field of action, adapting itself to changing circumstances.

Because specialists in recent years have been able to exploit the
sources more systematically and directly, we are much better informed
regarding the number of people tried by the Inquisition and the nature
of their crimes.

Through a methodical and detailed examination of more than forty
thousand trial summaries (relaciones de causas), sent by the regional tribunals to the Supreme Inquisition Council, Gustav Henningsen and
Jaime Contreras have presented an impressive summary of the Inquisition's activity during the years 1540–1700, the central period of its
existence.

We have formed an idea of the Holy Office's main activities at the
end of the fifteenth and beginning of the sixteenth century on the basis
of Jean-Pierre Dedieu's study of the Toledo tribunal and Ricardo García
Cárcel's study of the Valencia tribunal. T. Egido has investigated Inquisition activities by studying the *alegaciones fiscales* and the relaciones de
autos de fe. The catalog of alegaciones fiscales, excerpts from the cases
sent by the provincial tribunals to the Central Council before sentencing,
was recently published by Natividad Moreno Garbayo. The relaciones
de autos de fe contain, among other things, much information about the
prisoners and their crimes.

Although many other investigations of new sources still need to be
carried out, we now possess a more complete knowledge of inquisitorial
activity as well as of the evolution of the numbers of trials and the nature
of the crimes.

The first conclusion we arrive at based on completed studies is that
the Inquisition was an institution that evolved according to changing
circumstances. If it is an obvious exaggeration to speak of multiple inquisitions, we must distinguish among different periods of the Inquisition, as Jean-Pierre Dedieu has done. We can perceive the alternation
between periods of great intensity and periods of relative inactivity on
the basis of the number of individuals tried. The second half of the sixteenth century is a period of great activity culminating in the 1590s;
after 1620 there is a decline in the Holy Office's activities which continues throughout the seventeenth century. Except for specific instances,
the Inquisition gradually loses its importance and prestige during the
eighteenth century until its complete suppression is called for.

Besides the curve in the volume of people tried, the examination of the nature of their crimes eloquently reveals the areas of repressive inquisitorial activity. Henningsen and Contreras, basing their investigation on the same classifications used by the inquisitors, have organized crimes prosecuted by the Inquisition in the tribunals of Spain, Sardinia, Sicily, and America into ten categories: (1) Jews, (2) Moors, (3) Lutherans, (4) Illuminati, (5) *proposiciones*, (6) bigamists, (7) soliciting confessors, (8) crimes against the Holy Office, (9) superstitious individuals, (10) miscellaneous.

Between 1540 and 1700, the first four categories were considered capital offenses and made up forty-two percent of all cases, while the other fifty-eight percent were considered minor offenses. The number of individuals prosecuted from each category of capital offense corresponded directly to the political and religious circumstances of the period, depending considerably on the specific tribunal as well. We have observed, for example, that from the time of Portugal's annexation by the Habsburg monarchy in 1580, the number of trials of converted Portuguese Jews was very high in Castile until amnesty was conceded in 1605. The number of morisco trials was very high in Aragón, Valencia, and Granada during the period of prosecution (1605–1609) preceding the expulsion. During the period 1540–1559, when the fight against the Protestant Reformation was most intense, Lutherans made up thirty-one percent of all prosecuted individuals. Faithful Christians seduced by false mysticism, called the Illuminati, made up a very small percentage (0.03 percent), and appear only at specific moments and only in certain tribunals such as Llerena, Seville, and Logroño. We must also note the low number of executions: 826 cases throughout the entire period of 1540–1700, that is, 1.8 percent of all those brought to trial.

During the fifty-five-year period of 1560–1614, those tried for minor offenses made up approximately fifty-eight percent. The victims were Old Christians mainly from rural areas. The Holy Office's repressive actions were part of the evangelical campaigns to impose the Tridentine model of Catholicism. The concept of heresy was extended to include all propositions or affirmations contrary to Catholic dogma as well as acts based upon a supposedly erroneous interpretation of Catholic morality. Thus, for example, anyone who affirmed that fornication was not a sin for unmarried individuals was prosecuted for going against the teachings of the Church; the same applied to someone who married twice, because he had not respected the indissolubility of holy matrimony.

The Inquisition's control over religious life diminished during the seventeenth century. On the one hand, the Holy Office suffered a series of internal crises of a structural and economic character, and on the other hand, upholding the faith and morality of Trent was no longer among the Church's or the state's priorities. We have few monographic works dealing with the Holy Office's activity during the eighteenth century. T. Egido's investigations of fiscal allegations and autos de fe reveal a reduction in repressive interventions and a typology of criminal offenses including not only those defined above but new ones such as Molinism, Jansenism, and Masonry.

Civil and ecclesiastical institutions took increasingly contradictory positions in the eighteenth century, creating a wide gap. On one side, the regalist state tried to domesticate the Inquisition, and on the other side Enlightenment philosophy sought to base society upon rational law, dispensing with religious institutions altogether.

The existing tensions within Habsburg society that led finally to a dissociation between state and religion were reflected in the Inquisition, which, as a politico-religious organism, lost the justifications for its very existence. The French Revolution stimulated a new alliance between throne and altar, momentarily revitalizing the Holy Office as a repressive defensive instrument. The evolution leading to the abolition of the Inquisition, initially in 1812 and definitively in 1834, described by Francisco Martí Gilabert,[9] reveals the contradictory forces at work in modern Spain.

As an institution of religious and social control, the Inquisition based its justification upon the religious state. It ensured the survival of social institutions and values, maintaining the functions of certain modern policies.

AN ORGANISM OF CULTURAL REPRESSION

The Spanish Inquisition, besides being the tribunal of the faith, was responsible for censoring the press and thus fulfilled the functions entrusted to the congregations of the Inquisition and the Index by the Roman Church. In this field there have been many important investigations published during the past decade that, in leaving behind the old and sterile polemic on the Inquisition's influence on the evolution of Spanish science and culture, have studied censorship from different angles, beginning with a direct and systematic examination of the sources, such as the proceedings against the author and readers or owners of texts, inquisitorial legislation and regulation, and indexes of prohibited texts.

Antonio Márquez's *Literatura e Inquisición* is a description of censorious activity and Spanish literary production and provides information on a large number of Spanish writers and intellectuals. Recently Alfredo Vílchez Díaz compiled a useful list of Spanish authors and anonymous individuals on the inquisitorial indexes. A special issue of *Arbor*, entitled *Inquisición y ciencia*, appeared, including articles by various contributors, among whom A. Márquez (the editor), José Pardo Tomás, and Lucienne Domergue have offered partial answers to questions concerning the Inquisition's influence on Spain's scientific backwardness in the modern period. In various works directly studying the sources, principally in Virgilio Pinto Crespo's *Inquisición y control ideológico en el siglo XVI*, various aspects of the workings of inquisitorial censorship during the sixteenth century have been thoroughly investigated. Marcelin Défourneaux's book on the censorship of French texts during the eighteenth century, published in 1963,[10] has recently been supplemented by Lucienne Domergue's valuable contributions on culture and censorship during that century.

For more than ten years, Domergue and various collaborators at the Centre d'Etudes de la Renaissance de l'Université de Sherbrooke have studied the indexes of prohibited texts (including European texts in general, but principally Spanish and Roman ones), the results appearing regularly in the collection *Index des livres interdits*.[11] The first phase of the project focusing on the sixteenth century is composed of two volumes on Spanish indexes: the first volume (already published) covers the indexes of 1551, 1554, and 1559, and the second, soon to be published, covers the 1583 and 1584 indexes. Our investigation examines censored materials, that is, the content of the indexes of prohibited and expurgated materials. The prohibited material reveals the presence of a repressed counterculture struggling against the dominant official culture. The prohibited or censored writings are but the tip of the iceberg, opening avenues of exploration of the unsuspected underlying reality not immediately apparent in the collective consciousness. We sincerely believe that our study, like those previously mentioned, is of a positive rather than a speculative nature, and that its investigation of essential sources will allow us to determine the extent of inquisitorial censorship's influence on different aspects of Spanish reality: culture, religion, literature, political and social development.

THE FUTURE OF INQUISITORIAL STUDIES

We need to ask ourselves whether the interest awakened in inquisitorial studies during the past ten years is a temporary phenomenon, or whether we are breaking new ground regarding Spain's history which must continue to be studied in order for us to achieve a greater understanding of Spanish society's evolution in its totality. We have observed signs of weariness or apathy in some historians, attracted by more appealing and contemporary topics.

We believe, however, in a future full of possibilities for inquisitorial studies, although perhaps they will not continue to enjoy the notoriety and relevance of the past decade. Our faith in the future of inquisitorial studies is based on the following considerations:

The historians in the forefront—Henningsen, Contreras, Dedieu, García Cárcel, and others—have tilled the fertile field of inquisitorial studies, and not only do they continue their own investigations, but they have also attracted new students who will in turn undertake new investigations, armed with the renovated problematic and methodology as well as the assistance of modern technology.

The archival documents and other inquisitorial sources offer the fields of social and intellectual history an arsenal of extremely valuable material. We need only consider the data base of the relaciones de causas or the inquisitorial trials which will lend themselves to unlimited quantitative and qualitative surveys. Some of the investigations of the 1970s based on Inquisition trials—studies by Emmanuel Le Roy Ladurie of a French Midi town called Montaillou and by Carlo Ginzburg on a miller named Menocchio from the Friuli region—are good examples of the abundance and quality of the information yielded by analyzing specific trials with the appropriate methodology.[12] The inquisitorial sources also provide excellent opportunities for quantitative studies, as Michel Vovelle's methodology of compiling and analyzing a series of sixteenth-century wills from the French Province has proved.[13] Without dwelling upon or insisting only upon examples of *nouvelle histoire*, we are reminded that Jean Delumeau's work on fear and guilt in modern Europe[14] offers both a problematic and a qualitative model of analysis applicable to many inquisitorial sources.

Notwithstanding the destruction of archival sources from the majority of regional Inquisition tribunals, thousands of documents still exist, housed mainly in the Archivo Histórico Nacional in Madrid, whose systematic study will surpass the individual efforts of the majority of investigators. The individual investigator's procedure, which previously consisted of studying the inquisitorial archives in order to produce a monographic work on an individual or specific theme, can now be likened to the fisherman who casts his line into the water in hopes of finding a treasure. Such a procedure is completely anachronistic when we are now able to catalog and classify the sources according to clearly defined criteria and establish an integral and cumulative data base accessible to all investigators through the international channels of computer networks.

These are the concerns of a number of Inquisition specialists who have met on several occasions for the purpose of coordinating their efforts in the direction outlined above. Realizing that the Inquisition documents are not essentially different from those of other ecclesiastical or civil tribunals, they established contact with legal historians and organized the symposium on "Judicial Records and the Computer: Secular, Ecclesiastical, and Inquisitorial Courts," held at the Maison des Pays Iberiques in Bordeaux in October 1987 under the auspices of the European Science Foundation. Inquisition historians from Spain, Italy, and Portugal, members of the International Association of the History of Crime and Criminal Justice, and representatives from the Association of History and Computing are studying the possibility of adopting specific shared conceptual bases that would establish what elements should be in the data base, created from the *codaje* manual, at the service of historical investigation from both a quantitative and a qualitative perspective. Initiatives such as these bode well for the future of inquisitorial studies.

NOTES

1. E. Llamas Martínez, *Documentación inquisitorial: Manuscritos españoles del siglo XVI existentes en el Museo Británico* (Madrid: Fundación Universitaria Española, 1975).

2. M. Avilés, "Los fondos extranjeros," in *Historia de la Inquisición en España y America,* ed. J. Pérez Villanueva and B. Escandell Bonet (Madrid: Biblioteca de Autores Cristianos, Centro de Estudios Inquisitoriales, 1984), 1:83–89.

3. A. Selke, *El Santo Oficio de la Inquisición: Proceso de Fr. Francisco Ortiz* (Madrid: 1968).

4. J. I. Tellechea Idígoras, *Fray Bartolomé Carranza: Documentos históricos,* 6 vols. to date (Madrid: Archivo Documental Español. Real Academia de la Historia, 1962–1981).

5. *Inquisiçao: I Congresso Luso-Brasileiro sobre Inquisiçao: Resumos das comunicaçoes, Lisboa, 17 a 20 fevereiro 1987* (Lisbon: Sociedade Portuguesa de Estudos do Século XVIII, 1987), 128–129.

6. *Ibid.,* 131–134.

7. Nicolau Eymeric et Francisco Peña, *Le manuel des inquisiteurs,* ed. and trans. Louis Sala-Molins (Paris: Mouton, 1973).

8. J. L. González Novalín, "Las instrucciones de Valdés," in *Historia de la Inquisición,* 1:633–648.

9. Francisco Martí Gilabert, *La abolición de la Inquisición* (Pamplona: Ediciones Universidad de Navarra, 1975).

10. M. Défourneau, *L'Inquisition espagnole et les livres français au XVIIIe siècle* (Paris: Presses universitaires de France, 1963; Spanish edition, Madrid: Taurus Ediciones, 1973).

11. Five volumes have been published: (1) *Index de l'Université de Paris*; (2) *Index de l'Université de Louvain*; (3) *Index de Venise, 1549 et 1554*; (5) *Index de l'Inquisition Espagnole, 1551, 1554, 1559*; (7) *Index d'Anvers, 1569, 1570, 1571* (Sherbrooke, Quebec: Centre d'Études de la Renaissance, Éditions de l'Université de Sherbrooke, 1984–1988).

12. E. Le Roy Ladurie, *Montaillou, village occitan de 1294 à 1324* (Paris: Gallimard, 1975); C. Ginzburg, *The Cheese and the Worms: The Cosmos of a Sixteenth Century Miller* (Baltimore and London: Johns Hopkins, 1980).

13. M. Vollvelle, *Piété baroque et déchristianisation: les attitudes devant la mort en Provence au XVIIIe siècle* (Paris: Plon, 1973); idem, *Idéologies et mentalités* (Paris: François Maspero, 1982).

14. J. Delumeau, *La peur en Occident, XIVe–XVIIIe siècles: Une cité assiégée* (Paris: Fayard, 1978); *Le péché et la peur: La culpabilisation en occident, XIIIe–XVIIIe siècles* (Paris: Fayard, 1983).

PUBLICATIONS ON THE SPANISH INQUISITION, 1977–1988

Abellán, J. L. "La persistencia de la 'mentalidad inquisitorial' en la vida y la cultura española contemporánea, y la teoría de 'las dos Españas.'" In *Inquisición española y mentalidad inquisitorial: Ponencias del Simposio Internacional sobre Inquisición, Nueva York, abril de 1983*, edited by A. Alcalá et al., 542–555. Barcelona: Editorial Aries, 1984.

Alcalá, A. "Control inquisitorial de humanistas y escritores." In *Inquisición española*, edited by A. Alcalá et al., 288–314. Barcelona: Editorial Aries, 1984.

Alcalá, A. et al. *Inquisición española y mentalidad inquisitorial. Ponencias del Simposio Internacional sobre Inquisición, Nueva York, abril de 1983*. Barcelona: Editorial Aries, 1984.

Alfaro, G. "Los 'Lazarillos' y la Inquisición." *Hispanófila* 78 (1983): 11–19.

Alonso Burgos, J. *El luteranismo en Castilla durante el siglo XVI: Autos de fe de Valladolid de 21 mayo y de 8 de octubre de 1559*. El Escorial: Swan Avantos y Hakeldama, 1983.

Alvarez de Morales, A. "La crítica al Tribunal de la Inquisición durante la segunda mitad del siglo XVIII." *Estudis* 6 (1977): 171–182.

———. *Inquisición e ilustración (1700–1834)*. Madrid: Fundación Universitaria Española, 1982.

Amiel, C. "La 'pureté de sang' en Espagne." *Annales du C.E.S.E.R.E.* 6 (1983): 27–45.

———. "The Archives of the Portuguese Inquisition: A Brief Survey." In *The*

Inquisition in Early Modern Europe: Studies on Sources and Methods, edited by G. Henningsen and J. Tedeschi, in association with C. Amiel, 79–99. DeKalb, Ill.: Northern Illinois University Press, 1986.

Andrés, M. "Alumbrados, erasmistas, 'luteranos' y místicos, y su común denominador: el riesgo de una espiritualidad más 'intimista.'" In *Inquisición española,* edited by A. Alcalá et al., 373–409. Barcelona: Editorial Aires, 1984.

———. *La teología española en el siglo XVI.* 2 vols. Madrid: Biblioteca de Autores Cristianos, 1977.

Aranda Doncell, J. *Los moriscos en tierras de Córdoba.* Córdoba, 1984.

Asensio, E. "Censura inquisitorial de libros en los siglos XVI y XVII. Fluctuaciones, decadencias." In *El libro antiguo español. Actas del primer Coloquio Internacional* (Madrid, 18 al 20 diciembre 1986), al cuidado de M. L. López-Vidriero, y P. M. Cátedra, 21–36. Salamanca: Ediciones de la Universidad de Salamanca. Biblioteca Nacional de Madrid. Sociedad Española de Historia del Libro, 1988.

Aspe, M. P. "El cambio de rumbo de la espiritualidad española a mediados del siglo XVI." In *Inquisición española,* edited by A. Alcalá et al.: 424–433. Barcelona: Editorial Aries, 1984.

Avilés Fernández, M. "Los alumbrados en Andalucía." In *El barroco en Andalucía,* edited by M. Peláez del Rosal and J. Rivas Carmona, 137–152. Córdoba, 1984.

———. "La censura inquisitorial de 'Los seis libros de la República' de Jean Bodin." *Hispania Sacra* 37 (1985): 655–692.

———. "Delación a la Inquisición y otras reacciones de los lectores del 'Tratado de la regalía de amortización' de Campomanes.'" *Hispania Sacra* 36 (1984): 43–69.

———. *Erasmo y la Inquisición. El libelo de Valladolid y la 'Apologia' de Erasmo contra los frailes españoles.* Madrid: Fundación Universitaria Española, 1980.

———. "España e Italia en los escritos del antierasmista Luis de Maluenda." *Anexos de Pliegos de Cordel* 1 (1979): 225–239.

———. "La Inquisición en la Andalucía barroca." In *El barroco en Andalucía,* edited by M. Peláez del Rosal and J. Rivas Carmond, 153–167. Córdoba, 1984.

———. "Los inquisidores generales: estudio del alto funcionariado inquisitorial en los siglos XV y XVI." *Annuario dell'Istituto Storico Italiano per l'età moderna e contemporanea,* 37–38 (1985–1986): 261–284.

———. "Motivos de crítica a la Inquisición en tiempos de Carlos V: Aportaciones para una historia de la oposición a la Inquisición." In *La Inquisición,* edited by J. Pérez Villanueva, 165–192. Madrid: BAC, 1980.

———. *Sueños ficticios y lucha ideológica en el Siglo de Oro.* Biblioteca de Visionarios, Heterodoxos y Marginados. Madrid: Editora Nacional, 1981.

———. "Verdaderas y falsas imágenes de la Inquisición española." In *La Inquisición: Palacio de Velázquez del Retiro, Madrid, octubre–diciembre 1982,* 33–50. Madrid: Dirección General de Bellas Artes, Archivos y Bibliotecas, 1982. Exposition organized by the Ministry of Culture, 1982.

Avilés Fernández, M., J. Martínez, and V. Pinto. "El Archivo del Consejo de la Inquisición: Aportaciones para una historia de los archivos inquisitoriales." In *Revista de Archivos, Bibliotecas y Museos* 81 (1978): 459–517.

Azcona, T. de. "Aspectos económicos de la Inquisición de Toledo en el siglo XV." *V Simposio Toledo Renacentista* 1 (1980): 5–72.

Bataillon, M. "Humanismo, erasmismo y represión cultural en la España del siglo XVI." In *Erasmo y el erasmismo*, 162–178. Barcelona: Editorial Crítica, 1978.

Beinart, H. *Los conversos ante el Tribunal de la Inquisición.* Barcelona: Riopiedras Ediciones, 1983.

Bel Bravo, M. A. *El auto de fe de 1593. Los conversos granadinos de origen judío.* Granada: Universidad de Granada, 1988.

Bennassar, B. *L'Inquisition espagnole, XV–XIX siècles.* Paris: Hachette, 1979. Translated by J. Alfaya, under the title: *Inquisición española: Poder político y control social.* Barcelona: Editorial Crítica, 1981.

———. "Modelos de la mentalidad inquisitorial: Métodos de su 'pedagogía del miedo.'" In *Inquisición española*, edited by A. Alcalá et al., 174–183. Barcelona: Editorial Aries, 1984.

Benítez Sánchez Blanco, R. *Felipe II y los moriscos: El intento decisivo de asimilación 1559–1568. Estudios de historia de Valencia*, 183–202. Valencia, 1978.

———. *Moriscos y cristianos en el Condado de Casares.* Córdoba, 1982.

Blázquez Miguel, J. *La Inquisición en Albacete.* Albacete: Instituto de Estudios Albacetenses, 1985.

———. *La Inquisición en Castilla La Mancha.* Madrid: Universidad de Córdoba, 1986.

———. *Inquisición y criptojudaísmo.* Madrid: Ediciones Kaydeda, 1988.

———. *El Tribunal de la Inquisición de Murcia.* Murcia: Academia Alfonso X el Sabio, 1986.

Borromeo, A. "Contributo allo studio dell'Inquisizione e dei suoi rapporti con il potere episcopale nell'Italia spagnola del cinquecento." *Annuario dell'Istituto Storico Italiano per l'età moderna e contemporanea*, 29–30 (1977–1978): 219–276.

———. "Inquisizione spagnola e libri proibiti in Sicilia ed in Sardegna durante il XVI secolo." *Annuario dell'Istituto Storico Italiano per l'età moderna e contemporanea*, 35–36 (1983–1984): 219–271.

Burgarella, P. "Fonti d'archivi sull'Inquisizione spagnola in Sicilia." *Annuario dell'Istituto Storico Italiano per l'età moderna e contemporanea*, 37–38 (1985–1986): 143–160.

Burman, E. *The Inquisition: The Hammer of Heresy.* Wellingborough, Eng.: Aquarian Press, 1984.

Cardaillac, L. *Moriscos y cristianos viejos: Un enfrentamiento polémico. 1492–1640.* Madrid, 1979.

Carrete Parrondo, C. *Fontes Iudaeorum Regni Castellae. III: Proceso inquisitorial contra los Arias Dávila segovianos: Un enfrentamiento social entre judíos y conversos.* Salamanca, 1986.

Carrete Parrondo, J. M. *Movimiento alumbrado y renacimiento español: Proceso in-*

quisitorial contra Luis de Beteta. Madrid: Centro de Estudios Judeo-Cristianos, 1980.

Cascales Ramos, A. *La Inquisición en Andalucía: Resistencia de los conversos a su implantación.* Seville: Editoriales Andaluzas Unidas, 1986.

Castro, M. de. "El franciscano Fr. Luis de Maluenda, un alguacil alguacilado de la Inquisición." In *La Inquisición española,* edited by J. Pérez Villanueva, 797–813. Madrid: BAC, 1980.

Cobos Ruiz de Adana, J. "Sexualidad e Inquisición en Córdoba a finales del siglo XVI." *Axerquía* 2 (1980): 175–194.

Contreras, J. *El Santo Oficio de la Inquisición de Galicia: Poder, sociedad y cultura.* Madrid: Akal Editor, 1982.

———. "Algunas consideraciones sobre las relaciones de causas de Sicilia y Cerdeña." In *Annuario dell'Istituto Storico Italiano per l'età moderna e contemporanea,* 37–38 (1985–1986): 181–191.

———. "The Impact of Protestantism in Spain 1520–1600." In *Inquisition and Society in Early Modern Europe,* edited and translated by S. Haliczer, 47–63. London: Croom Helm, 1987.

———. "La infraestructura social de la Inquisición: Comisarios y familiares." In *Inquisición española,* edited by A. Alcalá et al., 123–146. Barcelona: Editorial Aries, 1984.

———. "La Inquisición aragonesa en el marco de la monarquía autoritaria." *Hispania Sacra* 37 (1985): 489–540.

———. "La Inquisición de Aragón: Estructura y oposiciones (1550–1700)." *Revista de Estudios de Historia Social* 1 (1977): 113–141.

———. *Inquisición española: Nuevas aproximaciones,* edited by J. Contreras. Madrid: Centro de Estudios Inquisitoriales, Ediciones Nájera, 1987.

Contreras, J., and J. P. Dedieu. "Geografía de la Inquisición española: La formación de los distritos (1480–1820)." *Hispania* 40 (1980): 37–93.

Contreras J., and G. Henningsen. "Forty-four Thousand Cases of the Spanish Inquisition (1540–1700): Analysis of a Historical Data Bank." In *The Inquisition in Early Modern Europe: Studies on Sources and Methods,* edited by G. Henningsen and J. Tedeschi, in association with C. Amiel, 100–129. DeKalb, Ill.: Northern Illinois University Press, 1986.

Coronas Tejada, L. "Estudio social de los familiares del Santo Oficio en Jaén a mediados del siglo XVII." In *La Inquisición española,* edited by J. Pérez Villanueva, 293–302. Madrid: BAC, 1980.

———. *El inquisidor de las brujas.* Jaén, 1981.

———. *Los judeoconversos en el reino de Jaén.* Jaén, 1978.

Cristóbal, M. A. "La Inquisición de Logroño. Una institución de control social." In *Inquisición española: Nuevas aproximaciones,* edited by J. Contreras, 127–158. Madrid: Centro de Estudios Inquisitoriales, Ediciones Nájera, 1987.

De Bujanda, J. M. "Censura e Inquisición en España en el siglo XVI." In *La Inquisición española,* edited by J. Pérez Villanueva, 179–192. Madrid: BAC, 1980.

———. "Censure romaine et censure espagnole au XVIe siècle: Les index romain et espagnol de 1559." *Annuario dell'Istituto Storico Italiano per l'età moderna e contemporanea*, 35–36 (1983–1984): 169–186.

———. *Index de l'Inquisition espagnole, 1551, 1554, 1559.* Index des livres interdits, vol. 5. Sherbrooke, Quebec: Centre d'Études de la Renaissance, Éditions de l'Université de Sherbrooke, 1984.

———. "Un índice de libros permitidos." In *Homenaje a Eugenio Asensio*, 311–319. Madrid: Editorial Gredos, 1988.

———. "Indices de libros prohibidos." In *Diccionario de Historia Eclesiástica de España*, 399–499. Madrid: Instituto Enrique Florez. Consejo Superior de Investigaciones Científicas, 1986.

———. "Indices de libros prohibidos del siglo XVI." *Arbor* 108, no. 421 (enero 1981): 7–14.

———. "Littérature castillane dans l'Index Espagnol de 1559." In *l'Humanisme dans les lettres espagnoles; XIXe colloque international d'études humanistes, Tours, 5–7 juillet 1976*, 205–217. Paris: J. Vrin, 1979.

———. "Luther et la censure catholique." In *Encounters with Luther: Papers from the 1982 McGill Luther Symposium*, edited by E. J. Furcha, 28–44. Montréal: E. J. Furcha, 1984.

———. "El primer índice de libros prohibidos." *Studia Theologica* 61 (1984): 443–450.

Dedieu, J. P. "Analyse formelle de la procédure inquisitoriale en cause de foi." In *Mélanges de la Casa de Velázquez*, 23 (1987): 227–251.

———. "Les archives de l'Inquisition: Source pour une étude anthropologique des vieux chrétiens: Un exemple et quelques réflexions." In *La Inquisición española*, edited by J. Pérez Villanueva, 893–912. Madrid: BAC, 1980.

———. "The Archives of the Holy Office of Toledo as a Source for Historical Anthropology." In *The Inquisition in Early Modern Europe: Studies on Sources and Methods*, edited by G. Henningsen and J. Tedeschi, in association with C. Amiel, 158–189. DeKalb, Ill.: Northern Illinois University Press, 1986.

———. "Les causes de foi de l'Inquisition de Tolède (1483–1820): Essai statistique." In *Mélanges de la Casa de Velázquez*, 14(1978): 143–171.

———. "'Christianisation' en Nouvelle Castille: Catechisme, communion, messe et confirmation dans l'archevêché de Tolède, 1540–1650." In *Mélanges de la Casa de Velázquez*, 15 (1979): 261–293.

———. "The Inquisition and Popular Culture in New Castile." In *Inquisition and Society in Early Modern Europe*, edited and translated by S. Haliczer, 129–146. London: Croom Helm, 1987.

Dedieu, J. P., and M. Demonet. "L'activité de l'Inquisition de Tolède: Étude statistique, méthodes et premiers résultats." *Annuario dell'Istituto Storico Italiano per l'età moderna e contemporanea*, 37–38 (1985–1986): 11–39.

Del Rio Barbero, M. J. "Censura Inquisitorial y teatro de 1707 a 1819." *Hispania Sacra* 38 (1986): 279–330.

Domergue, L. *Censure et lumières dans l'Espagne de Charles III*. Paris: CNRS, 1982.

———. "Inquisición y ciencia en el siglo XVIII." *Arbor* 124, no. 484–485 (abril-mayo 1986): 103–130.

———. *Le livre en Espagne du temps de la Revolution Française.* Lyon, 1984.

Domínguez Ortiz, A. *Autos de la Inquisición de Sevilla (Siglo XVII).* Seville: Servicio de Publicaciones del Ayuntamiento de Sevilla, 1981.

Domínguez Ortiz, A., and B. Vincent. *Historia de los moriscos: Vida y tragedia de una minoría.* Madrid, 1978.

Domínguez Salgado, M. del P. "Inquisición y Corte en el siglo XVII." *Hispania Sacra* 37 (1985): 569–584.

———. "Los orígenes del Tribunal de Corte (1580–1665)." In *Inquisición española: Nuevas aproximaciones,* edited by J. Contreras, 99–125. Madrid: Centro de Estudios Inquisitoriales, Ediciones Nájera, 1987.

Drochon, P. "Une polémique sur l'Inquisition en 1869." *Hispania Sacra* 39 (1987): 117–137.

Dufour, G. *La Inquisición Española: Una aproximación a la España intolerante.* Barcelona: Montesinos, 1986.

Echeverría, M., P. García de Yébenes, and R. de Lera. "Distribución y número de los familiares del Santo Oficio en Andalucia durante los siglos XVI–XVIII." *Hispania Sacra* 39 (1987): 59–94.

Escandell Bonet, B. "Estudios de una burocracia inquisitorial en términos funcionales: Las relaciones del Tribunal Romano y la Administración Virreinal como observatorio (1570–1600)." *Hispania Sacra* 37 (1985): 387–408.

———. "El 'Fenómeno inquisitorial': Naturaleza sociológica y pervivencias actuales." In *La Inquisición: Palacio de Velázquez del Retiro, Madrid, octubre–diciembre 1982,* 8–55. Madrid: Direccion General de Bellas Artes, Archivos y Bibliotecas, 1982. Exposition organized by the Ministry of Culture, 1982.

———. "La Inquisición como dispositivo de control social y la pervivencia actual del 'modelo inquisitorial'." In *Inquisición española,* edited by A. Alcalá et al., 597–612. Barcelona: Editorial Aries, 1984.

Escudero, J. A. "Los orígenes del 'Consejo de la Suprema Inquisición.'" In *Inquisición española,* edited by A. Alcalá et al., 81–122. Barcelona: Editorial Aires, 1984.

Eymeric, N., and F. Peña. *El manual de los inquisidores.* Madrid, 1983.

Ferrer Benimelli, A. "La Inquisición frente a masonería e ilustración." In *Inquisición española,* edited by A. Alcalá et al., 81–122. Barcelona: Editorial Aries, 1984.

———. "Inquisición y masonería: un problema político-eclesial." In *La Inquisición española,* edited by J. Pérez Villanueva, 737–781. Madrid: BAC, 1980.

García Arenal, M. *Inquisición y moriscos: Los procesos del Tribunal de Cuenca.* Madrid: Siglo Veintiuno Editores, 1978.

García Cárcel, R. *Herejía y sociedad en el siglo XVI: La Inquisición en Valencia, 1530–1600.* Barcelona: Ediciones Península, 1980.

———. "El itinerario de los moriscos hasta su expulsión (1609)." In *Inquisición española,* edited by A. Alcalá et al., 67–80. Barcelona: Editorial Aries, 1984.

———. "El modelo mediterráneo de brujería." *Annuario dell'Istituto Storico Italiano per l'età moderna e contemporanea,* 37–38 (1985–1986): 245–257.

———. "Número y sociología de los familiares de la Inquisición valenciana." In

La Inquisición española, edited by J. Pérez Villanueva, 271–283. Madrid: BAC, 1980.

———. "Trayectoria de la Inquisición valenciana." In *La Inquisición española,* edited by J. Pérez Villanueva, 411–433. Madrid: BAC, 1980.

García de Yébenes Prous, P. "Ventura Rodríguez: De arquitecto real a arquitecto del consejo de Inquisición." *Hispania Sacra* 37 (1985): 619–654.

García Fuentes, J. M. *La Inquisición en Granada en el siglo XVI: Fuentes para su estudio.* Granada: Universidad de Granada, 1981.

García Servet, J. *El humanista Cascales y la Inquisición murciana.* Madrid: Ediciones José Porrúa Turanzas, 1978.

Gil, Sanjuán J. "Fuentes documentales del Santo Oficio Granadino para el estudio de las minorías disidentes en Andalucía." *Hispania Sacra* 37 (1985): 729–749.

———. "La Inquisición de Granada: Visita a Málaga y su comarca en 1568." *Baetica* 1 (1978): 313–336.

Gil Novales, A. "Inquisición y ciencia en el siglo XIX." *Arbor* 124, no. 484–485 (abril–mayo 1986): 147–170.

Gómez Pastor, P. *Proyecto de reforma de la Inquisición en 1768: Historia económica y pensamiento social,* 87–95. Madrid: 1983.

González de Caldaz, M. V. "Nuevas imágenes del Santo Oficio en Sevilla: El auto de fe." In *Inquisición española,* edited by A. Alcalá et al., 237–267. Barcelona: Editorial Aries, 1984.

González Novalín, J. L. "L'Inquisizione spagnola. Correnti storiografiche da Llorente (1817) ai giorni nostri." *Storia della Chiesa in Italia* 39 (1985): 140–159.

———. "La Inquisición española." *Historia de la Iglesia en España,* vol. 3. Madrid: Biblioteca de Autores Cristianos, 1980.

———. "Luteranismo e Inquisición en España (1519–1561). Bases para la periodización del tema en el siglo de la Reforma." *Annuario dell'Istituto Storico Italiano per l'età moderna e contemporanea,* 37–38 (1985–1986): 43–73.

Gracia Boix, R. *Autos de fe y causas de la Inquisición de Córdoba.* Córdoba: Publicaciones de la Excma Disputación Provincial, 1983.

———. *Colección de documentos para la historia de la Inquisición de Córdoba.* Córdoba: Monte de Piedad y Caja de Ahorros de Córdoba, 1982.

Gracia Guillén, D. "Judaísmo, medicina y 'mentalidad inquisitorial' en la España del siglo XVI." In *Inquisición española,* edited by A. Alcalá et al., 328–352. Barcelona: Editorial Aries, 1984.

Gutiérrez, A. *Jean Bodin et Michel de Montaigne en Espagne (1590–1637): Textes de l'Inquisition.* St. Etienne: Université Jean Monet, 1978.

Haliczer, S. "The First Holocaust: The Inquisition and the Converted Jews of Spain and Portugal." In *Inquisition and Society in Early Modern Europe,* edited and translated by S. Haliczer, 7–18. London: Croom Helm, 1987.

———. "La Inquisicíon como mito y como historia: Su abolición y el desarrollo de la ideología política española." In *Inquisición española,* edited by A. Alcalá et al., 496–517. Barcelona: Editorial Aries, 1984.

Hamilton, A. *El proceso de Rodrigo de Bivar (1539)*. Madrid: Fundación Universitaria Española, 1979.

Henningsen, G. "The Archives and the Historiography of the Spanish Inquisition." In *The Inquisition in Early Modern Europe: Studies on Sources and Methods*, edited by G. Henningsen and J. Tedeschi, in association with C. Amiel, 54–78. DeKalb, Ill.: Northern Illinois University Press, 1986.

————. "El 'banco de datos' del Santo Oficio: Las relaciones de causas de la Inquisición española." *Boletín de la Real Academia de la Historia* 174 (1977): 547–570.

————. "La colección Moldenhawer en Copenhague: Una aportación a la archivología de la Inquisición española." *Revista de Archivos, Bibliotecas y Museos* 80 (1977): 209–270.

————. "Los daneses y la Inquisición." *Annuario dell'Istituto Storico Italiano per l'età moderna e contemporanea* 37–38 (1985–1986): 203–216.

————. "La elocuencia de los números: Promesas de las 'relaciones de causas' inquisitoriales para la nueva historia social." In *Inquisición española*, edited by A. Alcalá et al., 207–225. Barcelona: Editorial Aries, 1984.

————. "Las víctimas de Zugarramurdi: El origen de un gran proceso de brujería." *Saioak* (Revista des estudios vascos) 2, no. 2 (1978): 182–195.

————. *The Witches' Advocate: Basque Witchcraft and the Spanish Inquisition (1609–1614)*. Reno, Nevada: University of Nevada Press, 1980.

Henningsen, G., and J. Tedeschi. *The Inquisition in Early Modern Europe. Studies on Sources and Methods*. In association with C. Amiel. DeKalb, Ill.: Northern Illinois University Press, 1986.

Higueruela del Pino, L. "Actitud del episcopado español ante los decretos de supresión de la Inquisición (1813–1820)." In *La Inquisición española*, edited by J. Pérez Villanueva, 939–977. Madrid: BAC, 1980.

Huerga, A. "Fray Luis de Granada entre mística, alumbrados e Inquisición." *Angelicum* 66 (1988): 540–564.

————. *Historia de los alumbrados (1570–1630)*. 4 vols. Madrid: Fundación Universitaria Española, 1978–1988.

Huerga Criado, P. "Los agentes de la Inquisición española en Roma durante el siglo XVII." In *La Inquisición española*, edited by J. Pérez Villanueva, 243–256. Madrid: BAC, 1980.

————. "El Inquisidor General Fray Tomás de Torquemada." In *Inquisición española: Nuevas Aproximaciones*, edited by J. Contreras, 7–51. Madrid: Ediciones Nájera. Centro de Estudios Inquisitoriales, 1987.

————. "La etapa inicial del Consejo de Inquisición (1483–1498)." In *Hispania Sacra* 37 (1985): 451–464.

Idoate, F. *La brujería en Navarra y sus documentos*. Pamplona: Institución Príncipe de Viana, 1978.

Inquisiçao: I° Congreso Lusso-Brasileiro sobre Inquisiçao: Resumos das comunicaçoes, Lisboa, 17 a 20 fevereiro, 1987. Lisboa: Sociedade Portuguesa de Estudos do Século XVIII, 1987.

La Inquisición: Palacio de Velázquez del Retiro, Madrid, octubre–diciembre 1982.

Madrid: Dirección General de Bellas Artes, Archivos y Bibliotecas, 1982. Exposition organized by the Ministry of Culture.

Jiménez Lozano, J. "Supervivencia de cultemas islamo-hebraicos en la sociedad española o el fracaso histórico de la Inquisición." In *Inquisición española,* edited by A. Alcalá et al., 353–371. Barcelona: Editorial Aries, 1984.

Jiménez Monteserín, M. *Introducción a la Inquisición española: Documentos básicos para el estudio del Santo Oficio.* Madrid: Editora Nacional, 1980.

Jones, J. A. "Censuras acerca de la impresión de la 'Paraphrasis Chaldaica' de Andrés de León: Un aspecto de la amistad entre Benito Arias Montano y Pedro de Valencia." In *Homenaje a Pedro Sainz Rodríguez.* 4 vols. 1:339–348. Madrid: Fundación Universitaria Española, 1986.

Kamen, H. *Inquisition and Society in Spain in the Sixteenth Century.* Bloomington, Indiana: Indiana University Press, 1985.

———. "Notas sobre brujería y sexualidad y la Inquisición." In *Inquisición española,* edited by A. Alcalá et al., 226–236. Barcelona: Editorial Aries, 1984.

Kinder, Gordon A. *Spanish Protestants and Reformers in the Sixteenth Century: A Bibliography.* London: Grant and Lutler, 1983.

Lea, H. C. *Historia de la Inquisición española.* 3 vols. Madrid: Fundación Universitaria Española, 1982–1984.

Lera Garcia, R. de. "Cripto-Musulmanes ante la Inquisición granadina en el s. XVIII." *Hispania Sacra* 36 (1984): 521–575.

Llamas Martínez, E. "Secuelas de la acción de la Inquisición española contra los libros de Madre Teresa de Jesús." *Cultura, Historia e Filosofía* 5 (1986): 289–317.

Llorente, J. A. *Historia crítica de la Inquisición en España.* Pamplona: Ediciones Hiperión, 1980.

———. *Noticia biográfica: Autobiografía.* Con una "nota critica" de A. Márquez, y un "ensayo bibliografico" por E. Van der Vekene. Madrid: Taurus Ediciones, 1982.

López Vela, R. "Estructura y funcionamiento de la burocracia inquisitorial (1643–1667)." In *Inquisición española: Nuevas aproximaciones,* edited by J. Contreras, 159–231. Madrid: Ediciones Nájera, Centro de Estudios Inquisitoriales, 1987.

———. "La generación de funcionarios inquisitoriales de la época de Nithard." In *La Inquisición española,* edited by J. Pérez Villanueva, 233–241. Madrid: BAC, 1980.

Loy, J. R. "Los ilustrados franceses y su idea de la Inquisición." In *Inquisición española,* edited by A. Alcalá et al., 587–596. Barcelona: Editorial Aries, 1984.

Márquez, A. "Ciencia e Inquisición en España del XV al XVII." *Arbor* 124, nos. 484–485 (abril–mayo): 65–83.

———. "La Inquisición: Estado de las investigaciones inquisitoriales." *Revista de Occidente* 6 (1981): 147–156.

———. *Literatura e Inquisición en España (1478–1834).* Madrid: Taurus Ediciones, 1980.

Martínez Millán, J. "Las canonjías inquisitoriales: Un problema de jurisdicción entre le Iglesia y la monarquía." *Hispania Sacra* 34 (1982): 9–63.

———. "El Catálogo de libros prohibidos de 1559: Aportaciones para una nueva interpretación." *Miscelánea Comillas*, 37 (1979): 179–217.

———. "Estructuras de la Hacienda inquisitorial." In *Inquisición española*, edited by A. Alcalá et al., 147–173. Barcelona: Editorial Aries, 1984.

———. "La formación de las estucturas inquisitoriales." *Hispania* 43 (1983): 25–46.

———. "Los miembros del Consejo de Inquisición durante el siglo XVII." *Hispania Sacra* 37 (1985): 409–450.

———. "Los problemas de jurisdicción del Santo Oficio: 'La Junta Magna.'" *Hispania Sacra* 37 (1985): 205–259.

Martínez Millán, J., and Sánchez Rivilla. "El Consejo de la Inquisición (1483–1700)." *Hispania Sacra* 36 (1984): 71–193.

Méchoulan, H. *El Honor de Dios: Indios, judíos y moriscos en el Siglo de Oro.* Barcelona, 1981.

Mendoza García, I. "El padre Juan Everardo Nithard: Valido e inquisidor general." In *Inquisición española: Nuevas aproximaciones*, edited by J. Contreras, 77–98. Madrid: Ediciones Nájera. Centro de Estudios Inquisitoriales, 1987.

Meseguer Fernández, J. "Fernando de Talavera, Cisneros y la Inquisición de Granada." In *La Inquisición española*, edited by J. Pérez Villanueva, 371–400. Madrid: BAC, 1980.

———. "Diego Sarmiento de Valladares, Inquisidor General: Documentos para su biografía." *Archivo Ibero Americano* 40 (1980).

———. "Instrucciones de Tomás de Torquemada: Preinstrucciones o proyecto?" *Hispania Sacra* 34 (1982): 197–215.

———. "El Cardenal Cisneros, inquisidor general (1507–1517)." *Archivo Ibero Americano* 43 (1983): 95–194.

Mier, E. de. *El conflicto del poder y el poder del conflicto. (El familiar del Santo Oficio de la Inquisición, Toribio Sánchez de Quijano de Cartes.)* Santander: Ediciones Tantin, 1984.

Miguel Gonzáles, M. L. de. "Características económicas de la Inquisición aragonesa desde 1506–1516." In *Inquisición española: Nuevas aproximaciones*, edited by J. Contreras, 53–75. Madrid: Ediciones Nájera. Centro de Estudios Inquisitoriales, 1987.

Monter, W. "Protestantes franceses y tolerancia inquisitorial." *Hispania Sacra* 39 (1987): 95–116.

———. "The Mediterranean Inquisitions." In *Ritual, Myth and Magic in Early Modern Europe.* Athens (Ohio): Ohio University Press, 1984.

———. "The New Social History and the Spanish Inquisition." *Journal of Social History* 17 (1984): 705–713.

Moreno Garbayo, N. *Catálogo de alegaciones fiscales.* Madrid: Archivo Histórico Nacional, 1977.

———. *Inventario de los libros 1225 a 1281 con índices de personas, materias y lugares.* Madrid: Archivo Histórico Nacional, 1979.

Moreno Mancebo, M. "Breve biografía de Olavide." In *Inquisición española: Nuevas aproximaciones*, edited by J. Contreras, 257–296. Madrid: Ediciones Nájera. Centro de Estudios Inquisitoriales, 1987.

Morón Arroyo, C. "Ciencia, Inquisición, ideología: Temas de nuestro tiempo." *Arbor* 124, no. 484–485 (abril–mayo 1986): 29–43.

———. "La Inquisición y la posibilidad de la gran literatura barroca española." In *Inquisición española*, edited by A. Alcalá et al., 315–327. Barcelona: Editorial Aries, 1984.

Muños Calvo, S. *Inquisición y ciencia en la España moderna*. Madrid: Editora Nacional, 1977.

Nalle, S. "Popular Religion in Cuenca on the Eve of the Catholic Reformation." In *Inquisition and Society in Early Modern Europe*, edited and translated by S. Haliczer, 67–87. London: Croom Helm, 1987.

Navarro Latorre, J. *Aproximación a Fr. Luis de Aliaga, confesor de Felipe III e inquisidor general de España*. Zaragoza, 1981.

Netanyahu, B. "¿Motivos o pretextos? La razón de la Inquisición." In *Inquisición española*, edited by A. Alcalá et al., 23–44. Barcelona: Editorial Aries, 1984.

Nieto, J. C. "El carácter no místico de los alumbrados de Toledo, 1509(?)–1524." In *Inquisición española*, edited by A. Alcalá et al., 410–423. Barcelona: Editorial Aries, 1984.

———. "The Heretical Alumbrados-Dexados: Isabel de la Cruz and Pedro de Alcaraz." *Revue de littérature comparée* 52 (1978): 293–313.

Ocaña Torres, M. L. "El 'Corpus jurídico' de la Inquisición española." In *La Inquisición española*, edited by J. Pérez Villanueva, 913–916. Madrid: BAC, 1980.

Ortega Costa, M. *Proceso de la Inquisición contra María de Cazalla*. Madrid: Fundación Universitaria Española, 1978.

———. "San Ignacio de Loyola en el *Libro de alumbrados*: nuevos datos sobre su primer proceso." *Arbor* 107 no. 419 (noviembre 1980): 163–174.

———. "Tribulaciones de un tribunal: El Santo Oficio de Toledo (1530–1535)." In *Homenaje a Pedro Sainz Rodríguez*. 4 vols. 4:543–555. Madrid: Fundación Universitaria Española, 1986.

Pardo, Tomas J. "Obras y autores científicos en los índices inquisitoriales españoles del siglo XVI (1559, 1583 y 1584)." *Estudis* 10 (1983): 235–259.

———. "El paracelsismo europeo en los índices inquisitoriales españoles (1583–1640)." *Arbor* 124, no. 484–485 (abril–mayo 1986): 85–101.

Pérez, Ll., Ll. Muntaner, and M. Colom, eds. *El Tribunal de la Inquisición en Mallorca: Relación de causas de fe, 1578–1806*. vol. 1. Mallorca: Miguel Font Editor, 1986.

Pérez Bustamante, R. "Nóminas de inquisidores: Reflexiones sobre el estudio de la burocracia inquisitorial en el siglo XVI." In *La Inquisición española*, edited by J. Pérez Villanueva, 257–269. Madrid: BAC, 1980.

Pérez de Colosia Rodríguez, M. I. *Auto inquisitorial de 1672: El criptojudaísmo en Málaga*. Málaga, 1984.

Pérez de Colosia Rodríguez, M. I., and J. Gil Sanjuán. "Málaga e Inquisición." *Jábega* 38 (1982): 16–21.

Pérez Ramírez, D. "El Archivo de la Inquisición de Cuenca: Formación, vicisitudes, estado actual." In *La Inquisición española*, edited by J. Pérez Villanueva, 855–875. Madrid: BAC, 1980.

———. *Catálogo del Archivo de la Inquisición de Cuenca*. Madrid: Fundación Universitaria Española, 1982.

Pérez Villanueva, J., Director del volumen. *La Inquisición española: Nueva visión, nuevos horizontes*. Madrid: Siglo veintiuno editores, 1980.

———. "Algo más sobre la Inquisición y Sor María de Agreda: La prodigiosa evangelización americana." *Hispania Sacra* 37 (1985): 585–618.

———. "Felipe IV y la Inquisición y espiritualidad de su tiempo: Su figura desde tres epistolarios." In *Inquisición española*, edited by A. Alcalá et al., 434–461. Barcelona: Editorial Aries, 1984.

Pérez Villanueva, J., and B. Escandell Bonet, eds. *Historia de la Inquisición en España y América: El conocimiento científico y el proceso histórico de la Institución (1478–1834)*. Madrid: Biblioteca de Autores Cristianos. Centro de Estudios Inquisitoriales, 1984.

Perry, M. E. "Beatas and the Inquisition in Early Modern Seville." In *Inquisition and Society in Early Modern Europe*, edited and translated by S. Haliczer, 147–168. London: Croom Helm, 1987.

Peters, E. "Una morada de monstruos: Henry Charles Lea y el descubrimiento americano de la Inquisición." In *Inquisición española*, edited by A. Alcalá et al., 518–541. Barcelona: Editorial Aries, 1984.

Pinto Crespo, V. "La actitud de la Inquisición ante la iconografía religiosa: Tres ejemplos de su actuación (1571–1665)." *Hispania Sacra* 31 (1978–1979): 285–322.

———. "El aparato de control censorial y las corrientes doctrinales" *Hispania Sacra* 36 (1984): 9–41.

———. "La censura: Sistemas de control e instrumentos de acción." In *Inquisición española*, edited by A. Alcalá et al., 269–287. Barcelona: Editorial Aries, 1984.

———. "La documentación inquisitorial." In *La Inquisición: Palacio de Velázquez del Retiro, Madrid, octubre–diciembre 1982*, 93–106. Madrid: Dirección General de Bellas Artes, Archivos y Bibliotecas, 1982. Exposition organized by the Ministry of Culture.

———. "Los índices de libros prohibidos." *Hispania Sacra* 35 (1983): 161–191.

———. "Herejía y poder en el siglo XVI: Una propuesta de indagación." *Hispania Sacra* 37 (1985): 465–488.

———. *Inquisición y control ideológico en la España del siglo XVI*. Madrid: Taurus Ediciones, 1983.

———. Institucionalización inquisitorial y censura de libros." In *La Inquisición española*, edited by J. Pérez Villanueva, 513–536. Madrid: BAC, 1980.

———. "El proceso de elaboración y configuración del Indice y expurgatorio de 1583–1584 en relación con los índices del siglo XVI." *Hispania Sacra* 30 (1977): 201–254.

———. "Thought Control in Spain." In *Inquisition and Society in Early Modern*

Europe, edited and translated by S. Haliczer, 171–188. London: Croom Helm, 1987.

Reguera, I. La Inquisición en el País Vasco: El Tribunal de Calahorra (1513–1570). San Sebastián: 1984.

Represa Rodríguez, A. "Documentos sobre la Inquisición en el Archivo de Simancas." In La Inquisición española, edited by J. Pérez Villanueva, 845–855. Madrid: BAC, 1980.

Riera, J. "Expurgo de las Academias de Matemáticas de Barcelona y Segovia de 1790." Arbor 124, no. 484–485 (abril–mayo 1986): 131–146.

Rodríguez Besné, J. R. "Notas sobre la estructura y funcionamiento del Consejo de la Santa, General y Suprema Inquisición." In La Inquisición española, edited by J. Pérez Villanueva, 61–65. Madrid: BAC, 1980.

Rodríguez Sánchez, A. "Moralización y represión en la España del siglo XVI." In Homenaje a Pedro Sainz Rodríguez. 4 vols. 3:591–601. Madrid: Fundación Universitaria Española, 1986.

Rose, C. S. "Antonio Enríquez Gómez: Historia de un converso." In El barroco en Andalucía, edited by M. Peláez del Rosal and J. Rivas Carmona, 115–122. Córdoba, 1984.

Ruitz, T. R. "La Inquisición medieval y la moderna: Paralelos y contrastes." In Inquisición española, edited by A. Alcalá et al., 45–66. Barcelona: Editorial Aries, 1984.

Sala-Molins, L. Le dictionnaire des inquisiteurs: Valence, 1494. Paris: Editions Galilée, 1981.

Sánchez Ortega, M. H. La Inquisición y los gitanos. Madrid: Taurus Ediciones, 1988.

———. "Un sondeo en la historia de la sexualidad sobre fuentes inquisitoriales." In La Inquisición española, edited by J. Pérez Villanueva, 917–930. Madrid: BAC, 1980.

Santamaría Garraleta, J. L. "Orígenes de la Inquisición en Navarra." In La Inquisición española, edited by J. Pérez Villanueva, 405–410. Madrid: BAC, 1980.

Sarrión Mora, A. "El médico y la sociedad rural del siglo XVII: El proceso inquisitorial de Francisco Martínez Casas." In Inquisición española: Nuevas aproximaciones, edited by J. Contreras, 297–321. Madrid: Ediciones Nájera. Centro de Estudios Inquisitoriales, 1987.

Sendon de León, V. La España herética. Barcelona: Icaria, 1986.

Sesma Muñoz, G. A. El establecimiento de la Inquisición en Aragón (1484–1486): Documentos para un estudio. Zaragoza: Institución Fernando el Católico, 1987.

Tedeschi, J. "Organización y procedimientos penales de la Inquisición romana: Un bosquejo." In Inquisición española, edited by A. Alcalá et al., 185–206. Barcelona: Editorial Aries, 1984.

Tellechea Idígoras, J. I. "Don Carlos de Seso: Bienes y biblioteca confiscados para la Inquisición (1559)." Revista Española de Teología 43 (1983): 193–197.

———. "Don Carlos de Seso, luterano en Castilla: Sentencia inédita de su proceso inquisitorial." In *Homenaje a Pedro Sainz Rodríguez*. 4 vols. 1:295–307. Madrid: Fundación Universitaria Española, 1986.

———. "Molinos y el quietismo español." In *Historia de la Iglesia en España* 4:517–521. Madrid: Biblioteca de Autores Cristianos, 1979.

———. *Tiempos recios: Inquisición y heterodoxos*. Salamanca: Ediciones Sígueme, 1977.

Tomás y Valiente, F. "Relaciones de la Inquisición con el aparato institucional del Estado." In *La Inquisición española*, edited by J. Pérez Villanueva, 41–60. Madrid: BAC, 1980.

Ungerer, G. *La defensa de Antonio Pérez contra los cargos que se le imputaron en el proceso de visita (1584)*. Zaragoza, 1980.

Van der Vekene, E. *Bibliotheca bibliographica Historiae Sanctae Inquisitionis*. 2 vols. Vaduz, Liechtenstein: Topos Verlag, 1982–1983.

Vázquez Janeiro, I. "Cultura y censura en el siglo XVI: A propósito de la edición de Index des Livres interdits." *Antonianum* 63 (1988): 26–73.

Ventura Subirats, J. "Conversos, Inquisición y cultura en Valencia." *Mayurqa* 19 (1980): 251–276.

———. *Inquisició espanyola i cultura renaixentista al País Valencià*. Valencia: Eliseu Climent Editor, 1978.

Vernet Ginés, J. "Ciencia hispano-islámica y la mihna." *Arbor* 124, no. 484–485 (abril–mayo 1986): 45–55.

Vidal, J. *Quand on brûlait les morisques, 1544–1621*. Nîmes: Imprimerie Barnier, 1986.

Vilchez Díaz, A. *Autores y anónimos españoles en los índices inquisitoriales*. Madrid: Universidad Complutense, 1986.

Villa Calleja, I. "Investigación histórica de los 'Edictos de Fe' en la Inquisición española (siglos XV–XIX)." In *Inquisición española: Nuevas aproximaciones*, edited by J. Contreras, 233–256. Madrid: Ediciones Nájera. Centro de Estudios Inquisitoriales, 1987.

THIRTEEN

Historiography of the Mexican Inquisition: Evolution of Interpretations and Methodologies

Richard E. Greenleaf

When I began my archival investigations on the Mexican Inquisition in 1954, study of the Holy Office was still concentrated in the pioneering works of José Toribio Medina, Joaquín García Icazbalceta, Henry Charles Lea, Luis González Obregón, and Julio Jiménez Rueda.[1] The *Boletín* of the Archivo General de la Nación, in its first series, and the *Publicaciones del Archivo General de la Nación* dealing with the Holy Office and the Indians and the Inquisition and the Enlightenment, provided most of the published documentation available.[2] The fourteen folio volumes of the "Indice del Ramo de la Inquisición" constituted then and continue to be the most important research tool to investigators.[3] Studies dealing with the Mexican Holy Office, with a few exceptions, tended to recapitulate the data and tabulations contained in the printed sources.[4] Few scholars had perceived the true importance of Luis González Obregón's remark to the young researcher France Vinton Scholes when he first arrived in the Archivo in 1927. Don Luis said of the Ramo de la Inquisición "in these *legajos* you will find the social and intellectual history of colonial Mexico."[5] The three and one half decades since 1954 have brought great changes in Mexican Inquisition historiography. Splendidly trained scholars have examined the *procesos* and other documentation in the Inquisition archives both in Mexico and in Spain.

Beginning in the 1960s a new genre of Inquisition studies appeared. The first of many scholarly Inquisition symposia was held in Santander in 1976, followed by one in Denmark organized by the distinguished Danish folklorist and Hispanist Gustav Henningsen.[6] A magnificent exhibition on the Inquisition was mounted in Madrid in the Palacio de

Velázquez del Retiro by the Ministerio de Cultura in 1982,[7] in tandem with an important symposium at the Archivo Histórico Nacional. There followed a series of impressive scholarly conclaves in the Iberian peninsula culminating with one on Toledo in February 1988. Each of these meetings has generated publications. Largely responsible for these developments has been the Centro de Estudios Inquisitoriales, located in the complex that houses the Archivo Histórico Nacional in Madrid. It has nurtured a renaissance in studies of the Holy Office of the Inquisition in Spain and America, works based on extensive archival documentation and, for the most part, devoid of both apologias for and polemics against the Inquisition. Two senior scholars in Spain who direct research on the Spanish Inquisition (Joaquín Pérez Villanueva) and the tribunals of the New World (Bartolomé Escandell Bonet) have launched a massive three-volume history of the Holy Office with the collaboration of thirty-six specialists.[8] Volume 1 of the series on the state of knowledge and historical development of the Inquisition from 1478 to 1834 is followed by a volume on the bureaucratic structure of the Holy Office and a third tome on themes and problems of interpretation. The second and third volumes are currently in preparation.

Only a synoptic view of volume 1—1,548 pages in two parts with multiple chapters and subsections—can be presented here. An attempt is made for the first time to present a systematic history of the modern Inquisition "made by Spaniards who have risen above ideological biases and distortions" and who apply professional canons of historical research and methodology to their task (Centro de Estudios Inquisitoriales flyer). By applying academic rigor to their analysis of the Inquisition the team hopes to eschew tired clichés, outmoded interpretations, and crosscurrents of Black Legend-White Legend historiography. Interpretations tend to be more sociological than religious. Intolerance is dealt with within a political and societal framework rather than from a viewpoint of persecution and religious toleration.

French scholars of the Holy Office in Spain and the Empire are also making significant advances. Works by Robert Ricard, Marcel Bataillon, and Pierre Chaunu have been carried forward by Bartolomé Bennassar and his students, who are in the forefront of this movement. In the United States, Inquisition symposia organized by Angel Alcalá in New York in 1983 and by Stephen Haliczer and John Tedeschi in Chicago in 1986 have preceded this distinguished gathering in Los Angeles. Meetings in Paris and Rome have also focused on the Inquisition.[9] Obviously the greatest scholars of the Mexican Inquisition have come from Mexico, and their proud tradition is being carried on by seminars in the

History of Mentality and Religion in Colonial Mexico at the Department of Historical Investigation of the National Institute of Anthropology and History, and seminars on the Mexican Inquisition at the Universidad Autónoma Metropolitana. For several years now, the Centro de Estudios Lingüísticos y Literarios of the Colegio de México along with the Instituto de Bellas Artes, the Archivo General de la Nación, and the Universidad Nacional Autónoma de México have sponsored a project to catalog literary texts of New Spain found in the Inquisition series. The project has completed its review of the eighteenth-century material, and a book entitled *Catálogo de textos literarios novohispanos en el Archivo General de la Nación (México)* should be published within the year. Although the focus of this work is literature, it will include an appendix that will give information on, and references to documents on, witches and witchcraft, black magic, horoscopes, almanacs, and pacts with the Devil. The project is ongoing and plans eventually to provide the same type of information for the sixteenth and seventeenth centuries.

In a brief essay it is impossible to treat in detail individual studies on the Mexican Inquisition or to arrange a complete bibliography of article literature on the subject. Only the highlights can be brought into focus here. It seems that both a chronological and thematic presentation is needed to accomplish the task in the time allotted. From a chronological perspective it is necessary to remember that a Primitive Inquisition (Medina's phrase) operated in Mexico from 1522 to 1571, first under the aegis of friar inquisitors in the 1520s and then under an episcopal jurisdiction from 1535 to 1571 when Juan de Zumárraga, Francisco Tello de Sandoval, and Alonso de Montúfar were empowered as apostolic inquisitors. In Yucatán the monastic inquisition continued to operate outside the jurisdiction of Mexico City in the 1560s. In 1571 the Tribunal of the Holy Office of the Inquisition began to function pursuant to a decree of Philip II in 1569.[10]

THE PRIMITIVE INQUISITION, 1522–1569

Little known because only two hundred copies were printed is the section on Mexico's monastic and episcopal Inquisition prior to 1569 in José Toribio Medina's *La Primitiva Inquisición americana (1493–1569)*, 2 volumes. (Santiago de Chile: Imprenta Elzeviriana, 1914). Medina's narrative history of the Tribunal of the Holy Office in Mexico, first published in 1905, picks up the story in 1569. The 1954 reprint of his *Historia del Tribunal del Santo Oficio de la Inquisición en México* (Mexico City: Editorial

Cultura, 1954) has important added notes prepared by Julio Jiménez Rueda which refer to recent documentary discoveries and new viewpoints as of 1954. The important master's thesis of Yolanda Mariel de Ibáñez, *La Inquisición en México durante el siglo XVI* (Mexico City: Universidad Nacional Autónoma de México, 1945; reprint, 1979) contains one of the first important statistical tabulations of Inquisition activity. The copious *Herejías y supersticiones en la Nueva España* by Julio Jiménez Rueda appeared in Mexico City in 1946 and laid the foundations for generalizations on the various doctrinal concerns of the Holy Office.

Richard E. Greenleaf's 1957 doctoral dissertation published in revised form as *Zumárraga and the Mexican Inquisition 1536–1543* (Washington, D.C.: Academy of American Franciscan History, 1962) sharply focused on the episcopal inquisition during the first two decades of the colony and for the first time examined in detail the clash of Iberian Catholicism and Mesoamerican native beliefs. The work also examined the intellectual milieu of the first half of the sixteenth century as Christian humanism and Reformation ideas penetrated New Spain. Trials of the first Lutherans and crypto-Jews were treated in detail, as were the Holy Office's concerns with sorcery, superstition, and blasphemy, and the enforcement of morality in the first decades of conquest. Both Robert Ricard (1933) and Robert C. Padden (1967) used the Zumárraga Indian trials to exemplify clash of cultures in broader studies of the "spiritual conquest."[11]

Greenleaf's second volume, *The Mexican Inquisition of the Sixteenth Century* (Albuquerque: University of New Mexico Press, 1969), provided a series of essays based on archival documentation that exposed new sources and interpretations on the first decade of the Mexican Inquisition, 1522–1532, the Inquisition in Michoacan, trials of Protestants, physicians, and judaizantes, as well as an essay on the Montúfar Inquisition and the Mexican clergy, 1555–1571. Also included were analytical chapters on the operation of the Tribunal of the Holy Office from 1571 through 1601 and a detailed examination of the Mexican Inquisition and the first Calvinists.[12]

Confusion of Lutheran ideas and Erasmian thought in the early sixteenth-century colony was commonplace. Marcel Bataillon's *Erasmo y España, Estudios sobre la historia espiritual del siglo XVI*, 2 volumes (Mexico City: Fondo de Cultura Económica, 1950), has an appendix on Erasmian thought in the Zumárraga period, and Elias Trabulse has sharply delineated the influence of Erasmus in his study of Dr. Francisco Hernández in "El Erasmismo de un científico," *Historia Mexicana* 10 (1978):

224–296. José Almoina's *Rumbos heterodoxos en México* (Ciudad Trujillo: Universidad de Santo Domingo, 1947) is an important source on roots of Erasmian ideas in Mexico.

THE TRIBUNAL OF THE HOLY OFFICE OF THE INQUISITION 1571–1700

In the late 1960s a Frenchwoman from Mexico began her research on the Inquisition. Solange Alberro presented a three-volume dissertation that won her the coveted State Doctorate from the Sorbonne in 1984.[13] Two volumes have been published to date, a detailed statistical survey entitled *La actividad del Santo Oficio de la Inquisición en Nueva España, 1571–1700* (Mexico City: INAH, 1981); and *Inquisition et societé au Mexique, 1571–1700* (Mexico City: Centre D'Etudes Mexicaines et Centramericaines, 1988). François Chevalier, president of her doctoral defense committee, has characterized the work as "retrospective ethnography" or ethnohistory:

> The author offers an extraordinary picture of the social, picaresque, love, moral, political, and religious life and also of the "mentalities" of New Spain at that period. With this goal, she selected six or seven psychodramas with a human interest, an emotion, and an increasing transcendence from the first of the psychodramas (themes of witchcraft) to the last—the great tragedy of the persecution of the crypto-Jews of the middle of the century.[14]

Solange Alberro's many research articles and scholarly papers continue to enrich our knowledge of Inquisition and society in colonial Mexico.

After many years of archival research, María Asunción Herrera Sotillo completed her doctoral thesis at the Universidad Complutense de Madrid in 1982. Her study, entitled *Ortodoxia y control social en México en el siglo XVII: El Tribunal del Santo Oficio*, is a comprehensive treatment of all aspects of inquisitorial activity and is especially valuable for its many tabulations and statistical tables. The chapters on Mexican Inquisition bureaucracy and financial operation of the tribunal give researchers important new data. A sixty-page catalog of manuscript sources for study of the tribunal during 1571–1700 in the Archivo Histórico Nacional is excellent, informative, and a crucial tool for future research. Alberro and Herrera Sotillo worked independently of each other, each unaware of the other's research, and each study depended primarily upon the Inquisition manuscripts in Mexico (Alberro) or in the Archivo Histórico Nacional in Madrid (Herrera Sotillo).[15] Chapters 18 through 25 of Medina's *Historia del Tribunal*, pages 267–299 of Lea's *Inquisition in the Spanish Dependencies*, and sections 1–19 of Jiménez Rueda's *Herejías y supersticiones* trace the narrative history of the Holy Office to 1700. Only Jiménez Rueda offers interpretation of the data. Final chapters of Greenleaf's *Mexican Inquisition of the Sixteenth Century* provide analysis of the political stance of the tribunal as well as conflicts of jurisdiction, from which much is learned of bureaucratic mentality and grass-roots operation. Genealogies of Holy Office staff as well as *limpieza de sangre* of those appointed are contained in a work by Fernández de Recas. A compendium of tribunal deliberations on cases brought before the judges has been published for the early tribunal by Edmundo O'Gorman, *Primer libro de votos de la Inquisición de México, 1573–1600* (Mexico City: Archivo General de la Nación, 1949).[16] Julio Jiménez Rueda in 1944 published a brief biography of *Don Pedro Moya de Contreras, primer Inquisidor de México* (Mexico City: Ediciones Xochitl, 1944), which is amplified in the superb work of Stafford Poole, *Pedro Moya de Contreras: Catholic Reform and Royal Power in New Spain, 1571–1591* (Berkeley, Los Angeles, London: University of California Press, 1987).

In the sixteenth and seventeenth centuries, inquisitors were preoccupied with a feared Protestant menace in Mexico even though the new doctrines of the Reformation never constituted a threat to orthodoxy. Julio Jiménez Rueda has published a volume on trials of non-Spanish pirates as *Corsarios franceses e ingleses en la Inquisición de la Nueva España* (Mexico City: Archivo General de la Nación, 1945). Eleanor B. Adams suspects that the bays and coastal cities of Yucatán and Central America were the homes and business headquarters of many non-Spanish intruders. Her research article, "The Franciscan Inquisition in Yucatán: French Seamen, 1560," in *The Americas: A Quarterly Review of Inter-American Cultural History* 25 (1969): 331–359, is part of a forthcoming book to be entitled "Before the Buccaneers: Non-Spanish Intruders in the Caribbean, 1492–1610." G. Báez-Camargo, *Protestantes enjuiciados por la Inquisición en Iberoamérica* (Mexico City: Editorial Jakeg, 1960), has useful if somewhat misleading short biographical sketches of those thought to be Protestants.[17]

After one views the total documentation of the archives of the Mexican Inquisition both in Mexico and in Spain, it becomes increasingly clear that the most fundamental obligation of the inquisitors was to control the influx of printed matter which attacked or undermined the religious culture of New Spain.[18] For the sixteenth century the important documentary work of Francisco Fernández del Castillo, *Libros y libreros en el siglo XVI* (Mexico City: Archivo General de la Nación, 1914; reprint 1982), is essential for study of the process. Irving A. Leonard's many studies on the book trade, censorship, and the influence of books on colonial Mexican mentality are well known, especially *Books of the Brave* (Cambridge: Cambridge University Press, 1949), amplified as *Los libros del conquistador* (Mexico City: Fondo de Cultura Económica, 1953), and *Baroque Times in Old Mexico* (Ann Arbor: University of Michigan Press, 1959).[19] Almost unknown to scholars outside of the United States is Dorothy Schons's excellent review of Spanish archival documentation in the Ramo de Inquisición of the Archivo Histórico Nacional, entitled *Book Censorship in New Spain* (Austin, Texas: University of Texas Press, 1950), an analytical treatment of "Punitive Censorship in the Seventeenth Century." Both Manuel Romero de Terreros, *Un bibliófilo en el Santo Oficio* (Mexico City: Archivo General de la Nación, 1920), and Donald G. Castanien, "The Mexican Inquisition Censors a Private Library, 1655," *Hispanic American Historical Review* 34 (1954): 374–392, examine the library of Melchor Pérez de Soto, an astrologer. Considerably more article literature exists on books and men in colonial Mexico.[20]

One of the early uses of data in Inquisition procesos has largely escaped the notice of scholars of the Holy Office. Since virtually all provincial records of the New Mexico colony were destroyed in the Pueblo Rebellion of 1680–1681, most borderlands historians had been convinced that it was impossible to write the domestic history of the seventeenth-century colony. France V. Scholes was able to reconstruct the social, political, and religious history of New Mexico from the voluminous Inquisition procesos and ancillary manuscripts in the Archivo General de la Nación in his two volumes, *Church and State in New Mexico, 1610–1650* (Albuquerque: Historical Society of New Mexico, 1937) and *Troublous Times in New Mexico, 1659–1670* (Albuquerque: Historical Society of New Mexico, 1942). His methodological tour de force in this regard has never been properly recognized.

One of the most famous non-Jews tried at mid-century was an Irishman tried for insurrection, heresy, and other crimes and studied by Luis González Obregón, in *Don Guillén de Lampart: La Inquisición y la independencia en el siglo XVIII* (Mexico City: Archivo General de la Nación, 1908). Largely as the result of the scandals and the unprofessional conduct of Inquisition bureaucracy at mid-seventeenth century, Visitor Pedro Medina Rico formally established an organization designed to inculcate professionalism and to encourage morality, brotherhood, and charity in the Holy Office's personnel. Greenleaf's monographic article, "The Inquisition Brotherhood: Cofradía de San Pedro Mártir of Colonial Mexico," in *The Americas: A Quarterly Review of Inter-American Cultural History* 40 (1983): 171–201, examines this sodality from 1656 to 1837. A third volume by Greenleaf, "The Inquisition in Baroque Mexico" (for want of a better title and still in preparation), will focus on the 1640–1680 period, emphasizing prosopographical analysis. But it will also deal with the Holy Office's political, legal, and financial scandals explored in the same author's work, "The Great Visitas of the Mexican Holy Office, 1645–1669," in *The Americas: A Quarterly Review of Inter-American Cultural History* 44 (1988): 399–420.

In general, studies of the Holy Office bureaucracy are yet to be researched, especially the role of the non-salaried Inquisition police known as *familiares*. When Philip II founded the Tribunal of the Holy Office in Mexico, he attempted to circumscribe the privileges and immunities of Inquisition police and commissaries so that the bureaucracy of the Inquisition would not parallel the baroque and irresponsible corps of Holy Office functionaries in Aragón and Castilla. By royal decree, on 16 August 1570, the privileges of the *familiatura* in New Spain were regulated and strict limitations were placed upon the numbers of police allowed in urban areas and in the provinces. In general the familiares were given immunity from prosecution by the vice-regency in criminal cases, but they were subject to civil authority in civil cases. The king charged all of his subjects to report violations of conduct by the familiatura to the Tribunal of the Holy Office and to the Audiencia. On 13 May 1572, Philip II decreed that crimes committed by Inquisition officials against Indians were not covered by the familiatura's immunities. Within a decade after the 1570 decree it became clear that the familiares had entrenched themselves in colonial business enterprises and that they were repeating the patterns of personal aggrandizement which Philip II so deplored in Spain. Greenleaf's study of Familiar "Antonio de Espejo and the Mexican Inquisition, 1571–1586," in *The Americas: A Quarterly Review of Inter-American Cultural History* 27 (1971): 271–292, parallels one of Bartolomé Bennassar on Andalucia.[21]

Since there was an early and continuing relationship and pattern of migration from the islands of the Caribbean to Mexico and Central America, researchers will find Carlos Esteban Deive, *Heterodoxia e Inquisición en Santo Domingo, 1492–1822* (Santo Domingo: Universidad de Santo Domingo, 1983) valuable, as well as Ernesto Chinchilla Aguilar's *La Inquisición en Guatemala* (Guatemala City: Imprenta Universitaria,

1953). Jonathan I. Israel, *Race, Class and Politics in Colonial México, 1610–1670* (London: Oxford University Press, 1975) makes excellent use of Inquisition manuscripts. Richard E. Greenleaf, *Inquisición y sociedad en el México colonial* (Madrid: José Porrúa Turanzas, 1985) reproduces in Spanish translation twelve of Greenleaf's studies for the convenience of Spanish and Latin American scholars. Thematic analysis of Mexican Inquisition historiography dealing with Indians and the Inquisition, crypto-Jews, and problems of interpretation will follow the next section.

THE INQUISITION IN BOURBON MEXICO, 1700–1820

Until the late 1960s our knowledge of the eighteenth-century Inquisition rested on two excellent publications of the Archivo General de la Nación edited by Nicolás Rangel: *Los precursores ideológicos de la Guerra de la Independencia, 1789–1794*, vol. 1, *La Revolución Francesa*, vol. 2, and *La masonería en México: Siglo XVIII*, (Mexico City: Archivo General de la Nación, 1929–1932). The fine thesis by Monelisa Lina Pérez-Marchand, *Dos etapas ideológicas del siglo XVIII en México a través de los papeles de la Inquisición* (Mexico City: Universidad Nacional Autonóma, 1945) added to our understanding, but most authors relying on Medina, Lea, and Jiménez Rueda continued to interpret the Holy Office as a moribund institution in the eighteenth century.[22] Many works continued to assert that the Holy Office declined because it became a political instrument, citing the Inquisition trials of Miguel Hidalgo y Costilla, José María Morelos, and other Independence leaders as evidence.[23] Greenleaf's forthcoming volume on "The Inquisition in Bourbon Mexico, 1700–1820" takes issue with these interpretations and argues that while many scholars have called attention to the fact that the Holy Office of the Inquisition was a political instrument, what has not been examined in detail is the relationship that existed between heresy and treason during the three centuries of Spanish and Spanish-colonial Inquisition history. The belief that heretics were traitors and traitors were heretics led to the conviction that dissenters were social revolutionaries trying to subvert the political and religious stability of the community. These tenets were not later developments in the history of the Spanish Inquisition; they were inherent in the rationale of the institution from the fifteenth century onward and were apparent in the Holy Office's dealings with Jews, Protestants, and other heretics during the sixteenth century. The use of the Inquisition by the later eighteenth-century Bourbon kings of Spain as an instrument of regalism was not a departure from tradition.

Particularly in the viceroyalty of New Spain during the late eighteenth century the Inquisition trials show how the Crown sought to promote political and religious orthodoxy.[24]

Monelisa Lina Pérez-Marchand made an extensive study of the books prohibited in Mexico by the Inquisition, and her research determined that in the latter part of the eighteenth century, works of political philosophy predominated. It is important to note that the majority of books proscribed by Holy Office edicts during 1763–1805 did not simply question specific policies but rather challenged the theoretical existence or raison d'être of the state. This indirect attack made it possible for the colonist to read and apply general theories to particular circumstances— Spanish mercantilism, monopolization of office by peninsular Spaniards, monolithic religion, and so on. Because the colonists saw the French Revolution as an attempt to put these ideas into practice, accounts of it had to be zealously prohibited. Such works always carried heretical religious propositions. The banned *Lettres d'une péruvienne* (1797) are a case in point. The Holy Office charged that they were filled with sedition and heresy and were "injurious to monarchs and Catholic rulers of Spain . . . and to religion itself." The same decree also prohibited *Les ruines; ou, Meditation sur les revolutions des empires* by M. Volney and other works. A separate ban of the Volney tract alleged that its author affirmed that there neither is nor can be revealed religion, that all (people) are daughters of curiosity, ignorance, interest, and imposture, and that the mystery of the birth of Jesus Christ and the rest of the Christian religion are mystical allegories.

The Holy Office of the Inquisition did not limit its censorship to French books; English Enlightenment works were also a matter of concern. The works of Alexander Pope were most frequently mentioned in edicts of the Inquisition, particularly his "Cartas de Abelardo y Heloisa," a translation of "Eloisa to Abelard," telling the tale of a nun's love for Peter Abelard. Proscriptions of Pope occurred in 1792 and 1799, and by 1815 all of his works were banned. Other English books on the lists were *Gulliver's Travels* (1803) and *Pamela* (1803). The most important edict of the period was the one issued on 25 August 1805, for it presents a comprehensive and alphabetical listing of all books prohibited since 1789. Several hundred works appear on the list. The edict reflects concern not only with the French Revolution but also with the ascendancy of Napoleon.

In many cases the Inquisition found it necessary not only to prohibit political philosophy but to deny its content and validity. An example of this was the edict of 13 November 1794 with regard to a volume published in Philadelphia by Santiago Felipe Puglia entitled *Desengaño del Hombre*:

> The author of this book, writing in their own language, blows his raucous trumpet to excite the faithful people of the Spanish nation to rebellion of the most infamous sort. . . . The pedantic writer has made of himself a bankrupt merchant in such sublime goods as politics and the universal right, and [is] equally detestable for his impiety and insolence that, for his ignorance of sacred and profane literature and for the vile and ignominious style with which he speaks of Kings divined by God, imputes the odious name of despotism and tyranny to the monarchial regime and royal authority that arises from God himself and from His divine will . . . and the universal consent of all the people who from most remote antiquity have been governed by Kings. . . . [He attempts] to introduce the rebellious oligarchy of France with the presumption to propose that [it is] in reality the best example of desolation brought on by pestilences and anti-evangelical principles.

Of course many of the polemics of the rationalists were against the Inquisition itself, and to maintain its station in colonial life the Holy Office could not tolerate them.

To conclude that the Inquisition in Mexico declined in power and became decadent in the late eighteenth century because it developed into a political instrument seems clearly fallacious to this writer. The apparent decadence of the Mexican Tribunal after 1763 resulted from a whole complex of political and diplomatic circumstances which, in the end, led to a weakening of the institution. The shift of diplomatic and military alliances between Spain and France, and Spain and England, made it difficult for the Holy Office to punish foreign heretics within the viceroyalty of New Spain. It was equally difficult, if not impossible, to contain foreign political ideas. From the standpoint of domestic politics and Empire policy, the activities of the Holy Office were severely hampered and began to atrophy because of the tendency of royal and ecclesiastical officialdom to embrace philosophical eclecticism. Certainly in the case of the clergy this became a dangerous trend, since in the final analysis, the new philosophical and political ideas tended to undermine orthodoxy. Social and economic tensions in the Mexican colony, pragmatically evident, were reinforced by consideration of the new natural laws of politics and economics being expounded from abroad. On the threshold of this societal discontent, the Holy Office was often forced to make an ideological retreat, adopting an attitude of tolerance or inaction instead of its former firmness—in reality a new kind of "flexible orthodoxy."

The total documentation in the Mexican Inquisition archive for 1763 to 1805 reveals that the Holy Office cannot be indicted as loath to prosecute unorthodoxy of any kind. It only confirms the fact that overriding political considerations of the state made the inquisitors responsible for enforcing a rapidly changing "party-line" kind of orthodoxy, an almost hopeless task. It was impossible to police the far frontiers from California to Florida, from Colorado to Guatemala, from Havana to Manila, a problem as serious to the inquisitors as the problem of "flexible orthodoxy." Perhaps it was a sense of frustration in coping with the larger problems that led the Holy Office to concentrate on smaller ones. The tendency to engage in hairsplitting and tedious controversies over jurisdiction and judicial competencies was one result of this frustration. Another was the preoccupation with protecting the position and dignity of the Tribunal of the Inquisition.

The interpretation that the clergy (and the Inquisition) mirrored the times and the society to which they ministered is no doubt true of the Mexican experience during the second half of the eighteenth century. Would the Inquisition and the Crown have reacted any differently had the revolutionary political themes then in vogue been circulating fifty or one hundred years earlier? Probably not. At all events, the policies of Charles III (1759–1788) and Charles IV (1788–1808) did little to strengthen the Mexican Inquisition's mission to preserve political and religious orthodoxy. Indeed, the Spanish kings weakened the institution by failing to define the place of the Holy Office of the Inquisition in defining the Imperial self-interest.

Nicolás Rangel's volume of documents on the Inquisition and the Masonic movement in New Spain was used by J. A. Ferrer Biminelli to compose the Mexican section of *Masonería e Inquisición en Latinoamérica durante el siglo XVIII* (Caracas: Universidad Católica Andrés Bello, 1973); and Greenleaf's article, "The Mexican Inquisition and the Masonic Movement, 1751–1820," *New Mexico Historical Review* 44 (1969): 93–117, employed new documentation of the Jalapa Lodges, Los Caballeros Racionales, and other secret societies, linking Masonry with the independence movement. Often the transcendental views of Masons were transfused with the new social and political philosophies of the Enlightenment, and Masonic groups carried on political activities. The members kept their ideas within the group, and each depended upon the others to be loyal and to keep discussions secret so that established institutions would not feel challenged by the Masonic quest to better the human condition. The Holy Office of the Inquisition viewed Masons as social revolutionaries who were trying to subvert the established order.

Often the Tribunal of the Holy Office made no clear distinction among Masonry, Enlightenment philosophy, and Protestantism. As a result, after a century and a half of ignoring Protestants, the Holy Office began to be more interested in foreigners and obvious Protestants within its jurisdiction. William B. Taylor's Master of Arts thesis "Protestants before the Inquisition in Mexico, 1790–1820" (Mexico City: University of the Americas, 1965) and Richard E. Greenleaf's "North American Protestants and the Mexican Inquisition 1765–1820," *Journal of Church and State* 8 (1966): 186–199, investigate this new interest, and Greenleaf concludes that the primary goal of the Holy Office was to encourage Protestants to convert to Catholicism. The tribunal's function of religious instruction and conversion of non-Catholics was one of the most important activities of the Holy Office after 1765. Studies by Jacques Houdaille, "Frenchmen and Francophiles in New Spain from 1760 to 1810," *The Americas: A Quarterly Review of Inter-American Cultural History* 13 (1956): 1–29, and Charles F. Nunn, *Foreign Immigrants in Early Bourbon Mexico, 1700–1760* (Cambridge: Cambridge University Press, 1979) are based partially on Inquisition surveillance of foreigners and Protestants.

THE INQUISITION AND THE INDIANS

The question of the jurisdiction of the Holy Office of the Inquisition over the native populations in New Spain and the rest of the empire has been one of controversy and confusion since the earliest days of the conquest. The perplexing problem of enforcing orthodoxy among the recently converted Indians was linked with the debate over whether or not the Indian was a rational human being who had the capacity to comprehend the Roman Catholic faith and enjoy the full sacramental system of the Church. As in the case of the rationality controversy, the position of the Indian vis-à-vis the Holy Office of the Inquisition was not resolved articulately, and after the first decades of the spiritual conquest the question took on added importance as the Mexican clergy discovered recurrent idolatry and religious syncretism among their flocks.

Despite claims of traditional historiography, the Mexican Inquisition did try Indians from 1522 through 1571 as the friar inquisitors in Central Mexico and Yucatán prosecuted native transgressions against the faith and as the episcopal inquisition continued to discipline Indians. The Archivo General de la Nación published two important documentary compendia on the Indians and the Inquisition early in this century: *Proceso inquisitorial del cacique de Tetzcoco* (Mexico City: Archivo General de la Nación, 1910) and *Procesos de Indios idólatras y hechiceros* (Mexico

City: Archivo General de la Nación, 1912). Alberto María Carreño published in 1950 a documentary compendium *Don Fray Juan de Zumárraga: Teólogo y editor, humanista e inquisidor* (Mexico City: Editorial Jus, 1950) which gave some attention to the Indian trials and disputed Joaquin García Icazbalceta's claim in *Don Fray Juan de Zumárraga, primer obispo y arzobispo de México* (Mexico City: Editorial Porrúa, 1948) that the bishop was never an inquisitor. Robert Ricard, Robert Padden, and Jacques Lafaye have made varied use of the printed procesos, while Greenleaf has preferred to use the original documents because he has found difficulty with the published paleographic transcriptions.[25] France V. Scholes and Eleanor B. Adams edited the controversial *Proceso contra Tzintzicha Tangaxoan el Caltzontzin formado por Nuño de Guzmán, año de 1530* (Mexico City: José Porrúa Hermanos, 1952) as civil authority also assumed jurisdiction over Indian idolatry and sacrifice among the Tarascans.

In 1965 Greenleaf began his analysis of Indian Inquisition manuscripts for the entire colonial period in "The Inquisition and the Indians of New Spain: A Study in Jurisdictional Confusion," *The Americas: A Quarterly Review of Inter-American Cultural History* 22 (1965): 138–166, followed by a 1978 article with a selected documentary appendix in the same journal, "The Mexican Inquisition and the Indians: Sources for the Ethnohistorian," 34 (1973): 315–344. Even though the Tribunal of the Holy Office of the Inquisition was denied the right to hear Indian cases, an Indian Inquisition continued under an institutional framework quite similar to that of the formal Inquisition. After 1571 the Tribunal of the Holy Office acted as a fact-finding agency in the uncovering and disciplining of Indian transgressions against orthodoxy. Actual control over Indian orthodoxy reverted to the bishop's or archbishop's office and was placed under the care of the provisor, or vicar-general, of the diocese or archdiocese. The *provisoratos* contrived an entire bureaucracy of officials to cope with the new function, and they appointed delegates and commissaries in provincial areas. Following the tradition established during the period of the episcopal inquisition, the provisor and his commissaries often called themselves "inquisitors ordinary" and established tribunals and *juzgados* for Indians of the bishopric.

For several decades the provisorato set-up functioned without much competition or invasion of power by the Inquisition tribunal, but in actual operation of enforcement or orthodoxy there was still fusion and confusion of authority and responsibility of the inquisitorial and the ordinary functions. Quarrels over the competence of the provisorato and the tribunal in cases involving Indians in the seventeenth and eighteenth centuries occupy many pages of testimony in the actual procesos and comprise several *legajos* of administrative documents sent to Spain for resolution. Often, because many of the colonial Mexican clergy occupied several portfolios or exercised a multiple function, the personnel of the provisorato and the Holy Office were mixed in the conduct of trials, thus adding to the confusion over jurisdiction, especially in the remote provincial areas.

Investigatory activities of the Inquisition into Indian affairs continued throughout the colonial period of New Spain. Of particular concern were studies of recurrent paganism and idolatry and violation of the degrees of carnal and spiritual relationship permitted by the Church in the sacrament of marriage. The Inquisition usually kept meticulous records of these investigations, but because of the burden of work for ministers of the spiritual flock, the provisor or his agent kept sparse records or none at all. Therefore we must conclude that only the more serious deviations from orthodoxy came to light in the archives. Oftentimes materials on heresy and crimes against the faith are mixed with data on the spiritual activities of the regular and secular clergy. Between 1620 and 1700 concern focused on evaluation of missionizing techniques seen against the background of continued pagan practices and the process of religious syncretism taking place in many of the Mexican provinces. Friars of several of the orders were charged to write full reports, and these *relaciones* document fears of the inquisitors and ordinaries as to the extent of paganism in the supposedly Christianized viceregal area.[26]

In the aftermath of Zumárraga's Indian Inquisition, the Visitor to New Spain and apostolic inquisitor Francisco Tello de Sandoval launched a probe into paganism among the Mixtec Indians of Oaxaca.[27] The voluminous documentation was partially extracted for ethnological materials by Wigberto Jiménez Moreno and Salvador Mateos Higuera for commentary in their edition of *Códice de Yanhuitlán* (Mexico City: Museo Nacional, 1940), but they counsel the ethnohistorian that much data was left untouched. Other anthropologists have cited some of the data, but it was left to Richard E. Greenleaf to prepare a complete study with introduction in his *Mixtec Religion and Spanish Conquest: The Oaxaca Inquisition Trials, 1544–1547* (Madrid: José Porrúa Turanzas, 1991), and with ethnohistorical commentary by Maarten E. R. G. N. Jansen. Greenleaf's introduction also deals with the Oaxacan Inquisition of the Dominicans in 1560, when Indians from both Solá and Teticpac were subjected to an auto de fe. The Teticpac trials were examined from newly discovered archival documentation.

The climactic event of the sixteenth century Indian Inquisition came with the Landa idolatry trials in Yucatán during the period 1559–1562. In the 1930s, France V. Scholes discovered the corpus of the trials in

Spanish archives. He and Eleanor B. Adams published most of the materials in *Don Diego de Quijada Alcalde Mayor de Yucatán, 1561–1565,* 2 vols. (Mexico City: José Porrúa Hermanos, 1933), including a lengthy introduction that summarizes the trial records. France V. Scholes and Ralph L. Roys, *Fray Diego de Landa and the Problem of Idolatry in Yucatán* (Washington, D.C.: Carnegie Institution, 1938) give an in-depth analysis of the proceedings. Recently Inga Clendinnen has given a new interpretation of the Landa trials in *Ambivalent Conquests: Maya and Spaniard in Yucatán, 1517–1570* (Cambridge: Cambridge University Press, 1987). Building on several earlier research articles, she postulates that testimonies in the trial records may be unreliable and that incidences of idolatry and sacrifice may have been exaggerated. The Greenleaf articles on the Indians and the Inquisition and the Mixtec religion and Spanish Conquest deal with methodological problems of using the procesos de Indios as historical sources.

The procesos reveal fascinating data on the use of idolatry, sorcery, and sacrifice within a political context of native resistance to Spanish power. In general, the Indians attempted to manipulate inquisitional procedures by denouncing Spanish-appointed caciques as idolaters in order to deprive them of office. There are also denunciations for idolatry and human sacrifice by Indians who wanted to attack their own political enemies, hoping to replace them in the new political hierarchy. The procesos also illuminate subversive activities of Indian sorcerers, curers, witches, and seers who tried to perpetuate the old beliefs. Of particular concern to the Mexican Inquisition were groups of native priests and sorcerers who openly defied the "spiritual conquest" by establishing schools or apprenticeships among the young. The teachers made a frontal attack on Catholicism and Spanish Catholic culture. They ridiculed the new religion and urged a return to native religious practices. These men, branded as "dogmatizers" by the inquisitors, were considered especially dangerous by the missionary clergy. Thus the native priesthood preached a counterculture and a counter-religion and took the lead in performing sorceries and sacrifices. They supported the ancient practices of concubinage and bigamy as a symbol of resistance to the new religion—and the dogmatizers also ridiculed the Inquisition. Students of ritual humor among the Maya, notably Professor Victoria R. Bricker, in recent times have found survivals of plays and dances done in jest of the Holy Office. It is obvious that this same set of attitudes impelled native doctors or curers to continue the use of preconquest medicine, and to transmit Aztec, Maya, and Mixtec medical lore to future generations of Indians and mestizos in colonial Mexico.

Obviously, procesos de Indios initiated by the Inquisition are pe-

ripheral to other documentation about social discontent in sixteenth-
and seventeenth-century Mexico, but they are reliable benchmarks of
what was taking place. Trials of all genres of mestizos, pardos, and
others are indicative of developing syncretism, accommodation, and resistance to the culture of the conqueror. Most resistance to the Spanish
social structure, however, probably came in more passive ways, although
some writers would like to link forced acculturation with Indian rebellions in colonial Mexico. It is certain that native religion was important
in Indian rebellions and that paganism became a catalyst in the up-
heavals, but documentary studies of causal factors still await scholarly
investigation. Important to future studies will be analyses of peyote cults
and the use of other hallucinogens (yerba pipiltzintzin, ololiuqui) in
idolatry, sorcery, and in other patterns of pagan resistance.

Perhaps the thorniest problem faced by ethnohistorians as they in-
terprets procesos de Indios relates to classical procedures of historical
criticism: the art of determining the validity of historical sources. Do
the Inquisition manuscripts give a reliable picture of native religion or
pagan resistance? Did the monastic inquisitor or the provisor or the professional judge on the Holy Office tribunal correctly understand the
testimony of the evidence? Did the inquisitor project an image or an
interpretation of data in the procesos de Indios from an ethnocentric
Christian viewpoint? Did the scribes and notaries properly report the
proceedings? Were the interpreters really competent to transmit testimonies of Indians who did not know Spanish? While historians may
not be able to arrive at firm answers to these questions, they must
nevertheless be ever in their minds as they interpret. Given the nature
of these problems, distorted pictures and fanciful interpretations result
with alarming frequency.

The meticulous scholar must therefore examine a broad base of archival documentation and other sources in order to place the ethnohistorical data in proper perspective. Statements of historian France V.
Scholes and anthropologist Ralph L. Roys pertaining to *Fray Diego de
Landa and the Problem of Idolatry in Yucatán* may be applied to other
areas. They concluded that Indian testimony often "confirms, supplements, and clarifies our knowledge of Maya religion derived from other
sources," but they recognized that the evidence possibly "contains exag-
gerations, even certain falsehoods and that Indians may have called
upon memory of pre-Conquest practices as regards certain details." On
the whole, they concluded cautiously that "the testimony does provide
a generally valid description of actual cases of idolatry and sacrifice that
had occurred subsequent to the Spanish occupation and the beginning

of the missionary program."[28] Clendinnen, as noted, has explored these caveats and has taken issue with the traditional historiography on Landa and the Yucatán idolatry trials.

The careful scholar should always remember that it is important to let the documents speak for themselves whenever possible rather than to force them into a fanciful or preconceived framework, a framework often built on grand generalizations and untested hypotheses. Several dissertations and theses on the Indian Inquisition, and the Inquisition and mestizos and blacks, deserve to be published: Bradley W. Case, "Gods and Demons: Folk Religion in Seventeenth-Century New Spain, 1614–1632," (doctoral dissertation, Cornell University, 1977); Eva A. Uchmany, "La Conquista de México: El choque de dos culturas" (tesis de doctorado, Universidad Nacional Autónoma de México, 1971); Gloria R. Grajales, "Cristianismo y paganismo en la altiplanicie mexicana, siglo XVI" (tesis de maestría, Universidad Nacional Autónoma de México, 1949). Colin Palmer's *Slaves of the White God* (Cambridge, Mass.: Harvard University Press, 1976) uses Inquisition procesos to uncover the black experience in early Mexico.

Excellent examples of the use of procesos de Indios by anthropologists are Noemí Quezada, *Amor y magia amorosa entre los aztecas: Supervivencia en el México colonial* (Mexico City: Universidad Nacional Autónoma, 1975), which gives a critical survey of pre-Hispanic and colonial texts dealing with magical and religious aspects of love and sexuality, and, by the same author, "Hernando Ruiz de Alarcón y su persecución de idolatrías," UNAM/T, 1980: 323–354; studies of Ruth Behar, who is planning a volume on the eighteenth century building on her articles "The Visions of a Guachichil Witch in 1599: A Window on the Subjugation of Mexico's Hunter-Gatherers," *Ethnohistory*, 34 (1987): 115–138, and "Sex and Sin, Witchcraft and the Devil in Late-Colonial Mexico," *American Ethnologist* 14 (1987): 34–54; the translation and edition by J. Richard Andrews and Ross Hassig of Hernando Ruiz de Alarcón's *Treatise on the Heathen Superstitions That Today Live among the Indians Native to This New Spain, 1629* (Norman, Okla.: University of Oklahoma Press, 1984); and the anticipated work based on provisorato and other documents of Serge Gruzinski.[29]

CRYPTO-JEWS

The judaizante, or Jewish pseudo-convert to Catholicism, was a particular problem for the Mexican Inquisition. Judaizantes and conversos (actual converts to Catholicism) often came to Mexico under aliases to engage in conquest and commercial enterprises and, more importantly to the Inquisition, to practice the Jewish faith in private. Such people had come with Cortés and were tried in the 1520s by the first friar inquisitors. Their number rapidly increased all over the Mexican viceroyalty, especially in the central valley, Puebla, Nuevo León, and the far Northwest. In the last decades of the sixteenth century, members of the famous Carvajal family of Nuevo León were tried for relapsing into Judaism; and several of them, including some women, were burned at the stake. The Holy Office wished to use the Carvajal burnings as a threat to the Jewish community in Mexico; but it failed to eradicate the judaizantes, who continued to practice the old religion in private and to proselytize. The size of the Jewish or crypto-Jewish community continued to increase in the seventeenth century despite Church and state caveats.

Many scholars who have written about the Mexican Inquisition over the past few decades have tended to overemphasize the Holy Office's persecution of judaizantes. This is not unnatural because the majority of the authors have approached their subject from the perspective of Jewish history rather than Mexican history. As a result, the student of colonial Mexico gets a number of misconceptions. One mistaken impression is that the Inquisition was constantly preoccupied with prosecuting crypto-Jews throughout the colonial period. On the contrary, the vast majority of its cases dealt with breaches of faith and morals of the colonists: blasphemy, bigamy, superstition, doctrinal error, clerical morality, and Indian transgressions.

In-depth investigations in the Inquisition archive lead this writer to believe that there were many more Jews in colonial Mexico than is commonly supposed, and the documents hint that only a small number of these ever came before the Holy Office. For the most part, the Inquisition left them alone. They constituted a nebulous subculture in the colony, lending variety to the social scene and to the intellectual milieu. Except when they challenged the Church or Spanish authority in an open manner or when they particularly rankled the Mexican Spaniard as business competitors or as political rivals, these "heretics" did not appear in the halls of the Inquisition.

Pioneering works on the crypto-Jews before the Mexican Inquisition included Alfonso Toro, *Los judíos en la Nueva España* (Mexico City: Archivo General de la Nación, 1932), as well as his *La familia Carvajal*, 2 vols. (Mexico City: Editorial Patria, 1944). Rafael López's edition of *Procesos de Luis Carvajal (El Mozo)* (Mexico City: Archivo General de la Nación, 1935) added significantly to our understanding of the Inquisition and the Jews in late seventeenth-century Mexico and laid foundations for later narrative and interpretative studies. Pablo Martínez del Río's famous *Alumbrado* (Mexico City: Archivo General de la Nación, 1937) influenced the thinking of an entire generation of scholars. Greenleaf's chapter on "Zumárraga and the Judaizantes; 1536–1540," in *Zumárraga and the Mexican Inquisition*, pp. 89–99, and his "First Decade of the Mexican Inquisition, 1522–1532," in *The Mexican Inquisition of the Sixteenth Century*, pp. 7–44, present much new archival data on the auto de fe of 1528 and question the ethnicity of several "Jews" who were tried.

Arnold Wizmitzer began a synthesis of activities of the "Holy Office and the crypto-Jews in Mexico during the Sixteenth Century," *American Jewish Historical Quarterly* 51 (1962): 168–214 and, in the same journal, "Crypto-Jews in Mexico during the Seventeenth Century," 51 (1962): 222–268, both excellent surveys based on extensive research in both primary and secondary sources.

For more than twenty-five years the passionate scholar and indefatigable researcher Seymour B. Liebman worked on the history of the Jews in New Spain and in the rest of Latin America. Liebman's basic strength was his tenacity in ferreting out materials; his basic weakness was his passionate analysis and sometimes careless use of sources. Basic to researchers is his *A Guide to Jewish References in the Mexican Colonial Era* (Philadelphia: University of Pennsylvania Press, 1965). His major works included *The Enlightenment: The Writings of Luis Carvajal el Mozo* (Miami: University of Miami Press, 1967); *The Jews in New Spain: Faith, Flame and the Inquisition* (Miami: University of Miami Press, 1970); *The Great auto de fé of 1649 in Mexico* (Lawrence, Kans.: Coronado Press, 1974); *The Inquisitors and the Jews in the New World* (Miami: University of Miami Press, 1975); *Los judíos en México y América Central* (Mexico City: Siglo Veintiuno, 1971); *Valerosas criptojudías en América colonial* (Mexico City: Siglo Veintiuno, 1975). Liebman's books and his host of articles are excellent finding aids to research whether or not the researcher agrees with his point of view or his conclusions. His final book, published in 1982, was a touching tribute to his coreligionists, *New World Jewry, 1493–1825: Requiem for the Forgotten* (New York: Ktav Publishing House, 1982).

One scholar with whom Liebman had scholarly disputes is Martin A. Cohen, author of *The Martyr: The Story of a Secret Jew and the Mexican Inquisition in the Sixteenth Century* (Philadelphia: University of Pennsylvania Press, 1973), a well-documented study of the life of Luis de Carvajal the Younger. Also valuable to the researcher for quick reference is Dr. Cohen's compendium of reprints, *The Jewish Experience in Latin America*, 2 vols. (New York: American Jewish Historical Society, 1971).

The soon-to-be-published doctoral dissertation of Stanley M. Hordes,

"The Crypto-Jewish Community of New Spain, 1600–1649: A Collective Biography" (New Orleans: Tulane University Press, 1980) is a model study for imaginative use of Inquisition sources. See also Dr. Hordes's article "The Inquisition as an Economic Agent: The Campaign of the Mexican Holy Office against the Crypto-Jews in the Mid-Seventeenth Century," *The Americas: A Quarterly Review of Inter-American Cultural History* 39 (1982): 23–88. Greenleaf's "The Great Visitas of the Mexican Holy Office, 1645–1669," also sheds new light on the crypto-Jew in seventeenth-century Mexico, as does the Solange Alberro dissertation. The forthcoming work of J. Benedict Warren and Richard E. Greenleaf on *Gonzalo Gómez: Primer Poblador de Michoacán* (Morelia: Secretaría de Educación Pública, 1989) will integrate Inquisition manuscript sources with other corollary documentation on the early settlement of the Valladolid-Morelia Pátzcuaro area. Often linked with the mentality of the crypto-Jews were the mystics in New Spain: alumbrados, Illuminati Quietists, the circle that practiced *dejamiento*. An extensive literature exists on the mystics in Spain, but studies on Mexico are still sparse. Julio Jiménez Rueda's *Herejías y supersticiones*, chapters 13–15, pp. 139–182 is the most complete treatment of Alumbrados, pseudo-alumbrados, and mystics. Noemí Quesada's survey of "alumbrados del siglo XVII: Análisis de casos" in *Religión en Mesoamérica*, ed. Jaime Litvak-King (Mexico: Sociedad Mexicana de Antropología, 1972), pp. 581–586, is interesting. Dolores Bravo, *Ana Rodríguez de Castro, procesada por ilusa, y afectadora de Santos* (Mexico City: Universidad Metropolitana, 1984) has fascinating data. Alvaro Huerga's forthcoming *Historia de los alumbrados*, vol. 3, *Los alumbrados en Hispanoamérica* will include New Spain. Richard E. Greenleaf has prepared a catalog and extracts of all alumbrado trials in the Archivo General de la Nación from 1580 to the early nineteenth century with the hope of doing a complete study in the future.

The statistical tabulation of Mariel de Ibánez and Solange Alberro on procesos in Mexico, and Gustav Henningsen[30] and Herrera Sotillo on those in Spain, have placed crypto-Jewish prosecutions in proper perspective, showing that they constituted only a small portion of inquisitorial activity in the total picture of the Holy Office's attention to perceived heresy and correction of faith and morals in New Spain. A study of the Inquisition and clerical morality remains to be done on Mexico.[31]

PROBLEMS OF INTERPRETATION

There is considerable disagreement among historians over the proper role of religion in colonial Mexican society. Interpretation of the Church is made difficult because of the disagreement. Evaluation of the Inquisition is even more polemical because those who interpret the documents wish to do so from an Enlightenment and twentieth-century standard of political and legal theory, and they insist upon making religious toleration the central focus of their evaluation. Later this writer will suggest a wider sociological analysis of intolerance that seems more appropriate in understanding the problem.[32]

As a twentieth-century man, the author deplores repressive religious and repressive political institutions; but as a historian of religious institutions, he feels constrained to view them in a perspective of sixteenth- and seventeenth-century Mexico. Thus it seems fairer to judge the Mexican Inquisition from the vantage point of the prevailing judicial system and ideological structure of Spain and Spanish Catholicism than from the more equalitarian point of view. Some may call this a "White Legend" interpretation, but the writer prefers to see the Inquisition in the "historical present" in much the same way that the anthropologist would view the ethnographic present of the colonial period.

In Spain and in Mexico the Holy Office of the Inquisition was an internal-security organization charged with protecting a civilization and its culture—culture in its broadest sense: religious, political, and social. Even today the social scientist has great difficulty measuring the effects or the degree of repressiveness of internal-security organizations and their procedures. Enlightenment and twentieth-century political philosophy and jurisprudence certainly call into question rules of evidence, procedures, and judicial torture of the Mexican Inquisition. Prior to the legal reformism of Beccarria and the Benthamites, however, the Holy Office operated within a framework of procedures prescribed by canon law; these procedures were consistent with the rules of law of the era. Examination of thousands of Inquisition trial records has demonstrated to this writer that within the prescribed rules and regulations the inquisitors acted with zeal but also with fairness and common sense in the vast majority of cases. Again, one must add, this does not mean that we approve of these procedures today.

Critics of the Mexican Inquisition, and of the Spanish government, contend that the mere fact that the Holy Office required denunciations and proceeded with investigations is a good index of repression. Perhaps this argument can be supported on philosophical grounds, but it is more difficult to substantiate statistically. As social scientists using techniques of quantification to study modern police records, they encounter many of the same problems of analysis facing the investigator in the Inquisition archive. It appears that ninety-five percent of the total population of colonial Mexico never had any contact with the Inquisition. Of the five percent who did, five-sixths never came to trial because of insufficient evidence; and of that one-sixth who were tried by the Holy Office, perhaps two percent were convicted, with one-half of one percent being executed. These figures, while deplorable to the modern man, stand out in stark contrast with the accounts of the gothic writers on the Inquisition who give a distorted picture of the institution's outreach into society.

Gothic writing on the Holy Office has of course emphasized that the Inquisition surrounded its operations with extreme secrecy while recording them in meticulous detail, a procedure that some modern scholars feel led to the lurid myths about all phases of inquisitorial activities. It is perhaps true that obsession with secrecy fostered lurid myths about the Holy Office; but because the greater part of viceregal operations took place in a climate of extreme confidentiality, it appears that this interpretation has been exaggerated. Certainly, Protestant and Jewish historiography of the era contributed much to the distortions and luridness.

The almost universally held view that the Mexican Holy Office prosecuted heretics in order to line its pockets is open to question. Until competent scholars have analyzed many hundreds of volumes of detailed Mexican Inquisition account books and have proved the contrary, it would be difficult to sustain these charges. Certainly there is no clear evidence that the economic backwardness of the colonies can be ascribed to the Inquisition. Most generalizations about Mexican Inquisition finance have resulted from published data on the financial scandal of the middle of the seventeenth century when a group of impoverished and greedy inquisitors did indeed try to rob the Jews. However, this writer's preliminary investigations of the account books, and the study done of the scandal by Helen Phipps many decades ago, show that this was an atypical situation and that up until the middle of the seventeenth century the Mexican Holy Office was an impoverished institution. Researches by the author show that the wealth of the tribunal increased after the last quarter of the seventeenth century and throughout the eighteenth century—but that it did not increase appreciably from judicial fines or confiscations of property of heretics. The Holy Office received property and money in trust and in the wills of the faithful, and the rents and moneys were invested by the tribunal in the same manner that nunneries and other arms of the ecclesiastical establishment invested and increased their properties. The Treasury of the Holy Office was an investment institution serving primarily the economic needs of the creole elite.

In Mexico and in Spain, the phenomenon of intolerance—even with the presence of the Inquisition—can be studied meaningfully only if intolerance is related to a wide complex of historical circumstances. Henry Kamen has investigated these factors in the Iberian peninsula, and he has concluded that the religious issue was not the most prominent or the most relevant factor.[33] Greenleaf's research suggests that insularity, exclusivism, xenophobia, even racial attitudes, were more important factors than religion in developing the climate of intolerance that prevailed from the fifteenth century to the 1800s. In Mexico as in Spain, the Inquisition was not a tyrannical body imposed on the populace; nor was the Spanish Inquisition a logical outgrowth of Catholicism. Rather, it was a logical expression of prevalent social prejudices. The Tribunal of the Holy Office was neither a despotic body in control of a hypocritical nation nor was it by nature primarily anti-Protestant or anti-Jewish.[34]

During Habsburg times, and until the middle of the eighteenth century in Mexico, the Inquisition found ready support from the ruling elite and from the humble masses. For the most part, the focus of inquisitorial activities was on Indians and foreigners; thus, the Mexican populace regarded the Holy Office as a relatively benign institution that protected society and religion from traitors and fomenters of social revolution. The only real opposition to the tribunal came from conversos, the converted Jews. But even in the matter of the Jews, it should be remembered that anti-Semitism came first and then the Inquisition.

In colonial Mexico, the tribunal and its agents were never able to effect thought control over either the colonial population or Indian groups. Studies on colonial printing in Mexico, the book trade, literary production, scientific investigation, and colonial art show that a vital intellectual atmosphere prevailed and that the intelligentsia, both clergy and colonist, read, speculated, and wrote with a degree of freedom not found in Spain during the same era. In Mexico, as in Spain, those who wished to read about the new scientific ideas from abroad were allowed to do so, because none of those works ever appeared on the Index of prohibited reading.

Therefore, as an agency of social control the Mexican Inquisition worked as all such agencies do: to constrain but not to intimidate. Generalizations of the more popular writers to the contrary notwithstanding, actual evidence of intimidation is lacking in all but a very few isolated cases. There were debates, theological arguments, and ideological disputes within the clerical establishment, within the universities, and within the military and political bureaucracies—debates that might have led to security investigations in a more rigid intellectual milieu. But in Mexico they did not, at least until the middle of the eighteenth century. The political role of the Holy Office of the Inquisition tended to strengthen its mission rather than to weaken it.

Though they tend to disagree ideologically in their various researches and writings on the Church in Spain and in Mexico, Henry Kamen and this writer have independently reached similar conclusions. Those of the writer are tentative ones; Kamen's are articulated. The writer views the Holy Office as "an organic function of a corporate whole, inseparable from the social and economic forces which affected the whole body of society."[35] Kamen claims that "the ruling class of Spain was the demiurge of an ideology, which for good or ill, has dominated Spanish society into modern times," and he feels that "this class content in ideology cannot be too strongly emphasized as the main factor in the creation of the closed society of traditional Spain."[36] His research led him to conclude that "wherever it was established, the Inquisition drew its strength from the common people and the nobility over them, who together became the steadfast pillars of the traditional order in Spain."[37]

Research in the Mexican Inquisition papers has revealed the relevance of some of Kamen's ideas in the New World. The interesting thing that happened to Mexico, however, was that the ruling-class ideology of the creole elite and the common people changed at the turn of the nineteenth century; and with this development, the posture of orthodoxy changed. It became more flexible, more eclectic, and more amenable to attack on the Spanish monarchy from a political standpoint.

CONCLUSION

Revisionist studies have begun to view the Inquisition as a mirror of the Mexican society in which it ministered rather than as a causal force that brought social dislocations. Causal forces are difficult to substantiate, and political and social repressions are difficult to measure. The real importance to the historian of Inquisition trials may not be their religious content but the social and intellectual data which they contain. These data may well provide the social scientist with new viewpoints and revised interpretations within the framework of liberal historiography.

In any event, modern historians—no matter what their political affiliations and religious views—should be willing to do the documentary depth probes rather than rely on tired clichés when they interpret the coercive power of the colonial Church. Whatever their findings, the purposes of history will have been served by professionals rather than by polemicists.

NOTES

1. José Toribio Medina, *Historia del Tribunal del Santo Oficio de la Inquisición* (México: Editorial Navarro, 1954); Joaquin García Icazbalceta, *Bibliografía mexicana del siglo XVI* (Mexico City: Fondo de Cultura Económica, 1954) and his *Fray Juan de Zumárraga, primer obispo y arzobispo de México,* 4 vols. (Mexico City: Editorial Porrúa, 1947); Henry Charles Lea, *The Inquisition in the Spanish Dependencies* (New York: Macmillan, 1908); Luis González Obregón, *México viejo: Noticias históricas, tradiciones, leyendas y costumbres* (Mexico City: Fondo de Cultura Económica, 1959); Julio Jiménez Rueda, *Herejías y supersticiones en la Nueva España: Los heterodoxos en México* (Mexico City: Imprenta Universitaria, 1946).

2. *Proceso Inquisitorial del Cacique de Tetzcoco,* Publicaciones del Archivo General de la Nación, vol. 1 (Mexico City: Archivo General de la Nación, 1910; reprint, Guadalajara, 1968); *Procesos de indios idólatras y hechiceros,* Publicaciones del Archivo General de la Nación, vol. 3 (México: Archivo General de la Nación, 1912); Nicolás Rangel, *Los precursores ideológicos de la Revolución Francesa,* vol. 2, *La masonería en México, siglo XVIII* (Mexico City: Archivo General de la Nación, 1929–1932).

3. "El Indice del Ramo de la Inquisición" in fourteen typed folio volumes was microfilmed in three reels by the Library of Congress in 1949. Only two volumes of the Indice have been published by the Archivo General de la Nación: Guillermina Ramírez Montes, *Catálogo del Ramo de Inquisición,* 2 vols. (Mexico City: Archivo General de la Nación, 1979–1980). New documents from the huge Archivo Provisional, or Indiferente as it is often called, are added at intervals to the Ramo de la Inquisición. See Richard E. Greenleaf, "El Archivo Provisional de la Inquisición (México)," *The Americas: A Quarterly Review of Inter-American Cultural History* 31 (1974): 206–216, and the guide to documentary sources on the Mexican Inquisition in Richard E. Greenleaf, "Mexican Inquisition Materials in Spanish Archives," *The Americas: A Quarterly Review of Inter-American Cultural History* 20 (1964): 416–420. The Mexican Tribunal sections of Archivo Histórico Nacional, Madrid, have been microfilmed and are available to researchers. See Servicio Nacional de Microfilm, *Archivo Histórico Nacional: Sección de Inquisición* (Madrid: Centro de Documentación, 1972) for a catalog.

4. See for instance two of the many works of Boleslao Lewin, *Mártires y conquistadores judíos en la América* (Buenos Aires, 1954); *La Inquisición en Hispanoamérica (judíos, protestantes, patriotas)* (Buenos Aires: Editorial Proyección, 1962) among others on Mexico. The sections of Mariano Cuevas, *Historia de la iglesia en México,* 4 vols. (Mexico: Editoral Patria, 1946) are valuable syntheses of the works of Medina, Lea, González Obregón, and García Icazbalceta.

5. Richard E. Greenleaf, *The Mexican Inquisition of the Sixteenth Century* (Al-

274   RICHARD E. GREENLEAF

buquerque: University of New Mexico Press, 1969), vii. A Spanish translation was issued by the Fondo de Cultura Económica (Mexico City: Fondo de Cultura Económica, 1981) with a second printing in 1985.

6. See the proceedings edited by Gustav Henningsen, John Tedeschi, and Charles Amiel, *The Inquisition in Early Modern Europe: Studies on Sources and Methods* (Dekalb, Ill.: Northern Illinois University Press, 1986).

7. A beautiful catalog with articles and illustrations was published: *La Inquisición* (Madrid: Dirección General de Bellas Artes, Archivos y Bibliotecas, 1982).

8. Joaquín Pérez Villanueva and Bartolomé Escandell Bonet, *Historia de la Inquisición en España y América: Conocimiento científico y el proceso histórico de la Institución (1478–1834)* (Madrid: Centro de Estudios Inquisitoriales, 1984). See also Joaquín Pérez Villanueva, *La Inquisición Española: Nueva visión, nuevos horizontes* (Madrid: Centro de Estudios Inquisitoriales, 1980).

9. See Henningsen et al., *The Inquisition in Early Modern Europe*, 3–11, for a listing of the conclaves.

10. See Greenleaf, *The Mexican Inquisition of the Sixteenth Century*, 158–190, for the formative period of the Tribunal.

11. See Robert Ricard, *The Spiritual Conquest of Mexico: An Essay on the Apostolate and the Evangelizing Methods of the Mendicant Orders in New Spain, 1523–1572* (Berkeley and Los Angeles: University of California Press, 1966), trans. Lesley Byrd Simpson from the 1933 French edition, 264–282 and passim; Robert Padden, *The Hummingbird and the Hawk: Conquest and Sovereignty in the Valley of Mexico* (Columbus, Ohio: Ohio University Press, 1967), chapter 13, "Huichilobos and the Bishop."

12. Richard E. Greenleaf, *Mixtec Religion and Spanish Conquest: The Oaxaca Inquisition Trials, 1544–1547* (Madrid: José Porrúa Turanzas, 1991). The same author's study of the second archbishop "Alonso Montúfar and the Mexican Inquisition" is in preparation, and his other works on Indians and the Inquisition, including a new volume on Mixtec religion and Spanish conquest, are discussed in the thematic sections of this essay.

13. Solange Alberro Bechocaray, "Inquisition et Société au Mexique, 1571–1700," 3 vols. (Thèse d'Etat, Paris, 1984).

14. François Chevalier, "New Perspectives and New Focuses on Latin American Research" (Address before the Conference on Latin American History of the American Historical Association, Chicago, 29 December 1985).

15. Henningsen et al., *Inquisition*, 68, remarks that Alberro and Herrera Sotillo each analyzed cases not available to the other, and he counsels that the two sets of statistics need to be compared.

16. Guillermo Fernández de Recas, *Aspirantes americanos a cargos del Santo Oficio: Sus genealogías ascendentes* (Mexico City: Archivo General de la Nación, 1956).

17. See also the author's article written under the name of Pedro Gringoire, "Protestantes, enjuiciados por la Inquisición," *Historia Mexicana* 11 (1961): 161–179. Greenleaf, *The Mexican Inquisition of the Sixteenth Century*, has dealt with the

trials of Miles Phillips and Guillermo Orlando, and incorporates studies by
G. R. G. Conway, *An Englishman and the Inquisition* (Mexico City, 1927) and Frank
Aydelotte, "Elizabethan Seamen in Mexico and Ports of the Spanish Main,"
American Historical Review 58 (1942): 1–19.

18. See Greenleaf, *The Mexican Inquisition of the Sixteenth Century*, 182–186, for
"Books and Men."

19. Leonard's articles on the book trade are a mine of information. A series
of these were published in the *Hispanic Review* (HR) and *The Hispanic American
Historical Review* (HAHR): "On the Mexican Book Trade 1576," HR 17 (1949):
18–34; "On the Mexican Book Trade 1600," HR 9 (1941): 1–40; "On the Mexican Book Trade 1683," HAHR 27 (1947): 419–435.

20. See C. H. Griffin, "Some Aspects of the Book Trade between Europe and
the Indies in the Sixteenth Century" (Diss., Oxford University, 1982); Carlos
Millares de la Imperial, "La censura de publicaciones en Nueva España (1576–
1591)," *Revista de Indias*; "10 coloniales, 1585–1684," *Boletín del Archivo General
de la Nación* 10 (1939): 661–1006; "Libros mexicanos, 1553–1609," *Boletín del Archivo General de la Nación* 20 (1949): 1–63. Greenleaf has planned a study on
"Books and Men in Sixteenth-Century Mexico." His works on the literature of
the Enlightenment in Mexico and the important study of Monelisa Lina Pérez
Marchand are discussed below in this essay.

21. Bartolomé Bennassar, "Aux origines du caciquisme: Les familiers de
l'Inquisition en Andalousie au XVIIe siècle," *Caravelle*, no. 27 (1976): 63–71.

22. See for instance Lewis A. Tambs, "The Inquisition in Eighteenth-Century Mexico," *The Americas: A Quarterly Review of Inter-American Cultural History*
22 (1965): 167–181; "Incapacidad Operativa," in Pérez Villanueva and Escandell, *Historia de la Inquisición*, 1348–1353.

23. See Luis González Obregón, *Los procesos militar e inquisitorial del Padre
Hidalgo* (México: Archivo General de la Nación, 1887); *Procesos inquisitorial y
militar seguidos a Don Manuel Hidalgo y Costilla* (Mexico City: Editorial Navano,
1960); "El señor fiscal de este Santo Oficio contra don José María Morelos," *Boletín del Archivo General de la Nación* 19 (1958).

24. See Richard E. Greenleaf, "The Mexican Inquisition and the Enlightenment, 1763–1805," *New Mexico Historical Review* 41 (1966): 181–196. The same
author is writing a volume on "The Inquisition in Baroque Mexico," which deals
not so much with the great autos de fe of 1645 to 1649, when crypto-Jews and
many others were punished, as with the Visita de Hacienda and the probes
of Pedro Medina Rico and Marcos Alonso de Huydobro into procedural ir-
regularities and violations of rights of accused in all Inquisition trials from 1640
to 1657. Greenleaf builds on the early study of Helen Phipps, "Notes on Medina
Rico's Visita de Hacienda to the Inquisition of Mexico," in *Todd Memorial Volumes*, 2 vols. (New York: Columbia University Press, 1932), 2:78–89. He also has
built on the New Mexico studies of France V. Scholes to illuminate inquisitorial
activities in the Spanish Borderlands. His *The Inquisition in Bourbon Mexico* includes a chapter on the "Inquisition in Northern Mexico" and will incorporate

his "The Inquisition in Spanish Louisiana 1762–1800," *New Mexico Historical Review* 50 (1975): 45–72, and "The Inquisition in Eighteenth-Century New Mexico," *New Mexico Historical Review* 60 (1985): 29–59.

25. On Ricard and Padden see above. See also Jacques Lafaye, *Quetzalcoátl and Guadalupe: The Formation of Mexican National Consciousness, 1531–1813*, trans. Benjamin Keen (Chicago: University of Chicago Press, 1976), chap. 3, "The Inquisition and the Pagan Underground," 18–29. Greenleaf's *Zumárraga and the Mexican Inquisition, 1536–1543* contained the first in-depth analysis of the Zumárraga trials of Indians in two lengthy chapters.

26. The treatises are reprinted in Francisco del Paso y Troncoso, *Tratado de las idolatrías, supersticiones, dioses, ritos, hechicerías, y otras costumbres gentílicas de las razas aborígenes de México*, 2 vols. (Mexico City: Editorial Navarro, 1954), based on the original 1892 edition.

27. See Greenleaf, *The Mexican Inquisition of the Sixteenth Century*, 75–81, for the Indian Inquisition of Tello de Sandoval, 1544–1547.

28. Scholes and Roys, *Fray Diego de Landa and the Problem of Idolatry in Yucatán*, 600.

29. See Chevalier, "New Perspectives and New Focuses on Latin American Research." See the interesting works of Serge Gruzinski, *Les hommes-dieux du Méxique: Pourvoir indien et société coloniale, XVIe-XVIIIe siècles* (Paris, 1985), and "Matrimonio y sexualidad en México y Texcoco en los albores de la conquista o la pluralidad de los discursos," in Solange Alberro, ed., *Seis ensayos sobre el discurso colonial relativo a la comunidad doméstica: Matrimonio, familia y sexualidad a través de los cronistas en el siglo XVI* (Mexico City: INAH, 1980).

30. In addition to the statistical analyses of Alberro and Herrera Sotillo, see Gustav Henningsen, "El banco de datos del Santo Oficio," *Boletín de la Academia de la Historia* 174 (1974): 547–570.

31. Greenleaf, among his other planned studies, hopes to examine the *solicitantes*—those priests accused of solicitation of women in the confessional.

32. The following pages depend on Richard E. Greenleaf, "The Inquisition in Colonial Mexico: Heretical Thoughts on the Spiritual Conquest," in *Religion in Latin American Life and Literature*, ed. Lyle C. Brown and William Cooper (Waco, Tex.: Baylor University Press, 1980), 70–82.

33. Henry Kamen, *The Spanish Inquisition* (London: Allen and Unwin, 1965).

34. Ibid., 294.

35. Ibid., 301.

36. Ibid., 305.

37. Ibid.

CONTRIBUTORS

Jaime Contreras, faculty member of the History Department of the Universidad Autónoma de Madrid, has published numerous articles on the Inquisition and participated in many international conferences. His book, *El Santo Oficio de la Inquisición de Galicia: Poder, sociedad y cultura,* was published by Akal in 1982.

Anne J. Cruz, Associate Professor of Spanish, teaches Spanish and comparative literature at the University of California, Irvine. Her publications include *Imaitación y transformación: El petrarquismo en la poesía de Boscán y Garcilaso de la Vega* (John Benjamins, 1988); the coedition of *Renaissance Rereadings: Intertext and Context* (University of Illinois Press, 1988); and articles on Golden Age poetry, theater, and prose.

Jesús M. De Bujanda, who received doctorates in both history and theology, is Professor of History and also directs the Centre d'Etudes de la Renaissance de l'Université de Sherbrooke. He is author of *Index de l'Inquisition espagnole, 1551, 1554, 1559* (Editions de l'Université de Sherbrooke, 1984), volume V of *Index des livres interdits,* a multi-volume project that he directs.

Richard E. Greenleaf, whose scholarship on the Inquisition in Latin America commenced publication in 1960, will publish his ninth book in 1991, *Mixtec Religion and Spanish Conquest: The Oaxaca Inquisition Trials, 1544–1547* (José Porrúa Turanzas). Professor of History at Tulane University, he is also Director of the Roger Thayer Stone Center for Latin American Studies.

Stephen Haliczer is Professor of History at Northern Illinois University. Editor of *Inquisition and Society in Early Modern Europe* (Croom-Helm,

1987), his new book, *Inquisition and Society in the Kingdom of Valencia,* has just been published by the University of California Press.

Stanley M. Hordes is a visiting scholar in the Department of History and the Latin American Institute at the University of New Mexico, as well as principal consultant in the firm of HMS Associates in Santa Fe, New Mexico. As co-project director of "Crypto-Jews: New Mexico's Sephardic Legacy," he has published several scholarly papers, including "The Inquisition as Economic and Political Agent: The Campaign of the Mexican Holy Office Against the Crypto-Jews in the Mid-Seventeenth Century," *The Americas,* 39:1 (1982).

Richard L. Kagan is Professor of History at The Johns Hopkins University, where he specializes in early modern Spain. In addition to *Students and Society in Early Modern Spain* (Johns Hopkins University Press, 1974), and *Lawsuits and Litigants in Castile, 1500–1700* (University of North Carolina Press, 1981), he has published through the University of California Press both *Spanish Cities of the Golden Age* (1989), and *Lucrecia's Dreams: Politics and Prophesy in Sixteenth-Century Spain* (1990).

J. Jorge Klor de Alva, Professor of Anthropology at Princeton University, received a Guggenheim Fellowship in 1987–1988. Named Curator for the anthropology and history sections of Expo '92 in Seville, he has edited two books, *Encuentros interétnicos en el Nuevo Mundo: Interpretaciones contemporáneas,* and *Imágenes interétnicas en el Nuevo Mundo* (both forthcoming from Editorial Siglo XXI). His book, *Introduction to Aztec Culture: The Nahua Images of Self and Society,* will be published by the University of Utah Press.

Moshe Lazar, Professor of Comparative Literature at the University of Southern California, has carried out many years of research on the literature of forcibly converted Jews in Spain.

Angus I. K. MacKay is Professor of History at the University of Edinburgh. A specialist in medieval Spain, he has presented many scholarly papers and has published *Money, Prices and Politics in Fifteenth-Century Castile* (Royal Historical Society, 1981), and *Spain in the Middle Ages: From Frontier to Empire, 1000–1500* (Macmillan, 1983, Third Printing).

Geraldine McKendrick recently completed her doctorate at the University of Edinburgh and now holds a lectureship at King's College in London. Cambridge University Press will soon publish her book, *Franciscan Spirituality in Early Modern Castile.*

Roberto Moreno de los Arcos has taught history at the Universidad Autónoma de México and is currently Humanities Coordinator. His many publications include *Los nahuatlismos en el español de México* (Universidad Nacional Autónoma de México, Coordinación de Humanidades, 1989) and *Ensayos de bibliografía mexicana. Autores, libros, imprenta, bibliotecas. Primera serie* (Universidad Nacional Autónoma de México, Instituto de Investigaciones Bibliográficas, 1986).

Mary Elizabeth Perry, Research Associate at the UCLA Center for Medieval and Renaissance Studies, is Adjunct Professor of History at Occidental College. A specialist in research on the social history of Spain, she has published *Crime and Society in Early Modern Seville* (University Press of New England, 1980), and many articles on gender and deviance. Her most recent book is *Gender and Disorder in Early Modern Seville* (Princeton, 1990).

Noemí Quezada is investigadora titular in the Instituto de Investigaciones Antropológicas, Universidad Nacional Autónoma de México. An ethnologist who received her doctorate from the University of Paris, Sorbonne, she specializes in the cultures of colonial Latin America. Her publications include *Amor y magia amorosa entre los Aztecas* (Universidad Autónoma de México, 1984).

María Helena Sanchez Ortega, profesora titular of medieval and early modern history in the Universidad Nacional de Educación á Distancia, Madrid, has written extensively on sexuality in Spain and the Spanish gypsies, including *Los gitanos españoles: El período borbónico* (Castellote, 1977), and *La Inquisición y los gitanos* (Taurus, 1988). Her study, *La mujer y la sexualidad en el antiguo régimen* is in press.

Joseph H. Silverman was Professor of Spanish in the Adlai E. Stevenson College at the University of California at Santa Cruz before his recent death. He published many scholarly works on the literature of Golden Age Spain, including articles on the picaresque novel and Cervantes. Most recently, he published an edition of the folk literature of the Sephardic Jews (University of California Press, 1991), with Samuel G. Armistead and Israel J. Katz.

INDEX

Designer: U.C. Press Staff
Compositor: Prestige Typography
Text: 10/12 Baskerville
Display: Baskerville